THE EMERSON EFFECT

CHRISTOPHER NEWFIELD

THE EMERSON EFFECT

INDIVIDUALISM AND SUBMISSION IN AMERICA

THE UNIVERSITY OF CHICAGO PRESS
CHICAGO AND LONDON

Christopher Newfield is associate professor of English at the
University of California, Santa Barbara.

The University of Chicago Press, Chicago 60637
The University of Chicago Press, Ltd., London
© 1996 by The University of Chicago
All rights reserved. Published 1996
Printed in the United States of America

05 04 03 02 01 00 99 98 97 96 1 2 3 4 5

ISBN: 0-226-57698-1 (cloth)
      0-226-57700-7 (paper)

Library of Congress Cataloging-in-Publication Data

Newfield, Christopher.
    The Emerson effect : individualism and submission in America /
Christopher Newfield.
        p.   cm.
    Includes bibliographical references (p.) and index.
    1. Emerson, Ralph Waldo, 1803–1882 — Political and social views.
    2. Literature and society — England — History — 19th century.
    3. Emerson, Ralph Waldo, 1803–1882 — Influence.   4. Submissiveness —
United States.   5. Individualism — United States.   6. United States —
Civilization.   I. Title.
PS1642.S58N49   1996
814'.3 — dc20   95-23520
                                                                    CIP

CONTENTS

A Note on Emerson's Texts   vii

Acknowledgments   ix

Introduction   1

PART ONE
Liberal Troubles

1   The Submissive Center   17

PART TWO
Nature: The Corporatist Solution to Submission

2   The Authoritarian Language of Liberal Religion   43

3   Democratic Prophecy and Corporate Individualism   62

PART THREE
Individualism and Submission in Private Life

4   Friendly Inequalities: Emerson and Straight Homoeroticism   91

5   Loving Bondage: The Authority of Domestic Remoteness   129

PART FOUR
Late Emerson: Corporate Liberties

6   Market Despotism: "The Poet Affirms the Laws"   153

7   Corporatism and the Genesis of Liberal Racism   174

8   Continuations: Liberation from Management   209

Notes   219

Index   263

A NOTE ON
EMERSON'S TEXTS

I have tried to use versions of texts that are reliable, accessible, and complete. One modern work satisfies these criteria: for Emerson's published works through *The Conduct of Life* (1860), I have used *Essays and Lectures*, ed. Joel Porte (New York: Library of America, 1983), abbreviated as *Es and Ls*. For Emerson's later writings, I have used *The Complete Works of Ralph Waldo Emerson*, introduction and notes by Edward Waldo Emerson, Centenary edition, 12 vols., (Boston and New York: Houghton Mifflin, 1903–4), abbreviated as *ECW*, which is neither reliable nor particularly accessible. Emerson did not fully supervise the editing of his collections following *Society and Solitude* (1870). Although Emerson was a participant in the editing of *Letters and Social Aims,* much of the work was done by James Elliot Cabot and Emerson's daughter Ellen Tucker Emerson. Ralph L. Rusk provides this description of their methods: "A publishable passage was boldly wrenched from its old context and made to do service wherever Cabot and Ellen thought it could. 'In this way,' Cabot confessed, 'it happened sometimes that writing of very different dates was brought together.' Emerson himself could do little but take part in the search for materials" (*The Life of Ralph Waldo Emerson* [New York: Charles Scribner's Sons, 1949], 486). A new standard edition is under way, but has not yet reached the later volumes (*The Collected Works of Ralph Waldo Emerson,* ed. Alfred R. Ferguson, et al. [Cambridge, Mass.: Harvard University Press, 1971–]). For Emerson's journals, I have used *The Journals and Miscellaneous Notebooks of Ralph Waldo Emerson,* ed. William H. Gilman and Ralph H. Orth, 16 vols. (Cambridge, Mass.: Harvard University Press, 1960–82), abbreviated as *JMN*. All quotations from this remarkable standard edition of Emerson's journals have been modified to omit the editorial apparatus used by the editors to indicate Emerson's insertions, deletions, and other editorial notations. The printed text is the final result of Emerson's changes. I have also substituted American paperback versions of Freud for the Standard Edition.

ACKNOWLEDGMENTS

This book was written in a number of places, and has benefited from excellent company and commentary during very different stages of composition at Cornell and Rice Universities and finally at the University of California at Santa Barbara. I appreciate the valuable research and manuscript assistance of Bettina Caluori, Jon Hegglund, Toni Mantych, and David Zeigler at UCSB. I would like to express particular gratitude to Jennifer Stemmle, whose research for chapters five and seven enabled them to be completed, and to Avery Gordon, whose reactions always improved the book's arguments and whose presence allowed me to imagine life both during and after its completion.

INTRODUCTION

Radicalism and conservatism have been twisted entirely out of
shape by the liberal flow of American history.
— Louis Hartz

Although in fable and song the United States is the land of the free and
the home of the brave, its more everyday reflections attribute its suc-
cesses to the wisdom of moderation. In the center, it is said, lies the
balance of interests on which peaceful progress always depends. While
extremists and radicals raise hell and get things done, only centrists can
compromise their way to a reconciliation of the myriad differences that
typify complex modern societies.

Centrists are thought to accomplish a major reconciliation on which
all the others depend, as, for example, between the apparently competing claims of the individual and society. Too much insistence on individual rights makes necessary coordination, lawfulness, and mutual assistance impossible. Too much power to the community or the state erodes
the personal freedoms to which American life has long been devoted.
The center, then, is thought to be the place where individualism blends
with democracy, liberty with community. The genius of American political sensibility lies in its instinct for the comfort zone where extremes of
private or public power can't survive.

In what follows, I will dispute such claims for this tradition of moderation. I am not criticizing all moderation and compromise but a particular kind that has formed a historically crucial set of American
middle-class instincts about the political world. I will argue that ignor-
ing the origins and effects of this particular center has damaged American social and cultural development. My subtitle, *Individualism and Submission in America*, alludes to the main reason why. The major American
tradition of moderation rests less on the much-discussed balance between individual autonomy and popular sovereignty than on a habit of
submission to authority that weakens autonomy and democracy alike.

The book stars Ralph Waldo Emerson because I believe him to be
the principal architect of this tradition. He was not a political theorist,
of course, but took the private self as his lifelong subject, and had his
greatest influence through his descriptions of how democratic individu-

1

alists experience themselves. The most magical of these experiences has usually been thought to be that of maximum freedom, a freedom that is nonetheless in harmony with the needs of a democratic society. I will explain why I think this is a deceptive harmony. Emerson's celebration of democratic freedom has for too long obscured the important ways in which his sense of balance rendered both freedom and democracy secondary to large doses of submission to preestablished and unequal conditions.

Moderation in the United States is closely associated with the country's liberal tradition. In the popular political discourse of the last twenty years, liberalism has become a variant of the far left, but this is, of course, like asserting that Denver is on the continent's west coast, and this discourse should be seen not as a map but as a mockery of our political geographers. Be that as it may, liberalism has stood for a consensus about the American left's need to assimilate its ideals to the ways of the center. Besides performing this practical service of absorbing transliberal left thought into itself, liberalism offers some positive principles. These include enduring and somewhat incompatible ideas such as individual freedom of choice, the ceding of political choice to representative bodies, the sacred nature of private property, and the state regulation of private property. Liberalism's hybrid positions reflect not simply the incoherence of much left versus right political analysis, as my epigraph suggests, but more fundamentally, liberalism's preoccupation with "balance." In this book I will be regarding American liberalism as continually seeking harmony between such apparent opposites as private freedom and public order, liberty and union. And I will be suggesting that, in Emerson's powerful version, the reconciliation of terms diminishes both.

The contemporary scene offers a wealth of examples of this perennial U.S. liberalism. Here and elsewhere my examples will usually feature middle-class reformist American men. While I think they have been the major builders and beneficiaries of this liberalism, I also think the range of this liberalism's consciousness and practice lies far beyond the circle of its most favored advocates. Many of its deadlocks and retreats have marked moderate reformism throughout the history of the Christian West, and its dilemmas have, since 1800, filtered throughout American society. The relevance of an Emerson-like submissive individualism to this or that time and place will need to be decided by others. I do, however, invite connections that go beyond those offered below.

President Bill Clinton's secretary of labor, Robert Reich, writing in

The Resurgent Liberal, rejects simple notions of freedom as individual autonomy in favor of individuality as a kind of interdependence. He wants us to see "the team as hero." "To the extent that we continue to celebrate the traditional myth of the entrepreneurial hero, we will slow the progress of change and adaptation that is essential to our economic success. If we are to compete effectively in today's world, we must begin to celebrate collective entrepreneurship."[1] Unregulated self-reliance, Reich is saying, is old-fashioned. It has become economically dysfunctional, and must be replaced by sophisticated forms of cooperation, collaboration, and the coordination of individuals into flexible, mutually enriching groups. As conservatism placed increasing stress on the glory of economic individualism during the 1980s, liberals like Reich tried to distinguish themselves by calling for a revival of "civic republicanism," which is "as concerned with the moral quality of civic life and the relationships on which it is based as with the protection of individual liberties."[2] To put democracy into the hands of simplistic individualists is, for this liberalism, to hold prosperity hostage to that primitive American myth of liberal or "Lockean individualism." American greatness always depended on its ability to balance individualism with civic responsibility, simple liberty with community.

But if the liberal Reich is rejecting individualism, this is not because he is moving left toward an expanded notion of democracy.[3] While his liberalism downplays simple self-reliance, it does not replace self-reliance with public, cooperative sovereignty in politics and economics. Here's an example of what I mean from Reich's most influential book, *The Work of Nations.* "'American' corporations and 'American' industries are ceasing to exist in any form that can meaningfully be distinguished from the rest of the global economy. Nor, for that matter, is the American economy as a whole retaining a distinct identity, within which Americans succeed or fail together. . . . The standard of living of Americans, as well as of the citizens of other nations, is coming to depend less on the success of the nation's core corporations and industries, or even on something called the 'national economy,' than it is on the worldwide demand for their skills and insights."[4] Reich remains an individualist in the sense that the successful individual lives by her wits. She is not autonomous, however, as she has little control over the vast web she works and lives within, and she must always adapt and thrive through networks and groups. Nor can she turn to public powers to exert control on her behalf. Federal, state, and local governments have lost their real authority, national identity has devolved to corporate flagships, and even these corporations are dissolving into a global market in which power is everywhere and nowhere and yet entirely irresistible.

Reich offers a kind of corporate sublime in which power increases as it becomes more dispersed, invisible, and unfathomable. He repeatedly insists that the forces shaping modern economies are utterly beyond the control not only of individuals but also of public agencies, even of nations. He regards the U.S. economy as controlled far less by federal policy than by the world market, with its ostensibly unappealable laws of continuous wage reduction, its churning of communities and entire industries in and out of a society, and its tendency to increase social stratification within particular nations. While Reich's mapping of economic trends may be quite accurate, his response to some of their negative aspects shows no conviction that societies can exert public sovereignty over their own economic relations.[5] His solution is a misnamed "positive economic nationalism" which is distinguished by the evaporation of autonomous national policy; it amounts to the hooking of strategies of "cooperation" to existing patterns of market determination.[6] The autonomous individual has disappeared, but so has democratic sovereignty.[7]

Reich's analysis does not spring from nowhere. It features a balance between individual and community that forms *the* enduring tradition of American political sensibility. It expresses an explicit enthusiasm for the rewards of losing control. One can't affect anything, nor can one's federal government with its trillions in budget — and it is a good thing too. Losing collective control over basic economic forces is both inevitable and liberating; the forces of liberty should not resist this loss because they are enhanced by it. A liberal as humane and optimistic as Reich can argue with no visible distress that four-fifths of the U.S. population will lack input into economic governance, and that even the elite remainder, the "symbolic analysts," can work mostly at succeeding according to preestablished rules.[8] In the next chapter I will call this sensibility the Emerson Effect: individual autonomy and public authority vanish together before unappealable laws, but this leads to the enhancement of freedom. Emersonian liberalism does not so much invent the conceptual frame as develops the political sensibility that allows its loss of both private autonomy and public sovereignty to *feel OK*. This is at least as important a contribution as the conceptual frame itself.

In the present volume I discuss Emerson's development of his restrictive liberalism and individualism primarily in the context of particular forms of experience, forms such as race, divine spirit, gender, and sexuality. But I'm going to continue to outline some of the more abstract terms that will play a major role in my description of Emerson's political subjectivity. My premise here and throughout is that this political subjectivity has a intimate influence on passion and identity—on racial identity, on habitual erotic desire, on when one can and cannot speak. These political-cultural constituents of the liberal self, with their general descriptions like "democratic" or "individualistic," shape even the life known only to ourselves, one often far less thought than felt, which we mistakenly believe comes entirely from our more tangible identities of race, sexuality, and many others.

Corporate individualism is the term I'll use to describe the desired outcome of Emerson's liberalism: the enhancement of freedom through the loss of both private and public control. Appearing well before the familiar mode of business organization, this kind of individualism is "corporate" to the extent that it combines three major features. First, corporate individualism places great weight on individual merit and performance. Second, it regards this performing self not as isolated or autonomous but as an individual dependent upon a system of forces. Third, it undermines individual and public, political sovereignty over this system that, in much democratic theory, provides an alternative form of individual freedom. The decisive feature is the third, for it is this preservation of inequality within decentralized, diffused, and multidirectional modes of power that distinguishes corporatism from otherwise potentially egalitarian social structures. Corporate individualism rejects private and public control at the same time.

Corporate individualism is corporate rather than democratic. Both corporate and democratic individualism reject freedom defined as isolation and self-containment, but democratic individualism, in contrast, replaces individual submission with public sovereignty. It would be an extremely complicated, extensive task to enumerate specific cases in which individual power is acquired through participation in public sovereignty, and in this volume I must limit myself to outlining some of Emerson's incomplete inclinations in this direction. But one fundamental precondition of democratic individualism should be mentioned. Democratic forms of public sovereignty require equality. By equality I do not mean equality before the law or the specter haunting most discussion of equality in the U.S.: an equivalence of capacities that denies individual differences. I mean instead an equality of power between those who make the law and those whom the law governs. Though such equality insists on personal freedom, it ties freedom to participation in a full range of collective and explicitly political activities. When this kind of equality is in place, the citizenry in general, and not merely a small circle of leaders, wields public power. These political activities have final control over collective forces such as markets. They do not submit to markets in which private power is routine but public intervention is taboo. These activities exert a control over the making and executing even of market rules that is fundamental to democratic forms of individualism, but which is relinquished by corporate forms.

My purpose is to work through the components of Emerson's ambivalent, influential weakening of democracy. I will show how he substitutes corporate for democratic ways of living as an individual in mass society and does this in the name of individual freedom. His thinking resolves the tension between individual liberty and democratic group life by abandoning crucial elements of both. Individualism comes to include submission and democracy to include authoritarianism.[9] Emerson's international fame as a major prophet of the self makes his development of a submissive kind of individualism particularly astonishing and culturally important.

My purpose here is not to describe Emerson as essentially submissive or authoritarian but to encourage much greater attention to submission and authoritarianism as important determinants of the Anglo-American mainstream. Emerson's intellectual terrain contains no essences of freedom or bondage, democracy or tyranny, but harbors some of the most important, and most poorly understood, contradictions of U.S. life.

Within the liberal tradition, the most common way of dealing with an excessive teetering toward submission to fate or law is to beef up individualism. Liberalism is often said to originate as an ideology that celebrates laissez-faire government, stressing the right of the individual and his property to be free of outside interference. Liberalism in this view is thought to reconcile itself to state intervention only in the twentieth century, and before then to be always in touch with its laissez-faire roots. Emerson is most often read as a laissez-faire individualist, and radical individualism is usually thought to be his distinctive contribution to American culture. He is most famous for rejecting the authority of "society" or "custom" and chronicling the superior merits of self-reliance. According to this doctrine, truth and power depend on the self listening to its own instincts first, on insuring that all governance must flow continually from the innate legislative power of the individuals so governed. Individualism is also the most popular feature of Emerson's thinking, as it is in nearly any modern system of thought. "In the great contest of social systems, of modes of social life and organization, which filled the best part of [this] century, victory ultimately went to those who offered greater scope to individual creativity—inherent in every society but repressed in various ways by all sorts of idiotic, self-serving, exploitative or plain barbarous institutions."[10] Emerson is arguably U.S. culture's most formative theorist of this vision. In my argument, however, his individualism plays a different role. Rather than rejecting submission in the name of freedom, as we'd expect, his individualism defines freedom as submission to unmodifiable law.

In making this argument about the unexpected effects of individualism, I will not be denying American history's wealth of independent and sometimes spectacular individualist behavior. Nor will I be suggesting that any integration with social systems taints the authenticity of individual freedom. To the contrary, I assume throughout that plenty of nonsubmissive individualism turns up in American culture. I also think all real individualism is social, and that Emerson's most insightful and useful moments are when he shares this recognition with us (see, in particular, chap. 3 below). The issues for me are not whether individualism really exists (it does) or whether it can be collective and social (it must). The issues are what kind of individualism Emerson disseminated to the cultural "center" (submissive), and what kind of collective or social individualism might otherwise have been. I see Emerson as both drawn to a heroic kind of public, political, collective individualism and as instrumental in removing it from the centrist culture I am analyzing here. The center can be defined by this drastically modified individualism.

It is easier to see this modified individualism in Emerson once we modulate our sense of nineteenth-century liberalism. Even the early version, at least in Emerson's middle- and upper-class New England milieu, does not press for laissez-faire so much as it seeks to reconcile laissez-faire with regulation, a celebration of free selves and free markets with law, consensus, and regulation. The tensions in liberalism are everywhere visible in American society today, as the established political mainstream commits itself to large state programs that it then subordinates to private interests, lacking conviction in public and popular control but still embarrassed by its resort to private and elite direction. The liberal idea of a rapport between individual and community, like Reich's "collective entrepreneurship," is not a mistake but a tradition. The tradition extends back before Emerson's time. Its question is never whether but what kind of collective entrepreneurship to support.

Although my use of the term *corporate individualism* for the actual result of Emerson's and Reich's liberal balance owes much to strong work on corporate liberalism, in my view, this work incorrectly dates the beginning of the move away from laissez-faire after the Civil War, and thereby participates in an inaccurate assessment of liberalism as having moved from laissez-faire to big government over that period of time.[11] More accurate descriptions of the earlier phase of liberalism have arisen from two or three decades of work on early republican thought, which is rightly seen as having tempered whatever tendency antebellum Americans had toward a straightforward laissez-faire individualism.[12] Emerson's own liberalism emerged in a New England community moving from Federalism to Whiggery, where emphasis was put on combining individual conscience and moral development with civic virtue and duty.[13] Emerson himself spent most of his adult life moving between the Whig and Democrat parties, with the collective having an influence as strong as that of entrepreneurship. Most accounts see corporate liberalism rising well after the Civil War, with the onset of large business corporations and bureaucratic administration, in which rationality came to consist of following orders. Emerson's work, to the contrary, suggests that corporate liberalism and liberal individualism were always woven together.

I do not see liberalism as a form of laissez-faire individualism in Emerson's time and place that later shifted toward a regulatory view. But I do see a change in liberalism that I think receives too little attention. This is from a republican to the corporate form of liberalism I just outlined. Both of these rest on an attempted balance between individualism and collective order, but the former has democratic aspects, even where conformist and consensus driven, that the latter has stripped away. Reich does not, of course, describe his view as corporatist and instead uses the old term *civic republicanism* to describe a balance between "individual liberties" and "the moral quality of civic life." But in contrast to his own position, there was nothing fundamentally submissive about this community-minded individualism. It may have implied deference, but did not require the abandonment of public and private agency that came later in a supposedly emancipatory phase.

An example of still-republican thinking is the civic liberalism of the conservative Edward Everett, one of Emerson's Harvard professors and a prominent figure among Boston leaders. Speaking on the occasion of the fiftieth anniversary of the signing of the Declaration of Independence, Everett observed that "the fireside policy of a people is like that of the individual man. As the one, commencing in the prudence, order, and industry of the private circle, extends itself to all the duties of social life, of the family, the neighbourhood, the country; so the true domestic policy of the republic, beginning in the wise organization of its own institutions, pervades its territories with a vigilant, prudent, temperate administration; and extends the hand of cordial interest to all the friendly nations, especially to those which are of the household of liberty."[14] Individuality is inseparable from "all the duties of social life." Conscience is simultaneously private and public. The strength of the country's policies and moral example depends precisely on continuity between these realms. Liberty depends on "temperate administration." Everett's individualism is collective and conformist and deferential. But it is not submissive in the sense I mean: the "individual man" retains agency, developed at the "fireside" of the "private circle," which then becomes the basis of the control of policy. Control is retained rather than given up. Oddly, it is Emersonian individualism, as I read it, that does so much to undo the sovereignty assumed by predecessors far less liberal than he.

From the start, Emerson works in Everett's tradition of public or social individualism. Emerson's individual is invariably part of a larger whole. One critic has astutely noted that Emerson works with eighteenth-century notions of a community as an organism, in which persons find a place by virtue of a deliberative process in which they are "fitted to act in company . . . and they are the most happy men, whose hearts are engaged to a community."[15] Because Emerson begins and ends by devising various combinations of freedom and law, his career should not be viewed as a movement from deference to individualism, or from "freedom" to "fate," as Stephen Whicher's influential framework would have it, or from a possessive to a more democratic kind of individualism, as in Stanley Cavell's pragmatically intersubjective approach.[16] Emerson's influence has always depended on his ability to avoid simplistic libertarian types of freedom by effecting the liberal balances I've been describing. He implies that individualism triumphs, and yet does so not by avoiding the collectivizing implications of democracy (though this is the usual reading) but by incorporating them. Only at first does he appear to offer a liberalism of negative liberty in which liberty consists of an individual protected from encumbering social relations. Theorists of liberalism have customarily assumed that such a liberalism repudiated authoritarian forms of governance through its attack on external governance in general, even (or especially) when it was not quite ready to embrace democracy.[17] Emerson in fact devises a liberalism of moral relations, which is meant to suggest democratic interdependence; liberty exists only through ethical ties with the members of the overlapping communities to which one belongs. The liberty of solitude expresses itself in the liberty of collaborative governance. But this is not so much Emerson's innovation as his participation in a powerful ambient tradition. His innovation follows not on the question of whether to favor a relational individuality but on the question of what kind. His answer propels a very significant shift in the history of U.S. liberalism from a democratic toward a corporate kind of liberalism. It does so by introducing submission at the center of an extravagant American freedom.

In *The Emerson Effect*, I examine the convergence of forces traditionally discussed through political categories (liberalism) with those that have been treated as identity categories (white, heterosexual). My point is not to endorse the valid truism that identity is always political in the sense that private consciousness can never separate itself from social structures and forces, or to retranslate identities and behavior back into the language of politics. Rather, I am trying to analyze the conjunction between identity categories and the political subjectivity that comes to them from the long-range patterns of U.S. socialization. The everyday life of a middle-class intellectual like Emerson, with his family relations, male friendships, spiritual raptures, hidden desires, literary predecessors, and the rest of the tangled array of his changing identifications — all this is powerfully but often invisibly determined by feelings about the forms of one's social being, feelings which I'm calling political subjectivity. Who one's friends are of course has everything to do with their individual qualities, connections, and the context in which one knows them. But it also involves how submission feels, whether it feels better in groups or one-on-one, what kind of agency — communal, supernatural — one expects to protect one's submitting self. The book's chapters are organized around identity categories through which political subjectivity comes into play, but this subjectivity will remain an issue throughout, in the terms I've outlined here in a preliminary way.

The book is divided in four parts. In part 1, I describe the contradictions within Emerson's individualist political sensibility and outline the book's set of problems. Subsequent parts consist of pairs of chapters which stress first the submissive and then the corporate aspects of Emerson's individualism. In part 2, I redescribe the central drama of the transcendentalist manifesto *Nature* (1836). In chapter 2, I define Emerson's individualism by investigating his description of poetic voice as requiring the submission of the mind's autonomy to higher authority. In chapter 3, I argue that Emerson grounds this higher authority in collective solidarity but then redefines solidarity so that it lacks political control.

In part 3, I trace Emerson's development of relations with men and women as a collective and yet antidemocratic social sphere. I show in chapter 4 how his love of male friendship sustains a hostility to the masses and an eroticization of inequality. In chapter 5, I demonstrate how Emerson's notion of family life places domestic cooperation over male competition but corporatizes this domesticity in a variety of ways, yielding the subordination of reciprocal independence to a remotely controlled union, a union which seems liberal because it is flexibly gendered. The family conditions individuals not simply by establishing a gender hierarchy but by denigrating face-to-face knowledge, by tracing the weakness of femininity to a basis in local, hands-on, undetached, affective, and committed experience. Taking chapters 2–5 as a group, I sketch an anatomy of liberalism's submissive, corporate individualism: individuality depends on the imitation of existing, transhistorical being; individuality must retain impersonal ties to a collectivity that is not public and democratic but private and politically powerless; this male individuality is constituted by loving relations rather than by selfish autonomy, but any intimate relation must be noncollective and unequal; authority is most legitimate when it supervises and protects passive masculinity.

In part 4, I chronicle the results of Emerson's usually ignored later work. I describe his transformation of the public sources of poetic tradition into a marketplace in which private possession is combined with obedience in chapter 6. In chapter 7, I study Emerson's thinking about race relations before and after Emancipation. His views suggest that African American civil rights originate in a desire to limit civic agency, that whiteness functions as an unreal but ideologically effective equality, and that meritocracy historically preserves the stratifying powers of slavery. In chapters 6–7, I suggest that two major topoi of liberalism, free markets and merit-based integrationism, do not overcome but extend the conservative effects described in earlier chapters. Finally, in the conclusion, I offer a reading of a recent magisterial work of corporate prophecy, *Liberation Management* by Tom Peters, to suggest how completely emancipatory individualism has been absorbed by corporate individualism. In the conclusion, I state a precondition for developing a more democratic alternative to corporate individualism. The postorphic Emerson points toward a middle-class reckoning with what it has wished for — corporate rather than democratic individualism.

A range of commentators have argued that liberalism's ideals, while sound and emancipatory in themselves, have been derailed or corrupted by the circumstances of U.S. history, most of which are developed by the right: the rise of monopoly capital after the Civil War; racism and the failure of Reconstruction; the persistence of halfway social measures motivated by a misguided individualism; patriarchal dominance, including its penchant for violence and coercion; obsession with national union at the expense of difference; and the transition from a republic to a "national security state" after World War II. Although I believe that these socioeconomic conditions complexly, contradictorily, and powerfully determine the liberal theorizing that reforms and sustains them, Emerson's included, I also think that an exclusive focus on external social factors can underestimate the extent to which liberalism's problems are of its own making.

A dominant focus on historical context also underestimates the extent to which liberalism works less as a conscious, systematic ideology than as a structure of affect regarding social being. I am primarily concerned with this sensibility, though I will be tracing it, when necessary or helpful, to the social processes that created Emerson's world. I will not identify this sensibility with a particular political outlook, as though the issue could be explored by asking whether Emerson was for capitalism or really against slavery. I am not trying to expose Emerson's politics as suspiciously close to a moderate conventional wisdom with which I disagree. His influence is far more pervasive and subtle than his positions on major issues, and his influence would have been far less if it came in discrete units such as "free trade is freedom," which we could then accept or separate from those parts of his thinking that we liked better. I am interested in Emerson's understanding of social subjectivity, and when I say I am attending to his sensibility, I refer not to his specific analyses of culture and society or to his particular policy recommendations but to his frequently unconscious — and all the more influential — structure of feeling toward democratic authority.

This book is not so much about Emerson and American culture as about Emerson and the liberal imagination, which I think has mostly influenced a sector of the cultural center broadly termed the professional and managerial middle classes. This cluster of groups is diverse but generally includes people who create value by handling information and use information rather than force to control themselves and others. They have historically had a strong belief in the power of ideas to manage — though usually not modify — the institutional world. They are used to rising levels of prosperity and to overcoming privation, conflict, and oppression through the combination of prosperity and conceptual expertise. They were until very recently almost entirely white and male, but they almost never attribute their mobility to these qualities. Though their occupational structures are usually traced to the rise of professionalization in the decades following the Civil War, their sensibility and philosophy go back well beyond that and, in particular, to the liberal Christian clergy of the northeastern United States who elaborated their generic politics as a postrevolutionary, progressive centrism. Though this cluster of groups has produced many remarkable thinkers, their sage, their bard, their secretary of defense, was Ralph Waldo Emerson. Emerson's sensibility has traveled much further in the ranks than have his name or specific sayings.

Thus I will be most concerned with the effects of this outlook toward authority within white middle-class culture as it receives an enabling theorization from Emerson's thinking. Though my views about the implications of Emerson's thought for other groups will be clear throughout, I will not discuss Emerson's presence in these groups—either in a master class for whom domination was a social good and a fact of life, or in those groups made up of African Americans, immigrant Europeans and Asians, manufacturing workers, and most women, who were as often harmed as helped by this middle-class culture, and when helped, were helped one person at a time.[18] This middling class experiences itself as neither ruling nor ruled, and has been described by Pierre Bourdieu as the dominated fraction of the dominant class. Dwelling perpetually in a psychic and social middle zone, it is especially susceptible to mixed Emersonian modes like individualism without self-determination and democracy without group sovereignty. In reading Emerson, I will focus on the conflicting ways in which this group denied freedom to itself, denied itself freedom and therefore could not wish for freedom for others.

I sometimes think of this middle-class culture through the tradition of "halfway covenants" by which colonial Puritans democratized church membership while retaining hierarchy and passivity within the congregation. Emerson's is a halfway democracy: it defines freedom as individual movement and personal growth, but accompanies these with the pleasurable loss of self-governance.

Although I am critical of the political psychology that Emerson has authorized, I mean by these criticisms to honor Emerson's positive achievements and many of the idealistic uses to which he has been put. At no point do I wish to imply that the whole variety of uses of Emer-

son, and the spectrum of his effects, is mistaken or conformist. I do not
intend to homogenize his effects into a single kind, or to dismiss those
many readers who have found much in him to inspire greater liberties
of various kinds. Most of these readers were initially drawn in by his
ephemeral and yet unforgettable demand that individuals can and must
be allowed to control their fates, that finally, nothing matters but emancipation, that all systems of morality, of justice, of economy, of affection,
must serve that end. Emerson continues to inspire a remarkable range
of optimistic protest in those who believe that everyone can be far freer
than they are right now. Though some have charged him with a solipsis-
tic imperialism of the self, this is nearly the opposite of my lament. Emerson is at his best, in my view, when he demands liberation and demands it for everyone. I take these calls as genuine and yet object to
them insofar as they depend on the indissociable companion structures — unhappily constitutive of middle-class liberty — that block the
calls' unfolding.

I also do not mean to insist on group generalizations about the white
middle class. I wish instead to describe a widespread, psychosocial phenomenon that some of this middle class has had to consume far too
much energy struggling against. Nor do I wish to downplay, through
my criticisms, the liberalizing, middle-class radicalism of the Unitarian and Transcendentalist, abolitionist, pro-worker, and protofeminist
circles actively defining New England's middle classes throughout Emerson's life. Many middle-class people battled in various ways against
the crippling sensibility I will be detailing here. Like Emerson, these
women and men comprise an important strand in a diverse tradition of
American agitation for human and civil rights, for democratic independence through interdependence. This is a tradition which, though obviously not an American franchise, is the U.S. political legacy most useful
to the world. I admire the individuals who invented and sustained it
against convention and reward, and wish their writing and activity were
far better known.

But I also wish this tradition's limits were better known. Inspired by
Emerson's (and many others') powers of revision, I will detail the ways
in which his liberalism's political psychology obstructs the liberation his
career has symbolized. My aim is not to unveil obstructions or to de-
mystify or complicate his notions of freedom. It is, finally, to indicate
that this submissive freedom is unnecessary, that if the U.S. is to find a
new role in the world, it can and must be surpassed.

PART
ONE

Liberal Troubles

CHAPTER

ONE

The Submissive Center

1. Transcendentalism: Individualism and Democracy

Emerson is usually associated with a freedom narrative that is also assigned to the overall period of his active maturity, lasting roughly from 1828, the year of the first election of Andrew Jackson, to around 1872, after Emancipation and midway through Reconstruction. Its most unmixed version goes like this: the United States, conceived in liberty, achieved in the Jacksonian period a globally unprecedented freedom for the common man. The historian Robert Wiebe, writes, for example, that "after 1825 an extraordinary popular passion for personal freedom fought to extend the range of these exhilarating new rights in a self-fueling process that propelled the participants as fast and as far as their impulses drove them. In each area their objective was self-determination, and in sum they generated a revolution in choices that transformed the character of American society."[1] In spite of the crimes and failures of this period, the love of liberty decided the overall direction of American life.

Similarly, Transcendentalism is taken to express the opening of New England liberalism to democratic possibilities. Daniel Walker Howe notes that the Unitarian culture in which Emerson was raised followed "the Liberal clergy of the Congregational establishments in New England[, which] had been traditional opponents of both 'levelism' and 'tyranny,' and defenders of mixed 'Aristicrato-Democratical' government."[2] Born in 1803, Emerson was brought up in what Ronald Formisano calls "Deferential-Participant" politics, "a blend of deference, influence, party, and egalitarianism" that characterized Massachusetts through 1820 and sometime beyond.[3] The transcendentalists, in such accounts, broke with democratic deference through their alliance with a stronger version of democracy: "The greatness of the New England Transcendentalist writers lay to a large extent in their ability to invigorate their Unitarian literary heritage, reuniting its humanistic aspirations with an authentic Puritan ardor, and then synthesizing it with the American ideals of democracy and natural genius."[4] Their democracy began with their radical individualism, one rooted in their rejection of the primacy of Christian doctrine in setting religious truth. What came first for them, according to Anne C. Rose, was the original source of truth "in the heart," a heart whose wisdom had no need of mediation from minister, scripture, or the Unitarians' "historical evidences." By emphasizing exclusively individual resources such as "intuitive perception," "intuitive reason," and "consciousness," the "Transcendentalists . . . took the leap" beyond deference into the self-authorization of moral law.[5]

Transcendentalism is a complex and even disparate body of thought, but in most of its variants it assumes the balance between individualism and democracy that in the introduction I described as characteristic of U.S. liberalism. It expresses a fundamental liberal desire "both to unite individuals with the community and to preserve individual liberty in the face of community."[6] Transcendentalism attempts a symbiosis between two sides.

First, all of the transcendentalists were agreed on the power of an inward faculty of Reason to know truth that was out of reach of convention and society. George Ripley, for example, frequently argued that "the things that are seen . . . are dependent, in a great measure, upon our own souls."[7] Transcendentalism is in these moments "idealism in America," tied to a radical self-reliance that endowed it with an unprecedented power of making the world. But it fell to Emerson to create the astonishingly eloquent and uncompromising expressions of the individual's radical priority to all external systems of human life. "A man is a god in ruins," he exclaimed in *Nature*, and this divine individuality lives in thought and will, properly appreciated only by the transcendentalist who puts individual Reason before all other things. The Transcendentalist knows certain culturally belittled truths, and therefore

> does not respect government, except as far as it reiterates the law of his mind . . . His thought, — that is the Universe. His experience inclines him to behold the procession of facts you call the world, as flowing perpetually outward from an invisible, unsounded centre in himself, centre alike of him and of them, and necessitating him to regard all things as having a subjective or relative existence, relative to that aforesaid Unknown Centre of him.

From this transfer of the world into the consciousness, this beholding of all things in the mind, follow easily his whole ethics. It is simpler to be self-dependent.[8]

"His thought, — that is the Universe": in the face of his age's discovery of an "analytic of finitude," in which the ground of knowledge's possibility consists of the limits of knowledge, Emerson proclaims the self's infinitude.[9] This infinite Reason dwells within the self and constitutes individuality; this idealism produces a theory of radical individuality, and this in turn underwrites a politics. It is a politics of individualism in which the self "does not respect government, except as far as it reiterates the law of his mind."

But contrary to its reputation in some quarters, transcendentalism does not only place the individual apart from and ahead of the group. Its second impulse is to define the free self through equitable relations to others. As Norberto Bobbio defines it, in *democratic* individualism the state is a summation of individuals, but also "holds in the highest regard the individual's capacity to overcome isolation by devising various procedures allowing the institution of nontyrannical common power."[10] Liberalism becomes a popular creed in the United States by trying to establish a balance between laissez-faire individualism and a devotion to "common power." Even the Jacksonian Democracy, often as close to laissez-faire individualism as regular politics could come, attacked public institutions in the name of equalizing social relations.

A case in point is Andrew Jackson's message accompanying his veto of the bill to recharter the Bank of the United States in 1830. His theme of individual freedom from oppressive government is not simply a laissez-faire call for avoiding federal government, but for avoiding the undemocratic kind.

> Distinctions in society will always exist under every just government. Equality of talents, of education, or of wealth can not be produced by human institutions. In the full enjoyment of the gifts of Heaven and the fruits of superior industry, economy, and virtue, every man is equally entitled to protection by law; but when the laws undertake to add to these natural and just advantages artificial distinction . . . to make the rich richer and the potent more powerful, the humble members of society—the farmers, mechanics, and laborers—who have neither the time nor the means of securing like favors to themselves, have a right to complain of the injustice of their Government.[11]

Jackson wants not the elimination of government but equitable government. His description of equality is close to the definition I offered in the introduction: equality does not mean equalization of personal qualities or a leveling of differences. It does mean equality before the law and, more important, an equality between people and laws, between lawmakers and the law's subjects. Equality before the law requires equality of input into the laws, and Jackson claims to veto the bank charter because it reflects a gross inequity of influence between those who need loans and those who make them. Jacksonian individualism is liberal in the sense that it desires a balance between independence and an equitable community. This conjunction is so pronounced that a recent commentator describes Democrats as the party of paranoid individualism and the party of traditional face-to-face social relations.[12] The Federalists and Whigs were even more devoted to common laws of various kinds. Laissez-faire liberalism developed in the United States interactively with its merely apparent opposite, democratic liberalism; liberalism, again, defined itself by seeking a balance between claims of individual and law, freedom and equality.

Transcendentalism insists on the divinity of soul and of the democratic public. Orestes Brownson writes, "Great men do not make their age; they are its effect . . . A great man is merely the glass which concentrates the rays of greatness scattered through the minds and hearts of the people; not the central sun from which they radiate. To obtain an elevated national literature, it is not necessary then to look to great men, or to call for distinguished scholars; but to appeal to the mass."[13]

Margaret Fuller felt the individualist fear that the person who lives "too much in relations . . . falls after a while into a distraction, or imbecility." But she nonetheless claimed that "femality" was distinguished by a kind of genius for relations: woman is great "in an instinctive seizure of causes, and a simple breathing out of what she receives that has the singleness of life." Though this description of the feminine conforms to tired gender roles, it more particularly reflects Fuller's way of demanding social equality with men. If "man should esteem himself the brother and friend, but nowise the lord and tutor of woman," gender equality would help women spread their knowledge that true individuality is not lordship but friendship. "What woman needs is not as a woman to act or rule, but as a nature to grow."[14]

Similarly, George Bancroft explicitly links individual Reason to democratic relations. "If it be true, that the gifts of mind and heart are universally diffused, . . . then it follows, as a necessary consequence, that the common judgment in politics, morals, character, and taste is the highest authority on earth, and the nearest possible approach to an infallible decision. . . . if from the consideration of individual powers we turn to the action of the human mind in masses, we shall still retain our good hopes for the race. . . . If reason is a universal faculty, the decision of the common mind is the nearest criterion of truth."[15] Reason most perfectly expresses itself in the common mind, and thus individualism depends on democracy, and freedom on equality.

Emerson's thinking sometimes resonated with the general values of the nineteenth century workingman's and trade union republicanism—only corrupt practices, artificial legislation, or tyrannical cronyism could be responsible for inequality of wealth, since, in a polity of the virtuous, wealth and power naturally tend to diffuse themselves more or less evenly. Emerson could also draw on Whig efforts to link individualism to moral communitarianism. For example, the author of Massachusetts' Election Sermon for 1844 simultaneously celebrates "private rights" and the fraternal republic where "common weal . . . is intertwined with the fibres of our own hearts."[16]

A long tradition of Emerson readers continued to esteem exactly this union of radical self-reliance and the mutual determination of collective life. Emma Goldman also thought that Emerson combined individualism and the social good. Anarchism, she says, is

> the teacher of the unity of life; not merely in nature, but in man. There is no conflict between the individual and the social instincts, any more than there is between the heart and the lungs. . . . "The one thing of value in the world," says Emerson, "is the active soul; this every man contains within him. The soul active sees absolute truth and utters truth and creates." In other words, the individual instinct is the thing of value in the world. It is the true soul that sees and creates the truth alive, out of which is to come a still greater truth, the re-born social soul.[17]

Goldman first elevates the "active soul" to an Emersonian predominance but without pause describes it as the social soul. Anarchism is a socialized individualism. It finds in Emerson's idea of liberty a "free communism."[18] The doctrine of the soul is simultaneously the doctrine of the "social instincts."

More recently, Cornel West has described as Emersonian a culture not of competitive individualism but of "creative democracy," where "[s]ocial experimentation is the basic norm, yet it is operative only when those who must suffer the consequences have effective control over the institutions that yield the consequences."[19] Emersonian individuality is based in democratic self-determination. For Stanley Cavell, Emersonian self-reliance means reliance on the self's vision of an "attainable" yet "unattained" state that, though it cannot be found in existing society, arises from a social self that is "prepared to recognize others" as part of itself.[20] Again and again, Emerson is seen to stand for a reconciliation of personal freedom and otherness. This is Emerson the liberal, who envisions a moral community of those who know free individuality to be dependent on relations to the other.[21] Self-development is liberated from the demand for mastery and the fear of subordination; freedom develops out of equal relations.

2. Authoritarianism

This liberal balance of individualism and democracy will work only if both sides are preserved: it must deliver individual power and autonomy, however complex, and popular rather than higher, unreachable law. But when I looked to Emerson's transcendentalism for a synthesis of individualism and democracy in self-reliance, I found neither. I didn't find collective democracy, and I also didn't find his famous radical individualism that privileged the self-possessed individual over collective self-governance. Emerson did not repudiate democracy in favor of radical individualism in his youth, or vice versa in his maturity, for he consistently repudiated both at the same time.

Emerson's descriptions of self-reliance contain fascinating contradictions. He would repeatedly say, be free and not a slave, emancipate yourself, build your own world out of the revolutionary genius of your unique being—all the kind of statements most commonly associated with him. But the next minute he would redefine freedom as a rapturous servitude. In his flagship essay, "Self-Reliance," Emerson begins his third paragraph this way: "Trust thyself: every heart vibrates to that iron string." This is the clear anticonformism we expect from him. But he continues differently. "Accept the place the divine providence has found for you, the society of your contemporaries, the connection of events. Great men have always done so, and confided themselves childlike to the genius of their age, betraying their perception that the absolutely trustworthy was seated at their heart, working through their hands, predominating in all their being. And we are now men, and must accept in the highest mind the same transcendent destiny . . . obeying the almighty effort, and advancing on Chaos and the Dark" (*Es and Ls*, 260). This passage performs a series of moves that, in my view, typify Emerson's thought.

First, he summons the reader to reject conventional wisdom in favor of what he or she knows from within, from an instinct to develop one's inner being. This is Emerson the individualist radical, Emerson the anarchist, Emerson the creative artist, who insists that the truth requires that we first sever our ties to established knowledge and society. This is, in short, Emerson the radical liberal, putting self-possession first, but for the sake of any social change the soul decrees. To know, to be, is to break the chains.

But his next move defines this self-trust as a form of accepting one's place in precisely the "society of [one's] contemporaries" and in "the connection of events" that we might think self-trust was meant to evade. Genius turns out to be located in relationship rather than in autonomy. Self-reliance is not simple possessive individualism—self-ownership, freedom of contract, autonomy—but a complex relation to actually existing society.

Then, in a third move, Emerson locates the source of this insight or genius beyond his contemporaries in what he calls a "transcendent destiny." What is transcendent about it? As a transcendentalist, Emerson often refers to a natural/divine order beyond a realm of mere appearances such as social custom. But this familiar injunction to move beyond conventional understanding into harmony with Being means that one must "accept" and "obey." The transcendentality of the law does not appear as a specifiable rule or quality but as the rule of superiority, that which compels obedience. Superiority forms the content of transcendent law; accepting an external superiority is what makes "great men" great. Emerson imagines not those contemporaries who are extraordinary for their independence, originality, or freedom, but those who submit like children to the highest authority.

This three-step occurs again and again in Emerson's writing: defiance turns into obedience with such thoroughness that they become the same thing. Emerson moves from radical self-determination, through a second phase—mutual determination in relation to one's peers—and into a third, in which determination comes from a law transcending one's being and to which one "submits childlike," allowing one's body and mind to be filled like a vessel with an overmastering intelligence.

Here's a second example. Contemplating the dynamics of male friendship, Emerson writes, "I hate, where I looked for a manly furtherance, or at least a manly resistance, to find a mush of concession. . . . That great defying eye, that scornful beauty of [the friend's] mein and action, do not pique yourself on reducing, but rather fortify and enhance. Worship his superiorities; wish him not less by a thought, but hoard and tell them all. Guard him as thy counterpart."[22] Emerson first expresses his pleasure in an instance of "manly furtherance" or rugged individualism. Second, this vision of autonomy appears through a reciprocal intimacy; the speaker has influence over the "defying eye" of the friend, and can reduce or enhance it. Finally, Emerson transits from reciprocity to worshipful devotion. Keeping the comrade entails being overwhelmed and compelled to worship; Emerson both desires the counterpart and defines him as his superior, and sees him as a counterpart because he is superior.[23] He is equal because he is better. Concrete friendship does not offer a democratic alternative to pietistic submission but delivers that submission to one's friendship ties.

The second of the three steps manifests Emerson's democratic liberalism. Though he affirms self-reliance, his second step acknowledges the self's dependence on intersubjectivity and the vast web of social relations. It expands self-reliance beyond possessive individualism. He claims eternal essences in both the individual and the "transcendent destiny" in steps 1 and 3, and yet he also challenges their foundational narratives by affirming the importance of one's social history, of the continual revision of narratives of truth that a truly historical and intersubjective mind can perform. He offers a hopeful convergence of major motifs of modern liberalism: the social, public, historical nature of subjectivity; the revisionary power of antifoundationalist or antiessentialist criticisms of universalizing narratives; and democracy as composed by continually revising governing narratives in free consultation with one's community.

But this second position — of embodied, potentially democratic intersubjectivity — repeatedly gives way to deference and even absolute obedience to a higher authority. The second phase is one in which authority can be made and remade in common. It supports a participatory group subject. The third, however, acquires its sublime attraction precisely by invoking an authority beyond the group, one that makes but cannot be remade. It demands a submissive subject. The third step, preserving while overcoming the first two, combines liberalism with authoritarianism, democracy with despotism. Emerson links self-possession to submission to an absolute. Emerson's intersubjectivity, antifoundationalism, and democracy are compatible with and swept up into his authoritarianism. They all develop together in his work, and they are very hard to pull apart.

Again and again group life gives way to one's relation to an absolute law. As Emerson says in his essay "The Over-Soul," "When I watch that flowing river, which, out of regions I see not, pours for a season its streams into me, I see that I am a pensioner; not a cause, but a surprised spectator of this ethereal water; that I desire and look up, and put myself in the attitude of reception, but from some alien energy the visions come."[24] Emerson must look up to see and, more important, look up to receive what he cannot see when he looks.

In such a reading of essays like "The Over-Soul," I may appear to be attaching the label of authoritarianism to religious impulses generally. Emerson's authoritarian quality resides, as I see it, not in his religiosity itself, but in the specific ways he describes religious or ontological law, and how he applies it to social or personal questions. His interests in impersonal spirit might have led him to separate inner light from universal law on the model of, say, the Quakers, whom he often admired. His interest in the intersubjective nature of selfhood might have led him to tie spirit to some kind of collaborative holy liberation. Emerson demands neither the autonomy of inner life from divine law nor the return of divine law to the power of covenanted humans. In general, he alternatively seeks to preserve the rule of a "beneficent tendency" from a waning faith in a personal savior. His liberalization of Christianity rests on his aversion to liberalizing the role of absolute law in human affairs. In later chapters, which cover subjects like domesticity, male friendship, and race relations, I describe the implications, on nontheological subjects, of Emerson's lifelong translation of the loss of God into a gain for Law.

Why do we call this self-reliance? It repeatedly coexists with—and even defines itself through—social and ontological forms of subjection.[25] Harold Bloom once said that "Emersonian self-reliance is god-reliance," but that even radical individualists like Bloom think of this as an answer is itself the problem.[26] This confusion of autonomy with subjection is also a social problem: it expresses an unfortunate interchangeability between democratic liberalism and liberal authoritarianism. A symbiosis between public lawmaking and individual autonomy cannot be distinguished from a (flexible) law controlling public and private alike. Where individual and collective life might have interacted on reciprocally created and continually re-created grounds, they are each governed instead by an unappealable and preestablished principle of being.

As Emerson's thought changes and develops, his third position becomes less simplistically absolutist and far more capable of incorporating fluctuation, circulation, and mobility. Thus when I describe Emerson's thought, even as schematized in this three-step progression, as an important source of liberal authoritarianism, *liberal* is as important as *authoritarian*. Emerson's legacy to the contemporary liberal humanities has these two irreducible parts, which I bluntly summarize here.

The liberal: he argues that individual subjectivity depends on good community relations. These relations must be forever open and endlessly revised. The authoritarian: he insures that his community will be characterized by unilateral authority and control. Emerson condenses this double position in his essay "Poetry and Imagination": "thin or solid," he says, "everything is in flight, . . . everything undressing and stealing away from its old into its new form, and nothing fast but those invisible cords which we call laws, on which all is strung." Everything moves except for unchanging laws which supervise this movement. Emerson is liberal in defining the individual as constituted by ongoing negotiations between itself and others. Personal freedom rests on freedom of contract. Self-reliance, public and interactive, means the antifoundationalist critique of all authority. Emerson is authoritarian in demanding that these others can be part of negotiations only if they are superior. The superiority of the other insures that the rules that cover these negotiations cannot be modified, except by these same superiors. The superiority constitutes the negotiations. It insures that this superiority will remain in effect after the negotiations are over. As soon as the other's superiority wanes, Emerson will break off negotiations. Emerson's double legacy, then, is this: freedom means endless flexibility, and freedom means loss of control. Both sides of his thought are in continual operation. The tension is obvious in a concept like liberal authoritarianism, and suppressed when it appears as corporate individualism.

3. Liberalism as Structure

It has taken me a while to decide how much fuss to make about this double legacy. Liberalism forms a pervasive common sense in the United States, particularly among its predominantly white and white-collar middle classes. It thus makes unbelievers in its balances of individualism and democracy feel obtuse and irrational. Working on transcendentalism and reading its impressive body of secondary literature, I was continually instructed that Emerson's first two steps — self-reliance and embodied intersubjectivity — reflected a conjunction that defined the central tradition of American culture. For me to maintain that these were undermined by a third step in which a higher law returns seemed to evidence blindness to the subtlety of the conjunction of the first two.

All aspects of my higher education agreed that the individual subject is constructed, that freedom is consensual, that truth arises from community agreement, that consciousness is patterned and prestructured, that any opposition between individuality and power is epistemologically naive and politically immature. To mourn the loss of freedom and democracy to higher law implied, often to my own ears, that I must be mourning absolute forms of private and public agency that never existed. Liberalism's balance of freedom and democracy has always acknowledged the impossibility of self-created freedom and free self-determination; all agency is constituted by social relations, and all freedom is constituted by law. It was difficult to insist that personal freedom and public sovereignty were lost when they were always appearing in hybridized, mutually constituting forms.

The most sophisticated work in American Studies and cultural theory thus informed me that American history had to be read for its nuanced syntheses of liberty and order into "ordered liberty."[27] One scholar nicely condensed this wisdom: "The American cause was . . . the cause of 'union,' of liberty not as a final autonomy but as the freedom to choose one's bond."[28] In other words, "the genuinely self-reliant man would inevitably prove to be the perfect member; true individualism would yield 'union,' not anarchy."[29] Properly understood, individualism always meant that "one achieves selfhood by lacking the quality, the agency, so central to strong individuality" of the naive, atomistic variety; contrary to my own view, this "is not a contradiction, but rather a double movement in which the self is substantiated by the disappearance of its agency."[30] Noted cultural historians identified this double movement as especially advanced in the American version of democratic individualism: inheriting a "profound Puritan ambivalence towards selfhood," torn between "its own nature" and "God's decree," "Emerson's exhortation to greatness" manifests "the paradox" of American culture's unchanging devotion "at once to the exaltation of the individual and the search for a perfect community. Self-reliance builds upon both these extremes." Self-reliance is a simultaneous "total assertion of the self" and celebration of "the regenerate 'Americanus'" or regenerate national soul. This paradoxical individuality exists through an "ongoing corporate journey" that "enable[s Emerson] to dissolve all differences between history and the self."[31] In this way, Emerson reflects Louis Hartz's notion of the "liberal tradition," in which the "American democrat" lives out the nonconflict between liberalism's individual pursuit of property and the "egalitarian thunder of the Democrats."[32]

My contradiction was these critics' synthesis. Given their insights, it often seemed I should simply admit that *submission* was just a name-calling term for consent, as was *authoritarianism* for structure, as was *bondage* for our always-constructed freedom. Americanist interpretations of European theorists confirmed not only the pervasiveness but the historical importance of liberalism. My preoccupation with submission and bondage sometimes appeared to me as the fool's clothing of a projection of an illusory top-down, coercive, negative power onto intricate systems of complex circulations. Was I clinging to an outmoded protest model of free individuality and a naively, rigidly egalitarian model of true democracy? Most of this excellent and wised-up commentary implied good professional advice: calm down.

I have, but I still find little evidence of either autonomy or mutual determination in Emerson, and plenty of submission. His work can be used to illuminate the significant difference between a structured and a submissive individuality. Granting the structural, constituted, socialized basis of subjectivity says nothing about widely various relations to power possible within any system. Some bonds are chosen, some are imposed, some are chosen and imposed, and the very difficulty of the concept of choice asks us not to ignore domination but to watch for it more carefully. I am still stuck with this fact: even when I read Emerson with the knowledge that self-governance does not require an Enlightenment subject or absolute ego for its existence, and with the conviction that subject formation is always tied to subjection — and with the understanding that the whole point of democracy is that you might get personal liberty without sovereign self-invention — I still marvel at the extent to which Emerson's self-reliant individual seeks submission to an unalterable sovereignty. A description of Emerson's cultural ideal cannot be limited to the freedom to choose one's own laws, for that would overlook his ardent invocation of laws that are already given. In the present study, I work to avoid renaming consensus and structuration as submission. But I also try to outline the pervasive presence of surplus submission in the constitution of the quasi-secular middle-class political psyche.

Many of the theorists who deal with liberal subjectivity have been so liberalized themselves that they have trouble focusing attention on either private or public submission. Take Hegel, for example. In *Phenomenology of Spirit* he offers analyses of the relation between individual mind, human history, and spirit that intersect with Emerson's, and he goes well beyond Emerson in his treatment of lordship and bondage as a

constitutive element of Western democracy, which Emerson usually ignores. But Hegel emphasizes reciprocity in the relation between master
and slave, influentially arguing that the master's identity requires recognition from the slave. Many lessons can be extracted from this codependence, but chief among them has been the false one that the master's
domination coexists with a genuine reciprocity with the slave. Though
the master may be vulnerable and unhappy, this does not mitigate his
domination. Nonetheless, nationalist or spiritual unities among unequals are often read into romantic idealisms for which Hegel stands,
even when, as in the antebellum United States, they coexist with chat-
tel slavery.[33]

Freud's work has often led to a similar misreading. The important
concepts of incorporation and introjection correctly note the dependence of individual identity on the presence of the other in the self. The
distinct but related model of subjectivity based on oedipal masculinity
describes the "slave" position as an identification with the master that
eventually leads to the slave/son joining the master/father in a position
of power. Both models feature intersubjectivity and intrapsychic difference as constitutive of any individual subject. They should also allow us
to consider explicitly and systematically the central place of authoritarianism in democratic cultures. Explorations of incorporation analyze the
tyranny of the incorporated object over the incorporating ego, and por-
traits of oedipal sonship show the father's law controlling the son as the
condition of the son's acquiring any power at all. Nonetheless, many
uses of these models, including Freud's, also normalize the authoritarian
as nothing more than the fact of intra- and interpsychic relations. This
is particularly true of oedipal structures which, I argue at length in chapter 4, misdescribe the son's mandated submission as voluntary identification. Freud's work has often encouraged the mislabeling of coercion
and obedience as consent — consent as free as the psyche could manage.

Michel Foucault has been featured in a similar role. Many humanists
in the 1980s were rightly impressed by his extremely clear insistence
that power is not simple sovereignty that domineers like a tyrannical
father, that power is not properly tyrannical at all. Power is not "a mode
of subjugation which, in contrast to violence, has the form of the rule."
Power is "the multiplicity of force relations immanent in the sphere in
which they operate and which constitute their own organization."[34]
Power flows not from sovereignty but from relationships. But whatever
Foucault himself believed at various times, the multiple and relational
operations of power implied to some that coerced submission was pre-

modern — predominant mostly before the American and French Revolutions in those countries. Again, submission and domination became nothing more than the power relations that underwrite all social systems and subjects. Submission appeared as nothing more than the process of normal individuation through relation. Attention to such changes as the penal system's transition from physical coercion to psychic construction sometimes blocked awareness of continuities of coercion, inequality, and domination.[35]

The humanities in the 1970s and 1980s rediscovered the individual's constitutive bond to the other, but allowed the fact of subjection to power to be overshadowed by the fact that power works as a system or field. I came to regard this trend as itself Emersonian: it seemed the doctored rerun of Emerson's obsession with the rule of a coordinating higher law. What could claim to evade such total interdependence? The overriding fact was that of connection — connection between master and slave, top and bottom, inside and outside, nature and culture, self and other, self-reliance and god-reliance, dissent and conformity, freedom and submission. The question of freedom was naive, naively oppositional. Here's Sacvan Bercovitch on the subject: "In short, the issue was not co-optation or dissent. It was varieties of co-optation, varieties of dissent, and above all varieties of co-optation/dissent. America was a symbolic *field,* continually influenced by extrinsic sources, and sometimes changing through those influences, but characteristically absorbing and adapting them to its own distinctive patterns. And in the course of adaptation, it was recurrently generating its own adversarial forms."[36] Liberal America tolerates all, includes all. It assimilates, modifies, and rules and yet cannot be authoritarian because "American liberalism *privileged* dissent."[37] The absorption and domination wholly admitted to be liberalism's cultural role ought not be called liberal authoritarianism from this perspective for it merely connects, unites, changes, and absorbs.

How could the problem of submission to authority be rendered irrelevant by virtue of the fact of interconnection? What did power as connection say about what power did in its dispersed arrays? How could the structurality of power preempt the question of its uneven operation on different positions or groups (especially when Foucault himself was interested in such variations)? How was the presence of connection able to absorb the question of control?

Narrowing these questions to the case of Emerson, part of the answer has been the force of the liberal tradition itself: Emerson's readers are encouraged to locate moments of submission as only part of a larger dialectic between individuality and community. My rejection of these readings starts with the evidence of Emerson's texts: such a dialectic is, in fact, as I show in later chapters, secondary to submission to higher law and not the other way around. But I was able to see the importance of submission only after years of regarding Emersonian submission as in fact a really impressive and liberating kind of communal individuality. I was able to see the importance of what I've called the third step, the return of (flexible but unappealable) higher law only after a long time in which this submissive step seemed obviously unimportant compared to Emerson's first two steps, in which radical self-reliance and democracy are combined. I'm going to dwell on the difficulty I had in detecting this third step of higher law because of what it taught me about this step's importance to Emersonian liberalism.

4. Liberal Synthesis and Male Melancholia

The key to avoiding submission is equality. As I've noted before, I don't mean equality as a positive principle with particular notions about redistributing resources and public power. I mean equality as the trace of a usually absent capacity to match the power of those who give the laws we follow, and that therefore allows both autonomy and reciprocity.

Equality became an issue for me as I tried to explain my preference for Emerson's gloomy forebodings over his famous affirmations. His affirmations felt not simply mystical but constrictive. Faced with a choice between his mysticism and his skepticism, I joined many of his readers in preferring the latter, the second half of this "Plotinus-Montaigne," as James Russell Lowell named him. At the end of his essays, Emerson would always proclaim in one way or another that "the world is saturated with deity and with law." [38] These moments, though crucial to this thinking, were not the ones I liked. I preferred his outraged descriptions of how all things go astray. I enjoyed his turn from disgust at failure to a stabilizing fatalism. "Experiences, fortunes, governings, readings, writings, are nothing to the purpose; as when a man comes into the room, it does not appear whether he has been fed on yams or buffalo." [39] "The astonishment of life, is, the absence of any appearance of reconciliation between the theory and practice of life. Reason, the prized reality, the Law, is apprehended, now and then, for a serene and profound moment, amidst the hubbub of cares and works which have no direct bearing on it; — is then lost . . . and again found,

for an interval, to be lost again."[40] In passages like these, individual distinction is achieved through the inexorable tide of reality. Distinction
becomes as unnecessary as it is futile. Reading such passages provided
me a specific kind of freedom, freedom from individual struggle. Other
passages led further in this direction. Everyone's "sad muse loves night
and death, and the pit. His Inferno . . . is indeed very like . . . to the
phenomena of dreaming, which nightly turns many an honest gentleman, benevolent, but dyspeptic, into a wretch, skulking like a dog about
the outer yards and kennels of creation."[41] Buffalo, yams, and foraging
dogs fathomed a futility of possessive individualism that was repressed
by Emerson's more normative demands to take on nature/spirit's abundance of the "corn and the wine." Further descents on the scale of redemption would always ensue: "We fancy men are individuals. So are
pumpkins; but every pumpkin in the field, goes through every point
of pumpkin history." Such moments were my favorite Emerson. They
expressed the pointlessness of ambitious competition, and dismissed the
system that expected it as superficial.[42] Some relief was made inevitable
by these moments of competition's nonnecessity. In such melancholia
there was freedom from the failure to succeed according to the manifest
rules. It was far more satisfying to be liberated from the logic of authority than to fight for (and against) authority's approval.

The way Emerson performed this liberation was especially important. He negated the laws of individual performance by eliminating
the superior authority whose judgment brings the issue of performance
into existence. This negation arose in Emerson's strategic abjection,
which did not deny power to himself while acknowledging it in others,
but denied successful power to everyone. It established a state of general
dispossession in which one's own poverty could never be greater than
anyone else's. This mournful state was a triumphant leveler. It did not
"level down," either, but emptied illusive superiorities.[43] It was impossible to fail at appropriation and command when the entire system
of competitive property had been repudiated. Absent the demands of
possessive individualism, my apparent helplessness proved that, deep
down, I was part of the plan.

One might be skeptical of Emerson's utopian moments when everyone is included and can share. One might see these marking an attempt
to acquire unfair protections.[44] This skepticism, while astute, is also a
symptom of the competitive individualism Emerson sometimes tries to
suspend, for it reads all escapes from antagonism as regression or denial.
Emerson's gloom did not seem simply to reproduce a roundabout ego

defense but to imagine a system in which such a defense would be un-necessary. My gloomy Emerson held a positive notion of power in which power constituted all relations and structures and could be found in one's weakness as well as another's strength. In his moments of despair or scarcity he overcame his elitist gentility to propose the general dispersal of all forces, and even a literally democratic access to them. Power would then lead by its basic structure not to domination but to a continually changing equalization. Emerson offered a vision of individuals experiencing control and freedom that was compatible with cooperation and negotiation. To refer to the three-step quasi dialectic outlined earlier, these moments synthesized steps 1 and 2 — individuality realizing itself through interconnection rather than aggression. What seemed like mere resentment or melancholia offered something much more important — a vision of a successful version of liberalism's balance of individual and community. This was a vision of socialist liberalism, or Goldman's anarchism.

The legitimacy of the liberal balance depended entirely on the genuine presence of equality. Only equality neutralized a frightening subordination in a system devoted precisely to creating such subordinations as way of deciding who would fashion society. Emerson's fatalism offered inclusion in this process without asking for proof of mastery. This seemed equality enough, and indeed, genuine because decentralized and unplanned. Though I might well be a pumpkin, there was no history other than pumpkin history.

But after a while, this kind of equality, the only kind that I could find in Emerson, came to seem painful and unreal. Was equality actually an effect of this process? Were both sides of the idealized liberal balance actually present: (1) free personal agency and (2) equal agency among all participants? I decided finally that the answer was no. I came to recognize the content of these mournful pleasures to be in fact not the equalization of agency but the release from agency. Their main point was that there was nothing to be done. Conflict and competition made no difference. This did not mean that therefore I was taking possession of a power to re-create my historical situation. It meant nearly the opposite: the power of creation was superfluous and unnecessary. What seemed like a taking of force away from a superior and exclusive source and dispersing it lower down was nearly the reverse of the actual case. I was ceding force to this ulterior source. The main change was that the source had been deglamourized — made immanent and no longer transcendental. But the fact that it inhered in relations of interdependence did not mean that I had any active function within it. The fact of interconnection said nothing about relations of power or the distribution of agency. And agency remained entirely with fate, with the necessity that unfurled its bleak but encompassing history. Ultimately, the source of resolution was not myself or my immediate democratic community. It was still the father, my fate, "demetaphysicalized" into a sameness of pumpkins.

The outcome of these ostensibly equalizing moments had been the elimination of a feeling of helplessness and insufficiency. But they obscured this helplessness not by recapturing agency but by establishing the feeling's lawfulness and bringing it into the scheme. Emerson's skepticism provided not equal agency but a magical substitute: liberty as created and protected by the "moral sentiment" or "world-spirit." Equality was produced by relations to others soothed and governed by a superior common law.[45] Recognition did not arise from the collaborative interaction of peers that equality makes possible but from the workings of fate. Emerson's skepticism was indissociable from his faith. His equalizing could not be parted from his trust that whatever was missing in oneself would be supplied by "the moral design of the universe."[46] This promised merely that one belonged, no matter how low down one's place happened to be. It was the surrogate agency suitable to a deference culture, where one's activity reflects one's place in a structure one does not influence.

In short, I thought Emerson managed a connection between steps 1 and 2, a synthesis of egalitarian democracy and individuality, and that he evaded the antipathy between liberty and equality that has always haunted American liberalism. But this synthesis in fact depended on the presiding influence of the third step that I had previously overlooked — the guarantee of a flexible and utterly depersonalized dictator, "a law which is not intelligent but intelligence."[47] I don't mean to suggest that my period of felt but often unconscious belief in Emersonian liberalism can possibly represent the encounters of all of his readers. But my current understanding of this period convinces me that liberalism's balance of individualism and democracy may frequently depend on an unstated submission to flexible but unchangeable higher law. This is the authoritarian moment in the liberal imagination — submission to the right law makes equality irrelevant.

5. Equality and Corporatism

Modern Americans have come to see the world divided
into superiors and subordinates as naturally as the feudalists
saw it divided into masters and men.

— Jeffrey Lustig

The concept of equality is going to recur throughout my consideration
of Emerson's thought, and a few additional comments on the subject
may help clarify my initial assumptions about its place in liberalism and,
in a preliminary way, its relation to corporatism.

Nothing is more important about the idea of equality in the United
States than its widely assumed antagonism to liberty. I've already noted
that American liberalism can be distinguished through its attempts to
reconcile or balance the individual and the community, liberty and some
kind of public reciprocity. (I've also said that this book will chronicle the
extent to which this balance depends on submissive and authoritarian
elements.) Here it's crucial to note that liberalism, even as it seeks reconciliation, places liberty and equality in perpetual conflict. A sacrificial
logic rules the relation between them, and equality is the usual loser. In
the United States, nearly any attempt to increase equality in any area
except a widely accepted formal legal equality — to produce equality in
salaries, educational opportunity, political influence — is considered an
attack on the liberties of the people. For example, efforts to equalize
either political influence — by restricting large political campaign contributions — or the private market in media access have been ruled by the
Supreme Court to be infringements of free speech.

This conflict between liberty and equality comes as close as anything
in American life to constituting a national consensus. The notion that
equality impairs liberty unites what we call "liberals" and "conservatives" in an everyday way. Equality of condition, when sought with any
deliberation or system, strangles entrepreneurship, incentives to produce, and individuality itself. In short, actual equality means tyranny, or
at best, mediocrity. Although other countries, particularly in Europe,
have a long history of this same conservative-liberal discourse about despotic equality, as well as a similar Cold War tradition of regarding communism as the final refutation of egalitarian practice, they see liberty
and equality as more compatible, and have the smaller income gaps and
the larger systems of equal-access services to prove it. In the United
States, nearly any taint of egalitarian aims will doom a reform policy,
"redistribution" and other equality mechanisms having been banished

to the left-wing political wilderness. American liberalism owes much of its victory over socialism to its rejection of strong egalitarian aims. This may turn out to be a suicidal victory in the end. Having helped destroy national belief in the egalitarian principle that underwrites projects like government-supported health care, race-based affirmative action, paid maternity leave, public works, and even public education, liberalism in the last fifteen years has been largely swallowed up by a proudly anti-egalitarian, laissez-faire individualism of the political right. Whatever the future holds, liberty's ongoing priority to equality preserves a liberal-conservative consensus that has governed the nation since the time of Emerson's birth. In this light, the egalitarian liberalism of the 1960s looks like the aberration of an unusual time.

The liberal imagination has a difficult double mission. It must balance liberty and equality, but it must always maintain liberty in the dominant position. The imperative to balance liberty and equality is concurrent with the imperative to maintain the opposition between them. Nineteenth-century liberalism forms a bulwark against the more radically democratic view, well articulated by the late eighteenth century, that "equality and liberty are 'identical' in practice, because *neither* can true liberty go without equality *nor* can true equality go without liberty."[48] Emerson's liberalism, more intensely than most, revolves around this kind of claim for the mutual dependence of liberty and equality and is yet repelled by their conjunction.

In the academic humanities, most nonconservative work in crucial fields such as women's studies and ethnic studies has been rightly concerned with analyzing and protecting personal and cultural differences. Criticisms of academia tend to focus on moments in which it insufficiently supports the freedom to differ. The central problem, in one critic's words, is that "every single theoretically interesting project of postwar thought has finally had the effect of delegitimating our space for asking or thinking in detail about the multiple, unstable ways in which people may be like or different from each other."[49] This is an important point, but like most comments about large patterns in American life, it stays within the terms of that society's liberal political sensibility. Equality doesn't seem relevant to the liberation of sameness and difference. It doesn't seem part of either free choice or resisting coercion. Nonetheless, inequality or the perception of inferiority has always been crucial to stigmatizing difference as a problem: restrictions on equality support restrictions on freedom of difference. But we are all more or less subject to terms of debate in which it is hard to imagine how greater equality would enhance multiple, unstable, freely chosen sameness and difference.[50]

As noted above, in this book I use the term *equality* not to designate relations of equivalence or equalization established from outside these relations but something much like the opposite: a condition of reciprocal influence and agency. Equality cannot be reduced to a general rule of sameness, although that can be important in such cases as equal salaries for women and men or equal legal rights for documented and undocumented residents. Equality is the parity that allows negotiations to be continually made and remade by every side. It cannot be practiced by someone who, like me in my own liberal condition, careens between resenting systemic inequality and expecting it to be resolved by the sheer absence of a tyrannizing power and the abstract equality of things. Liking equality as a kind of general interconnection, I was not very good at actually laboring to produce actual equality. Resentment and its companion resignation are special psychic disasters less because they sap the Nietzschean will than because their submissiveness severs the individual from collaborative activity undertaken with peers. This sort of collaboration is not enabled by settled equations among different persons and groups, but instead itself constructs equality by actively working with one's equals, or with people who become rough equals through collaborative work. Such collaboration sees social relations as constituted not simply by relation itself, but by continual negotiations to produce equal agency within those relations. The major condition of this kind of continually constructed equality is a capacity to identify as readily with the un-Great as with the Great. This means, for my purposes here, not the denial of differences, including superior and inferior performances in particular contexts, but the denial of general superiorities based on these differences. Only the extremely various activity that creates and maintains reciprocal relations all over again every day gradually produces a collective system that has been sufficiently "delayered" by a history of open negotiation, a history of competition to control the rule of competition. This kind of equality does not mean the sort of fixed equating across differences that U.S. liberalism warns against but the leveling of the power of fixing rules.

Rather than invoking an essentialist metaphysics, such equality is, in fact, what would allow the creation of a truly postmetaphysical society. For it would enable the dismantling and reconstruction of systems of power by preventing the blocking of unauthorized inputs by a superior force. And it is the postmetaphysical labor of aggressively antiauthori-

tarian, dispersed collaboration that Emersonian liberalism, for all its
hostility to subordination, has the hardest time undertaking. Emerson's
three-step offers a self-recriminating resentment of inferiority that,
rather than building in its own way, awaits rescue from the superior
which it does not resent. Such waiting short-circuits the radical democracy for which Emerson's liberalism ambivalently longs.[51]

Liberalism exists in a continual state of tension between its usually
repressed sense that liberty depends on equality and its more common
view that liberty is threatened by it. The problematic position of equality, in liberalism, is resolved not through despotism but through corporate individualism. This both sustains and eliminates equality in the required fashion (see, esp., chap. 3). Corporate individualism triumphs
over the egalitarian variety in the Emersonian three-step I outlined
above. Autonomous individualism is replaced in his move to the second
step but becomes corporate only when he proceeds from the second to
the third. In the second step of embodied collectivity, equality is a condition of personally rewarding activity. In the third step, subjection to a
transcendental law, inequality is not simply overlooked but becomes a
positive necessary component of the law that binds. The potentially
democratic second position gives way to obeying a higher law of spirit,
which in turn underwrites society. Inequality is no longer seen as an
obstacle to free movement within a system but founds the system itself.
Even laissez-faire liberalism had the virtue of asking where the individual stands in relation to authority and whether that authority is despotic.
Emerson's corporate alternative accepts submission as part of the socialization process, allowing socialization and submission to seem the same.

Corporate individualism is a genuine individualism. It does not offer
an identifiable father, despot, demagogue, or other tyrannical sovereign
that crushes the self and makes obvious its loss of individuality to inferiority. As my own experience with the gloomy Emerson suggests, one
loses agency without actually losing it to a particular master. One becomes submissive without having a discrete superior to make submission obvious. Corporatism renders the superior law as unity and inclusion rather than as sovereignty. Unity makes equality unnecessary rather
than waging war on the idea. It eliminates the question of whether a
socialized environment is sufficiently egalitarian to allow for the kind of
reciprocal determination known as democratic, for it seems to accomplish the same thing as democracy — the administration of groups, the
rational reconciliation of differences — in a less conflictual way. It quietly
prefers union to any group agency that is different from obeying the

law. It rejects the distinction between the freedom to choose one's own laws and the "choosing" of laws that are already given. It says that all possible choice in modern democracies is comprehended by (freely) accepting the (democratic) values established by others.[52] The question of submission becomes moot.

This is what I mean by the Emerson Effect — the absorption of democracy into sociability, the loss of the distinction between democratic sovereignty and corporate administration. For corporate to replace democratic individuality with as little notice as it now receives, the difference must be part of mainstream culture. The Emerson Effect appears in the naturalness with which the fact of the self's constructedness in relation to a coordinating and superior law replaces (or settles) the question of the self's equality with the powers that perform that construction, of its power to control that construction. What Norberto Bobbio calls democracy's "autocratic power" does not involve a sovereign's coercion but only the pervasive sense of the irrelevance of talking about feeling dominated because one is not coerced. Authoritarian elements do not survive in U.S. democracy through the inherent logic of modern power or of human nature or of the complexity of our contemporary societies but through the power of corporate individualism to naturalize hierarchy by suggesting the irrelevance of equality to the facts of structure.

It is my task in this volume to analyze the construction of this kind of liberalism out of some surprising materials. It is my hope that this process might further inspire the creation of alternatives, particularly within Emerson's primary audience of middle-class information workers and managers.

PART

TWO

Nature:
The Corporatist
Solution to
Submission

CHAPTER

TWO

The Authoritarian Language
of Liberal Religion

Emerson's essay *Nature* launched his literary career by declaring a reconciliation between providential law and poetic self-making. While the essay repeatedly insists that the everyday world is grounded in absolute
Spirit, it also asserts that the world obeys the will of the true poet. The
"universal current" gives the poet life and yet sustains rather than replaces the poet's power as sovereign and lawgiver. The younger Emerson departs from the Neoplatonic tradition with which he is sometimes
associated by refusing to subordinate individuality to the absolute One.
He is closer to German idealism in wishing to combine sovereign law
with the priority of the individual ego. In this tradition, "the identity of
the 'I' does not mean only that abstract universality of self-consciousness
as such, but at the same time the category of singularity."[1] Singularity
depends on free subjectivity, and free subjectivity expresses itself
through individuated poetic voice. Poetry "alone is infinite, as it alone
is free, and its first law is that the poet's arbitrariness is subject to no
law."[2] The true poet is the founding father all over again: "It is the
sovereign, assertive, and objectifying ego whose practical freedom is
manifested through its struggle to realize itself by creating the world
and itself."[3] Emerson remains the national Orpheus for most readers:
while Hawthorne might stop at imagining "reform through continuity," Emerson, at least through the mid-1840s, is a "seer of 'perpetual
inchoation,' and rhapsodist of nonconformity."[4] He is "Mr. America,"

An earlier version of this chapter was published as "Controlling the Voice: Emerson's
Early Theory of Language," *ESQ: A Journal of the American Renaissance* 38, no. 1 (1992):
1–29. Reprinted by permission of the editor.

who "insists upon the necessity of the single self achieving a total autonomy, of becoming its own cosmos without first having to ingest either
nature or other selves."[5]

This reading of Emerson as the prophet of radical individualism has
been qualified in recent years, mostly by those who recognize Emerson's
willingness to admit otherness into the self, to grant a sizable place to
dependency, waiting, weakness, "mastery as listening," and "replacing
founding with finding."[6] But it is not easy to say what kind of independence is compatible with a great deal of dependence. How can the individual be receptive to "nature and other selves" while remaining free
from them? How much can one embed the individual in external structures of either cultural or metaphysical kinds while retaining "individualism" as a meaningful description?

As I noted in the previous chapter, Emerson's ongoing influence depends on his majestic expression of these two states as forming a coherent dual desire and not a contradiction. The Emersonian individual has
the best of both worlds in being radically free in self-development while
obeying the law. But the structure and operation of this dual subjectivity
remains more asserted than explained. Emerson commentary under-
standably tends to admire both sides of Emerson's double claim that
liberty for individuals means fulfilling a general spiritual law, yet this is
more a tribute to Emerson's ongoing influence than to our own critical
testing of these ideas, a testing which, collectively speaking, has never
had the persistence or scope to prevent Emerson's combination from
functioning with the complex but intuitive plausibility of a national
ideology.

This problem with the Emersonian notion of self-determination becomes particularly acute around the question of poetic language. Here
Emerson denies the power of meaning to the free poet by siding with
Neoplatonic realism against nominalism. In the debate between realism
and nominalism, the question was whether the particular, the apparent,
or the transient are bound ontologically to the universal, the essential,
and the permanent as the realist asserted, or whether these connections
arise from our autonomous acts of naming and reading. In the chapter
"Language" in *Nature,* Emerson favors realism. He claims that "particular natural facts are symbols of particular spiritual facts" and that, more
generally, "Nature is the symbol of spirit."[7] Emerson is here a Neoplatonist and not a romantic. Like Cratylus in the Socratic dialogue of that
name, Emerson holds in effect that the original users of language were
"legislators" who "invented names," but only by imitating the natures
of things; for Cratylus, a name must be "rightly imposed" if it is to name

the object at all.[8] The realist theory of language allots the poet only a limited role: he discovers the original "language of nature" in which the name, the thing, the soul of the thing, all correspond to each other in the One.

The realist view does not encourage invention but demands imitation. In this context, Emersonian invention is a variety of mimesis. Emerson's legislator represents preexisting laws rather than creating them out of his or her moral sense. Invention, to the contrary, depends on something like the nominalist's view, which Emerson repudiates in "Language."[9] The metaphysics, language theory, and cultural reception of Emerson's individualism do not entirely cooperate, for his individualism demands both obedience to universal law and the freedom of practical self-constitution. The collision affects the question of what "self-expression" actually expresses — an abstract and universal or a concrete and individual self.

In this chapter I describe the relation between invention and imitation as a contradiction within liberal individualism's notion of poetic language, and try to gauge the result. This might seem a doomed intention, since Emerson's readers not only notice the contradictions in his work but celebrate them as forms of higher consciousness, boldness, or complexity. For these readers, Emerson repeatedly finds himself in "an apparent self-contradiction" which turns out to be a "wise inconsistency."[10] Oppositional structures work roughly but symbiotically, hence universal and particular individuality or imitation and invention or Cratylian realism and possessive individualism coexist in mutual support. Emerson's readers need not actually claim a dialectical synthesis of these terms in which the strengths of each are preserved. They need only observe his empirical accuracy about subjective experience, which oscillates between freedom and obedience. They can also note his accuracy about the cultural effects of individualism, which might be said to allow its believers to refuse to choose between imitation and invention, and to have both at the same time. They can also argue that Emerson, following the most sophisticated philosophy of his time, defines the free self as constituted by its obedience of a law that it gives to itself.[11] This kind of reading might be based in romantic psychologism or Kant or Hegel or Foucault on the subject of power or American "consensus" historicism or all of the above — this is a question I leave to one side. I will instead stress the contradiction between (instead of the symbiosis of) opposing terms (invention and imitation, freedom and submission), and I do this not to claim individualism's poverty or breakdown but to redescribe its outcome and goals. Emerson's theory of language does not either succeed or fail adequately to imagine personal autonomy, for whatever its cultural reception has been, it does not seek autonomy in the first place.

1. The Rule of Law

In the context of the overall essay *Nature,* the "Language" chapter seems straightforwardly transcendentalist in making a central point that every other chapter of the essay also makes: the physical, intellectual, moral, and spiritual aspects of reality are echoing reflections of the universally interconnected Oneness of being. The "high argument" that begins with the chapter "Idealism" introduces human thought into the relation of nature and spirit only after this latter relation has been redundantly exemplified. The presence of spirit in the time-honored names for physical objects is one more example of the same.

In the previous chapter I outlined a three-step pattern which finds a presocial precursor in the "degrees" of "Language." This structure codifies gradations and differences within an ultimate Oneness:

> Language is a third use which Nature subserves to man. Nature is the vehicle of thought, and in a simple, double, and threefold degree.
> 1. Words are signs of natural facts.
> 2. Particular natural facts are symbols of particular spiritual facts.
> 3. Nature is the symbol of spirit. (*Es and Ls,* 20)

This series, which the chapter elaborates in some detail, moves from outward form to inner meaning and from natural to supernatural law. The term *degree,* probably borrowed from Coleridge, denotes harmonized movements within a preexisting unity rather than discrete entities coordinated after their separate creation by an independent human consciousness.[12] This scale becomes clearer when degree 2 is restated. "Particular natural facts" can be read as sense data and "particular spiritual facts" read as individual mental states, or "spirit" in the shape of the finite human mind. Revised in this way, the three degrees express three familiar levels of being:

1. physical nature;
2. individual consciousness;
3. spirit or the "oversoul."

Language is one more modality of the oneness of the individual with all being: a "thousandfold occult mutual attractions" between each particular is the means by which "Nature keeps herself whole" ("Nominalist and Realist," *Es and Ls,* 581, 584).

In the context of a generic transcendentalism, the language argument can be simply told:

> 1. Every word is originally "borrowed from some material appearance." (20)[13]
> 2. Every "state of the mind can only be described by presenting that natural appearance as its picture." (20)
> 3. "A [material] Fact is the end or last issue of spirit." (25)

The chapter therefore locates language in a hierarchical but unified chain of correspondences:

> 1. words correspond to nature;
> 2. thoughts corresponds to nature;
> 3. nature corresponds to spirit.

"Poetic," primitive, living words correspond to thoughts which correspond to nature and to spirit equally. On the present level of generality, Emerson's eloquent (though derivative) chapter can be summarized by a single sentence taken from one of his most likely sources, an article on Herder by Elizabeth Palmer Peabody, published two years before *Nature* and paraphrased, perhaps unconsciously, along with the work of Alcott, Reed, Oegger, Swedenborg, and Coleridge: "The human mind in its original principles, and the natural creation, in its simplicity" are parallel types "of the same creator, who has linked them for the reciprocal development of their mutual treasures" in linguistic signs no less than in any other aspect of being.[14] In short, "the Me and the Not-Me mirror one another in the Oversoul."[15] Pure poetic language expresses the reuniting of the subject and object of absolute knowledge.

This thinking locates its enemy in the "sensual" philosophy of Locke, which in this case means the Lockean belief that language is conventional. To the conventionalist, the word is an arbitrary signifier of the idea and is phonetic rather than iconic or pictographic or correspondent on the plane of Being. Emerson officially regards conventionalism as a symptom of trauma rather than of truth: language is not naturally conventional but is so only in its diseased state. Original language was united with the essence of things, but this relation has unfortunately been "broken up by the prevalence of secondary desires, the desire of riches, of pleasure, of power, and of praise, — and duplicity and falsehood take place of simplicity and truth, . . . new imagery ceases to be created, and old words are perverted to stand for things which are not; a paper currency is employed, when there is no bullion in the vaults." This linguistic coin, severed from its gold standard, represents not truth but absolute decay: "In due time, the fraud is manifest, and words lose all power to stimulate the understanding or the affections" ("Language," 22). The language of convention is the language of defaced coinage, blank humanity, white mythology,[16] empty ciphers, illegible spirit.

In the context of this critique of the language of convention, the poet has a very decided role.[17] He strips away encrustations of convention and false facades. He penetrates culture to the level of "Being as the category which contains essences in the same manner that the Idea contains particulars."[18] "Wise men pierce this rotten diction and fasten words again to visible things; so that picturesque language is at once a commanding certificate that he who employs it, is a man in alliance with truth and God. . . . A man conversing in earnest, if he watch his intellectual processes, will find that a material image, more or less luminous, arises in his mind, contemporaneous with every thought, which furnishes the vestment of the thought" ("Language," 23). The true poet resembles the honest citizen who understands commodities as objects that represent eternal laws rather than as objects that reflect merely their momentary value in the market. Corrupt words do not refer to things in their essential nature but only to other words: they are a "paper currency" in that they have meaning or value only in relation to other words whose meaning is in turn a function of relation, contingency, and exchange. Corrupt words exist only through their exchange value, for their use value—their inherent meaning—has been lost. True words have a fixed relationship to the underlying reality of "visible things," and the authentic poet, properly in harmony with general laws, can recover the "picturesque language" of visible correspondences.

How does Emerson's poet produce invention out of this? As I've said, commentators have tended to offer open, pragmatic, dialectical accounts, often making a double claim: the poet obeys and creates the law. This two-sided understanding of transcendentalist language theory often resembles Charles Feidelson's phenomenological notion of the symbol. Emerson, he says, "moves back and forth from self-expression to impression, from language as the power of mind to language as the potentiality of nature"; his thought rests on an "ambiguity of 'creation' and 'discovery.'" Feidelson sees this "paradoxical method of self-contradiction" as Emerson's great strength as a symbolist and protophenomenologist: "Emerson finds it necessary to invoke 'Mind' and 'Nature' in order to state a view that dissolves them . . . speech fundamentally refers neither to a preconception nor to an external thing but 'to that which is to be said.'"[19] Sacvan Bercovitch offers a similar combination. Emerson insists that language "is an exercise not in the powers of the individual imagination but in the philology of nature." But Emerson also believes that the use of natural language requires the poet's previous will to "choose (or invent) his identity, and then to impose his own patterns upon experience." To Bercovitch's romantic poet, reception is identically self-reception. Even "the imitation of Christ became for him the process of duplicating himself . . . a deific creation *ex imaginatione* in which *caritas* depended upon autonomy, and plenitude was narcissism extended to infinity."[20] Most influential commentaries have this dual form, melding freedom with determinism and metamorphosis with permanence.[21] In such accounts, the poet restores tarnished language through a dialectic between perception and creation.

The accuracy of this pragmatic transcendentalism depends on the dialectical presence of invention and imitation: the mind transcribes the invisible laws already given in nature and brings forth something that was not already there. The dialectical poet, that is, the liberal sage, must act as a "lawgiver" in Friedrich Schlegel's sense rather than simply in that of Cratylus, who traced the legislating of the first poet to a power of imitation. This poet must have a power not simply to designate but to figure forth. The power of troping is crucial to this independent status, and the trope most relevant to independence is catachresis. Catachresis knows the imitative aspect of the sign that it puts to a radically new use.

But at no point in "Language" does Emerson describe this kind of active yet "embedded" invention. His language chapter has the most impossible time trying to maintain any kind of dialectic between nature and independent mind. When poets pierce corrupt language and restore the original relation between words and things, they do so not out of a self-constituted power but out of "alliance with truth and God." The renewed, picturesque, material image arises spontaneously, from a noncognitive instinct. The poet watches his intellectual processes as though they were not part of his consciousness, but distinct from and prior to it, part of some other power. The process which commentators describe as dialectical in fact depends on one-sided reception. The first and second degrees of language use, which represent nature and mind, are finally subsumed by the third degree, or the Oversoul. Emerson appears to be in a tremendous hurry to end invention along with the histories of words and thoughts. He intrudes the Oversoul long before its allotted place in degree 3. The second sentence of (1), "words are signs of natural facts," leaps beyond the issue of the link between words and "natural facts" to say, "The use of natural history is to give us aid in supernatural history" ("Language," 20). And in (2), "particular natural facts are symbols of particular spiritual facts," the correspondence between natural facts and "some state of mind" dissolves into the omnipresence of the "universal soul."

> Who looks upon a river in a meditative hour, and is not reminded of the flux of all things? Throw a stone into the stream, and the circles that propagate themselves are the beautiful type of all influence. Man is conscious of a universal soul within or behind his individual life, wherein, as in a firmament, the natures of Justice, Truth, Love, Freedom, arise and shine. This universal soul, he calls Reason: it is not mine, or thine, or his, but we are its; we are its property and men. . . . Spirit is the Creator. Spirit hath life in itself. And man in all ages and countries, embodies it in his language, as the FATHER. (21)

Emerson is unable to describe individual mental processes without dissolving them into the One.

This does not mean that nature and mind mirror one another and retain their separate identities. Each collapses rather drastically and immediately into a spirit which annihilates its constituents' independence: the explicit condition of Reason is to have become the property of spirit, to be owned by this ulterior power, rather than to own oneself in some fuller way. This shift comes out of nowhere, as a non sequitur that ties the observer's consciousness of the stream as a type of influence (physical as well as metaphysical) to his consciousness of the universal soul. This discontinuity furnishes precisely the kind of sublime determinism that Emerson seeks: the Oversoul, though symbolized by nature, is that which is other to natural power, and which operates on principles which cannot, in spite of Emerson's theory of correspondences, be fully encompassed in, as, and through natural or cognitive activity. Intensifying this vein, the Oversoul becomes personified, and shifts from being an impersonal general Law ("a Law which is not intelligent but intelligence" ["Fate," 968]) to being a Father. The Father, unlike the Law, rules from outside and above and with ostentatious visibility; he cannot be internalized or sublimated as a nameless instinct belonging to oneself, but, even in his benevolence, is what can never even appear to be oneself.

In the second and third sections of the language chapter, Emerson's Neoplatonism is recurrent and undialectical: the empirical mind lacks creative power and discovers truth only by reuniting with the timeless

One who slumbers, already perfect, in the soul.[22] The individual soul is merely the One twice degraded (it is Plotinus's third hypostasis, the second being intellect). Rather than effecting a synthesis of differentiated terms, the soul wishes for a simple return and reunion with the absolute. The mode of this return is the most perfect reflection of this absolute, and the most perfect is the least reciprocal in bringing the least contribution from the fallen state of temporal being. As Emerson says in "The Poet," "Poetry was all written before time was," and the best poet is simply he who manages not to "substitute something of [his] own, and thus miswrite the poem" (449). The free poet does not, for Emerson, manifest the dialectic of personal sovereignty we usually attribute to the "American self." The poet, in a monkish solitude, transcribes the laws.

2. Empiricism's Supporting Role

I have not accounted for the empirical or organic side of Emerson's language chapter, though many readers have thought that Emerson's Neoplatonism in his second and third degrees of language use is qualified by his first and empirical degree. The latter strain is mixed with a Yankee pragmatism that already modifies his mysticism in *Nature*, dominates it by the late 1830s, and ostensibly repudiates it by the time of the "Swedenborg" essay of the late 1840s. Granting the significance of the first degree of language, Emerson then appears to combine idealism and empiricism in a higher reconciliation than could be found in either alone. If the first degree is meaningfully empirical, in other words, Emerson can be thought to recover the dialectic that seems missing from the other degrees. He is a naturalist as much as a mystic in this view, seeing the third degree without forgetting the first.

This reading has much in its favor. Emerson is certainly more compound and synthetic than a committed Neoplatonist like Bronson Alcott. Emerson does not quite declare with the latter that "Man's force, his individual will, his free-agency, cometh by submission to the superiour Force that ever presseth against him, penetrateth into his very centre, cometh forth from this centre and rusheth both out and into his very being."[23] Emerson grants some concrete freedom to the individual voice through the first degree of language, where things are given their first names by mankind, and these are modified and transferred over time through various historical processes. Does Emerson's first degree work like this?

His etymology casts words for things as part of the totality of creation, but it also distinguishes empirical from spiritual determinants of meaning.

> 1. Words are signs of natural facts. The use of natural history is to give us aid in supernatural history: the use of the outer creation, to give us language for the beings and changes of the inward creation. Every word which is used to express a moral or intellectual fact, if traced to its root, is found to be borrowed from some material appearance. *Right* means *straight; wrong* means *twisted. Spirit* primarily means *wind; transgression,* the crossing of a *line; supercilious,* the *raising of the eyebrow.* We say the *heart* to express emotion, the *head* to denote thought; and *thought* and *emotion* are words borrowed from sensible things, and now appropriated to spiritual nature. Most of the process by which this transformation is made, is hidden from us in the remote time when language was framed; but the same tendency may be daily observed in children. Children and savages use only nouns or names of things, which they convert into verbs, and apply to analogous mental acts. (*Es and Ls,* 20)

Emerson describes two phases of the "language of nature." First, "words are signs of natural facts" in the sense that words originally were imitations of the physical objects to which they referred. Language is natural because the original words for physical things imitated the objects to which they referred. Traces of this primary resemblance remain in existing words, and poetic uses of existing words reveal this original proximity to natural objects. In a second phase, "Every word which is used to express a moral or intellectual fact, if traced to its root, is found to be borrowed from some material appearance." The crucial differences here are that moral or intellectual words are traced to a linguistic root rather than to an object, and this root is itself a borrowing rather than an imitation. Words for ideas, emotions, concepts, and all nonmaterial entities derive from other words which designate objects only through the kind of mediation and displacement that Emerson calls "borrowing."

Emerson is working with two varieties of the language of nature that do not coincide. The first sort, involving words for objects, arises from a process of imitation. The second, involving words for concepts, feelings, and abstract systems, arises from a more complicated process which encroaches on several non-natural areas: cultural history, linguistic convention, imagination or invention, and the carrying over of meaning known as troping. Words imitate things, and second, words for spiritual things imitate words for physical things in a more complicated, even figural, way. This distinction between physical and spiritual words is often unstable and obscure, not to say simply untenable, but in the period's writing about language it designates a commonplace confrontation between innate and arbitrary traits, between spheres of necessity and of freedom.

For either variety of natural language, does Emerson free the realm of thought from the crude physical determinism of the sensuous philosophy? Critics have read his etymology as having "behind it much of the thought of Reed and Oegger and the Neoplatonists,"[24] but Emerson's reasoning is very close to that found in the Lockean textbook he used in college, Hugh Blair's *Lectures on Rhetoric*. On the first level, involving words for physical things, Emerson echoes (while diluting) Blair's observation that the words arose "by imitating . . . the nature of the object which they named, by the sound of the name which they gave to it."[25] Blair insists that the first words are natural rather than arbitrary, for "to suppose words invented, or names given, to things, in a manner purely arbitrary, without any ground or reason, is to suppose an effect without a cause" (102). In fact, the bulk of Emerson's first degree of language use is a paraphrase of the quintessential empiricist, Locke himself.[26] The conservative wing of the empiricist tradition asserts that, in Locke's phrase, "Nature, even in the naming of Things, unawares suggested to Men the Originals and Principles of all their Knowledge."[27] In the moment in which the sensualists allow the mind little creative latitude and trace "all . . . knowledge" to the suggestions of "Nature," Emerson does not repudiate but embraces them.

The status of poetry and human culture are at stake in the second variety of natural language, which involves words for nonphysical entities. Rather than protecting intellectual from physical words so that the former might arise from spiritual rather than physical processes, Emerson runs them together. Again he follows Blair. Blair considers the origin of language to have natural determinants and the development of language to rely in large part on convention, which presumably has a strong imaginative, cultural, invented, even arbitrary, component, but the strength of his faith in empirical causality reduces development (and idea-words) to origin (and object-words).

> Throughout the radical words of all Languages, there may be traced some degree of correspondence with the object signified. With regard to moral and intellectual ideas, they remark, that, in every Language, the terms significant of them, are derived from the names of sensible objects to which they are conceived to be analogous; and with regard to sensible objects pertaining merely to sight, they remark, that their most distin-

guishing qualities have certain radical sounds appropriated to the expression of them. (*Lectures,* 103)

Blair uses the term *derivation* with an authority that arises from commonsense notions of empirical determination. He carries this material linkage from the physical to the intellectual realm, thereby empiricizing and naturalizing the conceptual process of forming a word for an invisible or spiritual thing. He reverts to words for sensible things without noting any difference. Emerson's linkage of natural and supernatural history accomplishes the same assimilation.

Having followed Blair in assimilating these two processes, Emerson assimilates two different types of etymological examples. In the first case the word begins as a word for a physical thing and is applied to a spiritual thing based on an innate resemblance between the physical and spiritual thing. This innate resemblance is ratified by the natural history of etymology. "*Spirit* primarily means *wind,*" in Emerson's phrase (which is analogous to Locke's statement that "*Spirit,* in its primary signification, is Breath," and Noah Webster's claim that "In most languages, as far as my information extends, the terms used to signify *spirit,* or the intellectual principle, are primarily the names of *breath, air, wind*").[28] The literal meaning of *spirit* shifts from the physical to the intellectual sphere based on a resemblance between breath as the animating principle of the body (or wind as the animation of the air we breathe) and spirit as the life of the soul. This resemblance is based on what Rowland Hazard called a "primitive perception," and is verified by long linguistic usage.

In the second type of Emerson's examples, the word again has physical and intellectual referents. "We say the *heart* to express emotion," which is to say that *heart* originally signified *emotion.* In this case, however, the etymological link does not exist. The English word *spirit* does come from *spiritus,* meaning breath, breath of a god, or inspiration; *spiritus* arises in turn from the Latin *spirare,* to breathe. But *heart* comes from a Middle and Old English word that means "to place trust," while *emotion* comes from French and Latin meaning (at many removes) "to move" to "to excite," which can be the opposite of placing trust. *Heart,* the word for the spiritual thing, *emotion,* shows spiritual and physical meanings in unrelated difference rather than in innate, preexisting alignment. The absence of an etymological link suggests the absence of a perceptual, preexisting resemblance, and indeed the connection between *heart* and *emotion* derives from a process of figuration that cannot be regarded as the imitation of an innate likeness. While *spirit* and *heart* are alike in referring to their spiritual counterparts through acts of cognition or imagination that cannot be validated with physical evidence, the two examples denote two different types of linguistic development. And they result, in present use, in two different modes of reference: *spirit* refers literally to spirit, while *heart* refers figurally to emotion. In spite of this difference, Emerson lumps these modes together; he assumes kinship between troping (*heart*) and etymological naming (*spirit*). Without openly acknowledging this equation, Emerson binds the imaginative rupture of figuration to copying.

What explains this peculiar, even contradictory hybrid of troping and imitating, of intellectual and material determinations? Transcendentalists are, of course, reluctant to choose between naturalism and supernaturalism, as Carlyle first implied, since they believe that these levels correspond to one another in their common being without becoming interchangeable. As I have already noted, a long tradition of plausible, commonsense readings of this question has proposed that Emerson was shrewd and courageous enough to insist that the creation answers to our double wishes — we can have language more concretely tied to objects and have more autonomous self-expression. We want language to have both an imitative and an inventive (or self-expressive) power, and this is exactly what human language affords.

But this reading assumes that Emerson provides a separation of these two modes into different spheres or "departments," in Horace Bushnell's term; it assumes that Emerson acknowledges that, while obedience to the law of an object's essence is appropriate in some cases, breaking this empirical law or making the law anew or making one's own law is required in other cases — that freedom, or even the mere existence of intellect, assumes variable, local, temporal, provisional, and even newly created laws. This distinction between imitating and obeying, on one hand, and troping and inventing, on the other, is exactly what Emerson denies when he mingles these realms in each of his "degrees" of language use, including the paraphrasing and examples of degree 1. I realize this conflicts with the defiant Emerson who says "build, therefore, your own world"; nonetheless, his hybrid of troping and mimesis does not endorse free expression and reliable reference at the same time but anchors free expression in preexisting authority. Emerson implies that acts of troping are predetermined by rules much like those by which the primordial name was given by the referent's essence. By casting the transfer of spiritual meaning as empirically determined but then avoiding the literally empirical and concrete level of this determination, Emerson shows that language is free from a literal demand for the imitation of physical forms, but is nonetheless (or precisely at that moment) always governed by what physical life figures — necessitarian law.

3. Unexploited Openings

I'm arguing, then, that in "Language," Emerson calls first and foremost for controlling the voice. He performs this call by binding thought to spirit and nature where other theorists see some separation. This binding prevents Emerson from being read either as a conservative, for he still insists on invention, or as a romantic radical, for he authorizes only the utterance which agrees with existing law. He fully acknowledges the intellectual, internal, creative realm of ideas while subjecting it to an outside authority as immediately concrete as physical nature itself. The mind is granted its power of figuration but remains tied to a preexisting (spiritual and material) law. Invention and figurative usages do not for Emerson take the form of catachresis or passionate cries (Rousseau on language's origins) or of overflowing instincts or generalization (Adam Smith) but of governed mimesis.

This amounts to a formidable and seductive mixture of liberation and control. I didn't entirely grasp Emerson's position on this point until I systematically compared his views to those of the writers who loomed large in his own mind. I had, of course, been struck by his preference for Coleridge (especially the later, more theological Coleridge) over Shelley, Byron, and Blake, but was most helped by surveying figures he liked and disliked on the language question, and I summarize some of this now in order to sketch the extent to which Emerson's subjection of thought (as troping) to law exceeds that of his precursors. Many theorists (even spiritualist conservatives like Horace Bushnell) more carefully extract the independence of mind from their vision of divine Oneness.

Bushnell concurs with Emerson that "all religious truth is and must be presented under conditions of form or analogy from the outward state," but he nonetheless claims that "as physical terms are never exact, being only the names of genera, much less have we any terms in the spiritual department of language that are exact representatives of thoughts."[29] Though he limits spiritual signification to "a *logos* in the form of things," he also radicalizes the process by which spiritual meaning appears in figures. Such words are necessarily inexact, for a gap always remains between natural and spiritual (indeed, the spiritual is constituted by its difference from the natural). The inexactness of spiritual words requires that truth be approached through the multiplication of signs, through their ongoing struggle and contradiction: "We never come so near to a well-rounded view of truth, as when it is offered paradoxically."[30] Coleridge carefully sequesters Spirit from empirical results: "In disciplining the mind one of the first rules should be, to lose no opportunity of tracing words to their origin; one good consequence of which will be, that he will be able to use the *language* of sight without being enslaved by its affections. He will at least save himself from the delusive notion, that what is not *imageable,* is likewise not *conceivable.*"[31] James Marsh, Coleridge's early expounder in the United States, also denounces approximating spiritual knowledge too closely to natural signs: a spiritual fact must be "seen" with Reason alone for it to reveal its "inward and subjective nature."[32] Bronson Alcott insisted in his Temple School that "Rather than paying undue attention to the outside world, children should examine their spiritual depths and *then* look outwardly at the material presence. Nature was only to be made use of as 'imagery to express the inward life we experience.'"[33] Edgar Allan Poe vehemently links signs of spirit with nature's negation: he associates the malevolence of the black Polynesian sons of Ham in *Arthur Gordon Pym,* to take one example, with their immersion in a hieroglyphical language that appears literally as physical nature.

Unlike Emerson, these diverse transcendentalists manage to stress the role of physical nature and the distinction between the physical and spiritual "departments" of language use. European romanticism grants great power to the individual mind: I've already cited Schlegel; Rousseau's theory of primitive cries is well known; and Wordsworth, Shelley, and Hazlitt insist on autonomous invention far more than Emerson does in *Nature.* The bond within a language of thoughts, things, and spirit on which he insists was believed by these kindred authors to be fatal to thought.

Even the empiricist or historicist traditions that Emerson rejects allot greater latitude to consciousness; they stress language and poetry as *poesis* or, literally, making or creation. Vico serves as one notable example. Fontanier takes for granted the arising in the mind of a new idea which, lacking its own proper sign, can be represented only through the trope of catachresis.[34] Catachresis serves "as the foundation of our entire tropological system" precisely because it allows the poet, through "forced and [yet] necessary usage," to give a word a new meaning and to bring a new meaning into linguistic being. Condillac liberates poetic language from simple mimesis by regarding it as "characterized by the

association of ideas that governs the expression of passion and emotion."[35] Adam Smith's notion of the process by which proper names are
generalized to common nouns grants great authority to the process of
abstraction. Hugh Blair's historicism encourages him to cast the progress of language as the abandonment of fancy for understanding and
tropes for "proper and familiar names"; yet the ongoing construction
of language remains a human activity which has not ceased, and one
which remains fundamentally figural: "What a fine vehicle is it now become for all the conceptions of the human mind; even for the most
subtile and delicate workings of the imagination! . . . It entertains us, as
with a succession of the most splendid pictures."[36] Andrews Norton's
notion of the dependence of meaning on context similarly allows for a
huge variety of signification and for unceasing novelty and change. And
Locke's sense of the arbitrary nature of the link between idea and word
did not reduce so much as expand the possibilities of invention by making one's actual experience of the highest authority.

The empiricists of Emerson's acquaintance are, compared to him,
masters of the logos. They at least insist on the ambiguous complexity
of the relation between ideas and things that cannot be reduced to a
divine template, and use an array of methods far too variable for Emerson to legitimately reduce them to the copying of empirical data, particularly when a subtle advocate of copying is Emerson himself.[37] The historical variability of even scriptural meaning is the core of Andrews
Norton's thinking on the subject, and Emerson's move of spirit beyond
the bounds of scripture, though possessing obviously transgressive aspects, did not welcome spirit's significatory variability so much as offer
a way around it. In light of Emerson's veneration of the law, his sense
of being surrounded on all sides by lackeys would seem a textbook case
of projection. In this context, Emerson denounces sensualism not because it grants the mind too little freedom but because it grants too
much.

I want to emphasize that Emerson's "roads not taken" are exactly
those which lead to familiar intellectual destinations. First, in *Nature*'s
language chapter, he is not simply traveling toward the unity of all
things in which some independent, creative power is reserved for the
individual soul. Nor, second, is he heading toward an empirical theory
of the origins of language.[38] Nor does he move toward a repressive tolerance about tropes that Derrida describes as one aspect of a ubiquitous,
everyday Western logocentrism. One of Derrida's examples is Aristotle's
view that "what is proper to man is doubtless the capacity to make meta-
phors, but in order to mean some thing, and only one."[39] Aristotle may

regard linguistic liberty as what must be authorized by being univocal, but he grants a power of metaphor to the individual which is not determined in advance. Indeed, the relative autonomy of this power defines the individual as human. Meaning must be determinate, but it nonetheless expresses individual agency or, more accurately, the finitude of semiotic determinism. In the passages I've examined, even this restricted agency disappears from Emerson's notion of figurative language. He does not achieve liberalism's desired balance between freedom and order, subjective and objective, or expression and piety.

Where does he arrive, then? Emerson's actual destination is the place where figural signification mirrors the logos understood as "Spirit . . . the Creator," which living language calls "the FATHER" (21).

> The moment our discourse rises about the ground line of familiar facts, and is inflamed with passion or exalted by thought, it clothes itself in images. A man conversing in earnest, if he watch his intellectual processes, will find that a material image, more or less luminous, arises in his mind, contemporaneous with every thought, which furnishes the vestment of the thought. Hence, good writing and brilliant discourse are perpetual allegories. This imagery is spontaneous. It is the blending of experience with the present action of the mind. It is proper creation. It is the working of the Original Cause through the instruments he has already made. (*Es and Ls,* 23)

In a shocking shift, Emerson celebrates the "proper creation" of the mind only to attribute it to the "Original Cause." Once again, this does not mean that the freedom of the individual mind coexists with the Original Cause in harmonious autonomy or correspondence. For the moment of freedom is constituted by the moment of submission to superior, active power. "Brilliant discourse" retrieves the paternal source of all begetting. Emerson's excitement here is inseparable from this prospect that in language the father can never be replaced. He not only authorizes the living logos, but he remains its proprietor. Our language is great because it belongs to someone else. This someone else is not a pretender but a lawful sovereign. The potential for slavery that arises when our voice is owned by another is here written as benevolent paternalism.[40]

4. The Poetry of Abandoned Consent

Strong Emersonian individualism requires a paradoxical yet functional "balanced antagonism" of individual creation and providential law; but this "modified or mediated realism" is not what Emerson's language theory delivers.[41] It yields instead the elimination of the term *mind*, which ordinarily forms the bridge between nature and spirit. First, degree 2, or mind, is captured by degree 3, Spirit. But when Emerson turns from ontology to history and confronts temporal change in degree 1, or empirical naming, mind similarly disappears. The differences between spirit and linguistic history seem to him less important than how they can both be regarded as spheres of necessity where human thought is sublimely led. *Nature* summons the most intimate, private form of freedom — individual voice, literary creation, utopic imaginings, poetic self-expression — and subordinates it to preexisting law in both of the "departments" of being. Most of Emerson's idealist sources also fail to settle on a particular description of the sources of invention, but even the cautious pietists among them abandon invention less extravagantly than he. Rather than preserving a space for positing or troping under law, Emerson's "Language" chapter comprehensively submits all kinds of language use to the "superiour Force."[42]

The linking of historical to natural and spiritual law, the binding of invention to imitation, the definition of spontaneous selfhood as the return to the father — what should these ideas about language be called? Again, for them to express U.S. consensus liberalism, they would need to offer a sustainable, lawful liberty in which invention and mimesis each have their proper role. Such views of language would match a political liberalism which, from Emerson's time down to our own, imagines a harmony between union and freedom or "freedom and fate" (Stephen Whicher) — between private profit and the common good (Tocqueville). There is no doubting Emerson's emphasis on both sides of these familiar dualisms: he has inspired generations with his denial that we revolt against our habitual submissions to power and precedent even as he also says that this courage to be ourselves leads to lawfulness rather than dissent. There is also no doubting that Emerson links inspired utterance to receiving spiritual signals. But this point should be pressed further. Liberalism envisions the fulfillment of freedom in obedience yet insists that this obedience reflect free consent. This consent, in "Language," is precisely what Emerson rejects: obedience is spontaneous and unwilled, not willful and voluntary. I therefore prefer to call this theory of language "authoritarian." I do so knowing how inappropriate it seems as a description of a man who is read as the philosophical version of "live free or die." This only means that Emerson's authoritarianism does not reject individualism in the least. His notions of language endorse self-expression while promising that these expressions fulfill the father's law. I mean *authoritarian* to suggest that we should not derive a consensual liberty from Emerson's insistence that we cede rather than retain individual sovereignty.[43]

We can continue to call this liberalism if we wish since this stress on submission to an untouchable authority has been a practical outcome of actually existing U.S. liberalism.[44] But the ordinary invocation of liberalism redefines obedience as consent even where, as in "Language," consent is predetermined by spirit or nature. "Submissive individualism" more accurately conveys Emerson's influential, paradoxical demand that consent be suspended in the moment of the highest language use. My hope for the present study is not so much that it successfully labels Emerson as authoritarian, but that it describes one aspect of the history of our difficulty in discussing the authoritarian elements of U.S. democracy. We have long since moved past the point where our still-Emersonian culture can admit the presence of tyranny without analyzing it as the ordinary way in which freedom is constituted by law and power. I would be pleased if this consideration of Emerson's position on the theories of language of his period would help reopen the question of how much order freedom really requires, and how much obedience American liberalism is willing to excuse as the ordinary constituting of individuality.

CHAPTER

THREE

Democratic Prophecy and Corporate Individualism

Few things could be worse for the intellectual integrity of the
American democrat than the identification of the "capitalist" and
the "aristocrat" with the public action of legislatures.

—Louis Hartz

This capture signifies the dearticulation of Sendero Luminoso on
a national level. It cuts the brain from the organization. This
beheading, this loss of leadership, is why this is a transcendental
event.

—Alberto Fujimori

In his chapter "Language" in *Nature,* Emerson describes the expression
of individuality through submission to preestablished law. But what has
kept this submission from seeming central to Emerson's thought and
legacy? Part of the story lies in the tone of the essay's final chapter, "Prospects," which is most famous as an individualist rectification of all once
and future reticence. In this chapter Emerson declares that no self need
submit to anything but itself and its own law, for the external world is
in fact dependent on human life. Once the "laws of [man's] mind, the
periods of his actions externized themselves into day and night."[1] More
important, such will be the case again if he awakens and "perceives that
. . . his law is still paramount." God himself is nothing but our own
"alienated majesty" waiting to be reclaimed. Our submission to law is
submission to a law we once dictated out of a perfectly sovereign autonomy, which we have only temporarily forfeited.

This affirmation of the lordly self is not all of *Nature's* closing argument. Rather than burying submission with self-assertion, it attempts
to rearticulate submission as an ingredient in corporate relation. This

An earlier version of this chapter was published as "Emerson's Corporate Individualism,"
American Literary History 3, no. 4 (1991): 657–84. Reprinted by permission of Oxford
University Press.

emphasis on relation, which I will continue to explore in the next two chapters, gives Emerson something of a double role. As I stressed in the introduction, he develops a corporate notion of individualism in which individuality consists of obeying a massive (yet benevolent) administrative power which is private and out of one's control. But he also assumes the possibility of a public, collective agency which would reflect group sovereignty.

1. Individualism's Contradictions

Though it is still hard to associate Emerson and masculinist American culture with all this compromising of the self with history, institutions, and groups, the kind of submission discussed in the last chapter has been prominent in the observations of many politically minded foreign visitors to the United States. They have often agreed on at least one thing: U.S. democratic culture is as readily authoritarian as it is individualistic. As Maurice Gonnaud observes, "All the European travelers who visited America between 1825 and 1850, from Frances Trollope through Harriet Martineau and Tocqueville to Dickens, reported sadly or angrily on the distressing conformity of individual people, their entire and apparently unprotesting submission to the law of the majority."[2] In the mid-1840s, Alexis de Tocqueville was already foretelling a U.S. future in which social relations were determined not by citizens but by an "immense, protective power which is alone responsible for securing their enjoyment [and which] gladly works for their happiness but wants to be sole agent and judge of it."[3] Benevolent despotism, in this view, is not a corruption of democracy in America but is this democracy's essential structure. The United States substitutes democracy for the despotisms of the Old World only to make democracy despotic. United States liberty is conformity and its democracy is a liberal kind of authoritarianism. Sustaining the impressions of Tocqueville as well as those of other Europeans who found U.S. conformity where they sought its liberties, Jean Baudrillard declares them to be the same. "True freedom" here is the orgiastic adaptation to the "advertising effect" of fashion. "The liberated man is not the one who is freed in his ideal reality, his inner truth, or his transparency; he is the man who changes spaces, who circulates, who changes sex, and habits according to fashion, *rather than morality*."[4] Tocqueville's ruling "schoolmaster" has become Baudrillard's commodity market, but in each case the individual acquires freedom through obedience.

Tocqueville and Baudrillard regard this mobile but submissive free- dom not as a sign of U.S. backwardness but of its irreversible modernity. They form part of a tradition in cultural criticism that sees regulated freedom or "repressive tolerance" running deep in Euro-American middle-class culture. This tradition might have helped more of Emer- son's readers accept one of this book's major points: when liberal U.S. culture rejects the ideal of individual self-determination, it usually re- places it not with a notion of public, "democratic," collective self- determination but with individual obedience to the determination of larger or higher powers. Contrary to this reading, many American com- mentators have assumed that these deterministic higher powers are re- ally only versions of ourselves, so that the individual is likely to submit only to powers that he or she actually controls. "Obedience" would then be nothing more than a regulated freedom to which we must be re- signed as the partial subjects of postclassical public life, but which we control in a mediated way through the structures of democratic consent.

I should reiterate some material from previous chapters in the con- text of the corporate supplement of the market individual. Readings of American individuality under nineteenth-century market capitalism have for some time been rejecting the common portrait of a freely will- ing and possessing individual who imagined a private power over the external world through the metaphor of the "infinite self." In much re- cent work, personal identity is seen as mutual and relational rather than separatist, assertive, and absolute. A growing number of commentators regard the period's self-reliant individual as admitting a constitutive rela- tion to the social forces this individual often proclaimed to be alien. Modified, liberalized self-reliance, as I have noted, involves not the re- fusal but the incorporation of the other into the self.[5] This more re- ceptive individualist, though displaying a range of assertive positions, covertly and systematically replaced autonomy with more communal and consensual modes. The transcendentalist self now more obviously resembles the conscientious liberal citizen whose faith in the trans- formative power of the soul did not interfere with a concern for the health of civic life.

This modification of strong individualism boasts a number of con- ceptual advantages. It replaces the (usually white, well-educated, male) subject of simple self-differentiation with the more flexible subject of relation, "transition," and reception. It avoids screening the discourse of the period through a binary contrast between soul and history in which even the transcendentalists did not fully believe. When individualism is more consensual than assertive, it seems able to explain how the public and private spheres, far from the antagonists that Emerson described in his most polemical moments, can be continually married off. When asked whether America exists for each person or the people, for private property or national providence, the antebellum consensus liberal simply answered "both." Hence the appearance of strange words like "auto-American-biography" in our intellectual histories.[6] The agendas of self and state coincided, in these accounts, in a possessive *and* collective individualism that overcame the self's alienation from society through a system of highly structured and redemptive affiliations.

The doctrine of consent supports this reconciliation of receptive and assertive individuality. The obedience to a law which might seem subservient takes place within a liberal social contract in which a relinquished freedom is always relinquished freely. The liberal citizen finds freedom in consenting to laws that he (gender intended) can claim were legislated, if not by him directly, then by others in his name. The tradition that develops an assortment of kindred models includes Locke, Kant, Hegel, Madison, Freud, Lacan, and Foucault, to name only one crooked line that could also include Christ and Augustine. It is impossible to dismiss or expose the idea of freedom in obedience simply by pointing out that it is contradictory. The sovereign subject of representative democracy and the sovereign son of the oedipal scenario both acquire a delegated yet fully possessible power by consenting to a law which derives circuitously from themselves. Emerson's work exemplifies the gratifications on both sides of this combination.

The persuasions of Emerson and others notwithstanding, this individualism rests on a harmony between two distinctive ideal states whose compatibility is very uncertain. The self which is sovereign in Nietzsche's sense of making its own "measure of value" is not obviously compatible with the self that is sovereign in Kant's sense of free submission to a universal law. Schematically, Nietzsche finds freedom in a self-authoring of a unique moral law to which Kant counsels voluntary submission. The assertive self-positing individual has a notion of freedom that would ostensibly prevent him or her from desiring reconciliation with cooperative, other-directed, or universal modes: the idea of freedom as autonomy or independence is exacting and famously threatened by community systems.

Emerson's own vacillations show not only the power of combining Nietzschean and Kantian notions of sovereign individuality, but also the need for repression and heavy maintenance. Emerson might define "trusting yourself" as "accepting your place" and thus override a potential conflict (arousing a satisfied silence in the vast majority of his readers), but self-trust on other occasions means a radical disruption of precisely this kind of deference. There is no doubt that liberal individualism claims to have achieved a balance of freedom and order through consent, but this claim is contested from so many different directions in Emerson's time and ours that it is better treated as a myth than as anybody's psychological experience, including that of its defenders, or Emerson's. Emerson's writing dramatically illustrates how a voluntary Kantian submission to a moral law does not automatically absorb the structure of Nietzschean subjectivity's positing of its own law. The latter must continually look for other modes in which to utter itself separately from (if not in opposition to) the modes of submissive freedom.

Without attempting a more definitive statement about the relation between self-positing and consenting in antebellum liberal individualism, I note that their relation was neither of identity nor opposition, and was in need of constant mediation. Emerson and his contemporaries worked with a number of mediating structures. Emerson was particularly interested in the metaphysics of Oneness, in which all distinct individuals are united in being. A second mediation involves the "moral sense," which preexists and guides the nonetheless freely willing individual conscience. A third was filiopiety, in which obedience is rewarded with the passing on of the sanctioned power that grants the experience of freedom.[7] Political formulations of free consent, voluntary submission, and delegated self-governance, were also crucial. Political consent continues to receive a substantial boost from philosophical analyses of moral reason, in which submission is always submission to oneself. As Stanley Cavell makes the case, "Understanding Emersonian Perfectionism as an interpretation of Rousseau's and Kant's idea of freedom as autonomy means understanding it as questioning what or who the self is that commands and obeys itself and what an obedience consists in that is inseparable from mastery." Freedom does not mean eliminating obedience but making sure you are obeying something like your own best self.[8]

But consent was a mode of governance only when it was not a function of individual consciousness but of the consciousness of selves in groups. The group was an indispensable part of thinking through individualism's contradictions: how was obeying the public or the Constitution or the police like obeying yourself? How was the experience of a command from outside like that of a command from within? How did the outside express the law one gives to oneself, especially when the outside was impersonal or oppressive for reasons of race or gender or sexual preference? This need for mediation between individual and social agency sponsored an antebellum, middle-class obsession with concrete varieties of group life that sought a synthesis of free self and unifying law that was, as Bercovitch has it, simultaneously self and America. The antebellum "association" linked autonomy and unity in a tremendous range of ways, and the period was remarkable for being as much the age of associations as it was the age of the individual. Theological and psychological questions of the Oneness of souls, the moral law, and the master/slave dialectic continually manifested themselves as questions of social power. Thus Emerson refers to the "doctrine that man is one," but also notes how this means that "the individual, to possess himself, must sometimes return from his own labor to embrace all the other laborers."[9] For Emerson, as for his social and intellectual kin, U.S. individualism is perennially preoccupied with the meaning of the democratic group.

The stakes here were very high, for they concerned the power of individualism to present itself as the "American" outcome even in a social modernity driven by the forces of the party, the mass, the racialized community, the statistical aggregate, and the managed organization. The danger of socialization was that the public would revolt against an outmoded Jeffersonian individualism and allow publicly directed, collective agents some real authority over private property. Contra numerous insightful critics like the ones cited here, there is nothing about associations or other groups that readily supports possessive — though flexible — individualism. Emerson and his contemporaries had to puzzle out possibly *new* forms of individuality produced by the conjunction of the market with the business corporation.

2. Corporate Mediations

By the 1830s, Tocqueville was already suggesting that "corporation stockholders might be more representative of individualism than the self-sufficient yeoman farmer who is too often taken to embody the concept."[10] Speaking generally, the entities that mediated between autonomous and democratic types of individuality were not merely consensual but corporate forms. They were most frequently private collectives or associations, and were detached from the state. They were not socialist because the state, as the agent of the public, did not direct them. The corporate form was not limited to the business corporation, which gradually regularized its distinctive characteristics after 1850, but appeared in various kinds of voluntary associations as well as in the populations of involuntary ones like the extended family, the factory, and the prison. The business association was particularly important to an antebellum society trying to mingle the Lockean notion of the self as property with its communal or "republican" ideals, for this association squarely juxtaposed private possession to an increasingly socialized culture. The early corporation modernized individualism by bringing it from country to city, wielding a "concentrated moneyed power" in a way that other voluntary associations did not,[11] and removing the self from its "little society" of personal ties into a new tangle of relations to political economy.

The antebellum corporate form had several features of particular importance.

· It bridged the self and the state and structured the public realm the self experienced.

· It bound individuals in an association, which, unlike the family or neighborhood, did not provide face-to-face relations of "mutual agency" so much as the kind of impersonal transactions manifest as, for example, "transferrable shares."[12]

· It began as an instrument of public legislatures to be used for public purposes. Private profit was subordinate to the common good.

· At the same time, it consisted of a system that acted as a public institution while being controlled by private powers.

Such a structure had at least the potential to negotiate the conflicting demands of personal and collective agency, private and public power, by adapting the more isolated "possessive" self of classical liberalism to mass culture while claiming to sustain this possessive self. The corporation was not socialist but was a kind of privatized socialism: it formalized the collectivization of social power while allowing it to remain in private hands. The corporate form forestalled an age-old communist threat by "harnessing vast publics to a private interest . . . [and] entrust[ing] social production to private decision."[13] As wealth increasingly came to reside in collectives, these collectives were increasingly taken private. Liberalism could depart from a laissez-faire individualism that hampered capital accumulation, not to mention mass governance, for a corporate model. In various periods in U.S. history, corporate liberalism did not awkwardly straddle the contradiction between private and transcendent powers but synthesized them in a "double movement in which the self is substantiated by the disappearance of its agency."[14] It would seem, then, that corporate individualism was the paradoxical subjectivity that propped a paradoxical (yet highly functional) capitalism. Apparently reconciling Kant's free obedience and Nietzsche's radical sovereignty, corporate liberalism proposed that the more a person is corporate, the more that person is individual.

It makes sense, then, that some astute recent work favors corporatism as a reconciliation that works where clumsier solutions (the One, simple autonomy) had embarrassed themselves. Various critics suggest that by the end of the nineteenth century, American culture was ruled by a fully reciprocal connection between individuality and corporate being. Walter Benn Michaels reads Frank Norris and Josiah Royce as suggesting that "personality is always corporate."[15] But whatever might be contradictory about this — contradictory because corporate personality presumably conflicts with self-reliant autonomy — never actually appears. The "corporate moment" is "the moment when the nonidentity of material and ideal constitutes the identity of the person";[16] when, in other words, the person is said to have body *and* soul. For an individual to be a corporation is nothing more unprecedented or specific than to be a person with a soul. The corporate is, in this account, another word for *personality:* "Personality is always corporate," but "corporations must be persons even if persons aren't."[17] Similarly, Howard Horwitz identifies "Emersonian self-reliance" with corporate agency and Emersonian "virtue" with "self-eradication."[18] Self-reliant personal agency and the self willed by a "transcendence of personal agency" are interchangeable.[19] Lawrence Kohl suggests that "the world of contracts and constitutions, corporations and voluntary associations" issues in self-mastery and "inner-direction."[20] And David Leverenz argues that Emerson's "impersonal geometry" sustains rather than qualifies his "private infinitude."[21] These commentators regard personal autonomy as a function of corporate existence and see the corporate form producing an individual who is no less individual for being corporate. The corporate individual is an advanced model of the liberal individual adapted to the mass culture that begins to congeal in Jacksonian America. Finally, it is a democratic liberalism to the extent that it rejects the rule of domination. In a society based on the organization, "rules were not justified by hierarchy, but by the immanent contours of the process of social life; obedience arose not from discipline, but from persuasion."[22]

These critics accurately describe a particular liberal rhetoric that casts complex, dissonant communal forces as synthesizing totalities that individuate while corporatizing. This rhetoric had tremendous cultural power: it convinced most of its citizens most of the time that corporate capital preserved their freedoms rather than stole their sovereignty. It seemed to offer a good compromise individualism that allowed both coordinated force and personal greatness.

But is it actually a better solution to the contradiction between liberal individualism and democracy? How does corporate liberalism as a rhetoric or, more accurately, an ideology actually operate psychically, working as it did to justify particular interests in the guise of universality, and, throughout the nineteenth century, confronting a varying array of rival explanations and policies whose very existence it tried to conceal?

In fact, preliminary readings of earlier experiences of the corporate form suggest that corporatism, at least in its antebellum infancy, had a great deal of trouble making corporate life seem individualist. A range of writers simply rejected corporatism as the enemy of freedom and democracy. Even those who were interested in corporate subjectivity denied that it produced an autonomous individualism.

> Th[e] strong individuality of the South is the effect of the institution of slavery. The South without slaves would have had the same tendency to centralization that we have at the North. The cause of it here is the fact that no individual here feels himself of much importance by the side of the state. Individually he can do but little, and feels himself small. Hence his strong desire to lean on the state, his uncommon fondness for association, corporations, partnerships, whatever concentrates power and adds to individual strength. Then again our commercial and manufacturing pursuits also tend to make us desire somewhere the social power, we can call in to supply our deficiency in strength, capital, and skill.[23]

This northern writer (possibly the transcendentalist Orestes Brownson) agrees that the northern individual is a corporate individual. Nonetheless, the reviewer does not identify corporate individuality with autonomy but with dependence on external groups. Corporate life does not so much reconcile autonomy with socialization or private with public as it shatters the illusion that social systems result in a private sovereignty. One feels strength as a private individual only as a master of slaves; owning oneself entails owning someone else. The northern mode of individualism does not offer mastery but demands the strategic use of the association. Only associational selfhood allows the North to avoid the status of a slave democracy.[24]

Contrary to the consensus account, this association does not restore strong self-reliance. The individual draws strength from the state and practices a self-conscious search for "association, corporations, partnerships" that can replace the lordly self attributed to plantation masters. Here one of Emerson's contemporaries argues that the corporate person is not a private *individual* where "individual" involves strong independence.

This is not to deny that the corporate individual is a culturally powerful and pervasive phenomenon: the corporation "concentrates power and adds to individual strength." But this does suggest that corporate individualism, despite its apparent success as a synthesis, never resolves a contradiction between "strong individuality" and corporate individuality which this reviewer polarizes into the opposition between South and North.

The apparent synthesis stems from disavowing just how entirely dependent the corporate individual is on a very concrete corporate power. The individual must appear, to the contrary, to be able to spiritualize, internalize, and master corporate power. The corporation, preferably, must seem to be nothing more than the individual's own transcendent agency in all its projected majesty.[25] This creates the appearance of personal volition working in harmony with impersonal forces. This appearance must be systematically fabricated: it works, in this kind of liberalism, by making "communal being" out to be the subordinate of the self rather than its genuine other.[26] Corporate liberalism maintains freedom in subordination by obscuring or abstracting the corporation's goals and material instruments of subordination and rendering them agents of individual citizens.[27]

Since the coherence of corporate liberalism involves the dubious individuality of material corporate interests and power, one might wonder what would happen to its version of individualism were the actual divergence between corporate and individual agency to become obvious. Before the Civil War, the difference between the sovereignty of the public and that of corporations had not yet been concealed in the first place. In the last chapter of *Nature,* Emerson juxtaposes individual and corporate modes of poetic utterance without joining them together. In his discussion, Emerson uses the term "orphic" but not the terminology of chartered corporations or contract law. In discussing the latter, I am not trying to translate Emerson's ideas into a more secular idiom but want instead to clarify the fascination with nonindividualist subjectivity that he held in common with a wide variety of antebellum writers who were pushing against the limits of their increasingly paradoxical use of possessive individualism, and who often knew very well that the cultural future lay with entities more subtle than partnerships and scaled for the masses. The choice would not be between private autonomy and collective legislation but between two kinds of collectivity, one run in private from above, and the other run in public democratically. Emerson's orphic mode tries to imagine a corporate individuality that transcends individual autonomy. How does this attempt work out?

3. Oedipal and Orphic Corporatism

Emerson is well suited to articulate freedom in the North as corporatism. As I've noted, even his early writing, sometimes misread as a literature of rebellion, mounts a sustained summons to reliance on systemic forces. Does his work of the mid-1830s offer one "revolutionary ego" after another—the American scholar, the Young American, the Transcendentalist, the idealist, the orphic poet? Not exactly. Emerson's early ideal is less that of positing than of reflecting a preestablished and encompassing law: "The only prophet of that which must be, is . . . that Unity, that Over-soul, within which every man's particular being is contained and made one with all other."[28] As critics have suggested, Emersonian agency repeatedly involves the effacement of agency.[29] Emerson calls for resistance to a conformist social law the better to conform to spiritual law. Private power consists of external, higher powers and is obtained through merging with a metaphysical corporate body.

But Emerson's idea of freedom as obedience regularly overshoots piety in the direction of dissolution. In *Nature* he suggests that transcendent agency is not only submissive but is not agency at all. Spirit or "the Supreme Being, does not build up nature around us, but puts it forth through us, as the life of the tree puts forth new branches and leaves through the pores of the old. As a plant upon the earth, so a man rests upon the bosom of God; he is nourished by unfailing fountains, and draws, at his need, inexhaustible power."[30] This self is corporate in the sense of having its being as part of a system of laws and forces. It experiences itself as passive, but it is also more than passive: it is vegetative. In this figure, corporate being leads humble man toward the condition of the unthinking plant. To the extent that the corporate individual binds with absolute spirit or transcendent agency, to that extent it abandons personal agency. If the corporate individual is a subject of transcendent spirit, it is also self-contradictory. Personal and corporate agency are incompatible when the latter goes beyond locating agency in empirical associations (as the anonymous reviewer of *Slavery* had done) and locates it in transcendent spirit.

Partially in response to Spirit's extravagance, in "Prospects," *Nature*'s final chapter, Emerson tries to rescue individual identity while retaining some kind of transcendent spirit. But he does this not by simply reuniting individual and corporate states but by imagining a state in which individuality is best expressed through its corporate life, once divided from merely personal agency.

The voice of personal agency arises from George Herbert's poem on man, while the nonindividual comes from long fictional citations which Emerson attributes to the "orphic poet." For Emerson, Herbert represents a claim that the individual soul is the reflection of cosmological design, and this claim, although translated into a doctrine of the soul, renders the self as a reflection of Spirit.[31] Herbert's dependence on the law of the father makes him the explicitly oedipal son: his power consists of the paternal design "working through him." He rules creation as the father's deputy; his power, though real, is explicitly derivative. Unlike Milton, Wordsworth, and Emerson's other strong precursors, Herbert manages to live his belated sonship mildly and to write poetry without ever needing to rebel. But Herbert's obedience does not erode his personal agency or identity. Quite the contrary, like all loyal sons, he is rewarded with the ability to distinguish himself from the creation which fathered him. He merely resembles God, nature, and spirit, and does not merge into them. "'Man is one world,'" Herbert reports, "'and hath/Another to attend him.'"[32] The Herbertian poet boasts a stable personal identity and conscious, if not original, individual agency.

The chapter's second voice recaptures self-posited agency: "'Man is the dwarf of himself. Once he was permeated and dissolved by spirit. He filled nature with his overflowing currents. Out from him sprang the sun and moon; from man, the sun; from woman, the moon. The laws of his mind, the periods of his actions externized themselves into day and night, into the year and the seasons.'" Now man has shrunk, says the orphic poet, so that creation is no longer equivalent to him and springing from him. But the true poet is he who knows that man's pure originality can be recovered: "'He perceives that if his law is still paramount, if still he have elemental power, if his word is sterling yet in nature, it is not conscious power, it is not inferior but superior to his will. It is Instinct.'"[33] This poet knows that he does not simply reflect the creation but posits the creation because he ontologically preexists it. The orphic poet enacts Friedrich Schlegel's (rather than Herbert's) claim that "Poetry is republican speech: a speech which is its own law and end unto itself."[34] The poet supersedes existing sovereignty by expressing the original absolute self-possession that appears as instinct. The orphic poet's "untaught sallies of the spirit" and "continual self-recovery" arise from having established an identity between poetic will or Reason and its physical consequences.[35] In the words of Emerson's authority on the matter, the translator Thomas Taylor, Orpheus is nothing other than the "perpetual and abundant fountain, [from which] the divine muse of Homer, and the philosophy of Pythagoras and Plato, flowed."[36] In this reading, the orphic poet is not closer than other mortals to the fountain but *is* the fountain. The orphic poet owns the laws that constitute him, and owns himself as absolutely as Locke's God was thought to own the "Men" who were of his sole "Workmanship": he is his own God.[37] While Herbert explicitly obeys the external law of the father, Orpheus claims to have fathered himself, claiming thus to stand outside the oedipal cycle of filiopiety and parricide.

In Emerson's orphic poet, three qualities converge. The first is a power of self-positing or self-fathering, and the second is absolute ownership of the self as property. But surprisingly, neither of these qualities generates a poet who inhabits an individual sphere. For the poet's third quality is the embodiment of creation as a system, or corporate being. The poet distinguishes between now and then, history and prehistory the dwarf and the giant. To Emerson's radical idealism, the orphic poet is the corporate poet. The true poet does not only note correspondences as Herbert does, but knows himself as their original inventor. He constitutes the entirety of relations, forces, and laws that exist between all creatures. To constitute them, he must reject those ideas that tie him to the dwarfish notion of his mere "resemblance" to spirit in his individual person. He must abandon individuality itself. The orphic poet's body is a corporate body: it consists of "overflowing currents" which comprise "sun and moon, . . . the year and the seasons." Above all, its power to possess and posit absolutely is a corporate power that exists through the repudiation of personal power.

This dissociation of corporate power and personal identity is essential to the original myth of Orpheus. When Orpheus tries to retrieve Eurydice, his failure arises precisely from his power of possession. For Taylor, Orpheus acts as the sovereign will, "who by the melody of his lyre, drew rocks, woods, and wild beasts, stopt rivers in their course, and even moved the inexorable king of hell."[38] He possesses the law of objects so absolutely that he appears to posit them into existence. He appears as an exemplar of the ideal fusion of transcendent corporate agency and autonomous personal identity. But when Eurydice dies, Orpheus experiences a loss that one who had truly incorporated the world would not have felt. His mourning for her discloses a wound in his completeness or, in our terms, a gap between corporate union and the personal power of possession, a gap that only an oedipal structure can suppress. When Orpheus is offered a chance to rescue her from the underworld, he tries to retake her with the absolute personal power that assumes a link between personal and transcendent (infinite) agency. He is told, however, that he must let her follow him, meaning that he needs to refrain from direct possession and learn to let her follow with a will entirely her own. He is told, in other words, that corporate and individual agency are different: corporate reunion depends on relinquishing the kind of self that depends on personal possession. But Orpheus cannot maintain this suspension of his control and, succumbing to his familiar habits, turns to look at her and to verify her obedience. The underworld, indifferent to private property, reveals that this power, in a larger economy, leads to the object's withdrawal and the dissolution of the corporate structure. Orpheus doesn't learn much from all this, and his ongoing claim to have personal power and transcendent power over the corporate whole leads finally to the loss of his person. He is permanently separated from his beloved and ultimately dies by being separated from himself in a radically nonconsensual dismemberment into pieces that can never be reassembled.

"Prospects" seems to know the lesson of orphic power which Orpheus could not learn. The narrator is closest to Herbert, and he sets off his orphic utterances in quotation marks as though to announce their separation from his own pronouncements. Herbert's voice is successfully assimilated by the narrator, and though not originally the latter's, is now in his possession. The orphic voice, however, appears only in quotation.[39] When the narrator imagines the personal possession of orphic or corporate agency, however, he imagines a distinction between himself and that positing power. The voice that claims an originary power for the self arises from the self's other. The voice that arises from the self claims that its power is borrowed from another; it does not comprise a power that one could identify as personal identity. The power to own (oneself) is not owned but borrowed; the power of borrowing is all that is owned.

"Prospects" refuses the mythic combination of individual and transcendent agency that underlies corporate liberalism. The liberal individual in "Prospects" is Herbert, but his subordinate voice is not capable of a self-posited willing. Perhaps a poet could give up orphic pretensions to absolute self-possession in favor of Herbert's borrowed personal agency and identity. But according to "Prospects," the poet cannot pretend that this move toward Herbert would allow the self a self-legislating orphic will. Herbert's position offers individuality but not autonomy. The orphic will is omnipotent, but it is not individual. In part by the formal device of the quoted voice, Emerson blocks a dialectical rapport between these two modes of power, thus presenting as impossible the corporate yet individual personhood that the Orpheus myth shows to be disastrous.

The conflict within "Prospects" means that the corporate individual is a very loose notion: it does not denote an individual in the liberal sense. The division of the possessive will suggests that corporate and autonomous power, far from existing in harmony, are mutually exclusive. There is nothing about the orphic position in itself that supports possessive individuality. Orpheus is a corporate poet but he cannot be a corporate individual. When "Prospects" separates Herbert's voice from that of the orphic poet, the chapter avoids the kind of liberal individualism that affirms Emerson's receptivity to "otherness" or even to public or communal forces even as it claims to capture these for the private sphere.

"Prospects" offers a choice between at least two different readings of corporate individualism. The first, associated with Herbert and the oedipal sonship, issues in individuality through mimesis. This assumption rests on a traditionally "romantic" act of faith, a primal prosopopoeia, in which a human form is assigned to providential law; it proposes a familiar synthesis of reception and creation. The oedipal position assumes, in short, that submission to paternal power can yield complex collective agency. Herbert stands for the idea that possessive or liberal individualism and democracy — viewed as collective or collaborative voicing — are compatible. It is democracy that remains tied to paternalistic rule.

The second view, which here is orphic, regards the self-making autonomy that Herbert "borrows" as radically nonindividual. Herbert's corporate individualism appears as a contradiction in terms or, more accurately, a liberal fiction that ignores the antiindividual outcome of genuinely spiritual/corporate self-making. Orphic corporatism is corporate postindividualism. It suggests that democracy requires a loss of individual agency, that it entails embrace of something transcendentally collective, something that does not return to individual possession or simple identity. At the same time, orphic, corporate agency retains tremendous power, and indeed is the only genuine power that one can have in the world. This power arrives not through submission to the father but through repudiating submission. When Emerson, like the reviewer of *Slavery,* represents the relation between Herbertian and orphic, possessive and collective subjectivity as a contradiction, he protects the orphic from the liberal recuperation so common in Emerson's readers of every era.

I regard this as Emerson's most radical moment. By absorbing submission into collective agency, he figures a type of consent that arises from relinquishing separatist individualism in favor of direct contact with the corporate body. This contact furnishes an idea of a democratic sphere in which one becomes individually powerful by relinquishing submission in favor of nonindividualist collaboration. The corporate form joins democracy and individuality by surpassing individualism. That is to say, by abandoning possessive individualism, the self becomes more rather than less powerful. And by refusing to take possession as the model of individuality, the self embraces democracy. Orphic freedom is democracy without individualism.

4. Corporatism as Democracy

Emerson is not alone in this vision, for his thought in "Prospects" refracts a widespread middle-class interest in corporatism as a form of group life in which democracy would be inherent and orderly. Massachusetts Whigs, like many genteel progressives, looked to union to solve most social problems: "Faculty psychology taught an ideal of harmony within diversity, each of the human powers performing its appropriate function within an integrated whole. The model ruled out laissez-faire as a social philosophy, emphasizing instead the mutual responsibility of individuals and classes."[40] Such mutual responsibility expressed itself in the formation of associations, and indeed society itself was such an association writ large, and ruled by an elite whose preeminence was sanctioned by their benevolent wisdom. For William Ellery Channing, these associations extended freedom. "It is interesting and encouraging to observe, that the enslaving power of society over the mind is decreasing, through what would seem at first to threaten its enlargement; — we mean, through the extension of social intercourse." As "social being[s]" we need to "sympathize with others, and yet to determine our own

feelings; to act with others, and yet to follow our own consciences; to
unite social deference and self-dominion; to join moral self-subsistence
with social dependence; to respect others without losing self-respect;
to love our friends and to reverence our superiors, whilst our supreme
homage is given to that moral perfection which no friend and no superior has realized, and which, if faithfully pursued, will often demand
separation from all around us."[41] The ideal group offered this sort of
balance with a further, vital feature: the absence of a centralized leader.
"Associations often injure free action by a very plain and obvious operation. They accumulate power in a few hands, and this takes place just in
proportion to the surface over which they spread. In a large institution,
a few men rule, a few do every thing . . . a few are able to excite in the
mass strong and bitter passions, and by these to obtain an immense
ascendancy."[42] The kind of association most likely to behave like a plu-
tocratic tyranny was the "artificial" kind, such as a political party. But
the kind of association whose members "performed from a principle
within, performed without the excitement of an urging and approving
voice from abroad"—the kind of association that encouraged self-
reliance was spontaneous and natural, and "spring[s] from our very constitution."[43] These were families, neighborhoods, and towns, and not
"missionary societies, peace societies, or charitable societies, which men
have contrived." The natural association consisted simply of "common
daily duties of Christians in their families, neighborhoods, and business."[44] Good corporate life consisted of being in common, with no
despotic leader and no external restraint. It was simply the principle of
relation and interconnection, extended without calculation from the inner life of all the members. The natural association was democratic in
that there was no leader to submit to. It was also not strictly possessive,
since all individuality arose from an inner life held in common with all
the others. While possessive individualism contrasts private interior being and public being, Channing linked individuality to uncoerced, non-
dominated collective life.

For Channing and the reviewer of Channing's *Slavery,* northern individuality fulfilled these requirements. It evaded despotism and submission through equitable relationship; individuality "adds to individual
strength" by "lean[ing] on the state." And it acquired power without
possession which, once again, was figured as the possession of slaves.
Emerson's orphic poet offers a similar vision—democracy as corporatism, where individuality and possession separate, and power grows
through egalitarian freedom in common.

5. Contract and Possession

This vision of democratic corporatism is not simply undermined by market capitalism, for it expresses contradictions within that type of capitalism itself. These contradictions prevented corporate structures, even before the Civil War, from fully recuperating the forms of private property to which they were ostensibly consecrated.

Although Emerson does not often concern himself with political economy, he is preoccupied with the questions of subjectivity that were at issue in a variety of antebellum disciplines. The two types of poet in "Prospects" embody different descriptions of the fit between personal identity, private property, and mass or corporate forces. They are individualist and more than individualist responses to the dilemma of living in a culture which requires that the individual wield private power at the same time that power is becoming more socialized. Their divergence is not Emerson's eccentric invention. "Prospects" was written amid a quiet divergence between contract and corporation law, which officially complement each other, but whose legislated symbiosis does not necessarily extend to practical subjectivity. The contest there illuminates the tremendous difficulty that "individualism" has in pretending its hegemony.

Orphic corporatism is difficult enough to distinguish from the individualist kind in a culture that perennially seeks individualist resolutions to the overarching conflict between individual and collective forces. Contract was an especially attractive individualist solution, for it seems to allow the individual to enter the collective structure of the market entirely on voluntary terms. It worked within, while superseding, legislative statute and common law, both of which arose from a preexisting public sphere. In contract, "individuals, pursuing their own ends, made their own 'law,' perfected their own arrangements."[45] In short, they "built their own world" as Emerson's transcendentalism would have them do, and legislated independently of a prior law, which seemed limited to guaranteeing the contract's performance. This seemed like the best of both worlds of public and private: the public is sanctioned and also codified as a system of supports for private powers. In the "golden age of contract" in which Emerson dwelt, individualized deals were protected by public laws which refrained from "*ex post facto* tampering with bargains, for whatever reason."[46]

In contract, identity is personal. The theory claims that corporate power is fully captured and subsumed by the volition the contract expresses, and some famous cases after *Fletcher v. Peck* (1810) created a precedent for regarding the business corporation itself as a contract.[47] The full weight of contract law endorses the final victory of an individualist privatization of public resources and rights as embodied in the corporate charter. In Emerson's terms, Herbert speaks for the claim that corporate forces are absorbed by an individual contract. The doctrine of correspondence between self and creation affirms individualist corporatism. In other words, it expresses a contract made between God and his assenting creature (with God signing for both parties) which underwrites a resemblance between natural and supernatural forces and the individual. The self/spirit relation is a lawful yet voluntary face-to-face transaction.

In spite of this surprising power of contract to subsume everything, including Neoplatonic metaphysics, the satisfactions of contractual exchange do not provide the possessive individualist identity that these satisfactions seek. Corporatism initially articulates a public sphere in which the contractual "individual" is subordinate to public traditions and needs. To explain this, I must backtrack briefly. Contracts in the eighteenth century were judged by communally established notions of "substantive impact" and "fairness." Traditional standards routinely took precedence over the wills of the contracting parties.[48] The dominant view throughout the early nineteenth century was that a contract's terms must express a "natural justice and equity" to which individual volition should submit. But as the nineteenth century progressed, contract law referred with increasing exclusion to the individual will of a free agent. (This latter notion prevailed in part because it was more flexible than the concept of equitable value.) Intention rather than outcome increasingly functioned as the arbiter of a contract's fairness. The influential jurist William Story argued that "only 'an unnatural and artificial extension' of public institutions could create a 'power to overrule the express agreements of individuals . . .' since 'whatever men have consented to, that shall bind them, and nothing else.'"[49] This shift toward private consent is part of a battle that New England culture fought (and still fights) again and again so that liberal individualism, loosely construed, could escape a more "republican" organic solidarity.

In the process, the private consent meant to resolve a division became divided itself. Contractual will was supposed to sustain private intent in the realm of public exchange. But in so doing, it became torn between embodying individual property and representing a transitional place in a system of exchange. Contract law began to separate itself from property.

Contract began to be understood not as transferring the title of particular property but as creating an expected return.[50] Contract represented two somewhat different kinds of will: the immediate will to possession, and the will to engage in a network of transactions and contingencies. One form attempted to produce wealth by suspending contingency in favor of possession; the other sought wealth by inviting contingency. One excluded crowds of conflicting agents while the second invited them. The will in contractual exchange did not have the kind of immediate access to itself that the will as embodied in property ownership would theoretically provide; contract did not provide a personal identity based on unmediated self-possession.

Contract law addressed this (more or less unspoken) dilemma about the nature of the contracting will in part by making the will increasingly abstract through the 1850s. The will represented in free contract became the will to engage in controlled exchange. Though contract certainly sought to control market forces, this volitional control did not accomplish possession. No longer was property thought of "as entailing the right to undisturbed ownership free from all outside interference"; property was used in a transactional network in which it was "just another cash-valued commodity."[51] Legal agency had increasingly less to do with ownership and increasingly more to do with a transaction in which agency was itself a commodity. Formalizing the will did not resolve the status of legal agency but confirmed the split between possession and exchange.

If a contract did deliver inalienable possession—possession so secure as to allow personal identity to form around the power that delivered it—possession would lose its value. From the start, Emerson conceived even the natural forces ostensibly standing outside exchange to be forces supporting exchange: "All the parts [of nature] incessantly work into each other's hands for the profit of man. The wind sows the seed; the sun evaporates the sea; the wind blows the vapor to the field . . . and thus the endless circulations of the divine charity nourish man."[52] Were contract to deliver stable possession, the excess that is charity (and movement generally) would be missing. Charity represents the containment of the power of self-legislation in favor of a multiplicity of outcomes that the individual will does not intend. Contract is an instrument for protecting the individual against inalienable property and its old, inactive, and all too self-identical value. To will a contract is to agree to exchange as a way of avoiding possession. By the time Theodore Dreiser examines the instruments of credit and leverage in *The Financier*, the earlier, Emersonian fascination with the power of transition and circulation has evolved into the idea that only losers seek possession in the first place. The individual can own contracted property, but not in a way that furnishes autonomy.

Corporate liberalism in general insists that self-possession and contracted exchange are symbiotic and that the orphic and oedipal functions work together. But self-possession is not one of contract's outcomes. Accordingly, "Prospects" denies that the individual can get anything but nonindividualist ideas about him- or herself from the attempt to harmonize the modes of positing, owning, reflecting, and exchanging within the law. The divergence of the operation of power from personal agency allows Emerson to move toward the corporate nonindividual for his image of future splendor. "Prospects" participates in one prominent trajectory of market contract. This makes Emerson a spokesman for the market, but equally a spokesman for its internal conflict between the "oedipal" union of self-possession and circulation and the "orphic" loss of self in circulation.

6. The Public Basis of the Corporation

What kind of system emerges from a situation in which the most powerful mechanism of individualized corporatism — contract — does not sustain possessive individuality? The division in "Prospects" suggests that its speaker, experiencing himself only in relation to the other, cannot uphold the oedipal fiction that the conventional relation to otherness leads to self-ownership. I think it is worth noting for its own sake that contract fails to make market individualism a stable source of personal autonomy. But it is not immediately obvious what issues from this. The question needs to be asked in an especially pointed way because the answer might be nothing except the usual cycles of loss and recovery that sustain the oedipal desire for self-possession, a desire that survives in spite or, rather, because of the constant threat of its own ephemerality. We have been well warned that it is a mistake to "celebrate the subversive potential of the nonidentical subject" such as the subject of "Prospects," since "nonidentity . . . has so often [been] shown to be part of disciplinary processes."[53] Emerson commentary is a case in point for it has specialized in casting Emersonian nonidentity as "bipolar complementarity," "double consciousness," "alternation of opposites," "balanced antagonism," or a "receptive autonomy" that reads any conflict as part of a deeper plan for agonistic wholeness.

The paired poets of "Prospects" do not seem even to seek an alliance. The orphic poet flees from marriage with any individual. The poet sings less of each man and more of "Man" and finally of a "dominion," "house," and "world." At first, the poet affirms that "'A man is a god in ruins.'" However, he does not thereby affirm the "'will'" but, rather, "'Instinct.'"[54] Instinct for Emerson is spirit within the self, yet it is also a term that Emerson's texts associate with actual social groups. At the close of "The American Scholar," Emerson describes instinct indifferently as "the perspective of your own infinite life" which translates as "the shades of all the good and great."[55] One's own infinite life is beyond individuality in dwelling with "all the good and great" which leads to the formation of a more perfect "nation of men." "Self-Reliance," another early work, claims that the "aboriginal self," if defined as "Spontaneity or Instinct," is where "all things find their common origin."[56] Emerson describes instinct as the (orphic) voice which is not possessible. Sometimes he cannot possess the voice because it's God's and sometimes because it is a form of common property; I will return to these differences in later chapters. Overall, instinct is transcendent agency and, at other times, public agency — agency that, in belonging to all, is shared by all. Orphic power denies that agency rests with a superior individual and denies that it rests with oneself.

If one reads Emerson without expecting his metaphysical corporatism to lead to concrete individuality, one notes that it has potential to lead to concrete collectivity. In Marx's reading of liberal idealism, a refusal like Emerson's to separate corporatism from spiritualism produces the capitalist state's abstract commonality, one that can never supersede concrete individuality. But it is not so easy for an ongoing interaction to produce such a clear separation. Abstract commonality comes very close to being retained within Emerson's concrete individuality, and indeed he seeks this connection and refuses to use the poetic equivalents of contract and private property to subordinate this individuality to the state's abstract economy. The power of Emerson's orphic Spirit is that it does not quite fit with what Marx saw in Stirner and other bourgeois reformers, and it slides toward a corporate "Spirit" that heralds an actual "nation of men." This is a corporate form that cannot be described by a binary opposition between abstract and concrete, collective and individual.

This awkward transitional state puts Emerson midway between secular individualism and a quasi socialism authorized in part by his anachronistic Neoplatonism. He shows a displaced interest in materializing his spiritual corporatism that does not issue in an explicit attempt to restore the corporate form to public control. This interest is nonetheless urged beyond liberalism by the social and economic change that produced the all too concrete early business corporation. Even as Marx and Emerson wrote, the concrete was increasingly less and less individual. In its open, frontier phase, New England capitalism was not a free-for-all, but owed much of its advance to various forms of association. Emerson certainly can be found engaged in commonplace laissez-faire moralizing, but the fact is that world-making power in Emerson's time was already corporate. Individual enterprise recast the world like a modern Orpheus only by acting through chartered banks, railroad companies, interregional commodity networks, and large-scale labor operations. The remarkable dependence of market individuality on associations made corporatism an unlikely savior of the sovereignty of possession.

The ruling feature of the new corporate form was its privacy. Prior to the 1830s, "use of the corporate form was limited primarily to non-business, clearly public-related or noncontroversial activities such as municipalities and benevolent, religious, or educational societies."[57] Collective enterprises had public and communal legal status, and corporations were extensions of a general civic will as established by a legislature. But as the century progressed, various factors pressed corporate charters toward the private sector: "The [private] corporation began as a surrogate instrument for organizing essentially public functions. . . . Hampered by a lack of funds, poorly developed administrative structures, and a preference for private over governmental action, New York [among other states] resorted to private arrangements to provide transportation facilities and a system of currency and finance."[58] The shift from the public to the private corporation produced a massive increase in administrative efficiency, profit, and private capital. The corporate form supported individualist assumptions about personhood by explicitly harnessing collective forces to individual vision. By enabling the public interest to be privately owned, the corporation installed the collective, democratic will in a structure owned by possessive individuals.

But private property and the corporate form were consolidated in the later nineteenth century through a massive exertion of police power bought and wielded by a state-corporation alliance. Even then, the consolidation remained incomplete. I itemize a few of the vicissitudes of ownership that resulted when corporations attempted to privatize collective property. They are vicissitudes denied by oedipal and enacted by orphic corporatism.

First, the antebellum corporation offered the collective will access to forces far greater than those of private property. Before the Civil War the corporation was less a legal individual than it was an agent of collective opportunity. The wealthy Jacksonian David Henshaw put it this way: in England, modern economic development depends on individual wealth, but "our ancestors came here poor; the fundamental principles of their institutions were, to elevate the character, and improve the condition of the whole mass, by diffusing among all the citizens an equality of wealth, as well as of political rights and privileges."[59] The means they wisely chose were charters of incorporation, given "neither as monopolies nor perpetuities; they were particular, and peculiar laws, regulating particular bodies of men, for special and laudable purposes, the object being the common good, the individual interest of the corporators being secondary, and subservient to the primary object, the common good and general welfare."[60] Henshaw argued that the business corporation can serve the common good and in that way operate like a self-created commonwealth. The purpose of the business corporation was to join its members in relations other than those of private contract. As Emerson was composing *Nature*, other moderate progressives saw private accumulation as compatible with all aspects of public life, not only because public life was thought the natural servant of the private self, but because private accumulation was the servant of the commonwealth.

Second, the corporate form extended the private will only by altering it beyond recognition. The will became a network of shareholder obligations which did not result in shareholder agency. Only a handful of corporate owners managed the assets and did so more as a result of their status as manager or delegate than as owner. For nearly everyone, the corporation was the site of receiving the dividend rather than enacting the deed. Owners voted through their stock, but this vote expressed formal assent rather than substantive intent. Corporate consent and dissent appeared much more commonly through buying and selling stock in the market than through direct action. Structurally, it was then, as now, almost impossible for agency to escape the nexus of intracorporate exchange, and it almost never existed as positive substantive control. The corporation was not an agency to be owned, but was itself a market in its own shares, which represented a fully commodified agency. "Ownership" here simply meant access to this market. In the corporation,

investment and private control parted company: in one antebellum decision, a bank corporation was allowed to "*purchase,* absolutely" lands it
would not occupy, but nonetheless, "would *hold* them by a title defeas-
ible by the Commonwealth, and the Commonwealth alone."[61]

Third, the corporate charter in antebellum America did not simply
fracture the private will in the manner of contract but replaced it with a
public will tied to the legislature. While business partnerships were
founded through private agreements between persons who retained executive control over their organizations, corporations differed explicitly
from these in resting on a charter that functioned more as a constitution
than as a "mere license for private will."[62] These constitutions originated
in Emerson's time in the "affirmative law" of the state or federal legislature. While the idea of a "private corporation" may to us verge on
redundancy, the early corporation's status as private property hung by
the still-fragile thread of a controversial judicial construction of the charter as a contract under the U.S. Constitution. The idea of eliminating
public supervision of charters did not prevail until "long after 1855."[63]
Even when jurists were preferring the private rights of parties over restrictions on the charter by treating the charter as a private contract, the
founding charter remained visible as a creation of public power. The
United States Supreme Court, noted one Democrat, considered a charter like that of the Bank of the United States to render it a "public institution": "all acts of incorporation shall be deemed public acts."[64] The
chief justice of the New Hampshire Supreme Court ruled in *Trustees of
Dartmouth College* (1817) that "the property of these corporations exist[s] collectively in all the individuals of whom they are composed; not,
however, as natural persons, but as a body politic."[65] Even a conservative
advocate of property rights like Justice William Story simultaneously
sustained legislative sovereignty by noting in *Dartmouth College* "that a
legislature could avoid the effect of the decision by reserving in the charter itself the right to amend or repeal it."[66]

This idea survived the most sustained and varied series of challenges
by private interests. The corporation remained a shadow "body politic"
in the twentieth century, and the status of the "corporate fiction," the
"corporate personality," and other issues of private and public law remained active through the writing of George Canfield, John Dewey,
Harold Laski, Arthur Machen, Josiah Royce, Maurice Wormser, and
many others. The power of corporate agency to ignore legislative consent remains controversial enough to attract potentially successful law-
suits, at least regarding public authorities.[67] The "private" will, seen

apart from its fictions of autonomy was not so well expressed in contract as in an irreducible "association" dependent for many of Emerson's contemporaries upon legislative "concessions" that cannot separate themselves from a "body politic" or a "public will."[68] The orphic will manifests individual sovereignty as a collective will in this limited sense: though the orphic does not allow the collective will to become a public institution, it does not allow it, as does the law of corporate persons, to be taken private.

7. The Specter of Democracy

In insisting on the public aspect of the increasingly private antebellum corporation, I do not deny its ongoing privatization.[69] But I have suggested an instability in this privacy, and we fail to recognize immediately the public basis of private corporate forms only because of official actions that are part of the well-known policing of postbellum corporate capitalism. Contract law failed to ground the privacy and self-genesis of individual agency and failed because of its exposure to "public" forces in perpetual motion. The corporation builds more successfully on this public dimension. But the corporation manages to be neither private nor public, for even in its legal and fiduciary function as the arm of private interest, it encrypts the public within itself.

Pointing out the public or collective structure of private corporations does not in itself weaken the corporate grip, for we have no access to an "authentic" public sphere that would oppose the private version. The corporation has produced an oligarchical type of "public will" that has long substituted for a collectively governed community. Since Emerson's time the corporation has seemed to offer the best of both worlds: the scope and riches to construct ostensible public necessities like railroads, mass housing, and a global military, with none of the conflict and disorder of legislative activity. The corporation takes the form of a collective order without mutual agency or reciprocal influence; each individual exists as part of a group, but not as agent so much as shareholder. As long as we are construed as corporate individuals, we can neither move forward toward collective sovereignty nor backward toward autonomous individuality. Instead, we live in submission to decisions handed down from executive spheres tied to threads of fiduciary interest that lead toward even more remote regions of private capital.

Or so it seems. But though the corporate individual is individually helpless, she or he is also haunted by the specter of a public agency that dwells within mystified corporatism. Emerson moves in two directions at once on this matter, as is his lifelong custom. First, he insures that an individual's submission to a sufficiently gigantic and inaccessible collective instrument will seem like a spiritual triumph. His metaphysics of the One allows the community system controlled by private interests to seem literally providential. This metaphysics also allows personal agency to see being directed by a "transcendental" agency as coherent and individuating. Thus in our still-transcendentalist America, individuals compete in unending labors of self-differentiation while their social relations are managed from somewhere else.

But second, and often in spite of himself, Emerson reflects the cultural fact that the contractual and corporate supplements of simple possessive individualism lead toward a range of experiences of oneself that cannot be reduced to possession. "Prospects" implies that "oneself" exists most freely in a collective. Emerson replaces the simple relation of private and public with the relation between contradictory contracts and messy corporate instruments — between Herbert's submissive individuality and Orpheus's powerful commonality. Much of Emerson's work endorses the longtime American confusion of freedom with submission to laissez-faire private orders. On the other hand, it suggests that the powerful individualism that he associates with the orphic poet can acquire power only by eradicating its attachment to private individuality. Emerson here imagines an individual who has replaced his or her spiritualist adherence to "othered," or private, or otherwise inaccessible corporate bodies with a subtler understanding of agency as a participatory and collective activity. Corporate life would be controlled by a public legislative power rather than by private managers. This is Emerson at his most democratic, imagining a self liberated through its orphic embodiment of collective (and not transcendental) sovereignty. The antebellum prehistory of the collective subject imagined an individual free of corporate authoritarianism who has long since been buried. But it is difficult to judge the issue, since this is a prehistory that has not yet ended.

PART

THREE

Individualism and Submission in Private Life

CHAPTER

FOUR

Friendly Inequalities
Emerson and Straight Homoeroticism

A despot will lightly forgive his subjects for not loving
him, provided they do not love one another.
— Tocqueville

In part 2, I argued that *Nature* does not cure submissive Neoplatonic
metaphysics ("Language") with individualism ("Prospects"), but cures
individualism with corporatism. The latter is an ambivalent postindividualism that links power to quasi-public collective relations.

This corporate republicanism, as it might be called, could lead in a
number of directions. One might have been the utopian socialism that
attracted many of Emerson's transcendentalist peers. There was so much
of this in the air that even the skeptical Hawthorne felt a strong enough
curiosity about the Ripleys' commune, Brook Farm, to provoke him to
reside there for a number of months. Emerson famously resisted the
temptation himself, although, as I suggest below, his relation to socialism was more positive than is sometimes thought. The more immediate
settings for his explorations of social subjectivity are the home, which is
the subject of the next chapter, and clubs, where Emerson, who never
failed to belong to at least one, could pursue the comforts of male
friendship. Friendship offered what Tocqueville called a "little society"
of reciprocal relations. In civic friendship, Emerson might hope to find
a little democracy.

In small-scale group relations, individual desire and collective needs
were obviously more easily reconciled than was the case for citizenship
in a mass democracy. Male friendship did not, however, serve as a secure
retreat from life with the masses. Friendship could also represent the
possibility of democratic relations. Friendship was then the place in
which democracy had to be nipped in the bud, or at least modulated in

An earlier version of this chapter was published as "Democracy and Male Homoeroticism," *Yale Journal of Criticism* 6, no. 2 (1993): 29–62. Reprinted by permission of the
Johns Hopkins University Press.

accordance with the demands of overall social governance. Friendship did not represent the resolution of corporate postindividualism so much as another setting for a private life of quasi-public significance, and was contested for that reason. The two kinds of corporatism described in the last chapter are relevant here: would the male group, perhaps numbering only two, be created by joint submission to a common model or father-leader? Or would it make its own laws through some kind of egalitarian and mutual collaboration?

Large and complicated pressures direct straight male friends to the first possibility, being safely oedipal, ceding consent while maintaining group relations. Protecting oedipal from the more democratic bonding involves some serious patrolling of the border, lest identification with the father turn into identification with (or desire for) the brotherly friend. As I'll be arguing at some length here, the job calls for a strong phobia, specifically, homophobia.

The controversy over gays in the military furnished an example of the uses of homophobia in structuring relations in male groups.[1] One familiar explanation was that the straight nation's manhood is panicked by association with the simultaneously effeminate and predatory deviance that homosexuality is thought to represent. But the controversy introduced the group factor that I will be elaborating here. Male homoeroticism, when it becomes public homosexuality, threatens not just male but military order. It threatens the widely fetishized "unit cohesion" rooted in the despotism of unchallenged leaders. It threatens to undermine the despotism that has symbolically — and in fact — stabilized democratic society; it threatens by challenging not just straight homosociality in general, but a male homosociality that consists of submission to superiors.

The military crisis exposed a long tradition of sexualizing authority problems. American homophobia has proscribed male homoeroticism in part as a taboo on a kind of politics that takes democracy too far. Male homosexual identity emerged as the continuation of controls on sexual identity in the context of nineteenth-century attempts to validate and restrict the self-governance of the masses.

In a broad tradition most famously articulated by Walt Whitman, homoeroticism figures a faith in radical democracy, in a "brotherly love" in which a fusion of sexual and political identity defeats the competitive hierarchy that mainstream United States culture works especially hard to cast as the only viable mode of personal freedom. My interest here is not in whether Whitmanesque ideas are truly democratic but in the antagonisms to them, which are not. Two surprisingly parallel antagonisms are the "sciences" of the crowd and of the newly devised homosexual which, after long and jumbled preambles were launched within a few years of each other. Gustave Le Bon's *Psychologie des foules* was published in Paris in 1895, not long after the first development of the term *homosexual* in American medical journals and while Oscar Wilde's trials were helping construct homosexuality as a pathological identity.[2] At nearly the same historical moment, the man of the crowd and the man of "inversion" were transformed, with the invention of their "sciences," from being routine, dispersed, and politically ambiguous into psychic structures that threaten collective order. These distinct but parallel trajectories achieved synthesis in Freud's *Group Psychology and the Analysis of the Ego* (1921), where he, in effect, argued the impossibility of democratic group ties by describing civilization as the need to manage "homosexual love."[3] Emerson's deployment of civic friendship addressed similar problems with men in groups, but without the benefit of the sciences of the next century.

Freud's reading of the crowd remains a cornerstone of our ongoing system of administered democracy, based as it is on the assumption that hierarchy is crucial to freedom. This democratic order is not only masculine—a feature whose effects have been superbly described by feminist theorists and historians over the last 150 years. It is not only homophobic. It is masculine and homophobic in a particular way, in a way which constructs straight male identity through intimate and systematic inequality. Distinguishing between male homoeroticism and male homosexuality, I will explore how homophobia is politically charged by—though not reducible to—a phobia about equality.

1. Two Sodomies: Men and Mobs

> While the radicals of Europe were revolting in 1848 against the abuses of a tyranny whose roots were in feudalism, Emerson, the great radical of America, the arch-radical of the world, was revolting against the evils whose roots were in universal suffrage.
>
> —John Jay Chapman

Recent work in lesbian and gay studies has made real advances in understanding the fear of homosexuality by explaining the tension between male homosexual desire and heterosexual homoeroticism. Fear enters in the form of an uncertainty about whether one's putatively heterosexual bonding with other men might not be homosexual after all. The straight man's familiar patriarchal networking harbors within it a continual suspicion of deviance.

But in order for an uncertainty about one's possible homosexual desire (and about its unstable meaning) to lead to homosexual panic, one
must be panicked about homosexuality in the first place.[4] Describing
the tension between hetero- and homosexual identity illuminates the
mechanism through which homophobia is deployed, but this deployment depends on the tension's already being fraught with anxiety. Homophobia must previously exist for homoeroticism to pose such a terri-
fying danger. Continuing the examination of modern homophobia's
genealogy unveils a number of factors — the longstanding Christian taboo, legal histories, the increasing masculinization of commercial and
industrial areas of the antebellum city. But throughout the course of the
nineteenth century these factors acquire a new political weight. Homophobia's sexual regime takes its modern structure by miming the shape
of a national imperative. In the United States, this imperative appears
in antebellum panic about writers who did not distinguish sharply
between their hetero- and homosexual desires, and who attempted to
make a principle of public life out of a nonbinary, unpolarized notion
of male friendship.

First, the sounds of panic. Rufus Griswold, reviewing the first edition of *Leaves of Grass,* rejected its main theme as directly as offended
decency would permit.

> As to the volume itself, we have only to remark, that it strongly fortifies
> the doctrines of the Metempsychosists, for it is impossible to imagine
> how any man's fancy could have conceived such a mass of stupid filth,
> unless he were possessed of the soul of a sentimental donkey that had
> died of disappointed love. This *poet* (?) without wit, but with a certain
> vagrant wildness, just serves to show the energy which natural imbecility
> is occasionally capable of under strong excitement. . . . There are too
> many persons, who imagine they demonstrate their superiority to their
> fellows, by disregarding all the politeness and decencies of life, and, there-
> fore, justify themselves in indulging the vilest imaginings and shame-
> fullest license.

Whitman's major feature as a poet — besides his braying incompe-
tence — is the dirty excitability which identifies him as a man of the herd.
Like any member of a crowd, Whitman is imbecilic under the pressure
of "strong excitement," but adopts a false "superiority" that allows him
to disregard established rules and follow his own. As Griswold's review
proceeds in this vein, its repetitions link the presumptions of the mob
to a particular sexuality.

> These candid, these ingenuous, these honest "progessionists"; these hu-
> man diamonds without flaws; these men that have *come* — detest furiously

all shams; "to the pure, all things are pure"; they are pure, and consequently, must thrust their reeking presence under every man's nose. . . . In our allusion to this book, we have found it impossible to convey any, even the most faithful idea of its style and contents, and of our disgust and detestation of them, without employing language that cannot be pleasing to ears polite; but it does seem that some one should, under circumstances like these, undertake a most disagreeable, yet stern duty. The records of crime show that many monsters have gone on in impunity, because the exposure of their vileness was attended with too great indelicacy. *Peccatum illud horribile, inter Christianos non nominandum* [That horrible sin not to be mentioned among Christians].[5]

Griswold links Whitman's life with the masses to a social radicalism which he then figures as sodomy. Using Coke's well-known reference to sodomy as the sin "amongst Christians not to be named,"[6] Griswold sees in *Leaves of Grass* a revoltingly unashamed parade of "reeking" men, "coming m[e]n,"[7] "men who have come," men who "strut abroad unabashed in the daylight, and expose to the world the festering sores that overlay them" — men who "thrust" themselves on respectable men in ways which are simultaneously obscene and anarchic. Griswold reads sodomy in a double sense that should not be restricted to anal intercourse between men: "unnatural" relations between men and those unnatural (male) relations that lead to the "vagrance" of the masses, full as they are of ambitious, coming men who upset social hierarchy. Filthy poets like Whitman show that the "horrible sin" is (also) a form of insurrection. Griswold's disgust for sodomy already smolders, but it is fanned into flames by Whitman's unashamed self-direction.

When Griswold conflates sexual and political depravity he is working within the colonial definition of a sodomite as one of "Sodom's sinful citizens and their whole array of vices" and not as "persons guilty specifically and only of sodomy."[8] The antebellum urban novelist George Lippard makes a similar connection between the sexual and political forms of vile association. In a long dream described by the character Devil-Bug in *The Quaker City,* the sodomites are citizens of both genders and different sexual histories who fulfill the city's capacity for misrule.

One shriek went up to God from that vast crowd — one shriek of horror. Every eye beheld the corpse at the side of the King, and now — oh God of judgment! Every man in all that countless crowd, beheld the form of a grim Dead Man at his side! How the shriek of horror, rushed up at the clear sky, like thunder from hell! Yes, yes, every man beheld the form of a corpse at his side, every woman saw the leaden eyes gazing upon her

beauty, the very babes beheld the awful spectacle and hid their heads in
their mother's bosoms, and mingled their shrill cry of horror, with the
shriek of the millions.

   . . . look upon the wreck of the Doomed City . . . [and]shout "Wo,
WO UNTO SODOM."[9]

Lippard's sodomite is the woman or man of the crowd. Each member
of the mob is paired with a dead twin who once helped constitute a
couple but who had been disavowed by mob life. The sodomite is he
or she who favors mass life at the expense of pairing. The restored but
terminal pairing, in the case of the man, is with another man. "The city
of brotherly love" has become so promiscuous in its associations that
only the second coming of Christ will straighten it out. Devil-Bug
dreams the city's last day by scrambling together the two versions of
sodomy present in Griswold's review of Whitman: mob life and its exposed "truth" of same-sex intimacy.

    Sodomy's double meaning was facilitated by the elasticity of the term
prior to the twentieth century. Those who have studied the medico-
juridical discourse that finally did attribute "sodomy" to an intrinsically
"homosexual" male toward the end of the nineteenth century have mar-
veled at the ignorance about the details of same-sex intercourse that distinguished not only the public but also the police and the physicians
who presented the cases.[10] Although the connection to scriptural injunc-
tions remained alive, sodomy before 1890 did not so much convey an
idea of a specific deed as a form of compulsive male depravity.[11] Griswold and Lippard are not unusual in linking this depravity to the life of
the masses in large and chaotic cities. "Alabama, for example, had a town
named Sodom, not because of the sexual activities of the inhabitants
but because their neighbors regarded them as murderers, bandits, van-
dals, and general hell-raisers."[12] Sodomy, a social as well as a sexual
crime, is associated with a refusal to work and compete signaled by "la-
ziness," "sloth," and the neglect of business, and a willingness to congre-
gate for no practical purpose.[13] Male perversion appears in both the private and public domains in part because it is the activity that brings
private and public together: "Although one of the most frequently employed euphemisms for masturbation was 'the solitary vice,' from the
1830s forward it was the social pursuit of this nominally solitary activity
that is a constant target of anti-onanist writing."[14] The target of antebellum sodomy discourse — in addition to the frightening unthinkability
that surrounds the erotic taboo — is the unnatural intimacy created by
replacing private with public structures of desire and consciousness.[15]

Our own century is so powerfully under the spell of the relatively recent dichotomy between hetero- and homosexuality that it is hard to imagine sodomy as anything but a charged signifier of deviance from the heterosexual norm. And in the 1990s, the link between sodomy and mass democracy seems long defunct, especially when forms of direct democracy such as the ballot referendum are more easily used to repeal gay rights statutes than to install them. These referenda attack precisely those statutes which prevent gay citizenship from being revoked through prosecution, harassment, or violence. They attack what protects the democratic rights of the sodomite. When some respectable authors before the Civil War link the challenge of the mob to the sin of sodomy, it suggests that male homoeroticism per se—and not just its minority status or taboo—poses a distinctive and historically developed threat to crowd control. And a look at Ralph Waldo Emerson confirms that straight male homoeroticism, speaking anachronistically, begins to panic not so much at the prospect of loving a man but of encountering this love in a mass.

Emerson hates crowds but likes mysterious men. One-on-one male contact makes for pleasant serenity. "I begin to believe in the Indian doctrine of eye-fascination. The cold blue eye of [a student, thought to be Martin Gay] has so intimately connected him with my thoughts & visions that a dozen times a day & as often . . . by night I find myself wholly wrapped up in conjectures of his character & inclinations. . . . We have had already two or three long profound stares at each other. Be it wise or weak or superstitious I must know him."[16] Gay induces in Emerson the hypnotic and obsessional states that form an erotic captivity he finds liberating. I have been, he says,

> so full of pleasant social feelings—for a day or two past that the mind has not possessed sufficiently the cold frigid tone which is indispensable to become so *oracular* as it hath been of late. Although the praise and honor of my thoughts has not been as great as before, yet it acquires a greater joy and pleasure, since I believed I felt the beginnings of love. I saw a [male] friend, though an old one, unknown; I saw another [female] known and to be known; both, perhaps, if it pleases God, will make a part of life, a part of me.[17]

This passage has the tone of sanitizing revisionism, but lacks the expected revulsion for a forbidden love. Bondage turns out to be a private "social feeling" which does not prevent male object-choice. It relieves Emerson of the burden of oracularity, of a competitive and solitary quest for preeminence. It appears to replace autonomy with relation,

and domination with equality. Most important, egalitarian fraternity
does not mean the loss of desire. Though we should not confuse the
platonic friendship tradition with male homosexuality, Emerson finds
in Gay exactly some such confusion of free sociability and erotic compulsion.[18] As in Whitman, Emerson's homoeroticism does not stand
apart from his Platonized "social" feelings, for he is too strongly
attached to the feelings aroused by this single man.[19]

In one of his later essays, "Considerations By the Way," Emerson
again mixes platonic friendship and desire. Friendship, he says, is "a
serious and majestic affair, like a royal presence, or a religion."[20] But he
adds, "There is a pudency about friendship, as about love, and though
fine souls never lose sight of it, yet they do not name it." Referring not
only to the modesty of friendship but to its shame ("pudency"), Emerson says that male friendship is like love for a reason that, perhaps
following the sodomy topos of Coke and Griswold, is wisely left un-
named. And yet Emerson expresses no horror at the contact, but says,
"It is the only real society."[21]

Further instances of desire for men are scattered throughout Emerson's work. "Read the language of these wandering eye-beams," he
requests. They tell a story of a man's dependency on his friends. "Our
intellectual and active powers increase with our affection. The scholar
sits down to write, and all his years of meditation do not furnish him
with one good thought or happy expression; but it is necessary to write
a letter to a friend — and, forthwith, troops of gentle thoughts invest
themselves, on every hand, with chosen words."[22] Friends must be chosen on the basis of combined identity and difference: "Friendship requires that rare mean betwixt likeness and unlikeness, that piques each
with the presence of power and of consent in the other party."[23] Emerson cautions that friendship must not be allowed to take us away from
our "true self": "We must be our own before we can be another's."[24]
But with that in mind, he feels free to carry on. "I please my imagination
. . . with a circle of godlike men and women variously related to each
other, and between whom subsists a lofty intelligence."[25] This circle is a
necessity of the individual's radical dependence on the group: "Only he
may then speak who can sail on the common thought of the party, and
not poorly limited to his own."

This dependence of self on the other requires an intimacy that trans-
gresses the contracts and exchanges between the free individuals of a
market economy. Emerson makes this clear in his subordination of
"Gifts" to the love between equals. "No services are of any value, but

only likeness. When I have attempted to join myself to others by services, it proved an intellectual trick, — no more. They eat your service
like apples, and leave you out. But love them, and they feel you, and
delight in you all the time."[26] In transgressing the separateness of market
circulation, Emerson frequently invokes the imagery of fluids reminis-
cent of the "universal currents" flowing through his eyeball state in nature. "Late, very late, we perceive that no arrangements, no introduc-
tions, no consuetudes, or habitudes of society would be of any avail to
establish us in such relations with [friends] as we desire, but solely the
uprise of nature in us to the same degree it is in them, then shall we mix
as water with water, & if we should not meet them then, we shall not
want them, for we are already they."[27] Friendship overcomes the failures
of existing social relations to establish a genuine intimacy between two
beings, an intimacy here based on their common identity. The same
goes for the gift: "The gift, to be true, must be the flowing of the giver
unto me, correspondent to my flowing unto him. When the waters are
at level, then my goods pass to him, and his to me. All his are mine, all
mine his."[28] As a basis for masculine identity, Emerson obviously and
repeatedly rejects autonomy and a separate economy of fluids in favor
of a mixing of fluids and a fluid mixing that erodes the boundaries between man and man. In this mixing Emerson finds his (limited) version
of equality.

Such mixing is lovely between two men, but revolting when extended to society. Affection transported to groups shifts from friendship
to charity. "The worst of charity, is, that the lives you are asked to preserve are not worth preserving. The calamity is the masses. I do not
wish any mass at all, but honest men only, facultied men only, lovely,
sweet, accomplished women only, and no shovel-handed Irish, & no
Five-Points, or Saint Gileses, or drunken crew, or mob, or stockingers,
or 2 millions of paupers receiving relief, miserable factory population,
or lazzaroni, at all."[29] This is not the entirety of Emerson's feeling about
the working populace; let's just say it's the larger half. What makes them
so disgusting? It would divert us to get into Emerson's harsh theories
of natural selection, as reflected in his country saying, "Nature makes
fifty poor melons for one that is good." He offers a simpler suggestion
elsewhere: "Masses are rude, lame, unmade, pernicious in their demands and influence, and need not to be flattered but to be schooled. I
wish not to concede anything to them, but to tame, drill, divide, and
break them up, and draw individuals out of them."[30] The masses are
redeemed by division and individuation; their calamity is in their multi-

tudes. Government consists simply of breaking them up by undoing mass ties and turning them into singles again, singles who are always ready to be coupled.

These passages together suggest that Emerson discriminates between good and bad male bonding not by the presence or absence of (an ambiguous) eroticism but by bonding's number. The sodomy taboo asks not only "is it another man," but "is it private or public, coupled or collective"? While for Emerson and Griswold sodomy in such forms as male-male anal intercourse undoubtedly remains an abomination, Emerson openly desires aspects of male love with which sodomy overlaps. He openly dislikes that love, however, when it appears as the masses. Homosocial eroticism is spoiled by groups rather than by homosexuality, whose threat, as such, does not appear in Emerson's work. Fearful sodomy depends in Emerson less on the male/female difference in object-choice than on the difference between the couple and the crowd. He seeks not to suppress homoerotic intimacies but to privatize them. Given the short circuits between the democratic and the homoerotic kind of sodomy, Emerson's pleasure in ambiguous male friendship suggests that sodomy in antebellum America, as precursor to homosexuality, borrowed some of its powers of horror from a middle-class fear of mass democracy.[31]

2. Heads in the Crowd

I have been suggesting that some antebellum middle-class men may have had a more immediate hostility to public and multiple bonding than they did to same-sex bonding. But this raises the further question: what is so bad about public bonding?

Clarification comes from the rich and vivid loathings of social reformers. The liberal minister Edwin Chapin, in his often sympathetic 1843 work, *The Moral Aspects of City Life,* described the poor neighborhoods of New York City as a "swimming mist of hideous transactions and hideous faces," "pools dark with undistinguishable horrors" composed of masses of people "matted together in the very offal of debasement" from which could emerge only "surges of moral death."[32] In 1854, a decade of additional experience of New York has not changed Chapin's mind: "No one needs to be told that there are savages in New York as well as in the islands of the sea. Savages not in gloomy forests, but under the strength of gaslight . . . with warhoops [*sic*] and clubs very much the same, and garments as fantastic, and souls as brutal, as any of their kindred at the antipodes. China, India, Africa, will you not find their features in some circles of the social world right around you?"[33] Chapin's racism and class anxiety generate the polarization that was implicit in Griswold, Lippard, and Emerson: privacy or barbarism. Broadly speaking, this familiar kind of middle-class masculinity sees the point of male existence as self-differentiation, accumulation, and boundary defense, and sees America as the place where this is natural. Personal identity, embracing both harmony and competition, should never depend on someone else. Members of crowds diverge from this ideal autonomy; if they like crowd life, then they are primitives whose betrayal of individualist morality should not be allowed to spread.

Reformers loathe what they see as the savage deindividuation of a crowd's members. They loathe no less the crowd's fanatical leader. The leader is the principal target of New York's famous recorder and criminal judge, Richard Riker.

> All who reflected on the character of a mob, knew that it was a mere brute force which any bold and bad man might direct as an engine to gratify private revenge, and for the worst of purposes. It was devoid of discrimination [sic] and reflection; so that no matter how innocent or excellent a man might be, he is liable to become its victim. It was impossible to describe its evils. Hurried on by a blind fury, every thing became subject to its force, and the rights of property and personal security were lost and swept away, as it were, in an ocean of madness.[34].

For Riker, the mob's "evils" are unspeakable to a Christian because they endanger the private sphere of both property and person. But the problem Riker seems most concerned with is not that gangs of "savages" will roam the streets committing random violence. New York's gangs had been doing precisely that for years, wreaking intermittent but unfocused destruction on New York and each other. The "popular disturbance" was considered routine even by many Whigs (the 1833–35 period in New York City saw at least thirty-three riots large enough to be recorded) and was often sanctioned by the press and local authorities: "issues of a 'moral' character were particularly open to settlement by sanctioned violence and threats of violence."[35] Riker, instead, is worried by the combination of a savage mob and a despot at its head. He does not only fear a mob's "*blind* fury" but also a fury guided by the vision of a "bold and bad man" at the top. The dangerous mob has these two features.

Paul Weinbaum's survey of newspaper coverage of various disturbances suggests that organized crowds were perceived as more of a threat than spontaneous or violent crowds. But specifying the danger of these organized crowds is another matter. Riker's language points to the individual leader as the threat to order. Yet Weinbaum suggests that the strikes of 1836 were alarming because of the role of "unskilled workers": "The authorities and the press were alarmed by . . . strikes [as opposed to riots] because they did not expect orderly and purposeful behaviour from unskilled workers."[36] What Weinbaum calls the "demagogic view of rioting," which frightened middle-class observers with the specter of the omnipotent leader, also served as a screen for something still more frightening, something associated with a strike. The strike is characterized by "orderly and purposeful behaviour" not from leaders but "from unskilled workers." It is not the controlling leader but the conscious masses that the "authorities and the press" do not expect. The mob truly feared by the middle class was not a mob rioting without form or purpose, or rioting with a relatively nonpolitical goal such as affordable flour, or one rioting with an identifiable despot at its head, but the mob ruled by many heads and acting through collective analysis with rational aims.

Mob chaos was not as bad as mob order. Emerson's bitter complaint about the "calamity of the masses" is typical in referring to the latter. He is lamenting, after all, the "2 millions of paupers receiving relief," which is not a riot but a peaceful transaction which has arisen from a collectively articulated need. This reflects something apparently more repulsive than anarchy from below or lawgiving from above: lawgiving from below.

The response of the *Boston Daily Bee* to the urban leader Mike Walsh bears out this suspicion. He came as close to being an urban despot as most, but he remained for the genteel press a target of mocking patronization as long as he could be treated as "the idol of the rabble." The *Daily Bee* amiably pities his wish to "be popular rather than great" and to "lead the herd," and shrugs about his "trust and confidence" in members of "his own order," all of which suggests to the paper that Walsh is merely a popular demagogue. As long as the paper can regard Walsh as the head of the herd, the herd's threat does not arise.[37]

Similarly, Charles Loring Brace, who founded the Children's Aid Society in New York in 1853, feared neither organized despots nor disorganized crowds, but organized crowds. He enforced the rules for the poor developed by his society, and at the same time embraced the unsupervised children who lived in chaos all over the neighborhood. "Only 'the streets of New York,' he wrote . . . could have produced 'as bright, sharp, bold [and] racy a crowd of little fellows,'" and he is fond of what he calls the "happy race of little heathens and barbarians," those "'street rats' who 'gnawed away at the foundations of society.'"[38] But Brace abominates street children when they become an organized force: "Throughout the literature of the [Christian Aid Society], one finds comparatively few references to the wickedness, intemperance, profanity, or wildness of individual slum urchins. Rather, the danger Brace emphasized was their potential for destructive *collective* action. . . . Allowed to coalesce as a social force in the city, these urchins, grown to maturity, would 'come to know their power and *use it!*'"[39] The danger, in other words, is not that the grown-up urchins will be supine before any silver-tongued orator but that they will not. The real fear is that they will lead themselves. Like Riker and most of the rest of officialdom, Brace does not fear a brute mob so much as he fears a mob with a mind.

Granting, then, that the middle-class fear of the leader and/or the rabble is more fundamentally a fear of the orderly crowd, on what particular aspects of the orderly crowd does this fear focus? Part of the answer is certainly that in the long run an organized group is more powerful politically and socially than a flour riot or a lynching party. But this power is not so much the power to overwhelm elites as to ignore them. For example, the tenement life that obsessed middle-class reform societies offered not only crime and poverty but social independence. "The home was absent from the lives of urban laboring women, who observed no sharp distinctions between public and private. Rather, their domestic lives spread out to the hallways of their tenements, to adjoining apartments and to the streets below. . . . The major effort went into acquiring necessities — food, fuel and water — a task that took up hours of the day and entailed scores of errands out of the house. This work was by nature public, knitting together the household with the world of the streets. It generated its own intricate network of exchange among neighbors."[40] Tenement autonomy begins with the absence of the home, the reform society's special point of commonality and control. But what they denounce in poor neighborhoods is not lack of government, but rather local self-government. Here the street crowds follow neither savage instinct nor their appointed leaders (including their "betters" in reform societies and local government) but their own internally generated patterns of cooperation. The neighborhoods boast an abundant array of locally controlled, conflictual but stable working-class organizations that serve nearly every social purpose — mechanic's lyceums, workingmen's unions, grocery cooperatives, political parties, voluntary

organizations like the fire companies and tavern gangs, events like festi-
vals and parades, and a host of more informal practices, extensive kin
and friendship networks, and innumerable other forms of life and
thought unlike those of the middle classes and functioning well without
them, in spite of the neighborhoods' widespread poverty and brutaliz-
ing work. The "demagogue" theory of rioting, in short, justified the
control not only of demagogue-led mobs but of groups that lacked a
demagogue and which practiced self-rule.

The social relations of the neighborhoods around Five Points and the
Lower East Side were not only the outcome of economic and political
necessity but were also the source and effect of the working-class ideas
loosely termed "republican" or "agrarian" and generally intended as explicit alternatives to market individualism.[41] A columnist in the *Workingman's Advocate* invites his readers to

> look upon the human family as *one great family*. They are *really so* in their
> *interests* and in their *injuries*. . . . They have never ceased their manoeuver-
> ings to try to take each other prisoner, and bring each other and each
> other's children into the bondage of servitude. . . . *Wars* are nothing but
> large and powerful *mobs,* and *mobs* are nothing but smaller *wars;* and such
> is the end of the force which governments wield; they only *mob* the
> people into submission for the time being . . . I have been laboring for
> years to assist in spreading the truths of *equality* of the human race. . . .
> The right of every *human being* to all that it can *use* of these things is equal
> to its right to life itself. . . . I think I clearly see the way how the Monop-
> oly of the Land, and of its products, may *speedily* and *peacefully* be brought
> to a close, and every member of our great family . . . come to a treaty
> of amicable *peace with each other,* and all unite, eventually, in producing a
> *proportionate* share of what they consume.[42]

This writer opposes the regular government with its wars and its warlike
individualism and its ensuing "bondage of servitude." He calls instead
for a government of love and "the truths of equality." Living in the
crowded bosom of the "great family" of the neighborhood, the city, the
continent itself, the individual extracts liberty from a love rooted in an
equality of material resources, an idea common to the kinds of American
anticapitalism outlined by writers like Cornelius Blatchly, Langton Byl-
lesby, and Thomas Skidmore in the 1820s, and on through George Lippard and John Pickering in the 1840s.[43] The problem for elites was not
the masses' demagogic leader but a mass which led itself and, in addition, did so according to a belief in the "equality of the human race."
Worse, the existence of the working-class or immigrant neighborhood

implies that this kind of organic egalitarianism could spread throughout society. Mass neighborhoods that are neither anarchic nor despotic and in which residents can function imply that the redistribution of property might not destroy liberty and individuality. This in turn would suggest that democracy could grant some real sovereignty to unhierarchical group agency. In the streets, agency and identity are seen to survive their collectivization. The work of "reform" could then have been redefined as freeing up the masses rather than cracking down. Reform would have meant getting rid of the tyrannical local kingpins that respectable elites ambivalently used to maintain order. It would have meant replacing the Emersonian moral law with self-defined democracy.

3. Whitman's Homotopia: Loving the Masses

When Rufus Griswold singles out Walt Whitman with a special hatred, he is targeting the writer who most famously defined mass democracy as the expression of love circulating freely among independent men. Whitman ties democratic theory to the fluid social arrangements represented, in his view, by male friendship. Friendship does not transcend politics and justice but epitomizes their realization. Whitman renders male-male union and union with the masses interchangeable and codependent. "I say the mission of government, henceforth, in civilized lands, is not repression alone, and not authority alone, not even of law, nor by that favorite standard of the eminent writer, the rule of best men, the born heroes and captains of the race . . . but higher than the highest arbitrary rule, to train communities through all their grades, beginning with individuals and ending there again, to rule themselves."[44] Whitman defines democracy as community self-rule. He sees self-rule as involving the evasion of "heroes and captains," even when these are natural or "born." The relation of leader to citizen must not be based on that of father and child. But the lack of paternal, supervisory authority does not yield anarchy, as is so widely feared by Whitman's contemporaries. For a substitute bond exists, one that is equally adhesive and therefore as orderly as that between parent and child, but far less oppressive. This relation is likened to the egalitarian relation between brothers, but generalized to male society. "I confidently expect a time when there will be seen, running like a half-hid warp through all the myriad audible and visible worldly interests of America, threads of manly friendship, fond and loving, pure and sweet, strong and lifelong, carried to degrees hitherto unknown — not only giving tone to the individual character, and making it unprecedentedly emotional, muscular, heroic, and refined, but having the deepest relations to general politics. I say democracy infers such loving comradeship, as its most inevitable twin or counterpart, without which it will be incomplete, in vain, and incapable of perpetuating itself."[45] "Manly friendship," "fervid comradeship," "adhesive love" — for Whitman these masculine forces are mass democracy itself. Whitman's friendship avoids termination in monogamous privacy and opens out to the multitudes. Male comrades demonstrate a love that is public and look forward to a public that rests on general love.

Whitman's utopianism redefines the European male friendship tradition. His idea is not to establish a singular relation to the Other who, as Derrida argues, is then shown to correspond to "the law" as established by "a tribunal, a jury, some agency (instance) authorized to represent the Other legitimately, in the form of a moral, legal, or political community."[46] The Other (in Whitman's ideal) has no being independent of the living force of reciprocal adhesion, and hence its law consists of nothing more than the particular adhesion itself. For Whitman, the psychology of the crowd is the psychology of adhesion. Mass democracy can reject preestablished, unequal, or supervisory law once it has lived through the mutually created bonds and freedoms typified by friendly adhesion.

Whitman's conception resists the belief that interpersonal relations require the higher governance of preestablished and superior laws, whether these relations are conceived as economic, sexual, or political. For Whitman, friendship provides better governance because it creates equals. Private relations fulfill their political potential when they leave the family hearth and take to the streets, for, in the words of a later writer, "within the crowd there is equality. . . . All theories of equality ultimately derive their energy from the actual experience of equality familiar to anyone who has been part of a crowd."[47] Even in those passages where Whitman seems more auto- than homoerotic, he excites his readers' fear (or wish) that "masturbation is in the power of everybody;" and he envisions the "equalization of men which seriously eroded the traditional source of male identity."[48] The brothers' democracy contests the patrilineage and the family romance in favor of the ad hoc governance of the "adhesive" and "living generation."

Whitman's ideal is not unlike the mass democracy of the Paris Commune of 1871. Kristin Ross's description is illuminating: "Far more important than any of the measures or laws the Commune managed to pass was simply 'its own working existence': the expansive, thoroughly democratic nature of its social organization." As Marx put it, "The

Commune . . . was a revolution against the State itself . . . a resumption by the people for the people of its own social life."[49] The state becomes nothing more than personal ties and the everyday activities that arise from these; "politics becomes just another branch of social production."[50] This social production arises from a group life that replaces state structures and other hierarchical institutions, appearing as "the swarm," where individual and collective desire coexist: "the threat of the swarm and the threat of individual desire [to the bourgeois order] are the same threat."[51] Whitman anticipates the Commune's mass democracy and the more systematic Marxian anarchism of Mikhail Bakunin in understanding personal freedom only through mass freedom. Democratic life is a function of the "continued mutual dependence of individuals and the masses."[52]

"Democratic" subjectivity rests for Whitman on interdependence rather than private property. This is a significant break with post-Lockean liberalism. Powerful selfhood involves the elimination of the liberal distinction between private possession and public politics rather than its protective policing. In the third line of "Song of Myself," Whitman says, "For every atom belonging to me as good belongs to you"; this psychic socialism comes only two lines after the famous opening "I celebrate myself," and defines self-celebration as breaching self-possession. These lines express a theme that is everywhere in Whitman's writing.

This dependent, democratic, postpossessive individual should not be understood as submissive.[53] Whitman does not link intersubjectivity to servility, and does not insist on recovering autonomy in order to restore his virility. To take only one well-known example, the seduction sequence of stanza 29 of "Song of Myself" concludes in the next stanza in an erotic "reception" that lacks compensatory aggression.

> Blind loving wrestling touch, sheath'd hooded sharp-tooth'd touch!
> Did it make you ache so, leaving me?
>
> Parting track'd by arriving, perpetual payment of perpetual loan,
> Rich showering rain, and recompense richer afterward.
>
> Sprouts take and accumulate, stand by the curb prolific and vital,
> Landscapes projected masculine, full-sized and golden.

The sodomized narrator is not subordinated by the act, as he shows by experiencing enough equality with the penetrator to assume his vulnerability and ask about his mood. The rest of the stanza consists of images of reciprocity in nature, and furnishes scenes in which interconnection makes incoherent any inquiry into who dominates and who submits — does the rain control the seed, or the sprout lose by receiving the shower? My point is not to endorse Whitman's idealization here, or to deny the master/slave elements of any erotic attraction, but to note that he does not imagine his homoerotic bonds raising the problem of submission. On the contrary, he imagines that one can be penetrated and resist submission at the same time.

Further evidence that same-sex crowd subjectivity (or Whitman's "manly friendship") resists submission comes from a stranger quarter, that of the chronically panicked hygiene writer John Todd. In many ways Todd is Whitman's parodic opposite, endorsing repressed heterosexual union where Whitman evaded it, and defending the private, autonomous body where Whitman sought its violation. Whitman offends reformers, and Todd leads them.[54] Whitman is famous for his political homophilia and Todd for his fanatical defenses of controlled procreation. Whitman welcomes the streets and Todd denounces them. Whitman espouses a public libido which Todd bottles up in the single body. Whitman, for all his own abstraction and ephemeral spiritually, articulates numbers of bodies, while Todd describes crowds as an undifferentiated "tide." Todd really loses Whitman with his condemnation of masturbation on the grounds that it depletes the body's finite reserves of vital force. For him, "*all* sexual excitement was physically dangerous. Todd also feared that intercourse with women, like masturbation, robbed men of their physical powers."[55] He understood the "body as a system of energy or vigor, represented by a metaphor of liquidity," and the goal of moral control was to maintain the integrity of the private body's barriers.[56] Little could pose a greater threat to these bodily fluids than contact with the masses, or so we might infer from the fragility of Toddian man's little economy. And indeed Todd does claim that the young man must raise himself up against the influence of unattached women. In his book on the dangers of cities, he frets that "one impure look from a woman's eye . . . will do more towards . . . destroying the heart of a young man, than any amount of temptation from his own sex."[57]

But Todd resembles Whitman in seeing the young man's own sex as posing a more valuable temptation. In an instance when he does not stigmatize the crowd as female, Todd seeks its rupturing power. He eagerly pictures for his male reader the breaching of the closed equilibrium of vital energies by "the living mass around you, so alive, and so awake to every thing relating to this world — so eager for something new — so

FRIENDLY INEQUALITIES   109

delighted with any thing that can excite — so anxious to live in the swollen tide of human sympathies" (152). Contrary to expectation, the external tide does not "overcharg[e] the mind"[58] but fills it with life. Even as Todd consecrates his work to warning young men of the menace of urban "licentiousness," he represents another licentiousness which attracts him — an immersion in a "living mass" which (by default) remains masculine, and which offers the "sympathies" that dwell in its "swollen tide."

What does it mean that as odd a couple as Whitman and Todd wish to violate their "spermatic economies"? Todd's ordinary fear of crowds is a fear of conquest through a woman's erotic power; his momentary love of crowds derives from the male sympathy which causes no such fear. He senses in this crowd an absence of inequality that allows his normal defenses to relent. Todd manifests a fleeting, Whitmanesque delight in the masses and their "manly friendship" when they represent not subordination to the other but the absence of subordination in democratic sympathy.

I am not suggesting, in sum, that male friendship overcomes bondage in fact or that Whitman, much less Todd, outthink their misogynistic and authoritarian individualism.[59] The apparent equality of this friendship could be counterfeited and recuperated by market competition and male supremacy, and it is plain that fraternal associations were widely deployed in the service of bourgeois social policing.[60] Nonetheless, the power of this friendship tradition arose from its intersection with the existence and persistence of crowds. Antebellum homoerotic practices, vital and distinctive in themselves, are all but lost to history unless they provoked the forces of political order. Homoeroticism provoked not only by being "erotic" but by becoming egalitarian as well. The dangerously attractive eros was the eros of mass equality. Multiple relations, uncontrolled from above, cast the spell of illicit sexuality. Early crowd psychology and its deceptive "demagogue theory" serves as one of the branches of the science of sodomy. Though male same-sex desire was and is obviously different from mass democracy, and hounded for its own sake, this was a difference that the antebellum middle class often failed to register. Whether the result is sodomy or public equality, Sodom exists wherever the father is lost to view.

4. The Freudian Restoration, or, Heading for Jonestown

This link between "democratic" male bonds and male homosexuality (in later terms) continues to affect theories of democratic and of homosex-

ual relations. They converge in Freud's *Group Psychology,* where homosexuality becomes an essentialist personal identity in the same gesture
in which all true identity becomes personal — removed from the self-
dissolving promiscuity of the leveled group.

Freud's views have antecedents in the antebellum middle-class understanding of normative male intimacy. Friendship between two men was
not always regarded as a tie between equals. Bondage is the theme of a
reverie of Emerson's contemporary, Oliver Wendell Holmes.

> There is one very sad thing in old friendships, to every mind that is really
> moving onward. It is this: that one cannot help using his early friends as
> the seaman uses the log, to mark his progress. Every now and then we
> throw an old schoolmate over the stern with a string of thought tied to
> him, and look — I am afraid with a kind of luxurious and sanctimonious
> compassion — to see the rate at which the string reels off, while he lies
> there bobbing up and down, poor fellow! and we are dashing along with
> the white foam and bright sparkle at our brows — the ruffled bosom of
> prosperity and progress, with a sprig of diamonds stuck in it! But this is
> only the sentimental side of the matter; for grow we must, if we outgrow
> all that we love.[61]

Holmes's gladiatorial rapture celebrates the natural inequality that arises
from life's tests of personal ability. His jovial sadism relishes the fact that
the friend does not bob up and down to the rear because he has tried
and failed; he bobs there because Holmes has tied him up and tossed
him over the side. Holmes's half-facetious description of himself "dash-
ing along" over the "white foam" suggests a worried concealment of his
fear that precisely the opposite is happening — that, far from skimming
above the foam out of reach of the rejected loser, one is actually im-
mersed and adrift in a mob of losers resembling oneself. Like the ghostly
companions of Lippard's Sodom, Holmes's surpassed companion returns whenever Holmes looks behind. Bound and bobbing, the unwel-
come one offers Holmes the proof of his victory only at the price that
they remain attached.

Writers like Holmes can acknowledge their bonds only through displays of triumph. Freud clearly unites the ambiguously linked imperatives of maintaining inequality and controlling male homoeroticism.
His restoration of the father makes managing democracy much the same
as keeping men straight.

Group Psychology and the Analysis of the Ego (1921) takes up the conclusions of Gustave Le Bon's *Psychologie des foules* (1895).[62] Le Bon was,
among other things, a racist phrenologist and political reactionary who

had spent the decades following the collapse of the Paris Commune promoting regulatory sciences for the benefit of women and the "inferior" races. The professional tone of his book on crowds does not dissemble his preestablished equation between socialists, women, drunkards and members of assemblies, and tyrannical, insensible violence.[63] Nor is this an aspect of the work that Freud overlooks, for he accepts Le Bon's claim that to join a group means "a man descends several rungs in the ladder of civilization. . . . In a crowd, he is a barbarian — that is, a creature acting by instinct" (*Group Psychology*, 9, quoting *The Crowd*). Further, he agrees that "a group is extraordinarily credulous and open to influence, it has no critical faculty, . . . it thinks in images," and generally lives out unconscious drives. But the group is not only intolerantly, arbitrarily anarchic; it is simultaneously submissive. The crowd "wants to be ruled and oppressed and to fear its masters" (*Group Psychology*, 10–11).

Freud's *Group Psychology* sustains the crowd psychology that initially arose out of a proudly antidemocratic political agenda by tracing such politics to innate human psychology.[64] He verifies his theoretical moves by his concurrence with Le Bon's sociology. "Group spirit," Freud believes, is characterized by the demand that "every one must be the same and have the same. Social justice means that we deny ourselves many things so that others may have to do without them as well."[65] Collective governance, as a matter of empirical description, manifests a coercive equality. This equality is never, for Freud, characterized by mutual desire, agreement, or consent. It comes into existence through a homogenizing submission to the father-leader. There is always a substitute father. In the church, it is Christ, the loving big brother. "A democratic strain runs through the Church," Freud says, but only under a common lord. "Before Christ everyone is equal, and . . . everyone has an equal share in his love."[66] In a group, "all the members must be equal to one another, but they all want to be ruled by one person. Many equals, who can identify themselves with one another, and a single person superior to them all — that is the situation that we find realized in groups which are capable of subsisting."[67]

Freud's rejection of socialist or democratic claims is total. Collective structures (and not simply street mobs) may be marked by equality, but precisely to the extent that they are egalitarian, they will be distinguished by submission to a father substitute. The transistorization of nineteenth-century group circuitry only allowed libido switching to make a father out of anybody. Hence during the United States war with

Iraq, even a jittery mannequin like George Bush could play Dwight Ei-
senhower. The beauty of such a democracy is that it makes democracy
entirely compatible with hierarchical patriarchy. The subordination of
and traffic in women is one major ingredient in democratic patriarchy
but not the only one; not only must the brothers rule women, but the
fathers must rule the sons.

Freud's group psychology explains Le Bon's empirical descriptions
by tracing all peaceable public associations to one kind of identification with a substitute father. His summary is uncompromising. "The
uncanny and coercive characteristics of group formations, which are
shown in the phenomena of suggestion that accompany them, may
therefore with justice be traced back to the fact of their origin from the
primal horde. The leader of the group is still the dreaded primal father;
the group still wishes to be governed by unrestricted force; it has an
extreme passion for authority; in Le Bon's phrase, it has a thirst for
obedience. The primal father is the group ideal, which governs the ego
in the place of the ego ideal."[68] Freud brings demagogue theory to its
final frontier.

But how does he produce the inevitable yet flexible rule of the father
substitute? The entire weight of his argument turns on a transubstantia-
tion between two now familiar elements. He must show that multiple,
reciprocal connections between relative equals in all stable cases manifest submission to a single leader. Brotherly love must be a mask for all
the brothers' true objects of desire, the father superior. Desire among
male equals must really be a triangulated version of an Emersonian subjection to the great man.

Freud's conclusion here is placed in particular jeopardy by his countervailing knowledge that most male groups are neither straight nor
submissive. At times putting himself in agreement with writers like
Whitman, Freud argues that groups are built of love, a love which, as
he teaches better than anyone, flows in every direction. The group individual submits to the leader who has become his [sic] "ego-ideal," but
he also has powerful emotional ties with group members on his own
level. Through love, "intolerance" for strangers "vanishes, temporarily
or permanently, within the group." Love runs things and "alone acts as
the civilizing factor in the sense that it brings a change from egoism to
altruism." The libido attaches itself to "the people who have a share in
[the] process" of the "satisfaction of the great vital needs."[69] In these
admissions, Freud briefly echoes Marxian wishes in envisioning the removal of paternal tyranny and the replacement of competitive struggle
with variable libidinal attachment.

These collective attachments, for Freud, are homosexual. Though Freud does not describe this male love as sexual,[70] the male member of a group finds his homosexual and heterosexual attachments to be compatible. To use current terms, Freud's assertion that (male) group love is homosocial rather than homosexual obscures his knowledge of this distinction's fragility. Group ties in fact consist of a fraternal adhesion in which eroticism continually lurks. (Were homosexual desire missing or suppressed, homophobia would lose its charge.)

Freud uses male homoeroticism to bear out Le Bon's paradoxical claim that group ties make men into sheep while posing a revolutionary threat to order. For Freud, the ties between members of a group can overwhelm the tie between members and leader, causing the leader to be overthrown. "It may perhaps also be assumed," says a footnote, "that the sons, when they were driven out and separated from their father, advanced from identification with one another to homosexual object-love, and in this way won freedom to kill the father."[71] In the chapter in which Freud insists that even in modern groups a version of the primal father forces the sons "into group psychology," he is admitting the presence of the opposite event: the sons may feel identification with each other, an identification based on the common father ideal, an identification that coexists with mutual desire. At times, the sons reject the bond to the father in favor of bonds with each other. Homosexual desire enforces an egalitarian love that evades the tyrant. Freud imposes no time frame, so this process could look more like cooperation that revolution. These fraternal bonds — sexualized and desexualized — cannot in Freud's own account assure any more than they disrupt these father-son, top-bottom links.

This is one of those moments in Freud's writings in which a hugely unsettling vicissitude or reversal is avowed only to be conducted to a single outcome. He finally insists on the submissive, authoritarian pseudo equality of father-leader group psychology, one which oedipalizes society such that any destruction of one father produces the restoration of another. "The king is dead" always means "long live the king." And yet he cannot deny, and conceptually requires, the homoerotic reciprocity through which, in the time of revolt, the brothers rule themselves. This male group gives the father much libidinal competition. In a different way, women also divert investments from the leader. Individuals experiencing various forms of gendered desire show such powerful longings for group life that narcissism could be said to seek its own qualification. In short, Freud's work encompasses wanting to be loved by the father *and* "wanting to be fucked by the socius."[72] His text repeatedly confesses the possibility of antihierarchical movements that he officially subordinates to the father's eternal return. So to ask the question again, now in light of the conflict within Freud's own text, how does Freud restore the paternal order and its unchanging horde?

First, he declares group adhesion to be based on common features, and then he argues that these common features belong to the leader. Were this not the case, the common qualities that comprise the network of bonds might be properties the members of the group hold in common between themselves, properties like a contractual agreement, a temporarily overlapping goal, a shared activity, an accidental proximity, or a mutual desire.[73] Overcoming the dispersal of relations, Freud fuses these two distinct claims into one. In chapter 7, "Identification," he says that "the mutual tie between members of a group is in the nature of an identification . . . based upon an important emotional common quality; and we may suspect that this common quality lies in the nature of the tie with the leader."[74] By the end of the following chapter, "Being in Love and Hypnosis," the independence of the two claims has disappeared: "*A Primary group of this kind is a number of individuals who have put one and the same object in the place of their ego ideal and have consequently identified themselves with one another in their ego.*"[75] The group not only rests on common qualities, but these necessarily inhabit the ego ideal rather than the ego, and this ideal is entirely split off from the ego and superior to it. From mutual love to hypnotized bondage: as in all of his social writings, Freud manages to insist that the ego as formed in the family romance remains in the same condition in the group at the same time as he asserts the group's massive impact on that ego. And to maintain the dubious sovereignty of the ego ideal, Freud introduces homosexual identity.[76]

Freud has already defined the group as bound by "desexualized, sublimated homosexual love," but he now attributes a specific nature to active homosexuality.

A young man has been unusually long and intensely fixated upon his mother in the sense of the Oedipus complex. But at last, after the end of puberty, the time comes for exchanging his mother for some other sexual object. Things take a sudden turn: the young man does not abandon his mother, but identifies himself with her; he transforms himself into her, and now looks about for objects which can replace his ego for him, and on which he can bestow such love and care as he has experienced from his mother. . . . A striking thing about this identification is its ample scale; it remoulds the ego in one of its important features — in its sexual character — upon the model of what has hitherto been the object. In this process the object itself is renounced. . . . Identification with an object that is re-nounced or lost [that is, the mother], as a substitute for that object — introjection of it into the ego — is indeed no longer a novelty with us.[77]

The dissolution of the Oedipus complex normally produces a boy's am-bivalent identification with his father and an "affectionate" object-relation to his mother.[78] The "sudden turn" in this case means that the boy identifies himself with his mother instead of with his father. In the heterosexual instance, the identification with the father remains ambiva-lent, and the ego retains some independence from its own identification with the superior figure.[79] This ambiguous — and potentially egalitar-ian — homosociality characterizes the heterosexual, but not the homo-sexual. The latter's identification goes beyond the stage in which his ego remains distinct from the object, the mother with whom he identifies: "he transforms himself into her"; this identification "remoulds the ego . . . in its sexual character . . . upon the model of what has hitherto been the object."[80] The incipiently homosexual ego is effaced and remolded. It is no longer an ego capable of an autonomous, self-determined, or equal relation to the ideal object. The homosexual is the boy who has become his mother, sometimes to happier effects than those so deli-cately staged in Hitchcock's *Psycho*. He does not seek to possess objects that his remolded ego might desire but instead he "now looks about for objects which can replace his ego for him." One compromise reading of this moment suggests Freud's meaning to be that "the child . . . now identifies with his mother and selects future love objects who resemble himself,"[81] but this implies that Freud means that the intact ego is now homosexual because it desires a genital mirror of itself when in fact Freud states not that the ongoing ego desires such objects but that such objects are desired because they replace the ego. The homosexual ego is first and foremost not that which renounces its heterosexual, maternal object but the ego which, through its changed object, renounces itself.[82]

I'd like to emphasize three outcomes of all of this. First, Freud de-scribes the homosexual here not as a particular genital orientation but as a constitutive inequality between the ego and authority. This ego nec-essarily takes a submissive attitude toward the superego; it cannot, in other words, bring the ego ideal under the provisional sway of its own ego or model its law on impulses emanating from itself rather than from a superior. In contrast, the "normal" heterosexual ego — freed from the homoerotic energy of a group — will not only feel submissive tenderness toward the father but also a hostile wish to replace him.[83] The homosexual submits to the ego ideal and seeks to replace his ego altogether; the heterosexual can submit and/or rebel, feeling the "devouring affection" of straight sons and revolutionaries. Freud invokes a distinctively "homosexual" identity to eliminate the group ego's ambivalence about the leader, elevate this ego ideal beyond the reach of the ego, and render this ego a docile subject. Democracy in *Group Psychology,* to the extent that it is homosexual, is bondage to the substitute father. To melodramatize in the double usage of Lippard and Griswold, democracy, psychically, is the gathering of sodomites in the new Sodom, all calling for their own punishment.

Second, only "male homosexuality" allows Freud to generalize this submission to all social formations. Were the ego's submission a function of melancholia, hypnosis, or being in love (Freud's other models of the ego's subjection), it would be limited to temporary and/or specialized groups. Once he has defined male homosexuality as the condition of obedience to a superior ideal, Freud can fix his claim that the (always homoerotic) group's ubiquitous feature is "the tie with the leader" *rather than* with one's counterpart. He can exclude the possibility that individuals experience group life through submission and resistance to the leader and desire for one another such that each member is not blindly obedient to the chief but actively negotiating his relation to the variable and multiple chiefs that they all are to each other. He can exclude the possibility that group psychology contradicts rather than conforms to the subjugations of the family romance. He can exclude the examination of the historical variability of groups, and ignore the part played in their failed freedoms by the imposed demand — internalized or not — to follow your leader.

In Freud, the sublimation of male homosexuality and the regulation of collective life become the same thing. The leader, in all his kindly and dispersed authoritarianism, maintains collective order by sublimating same-sex male desire. Any democratic group life not controlled by redirecting homoeroticism toward the father he assumes will produce anarchy and destroy identity. Though it would be wrong to claim that love between men is inherently political or radical, Freud indicates that the science of psychoanalysis thinks as though it were. Emerson had demonized groups but preserved male intimacy, since joint and equal sovereignty was adequately blocked by the lordship and bondage of all true friendship. Freud, writing in an age in which private friendship could no longer be imagined to control politics, links good government to intimacy's desexualization. Freud's fusion of social peace with the control of male homoeroticism suggests the nature of the archaic threat which this homoeroticism poses: he says, to repeat, that ungoverned men "advanced from identification with one another to homosexual object-love, and in this way won freedom to kill the father."[84] Through his invocation of the homosexual ego (as melancholic), Freud transforms identification from a mechanism of diluting the bond with the cruel and superior ego ideal to the mechanism through which the ego ideal achieves its mastery. In a democracy, all real rulers first rule the homosexual within, who loves this rule.

5. Crowd Psychology and Submissive Friendship

Writing before the Civil War, Emerson could not invoke homosexual identity to regulate the contagion of public friendship. He regulates friendship by distinguishing between its private and public forms. What kind of relations does Emerson imagine between men in the private sphere? These would determine the kind of polity he imagines could be constructed by individuals, of materials they can control. If society at large is burdened with convention and the weight of material interest, the "little society," as Tocqueville called it, could furnish the ideal relations according to which larger society might eventually be reformed.

Once again, Emerson's notion that individuality entails dependence is not in doubt. This is the close of the chapter "Discipline."

> We are associated in adolescent and adult life with some friends, who, like skies and waters, are coextensive with our idea; who, answering each to a certain affection of the soul, satisfy our desire on that side; whom we lack power to put at such focal distance from us, that we can mend or even analyze them. We cannot choose but love them. When much intercourse with a friend has supplied us with a standard of excellence, and has increased our respect for the resources of God who thus sends a real person to outgo our ideal; when he has, moreover, become an object of thought, and, whilst his character retains all its unconscious effect, is converted in the mind into solid and sweet wisdom, — it is a sign to us that his office is closing, and he is commonly withdrawn from our sight in a short time.[85]

At first glance it seems that Emerson's friend, like Holmes's, is there to be exploited. All along he had provided not love but a principle of competition, a "standard of excellence." He is there to be used, and is converted into an "object of thought" as water is turned into power by a mill wheel. Friendship is instrumental, and the loser is vanquished after his principle has been extracted and abstracted into something "solid and sweet," a kind of money.

But Emerson does not triumph over his friend and achieve a desired solitude. He incorporates the friend instead of defeating him. He invokes the link between friendship and "waters" that he so often uses to spiritualize libidinal energy. The friend is "coextensive" with one's own idea, but this relation does not endow one with power but with its absence. Even after the friend disappears, he is remembered as an imposing force: "we lack power to put [them] at such focal distance from us, that we can mend or even analyze them. We cannot choose but love them." The loser retains a power of compulsion over the victor; the former is only withdrawn from our sight; "his character retains all its unconscious effect." Emerson's own rivalrous triumph incorporates the memory of his old desire to submit to the one who could compel his love. [86]

Evidence on this question is abundant. I've already cited Emerson's "eye-fascination" with Martin Gay; more canonical moments confirm his pleasure in overcoming autonomy. His more famous case of eye-fascination occurs in the early essay *Nature,* where he describes one moment of rapture as his having become a "transparent eye-ball; I am nothing; I see all; the currents of the Universal Being circulate through me." [87] In putting his feeling this way, Emerson parallels the language of Todd's remarks on onanism in *The Student's Manual,* published the year before *Nature,* in which Todd notes that the "mind must be continually filled up with new streams of knowledge" through the act of reading, which of course involves making the eyes transparent and thus open to the book's influence. [88] Emerson's sense of consummation derives from feeling permeated by alien fluids, being possessed by an invisible other which approaches him while remaining unseen. He actively desires an identity that derives from the violation of personal boundaries rather than from their maintenance. Though his official policy has been read to say, in sum, "I want to be alone," his moments of rapture usually derive from intimacy with a power that is ambiguously himself and not himself (recalling the way the word "onanism" linked masturbation and sodomy) and which entirely overpowers him.

Emerson's (liberal) views require masculine forms of receptivity and cooperation that, in the work of Todd, Holmes, and other instances of masculinity, were seen as moments of self-doubting failure. Friendship enables a receptivity that Emerson thinks can achieve the intimacy missing from public relationships. But something else begins to happen here. Emerson's genuine intimacy is sometimes expressed as a force that brings the couple back to the economy of the world. The gift, to recall a previous example, offers the model of reciprocal exchange within the friendly couple. "When the waters are at level, then my goods pass to him, and his to me."[89] The fluid mixing of the level waters sends them rushing over the barriers that separate man from man, but in so doing they also threaten the barrier between the couple and society.

As I noted earlier, Emerson distinguishes the male couple from "society." The latter offers a conformity and constraint which the couple surpasses. But Emerson also flirts with transgressing the boundary between the couple and the crowd so insistently enforced by authors like Lippard, Holmes, and most male hygienists. While Emerson repudiates the "calamity of the masses," he is ambivalently attracted to "associations," where these offer an ordered extension of friendship structures to groups without the anarchic dissolutions of identity he associates with mobs or with unselected society. "What is so pleasant as these jets of affection which make a young world for me again? What so delicious as a just and firm encounter of two, in a thought, in a feeling? . . . The moment we indulge our affections, the earth is metamorphosed; there is no winter, and no night; all tragedies, all ennuis, vanish, — all duties even; nothing fills the proceeding eternity but the forms all radiant of beloved persons."[90] These passionate delights lead away from "two" to larger assemblies, with the proviso that they be assemblies of the "beloved." The association need not be local or face-to-face; it can be defined through an abstract identification as long as this is based on love.

> Men have yet to learn the depth & beauty of the doctrine of Trust. O believe as thou livest that every sound that is spoken over the round world which thou oughtest to hear, will vibrate on thine ear. . . . Every friend whom not thy fantastic Will but the great & tender Heart in thee craveth, shall lock thee in his embrace; and this, because the heart in thee is the Heart of all, not a valve, not a wall, not an intersection is there any where in nature, — but one blood rolls uninterruptedly an endless circulation through all men, as the water of the globe·is all one sea, and truly seen its tide is one.[91]

Liberation means being locked in an embrace, where one is united with all the other lovers.

Emerson regards intimate fraternity to be materially transformative. "The earth is metamorphosed" by friendship, he believes. Through friendship "we weave social threads of our own, a new web of relations; and, as many thoughts in succession substantiate themselves, we shall by and by stand in a new world of our own creation, and no longer strangers and pilgrims in a traditionary globe."[92] Friendship, in this picture, is the site of democratic self-governance. Old relations are cast aside and new are made and remade by each generation and community as circumstances and desires demand. Individual transformation cannot be separated from the fate of the whole. "The individual, to possess himself, must sometimes return from his own labor to embrace all the other laborers."[93] "When we are finished men, we shall grasp heroic hands in heroic hands."

Emerson is so insistent on the web of love that links the brethren that at times he writes as though the only makers of the world are the democratic masses.

> But *great men:* — the word is injurious. Is there caste? is there fate? . . . It is a reply to these suggestions, to say, society is a Pestalozzian school: all are teachers and pupils in turn. We are equally served by receiving and by imparting. . . . As to what we call the masses, and common men; — there are no common men. All men are at last of a size; and true art is only possible, on the conviction that every talent has its apotheosis somewhere . . . heaven reserves an equal scope for every creature. Each is uneasy until he has produced his private ray unto the concave sphere, and beheld his talent also in its last nobility and exaltation. . . . One gracious fact emerges from these studies, — that there is true ascension in our love. . . . The genius of humanity is the real subject whose biography is written in our annals.[94]

The genius of humanity is the masses, masses made of men who are equal and who, most important, remain individuated without asserting superiority. Emerson's utopian thought conceives a state in which Holmes's competitive individualism vanishes without damage to the ego and shows individualism to have been a symptom of a traumatic bondage from which we might escape. Collective labor, when liberated from domination, will be revealed to be the only genuine source of history. Contra D. H. Lawrence, Emerson does not say, "henceforth, be masterless." He says, with a different emphasis, "there is no master." The idea is to reorganize society without antagonism or deference to the paternal function.

Emerson acknowledges that, in his own time, ideals of collective labor have become embodied in the communities or utopian associations. In contrast to the assumptions of our own anticommunist epoch, which sees in communists a desire for dictatorial control, Emerson saw in "beneficent socialism" a "wish for greater freedom than the manners and opinions of society permitted."[95] The communities are like joint-stock companies with the crucial difference that they express not only the desire for economies of scale but for mutual affection. The associations "were founded in love, and in labor. They proposed, as you know, that all men should take a part in the manual toil, and proposed to amend the condition of men, by substituting harmonious for hostile industry."[96] The "Communities aimed at a higher success in securing to all their members an equal and thorough education." Equality marks the communist difference, and Emerson feels compelled to give qualified approval: "It was a noble thought of Fourier, which gives a favorable idea of his system, to distinguish in his Phalanx a class as the Sacred Band, by whom whatever duties were disagreeable, and likely to be omitted, were to be assumed."[97] The communities establish individual freedom through equality and dispute the reality of any freedom without it. They see democratic freedom not in personal privacy but in the collectively self-determined creation of a commune that can replace the state.

Emerson, then, ties individual freedom to a man living through "his friendship, in his natural and momentary associations."[98] In saying this, I am not simply inverting the usual reading of Emerson's faith in individuality to claim that he favors associations to solitude; my point is that, having conceived of individuality as actualized only in male friendship, he likes to imagine an association based on some conglomeration of friendship. For such an association, his hostility to the masses is suspended. Where democracy is really like male friendship, it is not only bearable but necessary to the existence of free subjectivity. In straight and ambiguously homoerotic association, carefully built on male couples, individuality and democracy are found in delicate harmony.

6. Equality as Perversion

Why, then, does an Emerson who craves association not endorse the associations? He famously rejected George Ripley's invitation to join communal life at Brook Farm in 1840, saying that he could not expect "your community" to effect "my emancipation" more successfully than he could do himself.[99] On this basis, critics have erected a misleading (Cold War) contrast between individualism and socialism. If Emerson rejected utopian socialist communities then it must be in favor (and because) of his veneration of "individuality," a "belief in the absolute integrity, spiritual primacy, and inviolable sanctity of the self."[100] After

Emerson's refusal to join Ripley and Brook Farm, Perry Miller claims, "there were two opposing poles in Transcendentalism — the associationists and the Emersonian individualists."[101] And Emerson certainly makes statements that suggest individual autonomy is his primal instinct in rejecting communism. "The union is only perfect, when all the uniters are isolated."[102] On the basis of this citation and others, Sacvan Bercovitch has also argued that Emerson rejected socialism when he discovered "that he 'could not reconcile the socialist principle with [his] own doctrine of the individual.'"[103] A preoccupation with individuality blocked further experiment: Emerson's "own most daring venture in 'communatism' was to invite the servants to dinner one day in 1841 (an invitation which, once declined, was not renewed)."[104]

Emerson was not a socialist, but given his love of affectionate association, the reason does not lie in his "doctrine of the individual." If I am right in arguing that his doctrine of the individual was for him a doctrine of the self's inseparability from "manly bonds," socialism in itself would not threaten his individuality. Emerson's wish was not to be identified with one of Miller's poles of transcendentalism, but to be an associationist and an individualist at the same time. This is how he was read by Emma Goldman, as I noted in chapter 1, for whom the Emersonian individualist and the socialized anarchist come together. Given the doctrines of mutual bonds that make Goldman's reading plausible, the more common contrary claim — Emerson was not a socialist because he was an individualist — is inaccurate. But why, then, wasn't he an individualist or libertarian socialist, the genuine anarchist at which he sometimes played? What was it about the socialist associations of the 1840s, besides their collective relations (which Emerson often sought), that did threaten Emerson's sense of the self?

A clue lies in a passage in which Emerson tried to explain why reformers should not have put so much faith in "Association." "[Community] concert is neither better nor worse, neither more nor less potent than individual force. . . . What is the use of the concert of the false and the disunited? There can be no concert in two, where there is no concert in one. When the individual is not *individual,* but is dual; when his thoughts look one way, and his actions another; when his faith is traversed by his habits; when his will, enlightened by reason, is warped by his sense; when with one hand he rows, and with the other backs water, what concert can be?"[105] Without favoring the individual over the group, the individual prevails anyway. Emerson does not argue that concert suffocates individual initiative, nor does he express some other concern for "actual individualism."[106] Groups fail when they themselves cannot act like or as individuals. Emerson rejects association here not because it has too much unity to allow for the freedom of the individual, but because it has too little unity to act as though it were an individual.

The passage in fact rapidly becomes a critique of a certain kind of individuality rather than a critique of association. Emerson slams the self-divided individual and not the individual of the masses. The real problem here is the effect on the self of too little group government rather than too much.

What is the effect of too little government? It allows the individual self to fall into this state of self-division, to become "dual" rather than "individual." The problem with association appears not when it forces a monolithic identity on a complex and unique character, but when it fails to do this. Association betrays the self by providing a context in which it "with one hand . . . rows, [while] the other backs water." The crisis of "concert" and association comes down not to excessive regimentation or collective anarchy but to inward division.

A further question arises at this point, however: why in the world would Emerson blame association for self-division? The latter would seem more likely to occur in solitude, when external government provides no compulsion to choose. But Emerson does blame association, and the reason is that the self-divided individual is one pulled in different directions equally. The association threatens the self with self-division by not deciding on behalf of the self between different relations, by not establishing a hierarchy in which priority and primacy are manifest. Association divides the self precisely by providing the self with equal relations. Suspended in relations with others of equal strength, one could still choose between them, but this choice would have to be one's own. When the self is free to choose between equal ties, the result is self-division. A crisis of identity arises from too much power of self-help acting with too little hierarchy.

Emerson rejects association, then, not because of its anti-individualism (as he knew well, most communitarians were determined individualists) but because of its egalitarianism. Egalitarianism obliges the individual to choose without the guidance of unequal forces. The danger of association lies in its equality of relations rather than in relations themselves. This said, we have an easier time understanding the paradoxical individuality which desires individuality and association at the same time ("the union is only perfect, when all the uniters are isolated"). The contrary desires coexist on different planes. The Emersonian individual wants isolation from his equals, those who share membership in a community or institutional body. But this individual wants union with those who are above him, associated with Spirit, guidance, mastery, or force of some kind. The brother Emerson seeks is a big brother, he who can be imagined as a father. Far from replacing mass psychology with individuality, Emerson defines individuality as a function of stratified mass psychology. Individuality means not reciprocity with but submission to the other.[107]

This reading is borne out by abrupt shifts of theme in both of the 1844 essays on associations. In "The Young American," Emerson writes,

> This is the value of the Communities; not what they have done, but the revolution which they indicate as on the way. Yes, Government must educate the poor man. Look across the country from any hill-side around us, and the landscape seems to crave Government. The actual differences of men must be acknowledged, and met with love and wisdom. These rising grounds which command the champaign below, seem to ask for lords, true lords, *land*-lords, who understand the land and its uses, and the applicabilities of men, and whose government would be what it should, namely, mediation between want and supply. (224)

The revolution turns out to be the restoration of government. Government will respect individual differences by providing "lords, true lords." The lords return to run the government with "native skill"; these "natural workmen" are a sign that an increasingly contemptible "official government" will be met by "the increasing disposition of private adventurers to assume its fallen functions" (225). These "private adventurers" come not to bond as equals but to rule, and their office sign should say, "Mr. Johnson, *Working king*."

> We must have kings, and we must have nobles. Nature provides such in every society, — only let us have the real instead of the titular. Let us have our leading and our inspiration from the best. In every society some men are born to rule, and some to advise. Let the powers be well directed, directed by love, and they would everywhere be greeted with joy and honor. The chief is the chief all the world over . . . his duty and stint [are] to keep himself pure and purifying, the leaven of his nation. . . . Who should lead the leaders, but the Young American? (225–26)

Emerson is not simply saying that the "noble" is more in contact with the "private mind" and its "access to the totality of goodness and truth." He is saying that the noble is born to rule. This righteous lordship will be met with deference and submission from the masses. "New England

Reformers" transits more gradually, but leads to the same place. A man's "right relations with his mates," his "magnanimity," appears "in the preference . . . which each man gives to the society of superiors over that of his equals" (603). This repudiation of equality is highly functional, leading as it does to the "open channel to the highest life" that is "the first and last reality," the "Law alive and beautiful, which works over our heads and under our feet," and remains forever out of reach (607).[108]

A further feature of the above passage is crucial here: the young king's rule does not repudiate loving bonds but works through them. I noted in chapter 1 that Emerson's essay "Friendship" defines keeping one's "manly counterpart" as being overwhelmed and compelled to worship; he both desires the comrade and defines him as his superior. Emerson believes that this model of friendship is compatible with the democratic sharing of power. "It costs nothing to a commander to command: & every body, the most powerful, finds himself sometime also in the hands of his commander, it may be a woman, or a child, or a favorite, but usually it is another man organically so related to yo[u], that he easily impresses & leads your will, neutralizes your superiorities; . . . But this locally stronger man has his dragon also, who flies at his throat, & so gives the first his revenges. Thus every one has his master, & no one is stronger than all the others."[109] Men are born to be mastered, but each master has a master of his own. The effect is supposed to be a final cancellation and even equalization in which no one is stronger than anyone else. This eventual equality does not, however, contain lordship and bondage but is constituted by it. And this equality depends on an intimate similitude, a one-to-one correspondence, that reproduces the suppression of mutual desire in favor of paternal identification.

Emerson holds two distinct but interconnected views on male relations. Same-sex intimacy is "delicious" as long as it is "a just and firm encounter of two" rather than with a mob. But this male couple is most divine when it means relations between unequals, with pleasure rooted on subordination's side. Emerson ostensibly rejects the mind of the masses because those who are free in solitude become slaves in crowds. And yet he cherishes private friendship for its rewarding subjections. Group life harms Emerson's individual because it offers too much equality rather than too little freedom. The demand for submission some attribute to the association actually arises from this individual, unable, given its private life, to decide for itself among varying affinities.

7. Queerness and Homophilia

I have been expanding on how patriarchy arises not from male alliances in themselves but from Freudian and Emersonian democracy's management of them. Several conclusions follow from the parallels among anti-democratic crowd theory, Freud's deployment of homosexual identity, and Emerson's submissive, quasi-erotic friendships.

Emerson's corporatism leads away from earnest oedipality, but the result is not as democratic as it might potentially have been. One cannot separate Emerson's desire for democratic mixing from his desire to submit to the other. The moments which imagine the abandonment of independence in order to make, through mingling, "a new world of our own creation," are often the same moments in which he receives the new world from an unseen place. One-on-one relations offer a location for this fusion of reciprocity and submission. When Freud defines male homosexuality as this kind of submission, it becomes clear that, in their common tradition, homosexuality and democratic sovereignty are eclipsed by the same sexual politics. In Emerson's liberal imagination, this blocking structure is not heterosexual homophobia or possessive individualism, but a warmly homoerotic communitarianism, a heterosexual male bonding which displaces homoeroticism into hierarchical bonds.

Taken together, Freud's and Emerson's work suggests that male homosexuality is later blamed for a subservience which in fact defines male and democratic heterosexuality. Modern male homosexuality seems perverse in part through historical association with a "feminine attitude" or submissiveness that is actually the key to being straight. Liberal democracy builds on a submissiveness that is at once central to the identity of the normative male citizen and attributed to an egalitarian (Emerson) and homosexual (Freud) democracy.

Present-day discussions of patriarchal authority often build the assumptions of Emerson and Freud into their own adversarial analyses, and produce analytical handicaps. For example, Heidi Hartmann offers a general explanation for women's subordination when she defines patriarchy as "relations between men, which have a material base, and which, though hierarchical, establish or create interdependence and solidarity among men that enable them to dominate women."[110] What are the destructive elements in this male homosociality? As Eve Kosofsky Sedgwick asks, "What are the operations necessary to deploy male-male desire as the glue rather than as the solvent of a hierarchical male disciplinary order?"[111] Hartmann's formulation brackets hierarchy and declares the problem to be male solidarity itself. In saying this she sustains the outcome of Le Bon's and Freud's group psychology, which blames the effects of domination on the existence of the group. Here I do not mean that "men are victims, too," but hope to have suggested that the victimization of women and others should not be directly attributed to male attempts at collective relations. For sidestepping inequality's constitutive role encourages analysts to blame male bonding for the deeds of male competition. It slows development of alternatives to male rivalry where these depend on developing rather than dismissing (far more complex forms of) male solidarity. Critiques of patriarchy need to supplement their understanding of inequality between women and men, gay and straight, with better reckonings of the crucial role of inequality between apparently straight men.

The maintenance of inequality between men, I've argued, has required stigmatizing male homoeroticism as a tacit threat to hierarchy. Hetero-dominant patriarchy further depends on encouraging men to identify with and desire their marvelous superiors. These two pillars of patriarchy are related but should not be confused. Legitimizing gay male sexuality means making straight and gay men equals, but this does not in itself introduce equality into either straight or gay sexuality. My own wish for *queer* sexuality is that it will increasingly denote the place where men eroticize equality — where they feel the pleasure of not controlling other people. This would mean continuing to pressure homoeroticism beyond being constructed as egalitarian by straight rulers to actually enacting this equality within erotic life itself.

Of course "equality" seems utopian and even dismal in the realm of sexuality, where lack, yearning, overestimation, and subjugation play such constitutive and pleasurable roles; where the deployment of performance, fictionality, and difference seems so much closer to really making and unmaking power; and where queerness appears poised to wrest recognition from the straight mind that, without the rule of suffocating straightness, sexuality would free itself through "so many relaxed *signifiers* stiffening in no hierarchy but the continually flexible one instituted by desire."[112] I've been suggesting that such flexibility, controlled by democratic male sexuality, has its painful limits. I've argued that the limits appear as an affectionate subordination that has been hard to contest. The alternative to flexible subordination is not a vanilla equalization — quite the opposite — but the erosion of the eminence of the beloved. The means are many: parody, mixed signals, pushy spectacle, proliferated signifying, gender-fucking, fanatical queerness, politics in all the wrong places. But these will be incomplete unless they intersect with those psychic possibilities figured through the equality of democratic crowds.[113] The issue, therefore, though it alters much current attention to queer identity, is not only one of the gender of the object but of its status, not only of the sexuality of the heart you break but of its power. Flexibility without equality will not stay queer for long.

As for straight men, they live within the constitutive imperative of anxiously hierarchical, democratic heterosexuality: love no one as you love the master. I never get over my amazement at our national fatalism about the political stratifications that are sustained through a male sexuality utterly baffled by the ties between its desires and its competitions. Conditioned to a supporting humiliation from a cruel leader, a leader mimed by the unending train of nearly any willful boy or man in visible possession of empowering affinities, a nongay yet homophilic male may inaccurately associate the eroticization of his gay alliances with subjection to yet one more authority. The inhibiting fear, I would say, comes less from the stigma of his gay desire in itself—the desire within his conscious gay identification—than from the subjection he expects all male intimacy to make him suffer. The fear comes less from the uncertain presence and incipient shame of homoerotic desire than from the unwanted inferiority anticipated by this neither gay nor straight subject as the result of his experiences with the democratic regulation of same-sex contact. Given an apparent choice between one inferiority and another, this subject will choose that inferiority which offers protection—the consoling love for the dominant man. And it is this love for the leader that constitutes his straightness.[114] The straight homophiliac, always bled by this mistaken, this military love, will be able to confront homophobia only by confronting his need for inequality. And of this need, Emerson remains a masterful symptom.

CHAPTER

FIVE

Loving Bondage
The Authority of Domestic Remoteness

1. The Antebellum Family: Feminized or Liberalized?

In the previous chapter, a liberal kind of top-down authority appeared in the form of "egalophobia" between intimate, loving men. Emerson established a three-part position I've outlined before. He insists on individual freedom and greatness but defines these entirely in terms of interpersonal ties. But finally, this rich and libidinous self-reliance depends on the individual's inferiority and helplessness. For Emerson's genuinely liberal instincts, inequality was a blessing, and a democratic one at that. The pleasures of inequality underlay Emerson's democracy of male friendship, but it was the family and heterosexual love that translated submission into the corporate alternative to democracy.

Recent commentary on antebellum domestic and gender relations has taken a dim view of transcendentalist aspirations. While chronicling the radical social ambitions of the communitarian experimenters of the 1840s, commentators like Anne C. Rose emphasize the disappointingly conventional restrictions they placed on their women participants.[1] The causes of this disappointment seem to lie near at hand: the transcendentalists brought normative middle-class gender roles to their understanding of social and personal change; their critique of capitalist or at least of acquisitive, materialist society did not include a critique of patriarchy; they saw the new order in terms mostly of the nuclear family; even when they accepted such claims as Fourier's that postauthoritarian society depended on "freeing women's affections by the destruction of the fam-

An earlier version of this chapter was published as "Loving Bondage: Emerson's Ideal Relationships," *ATQ: Nineteenth-Century American Literature and Culture* 7, no. 3 (September 1991). Reprinted by permission of the University of Rhode Island.

ily,"[2] they were hemmed in by the notions and habits of male dominance. Hence even the increasingly woman-centered family of the time is now generally seen as furnishing "disciplinary intimacy" and "sweet control."[3] Antebellum men as well as women may have entered marriage because they wanted "to find intense, and reassuring, family sentiment," and the family may well have increasingly offered men paternal affection rather than patriarchal dominance, but the family can now be seen to have served men as a setting of uncontested preeminence: "Faced with a workplace that made men wonder about their self-determining power, husbands clung at home . . . to a patriarchal role."[4] The more flexible, democratic middle-class family defined itself around the woman's spiritual and functional prominence, yet the home brought the woman to the fore through her role as "subservient angel" in part so she could continue the work of the "network of 'fathers' who shepherded junior males" in earlier times.[5] David Leverenz places Emerson squarely in this perpetuation of male domination. "Emerson's ideal of manly self-empowering reduces womanhood to spiritual nurturance while erasing female subjectivity. 'Self-Reliance' takes for granted the presence of faceless mothering in the mind, an ideal state of mental health that he sums up in a memorable image: 'The nonchalance of boys who are sure of a dinner.'"[6] Such readings are confirmed by Tocqueville's contemporary musings: "Nor have the Americans ever supposed that democratic principles should undermine the husband's authority and make it doubtful who is in charge of the family. In their view, every association, to be effective, must have a head, and the natural head of the conjugal association is the husband. They therefore never deny him the right to direct his spouse. They think that in the little society composed of man and wife, just as in the great society of politics, the aim of democracy is to regulate and legitimatize necessary powers and not to destroy all power."[7] The democratic family and American democracy overall instruct children and citizens on all groups' need to be ruled by a head. Democracy's erosion of "barriers separating man and woman," which Tocqueville had earlier observed, coexists with hierarchy in general and gender hierarchy in particular. In the family, we might conclude, apparent feminization does not undermine patriarchal hierarchy.

While concurring with this conclusion, I have also been redescribing the structure and operation of *liberal* hierarchy. In this chapter, I will advocate shifting attention toward several factors. First, the change in the function of coercive power was not so much from external to internal, corporeal to psychological, paternal to maternal, although the rhetorical balance between these modes — cofactors since the Mayflower — tipped toward the latter. These categories are too individualistic, and fail to take the family seriously as a premier venue of antebellum group psychology. The question of this familial group psychology was not only how power could be internalized but how power could be made egalitarian without loss of authority. The yield here is not spurious male feminization, but a spurious group equalization.[8] Second, recent accounts have assumed that the feminized home teaches through (and teaches respect for) the mechanism of affective intimacy, when such a family, if Emerson's view is an instance, actually teaches reverence for power arriving from afar. Finally, though it is accurate to conclude that the feminized liberal middle-class family maintained gender inequality, this should not be taken to imply that liberal men sought preeminent, singular self-reliance for themselves and their sons. While the family did not deliver equality, it also avoided manly freedom. The liberal family democratized manhood by making its submissiveness count for something. In this family, men could get corporate security, that is, position without active agency. Their form of patriarchy would pivot on well-placed passivity.

2. Familial Democracy and Its Limits

For the liberal family man, the family served as a form of democratic imagining rather than as a refuge from it. Several features of the family made Emerson and his circle think of it as an important place to start developing a democratic sensibility.

The first has already been mentioned, and is often associated with Tocqueville's renowned description of democratic families in America generally. These families were less hierarchically oriented around a dominant father than were their predecessors. By the 1830s, the father was said to "abdicat[e] without fuss" to the son who becomes "his own master . . . without haste or effort." American daughters were also relatively autonomous, for "in no other country is a girl left so soon or so completely to look after herself"; democracy meant that "equality of conditions has swept down all the real or imaginary barriers separating man and woman."[9] The decline of domestic tyranny brought sons and daughters closer together in their parallel (and partial) emancipations from the authoritarian patriarch.

Second, the family minus its overtly despotic master was seen as a possible model for a more general kind of equality. Margaret Fuller,

writing in the *New York Daily Tribune,* and criticizing the "Prevalent Idea
that Politeness is too great a Luxury to be given to the Poor," suggested
that such equality could be instituted through a proper respect for domestic autonomy. Her piece attacked the kind of moral reform work
that presumes that the middle class can ignore the domestic economy
of the poor.

> An excellent man who was, in his early years, a missionary to the poor,
> used to speak afterwards with great shame of the manner in which he
> had conducted himself towards them. — "When I recollect," said he, "the
> freedom with which I entered their houses, inquired into all their affairs,
> commented on their conduct and disputed their statements I wonder I
> was never horsewhipped and feel that I ought to have been; it would have
> done me good, for I needed as severe a lesson on the universal obligations
> of politeness in its only genuine form of respect for man as man, and
> delicate sympathy with each in his peculiar position."

The family that is vulnerable to meddling from self-designated superiors
becomes a locus of subjugation and tyranny. An autonomous family,
protected by "politeness," signals mutual respect. As Fuller continues, it
becomes clear that she imagines politeness as a prerequisite if not the
backbone of democratic relations. "Charles Lamb, who was indeed wor-
thy to be called a human being from those refined sympathies, said, 'You
call him a gentleman: does his washerwoman find him so?' We may say,
if she did so, she found him a *man,* . . . treating her with that genuine
respect which a feeling of equality inspires."[10] A real man mixes gender
difference with equality rather than hierarchy. Without at all affecting
material conditions, manly behavior prevents public forms of inequality
from controlling the private body and mind. Its spirit of refinement, its
truly domestic sense of connection, bars social division at the entrance
to the household space in which self-formation occurs. The independent
family, containing its own "affairs," "conduct," and "statements," sponsors "refined sympathies" regardless of its formal social standing.
Though this avoids the question of material inequalities, these sympathies rest on a "feeling of equality" which protects weaker from stronger
classes by reducing the psychological effects of hierarchy — by installing
the democratic imagination in the mind.

Emerson sometimes approximates an idea like Fuller's: an equality
of domestic feeling that leaves actual class and gender strata intact.

> But though these partial values are as fluxional as broker's quotations,
> subject to every burst of sunshine or shade, and . . . raise or break our

confidence in popular intelligence, yet when we look over this constellation of cities which animate & illustrate the land, & see how little the government has to do with their daily life, how selfhelped & selfdirected all families are, knots of men in purely natural Societies, — societies of trade, kindred blood, of habitual hospitality, house & house, man acting on man by weight of opinion, of longer or better directed industry, the refinement & the refining influence of women, the invitation which experience & permanent causes open to youth & labor. When I see how much each virtuous & gifted person whom all men consider lives with & stands affectionately related to scores of excellent people who are not known far from home, & perhaps with great reason reckons all these people his superiors in virtue & in the symmetry & force of their qualities . . . — I see what cubic values America has. And she offers a better certificate of civilization than great cities or enormous wealth.[11]

This is one of those infrequent but profoundly yearning moments in Emerson when he does not replace the many with the great. He rejects mass democracy as usual, and envisions a society centered on one's superiors, as we would expect from the analysis offered in the previous chapter. And yet the result is not universal but local community. Families are "natural Societies," by which Emerson means not only blood kinship but men and women brought together by proximity, shared activities and purposes, and histories of association. Such societies are "selfdirected." They generate their own laws through something like Fuller's "refined sympathies," here called "man acting on man by weight of opinion" in league with "the refinement & the refining influence of women." This society is complete in itself, and needs no outside intervention. Its "civilization" is linked to and yet independent of the metropolitan and imperial versions; it is local, self-supporting, composed not of the great but of the near or, to be accurate, of greatness undiminished by its nearness, provincialism, or commonality. The community is self-sustaining because, if observed by a democratic mind, it can be seen to consist of "scores of excellent people who are not known far from home." Its typical figure is Fuller's "man": he who not only avoids subjugating others, but lives free of subjugation to a distant superior.

Emerson now and then explicitly declares that local society expresses the laws of general social equality.

> But *great men:* — the word is injurious. Is there caste? is there fate? . . . It is as real a loss that others should be low, as that we should be low; for we must have society.
>
> It is a reply to these suggestions, to say, society is a Pestalozzian school: all are teachers and pupils in turn. We are equally served by receiv-

ing and by imparting. . . . And if any appear never to assume the chair,
but always to stand and serve, it is because we do not see the company in
a sufficiently long period for the whole rotation of parts to come about.
As to what we call the masses, and common men; — there are no common
men. All men are at last of a size. . . . [12]

In a society where some are magnificently greater than others, it makes
sense to sacrifice direct relations to one's peers in order to gain contact
with them across any distance. But if all are fundamentally equal, local
destiny is as great as any other. Emerson is of course fully aware that
artists and intellectuals routinely despise local life for its apparent inferiority: maybe it is possible for the mayor of Santa Barbara, a surgeon in
Cincinnati, or a computer engineer in Houston to mingle as equals with
her colleagues in Paris, Tokyo, and Boston, but such coexistence between ballet dancers from Tucson and New York is far more difficult to
imagine. Nonetheless, Emerson here asserts that the greatness of the
remote is a delusion, that, as a Houston colleague of mine once observed, "a genius is someone from out of town." The apparent inferiority of one's neighbors is similarly delusional, and it is attributable to the
custom of hierarchical thinking, which examines people only for how
well they serve a general economy of performance and value (in skill, in
social amusement, in connection to greatness) and not for how they
serve their neighbors and themselves. In the local scene, Emerson finds
a paradoxical freedom from the restraints formed by competitive relations to everybody else. Provisionally counter to "our system," in which
"a man comes to measure his greatness by the regrets, envies, and ha-
treds of his competitors," the "little society," though in continual motion, refuses to be constituted by the worship of superiority: "in these
new fields there is room: here are no self-esteems, no exclusions." [13] The
family man learns from family life a lesson missing from his experience
of men: *greatness arises from equality,* and does not replace so much as
strengthen it.

Emerson sometimes associates these new fields of local reciprocity
with the expansion of home economics to public communalism.

Why should not I if a man comes & asks me for a book give it him? if
he ask me to write a letter for him write it? if he ask me to write a poem
or a discourse which I can fitly write, why should I not? And if my neigh-
bor is as skilful in making cloth, why should not all of us who have wool,
send it to him to make for the common benefit . . . ? As so let every
house keep a store-room in which they place their superfluity of what
they produce, & open it with ready confidence to the wants of the neigh-

borhood, & without an account of debtor & credit. . . . And is not the human race a family? Does not kindness disarm? It is plain that if perfect confidence reigned, then it would be possible and he asks how is confidence to be promoted but by reposing confidence?[14]

Emerson here imagines economic security issuing from the transgression of the laws of property. The psychic yield is the substitution of competition with "confidence," domination with face-to-face exchange. He comes quite close to Fourierist socialism, as paraphrased by the latter's American popularizer Albert Brisbane: "*Pecuniary dependency* poisons all social relations, and causes to a greater or less extent the renouncement of liberty, of that liberty which is most cherished, —*the Liberty of the heart with its sympathies and affections.*"[15]

Such passages in my view represent Emersonian culture at the summit of its imagination of an egalitarian version of capitalist democracies. He projects gender and class equality on the basis of the wisdom of Bancroft's "common mind," aggregated in local societies without supervisory control from centralized wealth and power. Their America would save itself by building a peasant civilization, retaining its sense of place and of the political superiority of place-based relations over those tied to remote and higher powers, universal rules, transcontinental scale, general circulation, and all the horrors of an unappeasable yearning for recognition from the distant great. Emerson's own town of Concord could serve him as a primitive, undeveloped anticipation of this ideal, for there he passed most of his adulthood within an utterly familiar village life while feeling little restriction on his international travels, national lecturing, and city connections.[16] While his notion of male friendship extols the pleasures of submissive brotherhood, he uses the heterosexual home structure to imagine a fulfillment of fraternity in a kind of spontaneous socialism. The family, economically deprivatized and opened to the neighborhood, translates one-on-one adhesion into a bigendered community of siblings outside the range of traditional patriarchal control.[17] The family, in contrast to male friendship, allows Emerson to display several important aspects of an egalitarian radicalism: it is collective, antipaternal, egalitarian, local, self-governed, and economically socialist. These features make manifest the fact that the individual can be "really great in little things . . . noble and heroic in the insipid details of everyday life."[18]

But this middle-class utopian imagining is both enabled by the feminized home and shattered by the presence of actual women and children. A sequence of journal entries from July 1839 suggests the problem. First, there's the idealizing presence of Waldo Jr. "I like my boy with his endless sweet soliloquies & iterations and his utter inability to conceive why I should not leave all my nonsense, business, & writing & come tie up his toy horse, as if there was or could be any end to nature beyond his horse. And he is wiser than we when [he] threatens his whole threat 'I will not love you.'"[19] The child puts immediate relations before transcendence. In so doing, he constitutes the home as a site of multiple and disunited wills, where outcomes need to be negotiated rather than referred to a general law. And young Waldo, apparently sensing what love means to his distracted father, redefines it as the creation and support—and not the spiritualizing rupture—of these intimate bonds. The two Waldos, affectionately different, comprise a system of self-governance that involves divergent desires. It requires a home economy that cannot standardize behavior on the basis of common principles but that must arise from ongoing negotiation and change. The home based on differential self-rule is sustained at the insistence of the childish son and not of the father, whose busy "nonsense" seeks meanings in nature that outlast whim.[20]

Several days later, Emerson expresses some exasperation with so much difference within the democratic home.

> I desire that my housekeeping should be clean & sweet & that it should not shame or annoy me. . . . I wish my house to be a college open as the air to all to whom I spiritually belong, & who belong to me. But is not open to others or for other purposes. I do not wish that it should be a confectioner's shop wherein eaters & drinkers may get strawberries & champagne. I do not wish that it should be a playground or house of entertainment for boys. They do well to play; I like that they should, but not with me, or in these precincts. Nor do I wish that it should be a hospital for the sick excepting only *my* sick.[21]

Emerson wants his home to be open but clean, and continues with further examples of those to be banished as insufficiently his. The preferable home is open only to spiritual kindred, which particularly excludes playing boys. The unpleasant home has a diversity of purposes and autonomous wills that do not achieve a unity of that kind that allows recognition of these others as himself.

The siege continues, and Emerson includes women along with the children as a problem to be solved. "The '*abandon*' of a scatterbrain, the 'abandon' of a woman, are no better than calculation; but the 'abandon' of a self commanding & reserved mind is like the fire of troops when the enemy is at the end of the bayonet."[22] The disorder of scattered women, pressing in through intimacy (like "the end of the bayonet"), must be escaped for an "abandon" that works like military force, and eliminates scattered elements in favor of a more disciplined whole.

The period in which Emerson is most preoccupied with the blessings of home life is also the time when he worries the most about housekeeping being overrun with diversity. This is yet another example. "Unroof any house & you must find there confusion. Order is too precious & divine a thing to dwell with such fools & sinners as we all are. See how in families where there is both substance & taste, at what expense any favorite punctuality is maintained. If the children, for example, are considered . . . then does the hospitality of the house suffer. . . . If all are well attended, — then must the master & mistress be studious of particulars at the cost of their own accomplishments & growth."[23] The journals of these years seek domestic sharing but shun domestic difference. They imagine a purification of the everyday home where its equalities are underwritten by "the eternal laws of mind which adjust the relation of all persons to each other by the mathematical measure of their havings & beings."[24] Emerson's introduction of woman into his little society induces him to call for the reduction of the family as a type of (disorderly) democratic community to a familiar kind of union.

3. Domestic Women, Disciplinary Distance

Emerson describes self-reliance as dependent on an egalitarian community; in so doing, he shifts from the first to the second stage of corporate individualism as described in chapter 1 above. He then expresses great discomfort with such a community. How does he retain its necessary element of collectivity and ostensible reciprocity while achieving the requisite sort of authority? He feminizes the receipt of unappealable authority.

Emerson divides his relationships along gender lines, and much of the time he has different names for them: "friendship" for his connections with other men, "love" for those with women. A great deal of contemporary thinking about the passions regarded these as two distinct types of feeling. Whitman used phrenological concepts to separate the "amative" feeling for women from the "adhesive" bond with men, and saw these as different psychological and political structures.[25] In his first series of essays (1841), Emerson divides love and friendship into consecutive chapters, and one difference in these feelings remains consistent. In "Friendship," male-male relations do not transcend rivalry but rest on a vexed conjunction of rivalry and detachment. "Love," however, insistently imagines a union that overcomes rivalry and even the individual identities of the participants. The dominant note in Emerson's thinking about women is his view that they represent and sustain a unity of self and universe underwritten by God. Emerson creates a division of labor between those who make singularity and those who make unity.

Emerson's straight view of male-male love, as we saw, has powerfully conservative consequences, though these do not appear as the will to power that is relatively easy to criticize. This friendship celebrates sameness,[26] yet it validates competition as central not only to economic efficiency but to love itself; and it teaches submission rather than autonomy—teaches submission to those superior enough to represent laws. This friendship veils male submission in the affectionate jostling that ensues when kindred men sense potential brethren; it conceals submission in the liquidating repudiation at friendship's end. By combining competition and submission, friendship confirms that freedom depends on maintaining hierarchy.

But when Emerson writes about women in "Love," rivalry has all but vanished in the transcendent union toward which the lovers continually move. The beloved woman is not so interesting to Emerson for herself as for her facilitation of a spiritual movement beyond the physical world and into the realm of unchanging beauty. First the "lover comes to a warmer love of [the] nobilities" of the beloved.

> Then he passes from loving them in one to loving them in all, and so is the one beautiful soul only the door through which he enters to the society of all true and pure souls. In the particular society of his mate, he attains a clearer sight of any spot, any taint, which her beauty has contracted from this world. . . . And, beholding in many souls the traits of the divine beauty, and separating in each soul that which is divine from the taint which it has contracted in the world, the lover ascends to the highest beauty, to the love and knowledge of the Divinity, by steps on this ladder of created souls.[27]

In male friendship, the two friends remains two, while in love, the (female) lover is a soul which serves as the rungs of an ascension that rapidly leaves her behind; their relationship gives way to the man's higher union with "all true and beautiful souls." The relationship is a devotional practice for the man where he learns to find faults and to avoid them on the road to "blend[ing] with God";[28] the bride, through her moral beauty rather than agency or identity, guides the way to God.

The temporal male-female relation is replaced by the husband's link to a society of souls. The earthly woman is replaced by the divine one; "Thus we are put in training for a love which knows not sex, nor person, nor partiality."[29] "When the [mere] affections rule and absorb the man," he is dependent on an individual female person. But in true love and murder, the lady vanishes.[30]

When domestic economy comes in contact with Emerson's version of the "angel in the house," the utopian features of his sociable home fall by the wayside. Antipaternalism is abandoned, as the climber pauses not to dwell with the rungs on the ladder but with the souls fused with God. Egalitarianism gives way to a sense that salvation depends on ascent out of the everyday. Whatever Emerson retains of the collective nature of salvation, of the soul's longing for "the society of all true and pure souls," requires the severing of "the particular society of his mate" and other ordinary relations. "Love"'s final paragraph notes that "there are moments when the affections rule and absorb the man, and make his happiness dependent on a person or persons. But in health the mind is presently seen again, — its overarching vault, bright with galaxies of immutable lights, and the warm loves and fears that swept over us as clouds, must lose their finite character and blend with God, to attain their own perfection."[31]

The rejection of women implied in this kind of idealization follows from Emerson's escape from the plurality and negotiation that comprise the little society. He construes marriage as perfect union or nothing. In his essay on Swedenborg, he rejects Swedenborg's faith in an eternal marriage in heaven. Real union requires the abandonment of the spouse for God.

> Of progressive souls, all loves and friendships are momentary. *Do you love me?* means, Do you see the same truth? If you do, we are happy with the same happiness: but presently one of us passes into the perception of new truth; — we are divorced, and no tension in nature can hold us together. . . . The Eden of God is bare and grand: like the out-door landscape, remembered from the evening fireside, it seems cold and desolate, whilst you cower over the coals; but, once abroad again, we pity these who can forego the magnificence of nature, for candle-light and cards. . . . For God is the bride or bridegroom of the soul. Heaven is not the pairing of two, but the communion of all souls. We meet, and dwell an instant under the temple of one thought.[32]

Loving women leads him out of marriage toward bondage with the multitudes unified under God.

Emerson does not wish simply to Platonize women into disembod-
ied vessels of divine law. Women must retain enough agency and autonomy to represent the living presence of a distant power.

Describing an evening outing in 1841, Emerson's description of the
moon suggests a desire for more than feminine receptivity.

> But on us sitting darkling or sparkling there in the boat, presently rose
> the moon, she cleared the clouds & sat in her triumph so maidenly & yet
> so queenly, so modest yet so strong, that I wonder not that she ever repre-
> sents the Feminine to men. There is no envy[,] no interference in nature.
> The beauty & sovereignty of the moon, the stars, or the trees do not envy:
> they know how to make it all their own. As we sail swiftly along . . . each
> moment, each aspect is sufficient & perfect; there is no better or worse,
> no interference, no preference, but every virtuous act of man or woman
> accuses other men & women . . . Blessed is Law. This moon, the hill, the
> plant, the air, obey a law.[33]

This seems like classical Emersonian Platonizing: the celebration of nature is a celebration of love without envy, the boat's movement reveals
unconflicted perfection, the stars and nature generally are undisrup-
tively sovereign. And yet the sovereignty is indissociable from femininity, which represents not only maiden modesty but also queenly
strength. Femininity gains its strength through its tie to the blessedly
distant law.

Emerson describes his ideal, a woman of *powerful* virtue, in a passage
about Anna Barker, whom Emerson seems to have adored from her first
appearance in 1839.

> Anna's miracle, next to the *amount* of her life, seems to be the intimacy of
> her approach to us. The moment she fastens her eyes on you, her unique
> gentleness unbars all doors, and with such easy and frolic sway she ad-
> vances & advances & advances on you, with that one look, that no
> brother or sister or father or mother of life-long acquaintance ever seemed
> to arrive quite so near as this now first seen maiden. It is almost incredible
> to me, when I spoke with her the other night — that I have never seen
> this child but three times, or four, is it? I should think I had lived with
> her in the houses of eternity.[34]

Having neutralized Barker's apparent seductive power by insisting on
her airy and childish quality, Emerson gets to cherish her for her power
of linking a standard kind of intimate femininity to the eternal. Powerful
intimacy possesses an erotic energy: Barker "advances & advances &
advances on you," he exclaims delightedly. She is as vivid, visible, willful,
and visibly looking as Emerson's harlot, whom I shall discuss below, but
her active nearness is delightful in league with the qualities that lead

him to call her "the holiest nun."[35] Barker is possessed of "celestial sincerity" and is yet more familiar than "brother or sister or father."[36] She is wholly domestic but also divine. This angel becomes such by expressing higher law in a local will. For linking local life to the absolute, Barker is the object of Emerson's love.

This need to elevate women's intimacy may explain why Emerson is unwilling to follow some domestic ideology in demanding women's subordination. In an 1855 address that must have had uneven effects on its feminist audience, Emerson waffles about equal rights but finally comes out and says that women "have an unquestionable right to their own property. And if a woman demands votes, offices and political equality with men, as among the Shakers an Elder and Elderess are of equal power, — and among the Quakers, — it must not be refused."[37] However qualified by a standard distribution of gender roles, Emerson's commitment to women's equal agency is significantly stronger than that of powerful domestic theorists like Catherine Beecher. After noting that "all men are created equal" is a Christian as well as a democratic concept, Beecher openly insists that "it is needful that certain relations be sustained, that involve the duties of subordination. There must be magistrate and subject, one of whom is the superior, and the other the inferior. There must be the relations of husband and wife, parent and child, teacher and pupil, employer and employed, each involving the relative duties of subordination. The superior in certain particulars is to direct, and the inferior is to yield obedience."[38] While Beecher regards democratic gender relations as satisfied by the voluntary nature of women's submission to men, Emerson suggests the need, if not for material equality, then for the kind of sufficient agency signified in his political economy by the power to own property.[39]

A virtuous woman should not be too submissive. But she should also avoid excesses of assertion. The attack on feminine assertion grows out of a more conventional Victorian polarization of angelic and fallen women. Emerson dislikes the "vulgar pretty woman" who insists on her visibility, in the form of loud clothes and cheap makeup.[40] She is unlike the "rare women that charm us" by giving society neither color nor any other visible presence but its "form, its tone."[41] He spells this out in a journal passage from September 1838:

> Forget as fast as you can that you exist, if you would be beautiful & beloved. You do not tell me, young maiden, in words that you wish to be admired[,] that not to be lovely but to be courted, not to be mistress of yourself but to be mistress of me, is your desire. But I hear it, an ugly harlot sound in the recesses of your song, in the niceties of your speech,

in the lusciousness (forgive the horrible word) of your manners. Can you not possibly think of any thing that you really & heartily want & can say so, & go the *straight* way in the face of God & men to effect, if it were only to raise a cucumber, or own a cat, or make a scratch cradle? Be it what it will, do that, chase your friend all over town; read, mark, *eat,* the book that interests you; any thing, no matter what, that interests you, that do, with a single aim, & forget yourself in it, & straightway you are a piece of nature & do share the loveliness & venerableness of nature. Therefore are tears *for another*[,] therefore is lively repartee, a good story, a fit action lovely & enlivening because in them the soul goes out of self & gives sign of relation to universal nature.[42]

A maiden is a harlot when she seeks to control Emerson through seduction, but his cure is not that she wait demurely for the man to move or that she retain chaste autonomy. Rather than remaining in the realm of sexual competition, Emerson finds remedy in the fallen woman rising by forgetting that she exists. He appears to be asking for a form of orthodox female submission in words much like those his wife Lidian uses to describe her sense of her duties within their own marriage: "God help me to have no aim in the future but to do his will in seeking the happiness of others — forgetting my own."[43] He asks that the harlot learn to be nothing but a "relation to universal nature."

The simplest explanation for Emerson's attitude would be a conventional sexism: he likes his men strong and his women weak. He really does revere self-reliance, this argument would go, but in men and not in women. Yet, as noted above, he also requires agency in women. Even this passage offers an unadmiring endorsement of female activity, in which a woman should chase a friend all over town, read, do "any thing, no matter what, that interests you," as long as it is done in self-forgetting. Similarly, Emerson feels an unsettled admiration for his phallic mother, Aunt Mary Moody Emerson, because, like the towering Daniel Webster, she "had an eye that went through & through you like a needle." Emerson accepts her own self-definition: "'She was endowed,' she said, 'with the *fatal* gift of penetration.'"[44] On the other hand, when he venerates a woman's humble piety, he sometimes does so to establish a model for his own male self. He notes of a liberal Quaker woman of New Bedford, Miss Mary Rotch, that she had discovered her inward spiritual life only when "she learned to have *no choice,* to acquiesce without understanding the reason. . . . Can you believe, Waldo Emerson, that you may relieve yourself of this perpetual perplexity of choosing? & by putting your ear close to the soul, learn always the true way."[45]

Waldo Emerson does not see self-reliant free choice as good for men
but bad in women; he sees it as good or bad depending on what kind
of self-reliance it is.

The harlot's crime is to make visible the contradiction between assertion and submission: the harlot is she who chases all over town without
managing to efface herself at the same time. Her sin is to act from her
own presence, to act out of herself, to have song, speech, and manners
which derive from her and not from "universal nature." The harlot's
failure to submit is a failure to be governed by distant powers; she is
not a piece of nature. Even by deciding what she will wear, she fails to
admit the superiority of these powers, and assumes her equal right to
make her own rules. She confronts a man who seeks power in obedience
to distant laws with power not as revolt but as a kind of everyday or
domestic self-direction. She asks Emerson to face his own official doctrine, now severed from the subservience to divine law that was all that
made the potential revolutions of self-reliance acceptably lawful to him
in the first place. Trashy self-reliance rejects its links to distant power.

Comparing Emerson's treatment of Anna Barker and the "harlot,"
we can see what a precarious line his virtuous women walk. They cannot
be too low and intimate, too merely local and absorbed with the household's needful doings. These women, though chastely harbored in the
home, are simply "scatterbrained," and represent the dissolution of order and meaning. Domestic virtue is not enough for Emerson. On the
other hand, women must not be too independent and self-directed.
These apparently opposed dangers — local intimacy and depraved visibility — have something in common: they each reject the presence of
remote authority. Emerson gains a significant social payoff here. Truly
seductive feminine virtue, like Barker's, does not replace the family democracy with directly authoritarian power. The woman who adequately
represents higher power manifestly retains her individual agency without the harlot's declaration of independence. The egalitarian form of the
family remains in place even as the chaos of internally diversified willing — the rule of intimacy — is replaced by distant laws. Seductive feminine virtue combines liberal and authoritarian elements and renders the
"little society" a training ground for avoiding both self-assertion and
obvious submission. Democratic tendencies are not nipped in the cradle
but affectively rewired, so that democratic equality and rule from afar
feel like the same thing.

4. The Power of Male Passivity

I've argued that Emerson dislikes the feminized circle of equal sovereignty that he seeks in the abstract, and that, in addition, he redefines
equal sovereignty by describing feminine virtue as the active expression
of distant law. The effect on liberal manhood remains to be described.

A dream begins the process.

> A droll dream last night, whereat I ghastly laughed. A congregation as-
> sembled, like some our late Conventions, to debate the Institution of
> Marriage; & grave & alarming objections stated on all hands to the usage;
> when one speaker at last rose & began to reply to the arguments, but
> suddenly extended his hand & turned on the audience the spout of an
> engine which was copiously supplied from within the wall with water &
> whisking it vigorously about, up, down, right & left, he drove all the
> company in crowds hither & thither & out of the house. Whilst I stood
> watching astonished & amused at the malice & vigor of the orator, I saw
> the spout lengthened by a supply of hose behind, & the man suddenly
> brought it round a corner & drenched me as I gazed. I woke up relieved
> to find myself quite dry, and well convinced that the Institution of Mar-
> riage was safe for tonight.[46]

The dream might be titled "The Rout of Reform; or, Reform Gets
Pissed Away," but that doesn't capture Emerson's own role here. The
defender of traditional marriage wields the hose, and Emerson identifies
with him and is impressed with his potent blasting and flooding of dis-
senters straight out of the meeting house. Emerson awakens with the
fear that he too has been pissed on as a dissenter on the topic of marriage, and is relieved to find himself dry. He implies that the institution
of marriage is safe in his own mind as well, and will be subject to no
negative speechifying from him. He is relieved to recall this paternal
figure, flaunting the indomitable hose, and vanquishing all internal
differences. At the same time, paternal power appears as an embar-
rassing type of comic violence. The embarrassment allows Emerson to
disavow his own relation to the paternal power of enforcement and control. Order and unity are enforced, marriage is assured, and yet Emerson
doesn't have to do the slightest thing. He can even imply his own en-
dangeredness at the hand of a power which he favors. Emerson, the
ambivalent, sidelined liberal male in his own dream, gratefully observes
the maintenance of a patriarchal institution by a viciously clowning patriarch without having to involve any degree of his own agency.

Even Emerson's more conservative defenses of "true womanhood" rebound to the quietude of the male in question. Emerson began his 1855 address to the Women's Rights Convention in Boston by affirming his belief that women are less important as creatures of reason than of intuition: "I think their words are to be weighed; but it is their inconsiderate word, — according to the rule, 'take their first advice, not their second:' . . . 'Tis their mood and tone that is important."[47] Here women lack safe, seductive agency and simply transmit impulses rather than originate thought. Emerson hastens to explain what this means for gender relations. "The general voice of mankind has agreed that they have their own strength; that women are strong by sentiment; that the same mental height which their husbands attain by toil, they attain by sympathy with their husbands. Man is the will, and Woman the sentiment. In this ship of humanity, Will is the rudder, and Sentiment the sail: when Woman affects to steer, the rudder is only a masked sail."[48] In a conventional reproduction of conservative domestic ideology, Emerson describes woman's role as the muse of rule-making man. His brief history of the evolution of women's rights begins with the development of the equality of the sexes and leads to the higher plane of sexual difference, which transforms equality into a gendered segregation of function between thought and feeling. This position leads predictably to Emerson's preliminary conclusion that, although the recent assertion of equal rights for women is not to be denied, it would be better for all if they did not insist upon its fulfillment. "Though their mathematical justice is not to be denied, yet the best women do not wish these things; they are asked for by people who intellectually seek them, but who have not the support or sympathy of the truest women; and that, if the laws and customs were modified in the manner proposed, it would embarrass and pain gentle and lovely persons with duties which they would find irksome and distasteful."[49] This boilerplate demands not submission to male authority per se but a voluntary avoidance of agency that would make submission inevitable. Men, as Emerson describes them, first and foremost, are the will itself (and not the act of willing); the important thing about them, as far as women are concerned, is simply that they have power. Emerson assumes these men will not be despotic, but granting them immanent authority nicely expresses the authoritarian element in Emerson's benevolence.

Nonetheless, Emerson winds up proclaiming the priority of women's "sentiment" to men's "will." The address concludes with Emerson saying, "The new movement is only a tide shared by the spirits of man and woman; and you may proceed in the faith that whatever the woman's heart is prompted to desire, the man's mind is simultaneously prompted to accomplish."[50] Though women need men to be their guardians, and though the "will" belongs exclusively to men, the male will here takes direction from women's desire rather than from itself. Whether inside or outside the home, women remain the most important source of male authority. Men have wills but they do not so much originate their will as respond to women's impulses. In spite of men's practical dominance, their agency arises from women's sentiment.

This power of sentiment is certainly not a blessing for women, but it is a benefit for men — without losing social position, they are endowed with a certain inalienable passivity. Women's sentiment has a collective outcome, one that produces unity while remaining a "tide," advancing and dynamic. Men are not the source of social relations or historical change. "The new movement is only a tide shared by the spirits of man and woman"; society is therefore structured by spirit and not its male members.

The presence of women in the domestic circle offers a solution to the divisions that perplexed Emerson's mid-career. His most canonical essays — "Experience," "Montaigne," and "Fate" — note a disjuncture between individuality and law, desire and reality that he overcomes in the final lines of these essays only through the invocation of cosmological magic. The divisions are profound. My own favorite moment of frustration occurs near the end of "Montaigne."

> Charles Fourier announced that "the attractions of man are proportioned to his destinies"; in other words, that every desire predicts its own satisfaction. Yet, all experience exhibits the reverse of this; the incompetency of power is the universal grief of young and ardent minds. They accuse the divine providence of a certain parsimony. It has shown the heaven and earth to every child, and filled him with a desire for the whole; a desire raging, infinite; a hunger, as of space to be filled with planets; a cry of famine, as of devils for souls. Then for the satisfaction, — to each man is administered a single drop, a bead of dew of vital power, *per day*, — a cup as large as space, and one drop of the water of life in it.[51]

Such conflicts potentially call for heroic effort — great labors of poetry or commerce, huge attempts to realize the self in a world unmindful that, deep down, mankind is its master. No such willing takes place, in part because Emerson repeatedly reveals its futility. On the next page, Emerson heals the split between desire and law with the "Eternal Cause," but not before he has mocked such a healing as envisioned in the socialism of Fourier. By invoking domestic life, Emerson can sustain the status quo without staging a ride to the rescue by self-reliant man or God.

An example appears in "Domestic Life," published in 1870. Emerson writes that domestic life is the "real history of the world" and the real "spirit of the age," more so than the "state-house or the court-room." "Is it not plain that not in senates, or courts, or chambers of commerce, but in the dwelling-house must the true character and hope of the time be consulted?"[52] The premise for this kind of argument, though it comes at the close of the essay, is the correspondence between domestic relations and eternal law. "Will [man] not see, through all he miscalls accident, that Law prevails for ever and ever; that his private being is part of it; that its home is his own unsounded heart; that his economy, his labor, his good and bad fortune, his health and manners are all a curious and exact demonstration in miniature of the Genius of the Eternal Providence? . . . Let religion cease to be occasional; and the pulses of thought that go to the borders of the universe, let them proceed from the bosom of the Household."[53]

For the older Emerson, domestic life unites intimacy and higher law, although during the middle course of his career these had seemed cruelly at odds. Now they are reconciled by tranquility among local relations. "I honor that man whose ambition it is, not to win laurels in the state or the army, not to be a jurist or a naturalist, not to be a poet or a commander, but to be a master of living well, and to administer the offices of master or servant, of husband, father and friend."[54] Living well means avoiding mastery and singular exertion, and letting the distant law prevail.

Clubs offer the benefits of familial passivity to all-male groups. The rivalry and hierarchy noted in the last chapter lead toward domestic union. The men who attract Emerson are those that intimate competitive superiority. "Our fortunes in the world are as our mental equipment for this competition is. Yonder is a man who can answer the questions which I cannot. Is it so? Hence comes to me boundless curiosity to know his experiences and his wit." But the struggles give way to the homely sense that "in spite of seeming difference, men are all of one pattern. We readily assume this with our mates, and are disappointed and angry if we find that we are premature, and that their watches are slower than ours. In fact the only sin which we never forgive in each other is difference of opinion."[55] Competition yields to kinship. Men together have a goal—familiarity governed by a higher unity—whose social (rather than metaphysical) version Emerson developed during the 1840s in his thinking about ideal women and the home.

The best club of all is West Point, which Emerson visited in 1863.

> West Point Academy makes a very agreeable impression on me. The inno-
> cence of the cadets, the air of probity, of veracity, & of loyalty to each
> other struck me, & the anecdotes told us confirmed this impression. I
> think it excellent that such tender youths should be made so manly &
> masterly in rough exercises of horse & gun & cannon & mortar . . . I
> think their ambition should be concentrated on their superiority in Sci-
> ence, — being taught, that, whoever knows the most must command *of
> right,* & must command *in fact,* if just to himself. Let them have no fears,
> then, of prejudices against West Point. "West Point a hot bed of aristoc-
> racy," is a word of some political hack, which seems to rankle in their
> memories. Rather let them accept it, and make West Point a true aristoc-
> racy, or "the power of the Best," best scholars, best soldiers, best engi-
> neers, best commanders, best men. . . . They will be the shop of power,
> the source of instruction, the organization of Victory.[56]

Rather than reading West Point as an unpleasant necessity, even during
a Civil War, Emerson imagines it as a model of good government. Domestic intimacy underlies its ideal order: a "sublime point is the value
of a sufficient man: cube this value by the meeting of two or more who
perfectly understand & support each other, you have then organized
victory."[57] It shows that command can be made absolute on the basis
of science. Those who have this science will be a society's ruling class
(based on "the power of the Best"). And the "best men" will affirm the
hierarchical nature of scientific social order.

Equally important is the ongoing condition of these military aristocrats. Military hierarchy maintains their "innocence" — it keeps them
"tender youths" not unlike maidens. They demonstrate a maidenly lack
of even Anna Barker's sort of agency. In the Academy, "they are once &
forever freed from every question by means of martial law. Every cadet
is instantly responsible to his superior officer, for his behavior . . ."[58]
West Point is the ideally self-contained home for men,[59] and the result
is a hierarchical society based on obedience and leading to a perfection
of male passivity, a passivity that offers its possessor protected status
rather than subordination.

5. Domestic Corporatism

The older Emerson is often read as manifesting intellectual decline in
meandering essays like "Domestic Life" and "Clubs" and in later journal
passages, but it is more likely that he had finally found what he was

looking for. Where "Montaigne" and "Fate" fret about the individual alone with his powers, "Domestic Life" builds on his earlier thinking about the feminized home to reveal family man's corporate destiny. We may miss the agon of individual striving, the drama of the contradiction between higher law and human desire, and be more impressed by his ontological than his fireside reconciliations. But this reconciliation has been central to his idealism from his earliest days. Two of its aspects are worth itemizing in conclusion.

First, his domestic theory fulfills his corporate individualism. Individuality is competitive (step 1), but achieved only in some semblance of equal and reciprocal ties (step 2), though these do not feel comfortable with much diversity of willfulness. This relatively egalitarian group is subjected to a rule from above (step 3); here the agent is the woman of domestic virtue, dignifying the democratic wish by retaining some autonomy while veiling authoritarian top-down law with her femininity. The liberal notion of domestic equality confounds the feelings of reciprocal intimacy with unification arranged somewhere else. The male position remains untouched, not because of his dominating will but because of the abnegation of his male will, which is replaced by a structural security arisen from a family closeness that lacks internal negotiation. The "best men," those who preside benevolently and even scientifically, have shed their social agency. This absence of agency undermines the democratic alternative Emerson sometimes wished for, maintains traditional stratifications, and creates an air of undominating benevolence that is difficult for women to attack.

Second, much of what has been attributed to the feminization of American culture should be assigned to its liberalization.[60] Some commentators have argued that sensitive, intellectual men like Emerson, marginalized by conventions of commanding masculinity, accepted feminized power as second best. I've suggested, instead, that Emerson helped develop the best sort of masculine power for the middle and professional classes—liberal power. Liberalization has little interest in actual equality and agency, and insists instead on the moral authority of an interdependence in which the nature of the bonds is rarely investigated. Usually these bonds are considered adequate if they suggest unity. It is as a liberal more than as a feminine or feminist domestic theorist that Sophia Hawthorne speaks when, writing about Margaret Fuller's *Women in the Nineteenth Century* to her more radical mother, she says, "If [Fuller] were married truly, she would no longer be puzzled about the rights of woman. . . . In perfect, high union there is no question of supremacy. Souls are equal in love and intelligent communion, and all things take their proper places as inevitably as the stars in their orbits. Had there never been false and profane marriages, there would not only be no commotion about woman's rights, but it would be Heaven here at once."[61] Hawthorne here describes a corporate heaven. It is feminized only in that ideal women are the means by which supremacy is liberally maintained. Liberalization is not the diminishment of analytical reason or the belief in a community of Christian sympathy but the circumvention of political agency, the loss of the belief that the absence of such agency is a loss. Liberalization is not the feminization of rational critique but the vanishing of what agency involves — an awareness of social relations, and of the inequalities on which middle-class living depends.

PART

FOUR

Late Emerson:
Corporate Liberties

CHAPTER
SIX

Market Despotism
*"The Poet Affirms
the Laws"*

1. Freedom from Foundations

A number of contemporary issues brought out the policy progressive in Emerson. He bitterly though quietly opposed Cherokee removal, and later, more publicly supported John Brown. From time to time he became active in opposing certain especially conservative policies promoted by eastern Massachusetts elites, as when he joined friend and railroad builder John Murray Forbes in blocking the nomination of the antiradical Benjamin Franklin Thomas as justice of the state supreme court. As I have noted before, critics often agree with F. O. Matthiessen in regarding Emerson's transcendentalist self-reliance as an ideology that promoted "the rise of the common man."[1] Faced with persistent conservatism, Emerson could be found to say, at least to his journal, "There must be a Revolution. Let the revolution come & let One come breathing free into the earth to walk by hope alone."[2] Emerson has thus been summoned as sponsor of the liberating revisability of a democratic culture composed of those breathing free of conformity, guided only by their moral sense.

But it is also the case that Emerson holds a number of standard conservative-liberal views that lend his overall record the equivocal complexity that has engaged generations of scholars. As an alternative defense of Emerson's positions on society or policy, which are never considered to be his most interesting thought, many of Emerson's readers link his democratic individualism to a liberation in philosophy. Cornel West traces Emerson's power to define "creative democracy" to his belief in "the primacy of power-laden people's opinion (*doxa*) over value-free philosophers' knowledge (*episteme*). Emerson's swerve was a democratic leveling of the subordination of common sense to Reason."[3] Two

books by Stanley Cavell offer detailed readings of Emerson as a philosopher whose democratic thought appears as his views on the intersubjective yet self-trusting process of knowledge formation.[4] Similar views
prevail among literature scholars. Julie Ellison, for example, traces Emerson's importance to his notion of "perpetual transition," in which he
"finally takes more pleasure in the motion that makes [influence and
invention] almost simultaneously possible than in the exercise of authority" and the fixing of truth.[5]

   In readings like these, Emerson endows individuals with a complicated, constructed freedom because he grants them the epistemological
preconditions for making "truth" either alone or in groups. Emerson's
rejection of conformity entails not so much changing what the facts
are but changing our understanding of what a fact is. He is less interested in transforming who has knowledge and to what effect than in
transforming our understanding of the status of knowledge. When the
individual and/or the community has learned something about the epistemological status of these realities — that they lack independent, absolute, or transhistorical foundations — this may (though it certainly need
not) undermine their authority. Emerson is useful, in this tradition, not
so much because he is a romantic individualist or a social democrat but
because he is an "antifoundationalist" about the status of knowledge.

   Antifoundationalism had been central to Anglo-American philosophy and political theory long before its ascendance in literary studies.
Philosophers like Cavell are right to look as far back as Emerson for the
early stages of a U.S. tradition that rejects mainstream epistemology's
longtime quest for the grounds of objective certainty. As an antifoundationalist, Emerson avoids a standard understanding of truth as a representation of a reality that is independent of the thought and language
of the observer(s). He ignores the project of developing settled criteria
by which objective knowledge can be distinguished from subjective
opinion. He rejects the claim of conventional epistemology that some
knowledge refers to "given" things while other knowledge is "added by
the mind." He further rejects the notion that epistemology can serve
as a foundational discipline in being able to distinguish knowledge
founded in objects from beliefs that arise from speculation, poetry, culture, or social practice. In his antifoundationalist phases, he refrains
from defining scientific or moral law as "truths which are certain because
of their causes," and traces them instead to "argued belief."[6] Like other
antifoundationalists, Emerson "teaches that questions of fact, truth,
correctness, validity, and clarity can neither be posed nor answered in

reference to some extracontextual, ahistorical, nonsituational reality, or rule, or law, or value; rather, antifoundationalism asserts, all of these matters are intelligible and debatable only within the precincts of the contexts or situations or paradigms or communities that give them their local and changeable shape."[7]

Epistemological radicalism takes on increased importance in the context of my conclusions in the preceding chapters. Poetic self-expression, possession and contract, a free, fraternal social sphere, and domestic intimacy have not been found to deliver constructed autonomy. But things might look better for a revolution in knowledge. Such a revolution, rather than requiring mass movements or state power to remake social relations, can delegitimate existing relations by rejecting the status quo's claim to be grounded in reason and moral law. Institutions often enforce acceptance by adopting an air of inevitable reality. They are vulnerable, then, to criticisms that do not focus only on substantive flaws but target the false objectivity on which such airs are grounded. The most effective critique is thought to be not that which proposes alternative moral values or desires or visions of the good, but that which destabilizes the system's claim to truth. For example, one could criticize male preponderance by arguing that gender equality is better than male superiority, but this amounts to little more than one's own truth claim against another's. Instead, one can show that the claims of male supremacy are fraught with internal contradictions, unacknowledged and unjustified assumptions, and secret ties to what they reject. Rather than making one's own foundational arguments, one criticizes the foundations of the adversary. At least initially, much pragmatism, deconstruction, feminism, and other insurgent antiuniversalisms share this sense of the superior salience of the critique of foundations over the critique of values and politics and positive principles. In this context, Emerson's value lies not in, say, his cryptosocialism, but in his antifoundationalism.

Antifoundationalists do not (or should not) argue that we can escape or change conventions simply because we know them to be conventional rather than absolute.[8] Nonetheless, their practices may assist a historical shift in the location of interpretive authority — they can "democratize" culture in the sense that they can strip tradition and entrenched elites of assumed authority and thus help individuals and groups to live by laws of their own making, laws which are justified by ongoing discussion among citizens rather than by correspondence to reality. Whatever one's politics, antifoundationalism demystifies the sheer weight of what is. It allows discussion of knowledge's interests and effects, producing "truth" out of conflicts among a variety of issues, forces, and groups.[9]

Antifoundationalism displays one of the principal features of American liberalism: opposition to fixity and absolutes. Liberalism has never been as interested in positive, settled arguments for its own preferred system of, say, capitalist democracy, as in painting its opponents as anachronistic dogmatists. Whether it be manufacturers rejecting deference to large landowners in England in the 1830s or American journalists dissecting the failures of Soviet-style command economies in the 1990s, practical failure and political tyranny are associated with foundational claims.

A second connection between antifoundationalism and liberalism is the presence of markets as the generic alternative to foundations. Though logically distinct, the market offers a culturally pervasive model for ungrounded, systemic interconnection. Markets appear to exemplify the principal features of nonfoundational truth or identity: meaning and value develop through exchange or circulation and produce meaning and value differentially — they offer an exchange value constituted by relations among various entities rather than by reference to an essence or object or other alleged grounds. Once on the market, texts, commodities, or individuals are defined through transaction rather than self-possession, through others rather than through inner being, and through change rather than through absolutes. As Barbara Herrnstein Smith describes the idea, "the market does not characteristically operate as the site of desecration but, rather, as the arena for the negotiation, transformation, and redistribution of value, including social-symbolic-cultural value; and the traditionally despised trader, banker, and merchant ('panderer,' 'usurer,' 'shopkeeper') are seen, accordingly, as the most visible mediators of *change* as well as the most obvious profiteers of *exchange*."[10] These links among antifoundationalism, the free market, and continual openness to change, have been extremely powerful in political and cultural discourse in the United States. They have meant that opposing something's market value can be equated with opposing an uncoerced and accurate estimate, with opposing the collective estimate of the masses (in the form of consumers) — even with opposing freedom itself. Markets and their popular equivalent, "business," receive widespread and enduring support not necessarily because most individuals directly feel their benefits, but because to oppose them is to befriend tyranny, dogmatism, or escapism. When Emerson shifts away from the foundationalist Neoplatonism of his early writing and describes truth and identity in terms of circulation and exchange, he would in this reading seem to be liberalizing his metaphysics in harmony with a political evolution from deference to market democracy.

2. Culture as Collective Sovereignty

Much evidence can be found for a view like Cavell's, which sees Emerson's advancing career as a shift from Neoplatonic essentialism to antifoundationalism. The youthful *Nature* is indeed obsessed with grounding language in a nature causally linked to spirit. The reader may remember my argument in chapter 3 that the younger Emerson links historical to natural and spiritual law, binds invention to imitation, and defines spontaneous selfhood as the return to the father, all of which constitute a case study in that abandonment of consent best described as authoritarian. But in Emerson's later prime, his epistemology becomes more flexible and pragmatic. He comes to see language less as the mimetic reflection of an unchanging One, as he did in his "foundational" phase, than as the result of perpetual motion in actual cultural practice. While once he may have thought that the essential is permanent and all conflict superfluous, he begins in the late 1830s to believe that every level of being undergoes perpetual metamorphosis. No linguistic sign, in this case, literally and permanently hooks onto an independent object. Emerson had once believed in the Swedenborgian doctrine of correspondence between spirit and nature but comes to read this as miscasting both terms: nature does not reflect unchanging spirit, but figures it through the endless flux in spirit itself. "The slippery Proteus," Emerson says, "is not so easily caught."[11] By 1840 he is arguing, even in the residually Neoplatonic essay "The Poet," that "all symbols are fluxional; all language is vehicular and transitive, and is good, as ferries and horses are, for conveyance."[12] For "progressive souls, all loves and friendships are momentary."[13] After this stage in his thinking, Emerson sees no preestablished and permanent essence in words, but only change. As one critic concludes, "With the notion of poetry consisting of a perpetual play of tropes, which aims to represent infinity not analogically but successively (like Kant's mathematical sublime), Emerson is finally weaning himself from the concept of origins that had tantalized him for so long."[14]

Emerson does not conceive of this play of tropes individualistically. He tends to replace his original "language of nature" with a language of history. The Divinity School "Address" (1838) began by describing nature as the harmonious symbol of spirit, which offers its secrets through its sheer presence: "The corn and the wine have been freely dealt to all creatures." "Quotation and Originality" (1859) also begins with an image of the organism taking nourishment from nature, but the "creatures" here are "flies, aphids, gnats and innumerable parasites," and nature's gifts are "taken in suction."[15] In this later essay, the authentically harmonious relation between world and soul appears not through nature but through culture. "We prize books, and they prize them most who are themselves wise. Our debt to tradition through reading and conversation is so massive, our protest or private addition so rare and insignificant, — and this commonly on the ground of other reading or hearing, — that, in a large sense, one would say there is no pure originality. All minds quote. Old and new make the warp and woof of every moment."[16] The poet does not only activate root meanings but disseminates traditional meanings borrowed from the archives. He quotes, anthologizes, rebroadcasts, and syndicates a commonwealth. Of course none of this means that Emerson's poet need not make it new. But by replacing nature with tradition, and making the poet receptive, Emerson partially socializes the structure of invention.

This redescription consists only partly of granting that invention has an external source: as I've argued in earlier chapters, Emerson assumes this idea from the very beginning of his career, and with him it is usually a very pietistic and conservative one. His more radical claim in "Quotation and Originality" is that the external source is multiple rather than united. Not only is law less an origin than an activity, but this activity is explicitly collective. "Mythology is no man's work," he says, and "truth is the property of no individual, but is the treasure of all men."[17] "We admire that poetry which no man wrote, — no poet less than the genius of humanity itself."[18] The active agent becomes personhood as a mass, and even the voice of the mystic preaches groups instead of solitude. With a characteristic irony, the older Emerson stresses empirical collectivity while retaining continuity with the old paradigm of divine forms.

> Swedenborg threw a formidable theory into the world, that every soul existed in a society of souls, from which all its thoughts passed into it, as the blood of the mother circulates in her unborn child; and he noticed that, when in his bed, alternately sleeping and waking, — sleeping, he was surrounded by persons disputing and offering opinions on the one side and on the other side of a proposition; waking, the like suggestions occurred for and against the proposition as his own thoughts; sleeping again, he saw and heard the speakers as before: and this as often as he slept or waked.[19]

Swedenborg's absolute is for Emerson a "society of souls." The individual receives its power of meaning from this society, which is no less spiritual for being collective. The individual never grows up to leave a maternalized social body, whose blood continues to circulate in it in the form of the inescapable, conflictual voices of this nonuniform collectivity. One does not awaken from society to one's visionary individuality; one dwells permanently inside society, where the group is as constitutive of one's mind as is one's own bloodflow.

Emerson repeatedly defines originality as a communal tradition in which history is irreducibly collective. He admires those products of consciousness that do not reflect a private interior essence but that, "passing through long time, have had a multitude of authors and improvers." "What we daily observe in regard to the *bon-mots* that circulate in society, — that every talker helps a story in repeating it, until, at last, from the slenderest filament of fact a good fable is constructed, . . . the legend is tossed from believer to poet, from poet to believer, everybody adding a grace or dropping a fault or rounding the form, until it gets an ideal truth."[20] Again, discursive truth achieves ideality by being communal. "Great genial power, one would almost say, consists in not being original at all; in being altogether receptive; in letting the world do all, and suffering the spirit of the hour to pass unobstructed through the mind."[21] The agent here is not the soul but the world, not spirit but "the spirit of the hour." The same holds not only for poem and fable, but for Scripture itself. The Bible is like all "religious literature, . . . a fagot of selections gathered through ages, . . . at last the work of the whole communion of worshippers."[22] "The Bible itself is like an old Cremona; it has been played upon by the devotion of thousands of years until every word and particle is public and turnable."[23] Even the Bible is not transcendent logos but an effect of the energies of mass life, one where individuality has been lost across the ages of unceasing transmission. Holy Writ is continually rewritten by the imagination as a public and collective force. It is composed of language, and "Language is a city to the building of which every human being brought a stone."[24]

The great texts, in addition to their collective or public nature, are also those which remain public, whose collective origins continue to be part of their identity and cultural reception. "Ideal truth" is that language which is not privatized and internalized, but which remains in permanent circulation and continual "metamorphosis" and which stays in the "commonwealth."[25] Great texts are they which reflect the congregated action of human history. These world-texts may be attributed to a single genius, like Shakespeare or Montaigne, but this may occur only when the author has been able to convene the multitudes. Like "every master," Shakespeare "has found his materials collected" in a "great body of stage-plays."[26] His greatness arises not simply because of his vast "sympathy with his people, and in his love of the materials he wrought in"; it lies in knowing about the people's creative precedence. "Shakespeare knew that tradition supplies a better fable than any invention can."[27] He likes how the English stage circulates "soiled and tattered manuscripts" "treated, with more or less skill, by every playwright" so that "It is now no longer possible to say who wrote them first."[28] Shakespeare is Shakespeare because he proclaims that he "did owe debts in all directions." The greatness of the text depends on its collective origin remaining apparent.[29] Possessive individualism and poetic genius obstruct each other. In Emerson's view, when we are most tempted to see poetry as depending on the poet's disavowal of all precursors in gestures of radically private originality, we must instead recognize at that precise moment that the poet's greatness arises from achieving some identity with the masses. Feeling greatness for Emerson consists of knowing that great texts are "somewhat far transcending any private enterprise!"[30] The strong reader realizes that fully poetic meaning is not only different from private property, but exists in conflict with it. The identity based in utterance is most powerful when most visibly public.

Emerson is doing more than acknowledging that meaning, which once seemed dependent on spiritual creation and/or imitation, is in fact based on social consensus. He describes a poetic communitarianism where private possession ceases merely to be in productive tension with public exchange in order to suggest that meaning entails the relinquishing of possession and even of separate identity.

Accordingly, Emerson defines the poetic sign differently than he defines a (possessible) commodity. In *Nature*'s chapter on "Commodity," Emerson says that "The private poor man hath cities, ships, canals, bridges, built for him. . . . the human race run on his errands . . . the human race read and write of all that happens, for him . . . nations repair his wrongs . . . and cut a path for him."[31] Here Emerson assumes that the private "man" and his "errand" preexist the general circulation of goods and services. Emerson says almost the opposite about signs: regardless of the variations in his sense of the sign's "origin," whether divine or social, it is external to and prior to the private man. Signs take their meaning in the public sphere and they remain there. They are not commodities which have a use value established prior to exchange. Nor do they have an exchange value which is settled by the market, by a general consensus, where this supposedly reflects the sum of a number of private judgments. For Emerson, anticipating Wittgenstein, there is simply no such thing as a private language. He combines transcendentalist spiritualism with a strong sense of the collective history that creates culture, as when he says that "genial power" means letting "the world do all, and suffering the spirit of the hour to pass unobstructed through the mind."[32] The mind must be receptive to Spirit, but it is not the absolute but "the spirit of the hour." The individual does not own and does not even hold meaning as part of himself, for this can belong only to the world. Rather than saying that Emersonian signs remain public and collective, it would be more accurate to say that they undermine individualism's distinction between private and public. A sign is not something that can circulate in society but can also be held as private property. The sign is both public and private in that its ownership remains a form of social lending to the individual. The title, however, stays public. Poetic property is a social and not a personal or natural fact.

Emerson rejects a simple individualism of possessive autonomy. There is something radically democratic about a realm of freedom that imagines the transformation of private ownership of truth into common knowledge and collaborative creation. It is this radical element in American pragmatism that rejects the contrast between freedom of thought and public forces, and which sees individuality expressed (even to itself) only through its collective being. Freedom and determinism, for this pragmatism, cannot be mapped onto the private and the political, for they exist in a much more complicated interconnection. Rather than finding intellectual freedom in private escape from the market and from social forces generally, Emerson assumes that language exists only in a common history that the individual is always within. The poet affirms the polity as the source of its living agency — affirms generically democratic relations as the principle by which poetic self-making encounters its own inspiration.

3. The Market in Quotations

Whatever amounts to a liberalization in Emerson's later, antifoundational understanding of meaning involves this collective element. But Emerson is also under considerable cultural pressure to attach meaning to individual consciousness. Does he successfully resist this? The issue appears in Emerson's later understanding of quotation.

Quotation has a two-sided function in "Quotation and Originality": "Next to the originator of a good sentence is the first quoter of it. Many will read the book before one thinks of quoting a passage. As soon as he has done this, that line will be quoted east and west. Then there are great ways of borrowing. Genius borrows nobly."[33] Genius quotes and borrows like everybody else, and the act of quotation issues less in possession than in dissemination: the outcome of the individual intervention is the line being "quoted east and west." Some pages later Emerson says something different. "There remains the indefeasible persistency of the individual to be himself. . . . He must draw the elements into him . . . However received, these elements pass into the substance of his constitution, will be assimilated, and tend always to form, not a partisan, but a possessor of truth. To all that can be said of the preponderance of the Past, the single word Genius is a sufficient reply. The divine resides in the new. The divine never quotes, but is, and creates. . . . And what is Originality? It is being, being one's self."[34] The cited "elements" are here not passed on but internalized. They join "the substance of his constitution." They render him a "possessor" and not a "borrower" on equal terms with all the other speakers. As Emerson continues, borrowing from the world becomes possession and this in turn transmutes into creation out of one's separate essence. Emerson insists on a distinction between private and public that at other times he undermines. The private is something separate and prior to the public. Indeed, Emerson sometimes uses the act of reading or quoting as the occasion to reflect on how each individual precedes all of history: "The ministrations of books, and of other minds, are a whiff of smoke to that most private reality with which [the poet] has conversed."[35]

Emerson here adapts his more unusual description of borrowing to a culture rooted in private property. Quotation is of course a borrowing, but now it requires no return. Those debts to common usage and collective genius were really only debts to ourselves all along. This is why Emerson says that this debt does not make us bankrupt. The poet cites the common sense because he regards it as a version of what he already has. One quotes because one sees in the words of another the "common sense." Quotable language, in this view, expresses the deep elements of our common humanity, and lies waiting to be used like nature or some other public resource. However and whenever one quotes, one takes possession of what is most essential about oneself.

Emerson invokes Goethe as an exemplar of this procedure. "What would remain to me if this art of appropriation were derogatory to genius? Every one of my writings has been furnished to me by a thousand different persons, a thousand things: wise and foolish have brought me, without suspecting it, the offering of their thoughts, faculties, and experience. My work is an aggregation of beings taken from the whole of Nature; it bears the name of Goethe."[36] Goethe acknowledges that genius arises from "a thousand different persons." He grants their difference as well, distinguishing between "wise and foolish" and assuming the variability of the unnumbered contributions. But in a sudden, second move, Goethe says that all these contributions will, once he assembles them, be called "Goethe." He does not mean that "Goethe" expresses the preexisting essence of a thing, but that he will be applying his own name to an "aggregation" of disparate beings who differ from him; he acknowledges the other's autonomous circulation by identifying the naming or the use of the name as a quotation. The otherness of the phrase is granted and appropriated at the same time. The phrase is identified as originating in the public domain even as it is taken private. Contrary to the tendency in Emerson that I outlined above, which is to insist on the permanent independence of the public sphere (as poetic tradition) from all individual claims, Emerson here uses Goethe to describe commonwealth as a private resource. Quoting turns out to be something like homesteading, for which the Western lands were public but considered empty and unable to signify anything in a civilized polity until they were converted to private use.

Accordingly, Emerson has contempt for quotation which fails to be appropriated into one's own private property by announcing the name of the actual author of the lines. "Quotation confesses inferiority" when it is a direct quotation in which a statement bears quotation marks, retains the name of another as its original author; this signals that the quoters do "not recognize their own."[37] Quotation displays superiority when it means borrowing without acknowledgment, when it is indirect quotation that speaks the words of the other as though they had all along really been one's own. To say "Only an inventor knows how to borrow" is to say that only an inventor knows how to redefine the quotation as a product of his or her deepest self. Once fully appropriated, the quotation becomes originality. The great poet is like the rich man, described elsewhere by Emerson as one "who can avail himself of all men's faculties. He is the richest man who knows how to draw a benefit from the labors of the greatest number of men."[38] Quotation, like market circulation, is more than a series of transactions. It does not mean borrowing in order to return, but concealing the borrowing in order to accumulate. Quotation means to plagiarize and nobly steal or, more accurately, to privatize a public sign/commodity in the routine and sanctioned way in which the individual's private sphere effortlessly absorbs collective resources, whether these be thoughts or labors.[39]

The free market is not capitalist in itself; locally or self-regulated transactions are compatible with many different patterns of ownership and economic relations. The market under capitalism must do more than exchange, however, for it must form capital through a well-known process of accumulation. The capitalist market must extract value in circulation, must prevent it from circulating endlessly. Rather than tending toward a homeostasis of random distribution, of distributions endlessly revised under the antifoundationalist ideal, value must be absorbed, condensed, and monopolized for it to become capital in the first place. Value's freedom of movement must be restricted for it to become capital. By acknowledging this kind of appropriation, Emerson associates the formation of cultural capital with ambiguously plagiaristic quotation.

Emerson's liberalism appears here as oblivious to any incompatibility between private accumulation and public freedom. He insists on the two tendencies at the same time—the sovereignty of public, collective culture and culture as private property. His liberal, dialectical understanding admits the social nature of subjectivity while insisting on the ongoing importance of individual imagination. An activity like quotation becomes a problem when it reflects "an aggressive, 'capitalistic' ethos of mastery over nature,"[40] but otherwise, it is liberal communitarianism showing up in a theory of poetry—private property governed by a sense of the common good. From his liberal perspective, Emerson's return from a communism of linguistic agency to a market notion of private possession not only reflects his actual society but also links his utopian idealism to the individualism that makes it so valuable. "Quotation and Originality" develops the last two steps of the three-step structure that we have seen elsewhere in his work: it approaches a socialist idealism that elevates the collective sovereignty of the people over private individuals; but in the midst of its emphasis on the common wealth and shared humanity, it simultaneously insists on a higher truth in the "organic motion of the soul."[41] Can these be reconciled?

4. Free Market Despotism

I've argued that the third step of that structure marked Emerson's authoritarian foundationalism, but this would seem to be repudiated by the presence of the market in his mature work. A writer may acquire the quotation as his or her property, but this acquisition is supposedly balanced by the receptive nature of language use which rests on free circulation and exchange, that is, on quoting and borrowing. Again, the market is antifoundationalist: the poet understands that meaning lacks foundations and arises from its own circulation and play, and sees that taking possession of one's meanings is indissociable from their ongoing circulation. Making language one's own is a form of liberty which co-exists with reciprocal lending and borrowing through a free and open process of circulation which excludes no one. Private property, once de-essentialized by the market, appears to manifest the reciprocity of private and public that underwrites American freedom. Spirit becomes the market, and the logos is demystified into the individual choices of multitudes over time brought together in the market. Authoritarian command is replaced by liberal exchange.

Liberalism is often popularly associated with statist regulation and rigid bureaucracy. This aspect finds its major compensation in antifoundationalism, whose popular approval would seem proportional to antifoundationalism's resemblance to a chamber of commerce-type free-market economy, "one under which the instruments of production are privately owned by many individuals; where the determination of what is produced, and by what means, and for what distribution, is made at the marketplace through the price mechanism. Under the free market, the consumer ultimately governs and directs production."[42] In Rorty's understanding of liberal cultural behavior, antifoundationalism replaces essentialist decisions about truth: "It is central to the idea of a liberal society that, in respect to words as opposed to deeds, persuasion as opposed to force, anything goes. This openmindedness . . . should be fostered for its own sake. *A liberal society is one which is content to call 'true' whatever the upshot of such encounters turns out to be.*"[43] Emerson's third step, rather than crushing individual autonomy (step 1) or democratic sovereignty (step 2), apparently provides the venue for their reconciliation. This venue is not the political arena, but the marketplace.

This idea that Emerson finds a vital center depends on seeing his liberal position as stressing collective development and individuality and then refusing to choose between them. But, to repeat, does the market forum of exchange and appropriation help sustain traits of individuality such as autonomy, originality, or difference?

In his Neoplatonic moments, Emerson tied discourse to a process of imitation rather than to individual invention. But imitation dominates *market* poetics as well. Emerson's later theory of language revolves around quotation rather than wild inspiration or reflective solitude. Quotation establishes meaning as a relation between two signs. Unlike other types of linguistic relation, quotation links the later sign not to something different but to something the same.

This function of quotation is not mysterious. Using and appropriating quotation requires an inaugural imitation very similar to the old-fashioned imitation of a natural essence. One's power of appropriation rests on the power to follow the rule of resemblance. Signs can be traded only when they can stand for each other. Like commodities, they are always traded at a fair value in the sense that they are exchanged at the moment when they are equivalent or interchangeable. The relation between two signs lacks foundations for the later Emerson in that it does not inhere in an external or spiritual reality but changes along with changes in public conventions and uses. Yet this does not mean that the reference from one sign to the other is any less dependent on an equivalence between them. The sign now imitates another sign rather than a Neoplatonic origin, but it is no less an act of imitation. Quotation goes well beyond taking inspiration in the exactitude that it requires. The quoted sign is predetermined and correspondent through the semiotic matching.

This matching also implies an inner resemblance between writer and precursor, since the need and even the capacity to quote means that the spirit of the precursor is already in the possession of the second poet. The act of individual possession is based on an identity between the spirits in question. As Emerson noted in his journal, "It plays into my chapter of Quotation to find this necessity of repetition. If man takes any step, exerts any volition, initiates anything, no matter what, it is law of fate that another man shall repeat it, shall simply echo it. The Egyptian legend got this tyrannical currency, ploughed itself into the Hebrew captives."[44]

All this sheds new light on why explicit "quotation confesses inferiority." It is not that it shows how unoriginal you are, but that it makes you too original, too different — it distinguishes you from your source. Borrowing without attribution, on the other hand, maintains your identity and interchangeability with the source. When, in the spirit of plagiarism, you repress the name attached to a quotation, you confirm "that truth is the property of no individual" and thus affirm priority of sameness to the self. You confirm the rule of nondeviation that founds exchange.[45]

Ungrounded exchange has no trouble generating a conserving continuity.[46] Emerson's continuing celebration of "being one's self" takes place within that system of resemblances he calls the "identity of law."[47] As a precocious antifoundationalist, Emerson can find determinism without foundations in a logic of identity that crosses fluid distances.

This does not mean, of course, that Emerson thinks of culture as the repetition of the same meanings from beginning to end. Differences, swerves, tropes, and originality generate unceasing change. Nonetheless, he locates originality not with the poet's will but with the interruption of the will by an unseen power. The individual certainly has an "indefeasible persistency . . . to be himself," but individuality is not properly the source of Genius. "The divine resides in the new. The divine never quotes, but is, and creates."[48] Emerson works divinity around into the place of agency, and sandwiches allusions to the self between them. "Genius," after all, "is in the first instance . . . the capacity of receiving just impressions from the external world," and "original force" enters not as invention but as "right distribution and expression." Emerson, as I've had other occasions to remark, is astonishingly tireless in pairing each outburst of anarchic selfhood with a preformatting receptivity. Near the end of "Quotation and Originality" he says, "'Tis certain that thought has its own proper motion, and the hints which flash from it, the words overheard at unawares by the free mind, are trustworthy and fertile when obeyed and not perverted to low and selfish account."[49] The mind's freedom is the freedom to overhear and to obey. When something interrupts the market's identity between signs, it is divine inspiration.

Emerson's antifoundationalism supports the same system of authority as did his Neoplatonic foundationalism. In the late language essay, "Poetry and Imagination" (1872), Emerson revolutionizes and retains the vision of language use in *Nature*. There, Emerson's three degrees of language use had expressed three distinct levels of being:

1. Every word is originally "borrowed from some material appearance."

2. Every "state of the mind can only be described by presenting that natural appearance as its picture."[50]

3. "A [material] Fact is the end or last issue of spirit."[51]

Decades later, and in a metamorphized America, he moves through a similar pattern in "Poetry and Imagination."

1a. "The perception of matter is made the common sense."[52] Common sense and common language arise from material fact.

2*a*. Nature is "steeped in thought, [does] everywhere express thought."

3*a*. Throughout material life, in all its variety, "nothing [is] fast but those invisible cords which we call laws, on which all is strung."[53]

As in *Nature,* Emerson traces words and thoughts to nature (1*a* and 2*a*), and then grounds nature in spirit. This anchoring permits a characteristic move: he first asserts "the independent action of the mind."[54] Then in the same sentence he notes that "this closer inspection of the laws of matter" shows "a certain tyranny which springs up in his own thoughts," a tyranny which is really the "Identity of law."[55] In late as well as in early Emerson, troping does not manifest the individual's intellectual mobility but the most accurate mimesis of the law from which thought and matter take their being.[56] Significantly, Emerson's chief trope is metonymy: far from forming a new sense, this trope consists of "seeing the same sense in things so diverse."[57] In the marketplace of ideas, the isolated mind is never off a leash woven of "invisible cords." Market exchanges of signs offer the friendly despotism of equivalences, equivalences that, in Emerson's view, are what make culture's existence possible.

Its logic of equivalences allows a cultural market to operate as Spirit—continual circulation is governed by uniform order. As Emerson notes in "Culture," "culture must reinforce from higher influx the empirical skills of eloquence, or of politics, or of trade, and the useful arts. There is a certain loftiness of thought and power to marshal and adjust particulars, which can only come from an insight of their whole connection. The orator who has once seen things in their divine order, will never quite lose sight of this, and will come to affairs as from a higher ground."[58] Markets are not simply the sum of individual movements but are "webs of relations" in which difference exists within an encompassing resemblance that reflects higher law. As a web of economy, the market in quotations is another example of how "relation and connection are not somewhere and sometimes, but everywhere and always. The divine order does not stop where their sight stops. The friendly power works on the same rules, in the next farm, and the next planet."[59] Emerson sometimes puts connectedness into motion as "rotation," but to similar effect. "The universality being hindered in its primary form, comes in the secondary form of *all sides:* the points come in succession to the meridian, and by the speed of rotation, a new whole is formed. . . . Really, all things and persons are related to us, but according to our nature, they act on us not at once, but in succession."[60]

Quotation is like the exchange of goods — an endless succession of relations that expresses deep harmony and resemblance.

The market enfolds autonomy in unity. Where it fails to conserve unity among its circulating signs, Emerson rejects it. He laments systems of competition, conflict, and scarcity, for in these "Nobody is glad in the gladness of another, and our system is one of war, of an injurious superiority."[61] Superiority injures when it reflects disunity. A quotation's expression of equivalence eliminates this problem by affirming unity. It affirms market relations, but only when the market is regulated rather than fully competitive. A competitive market does not transmit common meaning or value but expels one meaning regardless of whatever underlying connection it might have to another. Emerson's later work shows great skill at purifying the cultural market of the kind of competition which suggests the absence of governing laws. Poetic equivalence supersedes competitive difference: "in these new fields there is room: here are no self-esteems, no exclusions."[62] Quotation is a form of relation to a powerful other that replaces the differentiating superiority and excess of self with the useful superiority of lawful precedence and continuity. Liberalism's esteem for circulation, where equity is proportional to exchange, is in a symbiotic relationship with the order of uniformity.

For Emerson, then, markets homogenize multiplicity rather than underwrite autonomy. Though this idea may be strange to us, it was familiar in Emerson's progressive Whig circles. It was also remarkably consistent across time. In 1837, not long after the publication of *Nature* and its "Language" chapter, Daniel Webster focused on exchange as "establishing one commerce for all the States." "Every man, Sir, who looks over this vast country, and contemplates the commercial connection of its various parts, must see the great importance that this exchange should be cheap and easy." To sustain this fully national market, Webster rejects local self-regulation and other market "freedoms" (like independent state banks) in favor of a federally sponsored uniform currency. Such forms of authority, he tells his adversaries, are "not so much *regulations* of commerce, in a strict sense, as they are aids and assistances to commerce." Webster makes no attempt at all to appease Democrats or other laissez-faire individualists by celebrating the market's gifts to personal freedom. For him, a commercial market must enforce unity rather than freedom; its means is not free contract but a uniform currency, one in which a central power guarantees the mutual resemblance, the perfect correspondence, of all signs of value.[63]

In 1874, Emerson's acquaintance Edward Atkinson developed the
same interest in the market as a uniform government. Parties enter exchange "because both parties gain by it, or because both parties expect
to gain," but regarding the common medium or tokens of exchange,
dollars themselves, parties demand "only uniformity in their value or
estimation." Sound currency expresses the unifying power of open markets: "We are members one of another, and each works for all, with
hand or brain; the money was as needful to each and all as the miner's
pick and pan . . . and it works as much harm to each and all if the money
be bad. . . ." National life is not the sum of countless free choices but
the result of market uniformity. Where power has become too centralized, the cure is, again, not deregulation of individual behavior but "a
more widely extended system of banking, and the multiplication of
banking offices if not of banks themselves."[64]

Webster and Atkinson together expressed the extent to which, for
their kind of business liberalism, the market in America had always functioned as a corporate body. It provides unified governance through a
decentralized extension of sameness. Market circulation serves to refine
this governance far beyond the crude forms of sovereignty, inferiority,
or passionate obedience of more authoritarian circles. Although the
usual vision of the free market imagines its agents unconstrained by
history and living entirely in the immediate moment of choice, a commercial structure, like an "extended system of banking," uses movement
to establish habitual and even formal institutional relations of influence
and command. These relations, though they may be codified, often act
in the diffuse manner of a commercial "common culture." Emerson's
use of quotation makes the question of control much more explicit, for
the continual exchange of shared meanings generates a cultural tradition
which governs further exchange. For all three men, authority is not rein-
vented anew with each transaction but is embedded in the principle of
uniformity itself. This authority lacks an origin or center, and yet is as
determinate as any overt sovereign. Webster and Atkinson imagine that
a uniform system will stabilize an arena in which a variety of choices can
be devised, though in practice this system eliminates numerous local
(and locally controlled) arrangements. Emerson's equivalents, however,
do not simply make the background but influence the actual content of
culture; they regulate the concepts that coexist with the choices. The
market's antifoundationalism supports its corporate sovereignty.

With this in mind, I would like to reopen the question of how Emerson's later language theory connects to the three-step paradigm I have
outlined: Emerson affirms competitive, autonomous individuality, sub-

sumes this within self-regulated group life which in turn yields to hierarchical and unappealable authority. Since antifoundationalists believe in
nothing if not their contrast with foundationalists and associate authoritarianism with the latter, it would seem that Emerson's rejection of his
earlier foundationalism has moved him toward democratic governance.
But the absolute law that subsumed other elements in Emerson's third
step has been replaced not by market movement but by mobile market
union. Absent an insistence on diverging or creating, quotation does
little to diminish the control of the preexisting law as represented by the
quoted material, and indeed passes it on without the need of a sovereign
logos. Antifoundationalism updates the power relations installed by
foundational claims.

The present state of market corporatism continues to cast suspicion
on the power of antifoundationalism to critique foundational power in
a liberal society. It's hard to miss the compatibility between revolution
and uniformity wrought by globalized markets—revolution in industries and national production, and uniformity in standards and instruments of authority. One symptom has been the anxiety—particularly
among Emerson's moderate liberal male heirs—over the loss of an allegedly existing common culture that supposedly harmonized an earlier
American society. Another is the fatalism, if not the eagerness, with
which a similar group of relatively progressive policy jocks face the
standardizing effects of globalized production, to say nothing of global
media culture. President Bill Clinton's first address to the United Nations suggested that the United States should support "market democracy" until it has united all nations in their fundamental socioeconomic
values. The market's maximization of flexibility without foundations
also maximizes uniformity across national and cultural borders, and
there is no reason to think that more antifoundationalism will suddenly
begin to diminish the coercive founding narratives that it backhand-
edly supports.

Sovereignty without grounds: this rule distinguishes our officially
postauthoritarian society. Accordingly, in his later revisions of his third
step, Emerson was neither liberal nor authoritarian but a combination
of the two. Because the market determines a law that claims to be preestablished, coherent, even self-identical, its operations are authoritarian.[65] But, once again, it is a liberal authoritarian power that does not
present itself as law and order so much as free mobility, and that can be
associated with the transition from tyrannical to hegemonic forms of
power that were well under way by the nineteenth century.

In spite of this, it is worth recalling that Emerson's interest in market circulation, uniformity, and privatization of public resources is only one of two options present in his work. The other is the tradition founded and refounded and founded again, each time through varying conjunctures of disparate elements. This is an ungrounded activity, but it differs from antifoundationalism's stress on the mobility of market exchange by acknowledging the immobility of the actors, their difference from each other, and the irregularity of the nonsystem which they produce as their "culture."

The collective itself is foreshadowed as what cannot be assimilated through the logic of equivalence. It comprehends those parts of society that cannot be exchanged or generally circulated because they live out history in the differences and mutual otherness of their positions and experience. This public history consists of irreducible conflicts and untranslatable differences that are not represented or subsumed by that from which they differ. Market exchange allows transmission only of that which can find its equivalent or near twin. Through quotation, the history of poetry loses not only its capacity but its need to present a heterogeneous public system, and makes history out of those ideas which are interchangeable. Literary and philosophical canons crystallize the repeatability that perpetuates fluctuating equivalence. Emerson periodically feels what has been lost. Contrary to a common assumption, it is not the market that represents what Foucault called the "multiplicity of power relations" and that therefore, being full of "disjunctions and contradictions," cannot be likened to a system of domination.[66] Rather, multiplicity appears in what the market cannot readily identify — those mass utterances not picked up through the soul-making and canon-building functions of quotation.

Emerson's treatment of poetic language shows the antifoundationalist poet affirming the laws. But his antifoundationalism is finally unable entirely to reduce collective utterance to exchange — the English stage, common speech, "tradition," the "devotion of thousands," "somewhat far transcending any private enterprise!"[67] Most of the time, Emerson sanctions that process by which individualism comes to accept the market as friend rather than enemy and becomes submissive in the process. He encourages the movement from what I have called the second to the third stage of corporate individuality, in which a self-controlled group abandons control to higher powers. But sometimes, Emerson describes language as representing an agency that is not reducible to a few "representatives," and that requires its own distinct appearance. The substantive importance of this collective agency, modest as it may be, lies in its vision of transactions between nonequivalents, transactions which cannot be privatized on the basis of their purported equivalence with one's own being. Emerson's sketchy but recurrent gestures beyond the market reflect liberalism's repressed longings and reflect badly upon the antifoundationalism that does the repressing.

CHAPTER
SEVEN

Corporatism and the Genesis
of Liberal Racism

1. Latter-Day Liberalism

Like many of his peers, Emerson regarded the Civil War as the defeat of despotism and a triumph for liberty. He was so happy with these effects that some readers fear his delight may have damaged his mind. Maurice Gonnaud writes, "in Emerson's eyes the war became nearly identical with the grand cosmic operation of providence, so that when the north had won he found himself incapable of recovering his independence of judgment. With its hopes too abundantly gratified, his thought could not resist the illusion of security."[1] The gratification was indeed great, for he felt that tyranny henceforth would be blocked and liberty guaranteed by the restoration of the moral law in national politics. But equally great, in the view of most readers, was the new banality of his work.

Emerson's postwar writing is certainly disappointing in its lack of complex thought about the still unresolved questions of freedom and democracy that had haunted his 1850s thinking. On the other hand, his later thoughts about society add an air of finality to his views from before the war, which they strongly resemble. Given the consuming nature of his commitment to antislavery and national destiny, it should hardly be surprising that the war's vindication of his beliefs would encourage some complacency in their reiteration. But his response to the end of the war is neither unpredictable nor redundant. Rather than attributing it to age or excess satisfaction, we could more appropriately see it as an ongoing response to still unfolding postwar conflicts. The war hardly produced the end of history, and Emerson, rather than failing to respond, was responding actively, and in responding, was disseminating, during the period of his greatest fame, his kind of liberal common sense.

Given his long history with the idea of "self-reliance," we might have expected Emerson's emancipation rhetoric to be full of enthusiasm for the new future of black labor and black fulfillment. "Build, therefore, your own world," the great saying of *Nature,* would, in the emancipation context, have a whole new life. So would the old comparison of the common and the great, in which the relations, after a moral revolution, are reversed: "All that Adam had, all that Caesar could, you have and can do. . . . Line for line and point for point, your dominion is as great as theirs, though without fine names."[2] When, if not through black emancipation, could such a thought have achieved perfection, since it would then form an epitaph for the Caesars of the South, and criticize in advance the rise of the new Caesars of American industry? And yet none of this expectation of a self-created, remade world returns on the evening of emancipation. The rebirth of self-reliance for African Americans is, in Emerson's later work, subordinated to more pressing themes.

Emancipation had placed self-reliance in a historically momentous perspective. Classical liberalism, as noted earlier, is often characterized by its sense of a tension between liberty and equality. Black emancipation made American liberalism — its radical wing, at any rate — regard liberty and equality as interdependent, at least for a time. Slavery was the most vivid possible demonstration that liberty could be destroyed by equality's absence. The resentments of the defeated South threatened freedpersons' return to servitude. Racial reconstruction hinged on the belief that continuing liberty depended on a militant defense of civil equality. W. R. Brock makes the point well. While a sufficient equality was usually taken for granted as the normal outcome of the possession of personal liberties, "with the negroes this assumption could not be made: what was required was protection, maintained by enforceable law, at every point where the power of the dominant race was likely to impinge upon the weaker."[3] After Emancipation, equality was not a desirable side effect of liberty but its constituent. Small wonder, then, as Eric Foner argues, that though radicals disagreed about what equality might mean, they stood fast on "the core of the ideology — the idea of a powerful national state guaranteeing blacks equal standing in the polity and equal opportunity in a free labor economy."[4] Without equality, Emancipation would simply collapse. W. E. B. Du Bois crystallized the new linkage in his term "abolition-democracy": as democracy's expansion had required abolition, so the preservation of abolition now depended on democracy's expansion.

The simple liberal contrast between liberty and equality died in the war. Though the belief that equality was obsolete, inefficient, and immoral ran rampant in postbellum America, clear versions of this belief became increasingly "conservative." Liberal reformers, though always believing that equality could get out of hand, and certain that mobs and mass democracy endangered freedom, nonetheless established themselves in contradiction to those who saw the hierarchies of laissez-faire as entirely compatible with American ideals. Though Emerson's entire career, I've argued, shows the dependence of self-reliance on visions of collective life, this only put him ahead of his time, the time when self-reliance would, for the cultural center, openly turn on some sort of meaningful reciprocity among different segments of the polity.

This detente between liberty and equality defines white middle-class utopianism, and appears, after long absences, in those penitential recuperations from a convulsive struggle when liberalism and radicalism converge. But the fragility of this convergence cannot be attributed solely to the overwhelming power of its enemies. Such utopianism really didn't favor a future that belonged to these other forces, yet it did, and the inexorability of this process needs to be explained. The breakdown of the conjuncture of liberty and equality came partially from within and, oddly, at the moment in which their political and cultural momentum seemed at long last under way. This internal breakdown was indispensable to the undoing of Reconstruction, and operated above and beyond the deeds of its external opponents and the thousand cuts received from the buffetings of national politics.

What unraveled the liberty-equality link forged by Emancipation? The excellent historiography of Reconstruction favors a cluster of three sources. First, in the background, lie the limitations of nineteenth-century understandings of equality in general. These stress equality "*in* the eyes of God, *under* the law, and *of* opportunity" without demanding equality of outcome.[5] The other two common sources are the rejection of racial equality and a faith in free-labor, free-market solutions to all questions of social development. Andrew Johnson combined these last two beliefs in an 1864 address, where he defined the recently freed "Negro"'s "political freedom" as "liberty to work. . . . If he can rise by his own energies, in the name of God, let him rise. In saying this, I do not argue that the Negro race is equal to the Anglo-Saxon. . . . If the Negro is better fitted for the inferior condition of society, the laws of nature will assign him there!"[6] Johnson expects Negro inferiority and looks to the natural laws of market success to settle the issue. What one scholar has said about postwar black economic history is applicable to postwar U.S. social and cultural change more generally. It "makes sense only when interpreted as an interplay of two systems of behavior: a competitive economic system and a coercive racial system."[7]

A misleading story can be constructed from these undeniable factors. We could think that liberty and equality, though esteemed in the bosom of liberalism, remained somewhat underdeveloped and mixed with errors. So equality remained identified with, say, equality of opportunity or equality before the law; liberty was too often linked to laissez-faire economics; but all in all, the general direction was toward the enhancement of egalitarian freedoms. The postwar Emerson would then display nothing more than an excessively complacent optimism when he said that working for "justice, love, freedom, knowledge, utility" means to "ride in Olympian chariots by putting our works in the path of the celestial circuits," thereby allowing them to "harness also evil agents, the powers of darkness, and force them to serve against their will the ends of wisdom and virtue."[8] This reading assumes that Emerson desired freedom and love, but unfortunately sought them through a laissez-faire means that paralleled those used to justify the racial and economic inequity, that, for most of the postwar period, increased in matching step.

The present study has offered quite a different explanation. Emerson's thought, representative of and influential in the liberal reform center, did not simply lend halfway support to but actively opposed substantial forms of liberty and equality. His beliefs in laissez-faire and black inferiority arose not simply from contingent impurities but from deep and unsuspected allegiances to authoritarian elements in liberal order.

In this chapter I will argue that the cultural center, intellectually close to transcendental liberalism, rejected a free market in favor of a corporatist understanding of natural law; that this transition depended on a liberal form of racist thinking; and that this combination of corporate and liberal-racist understandings of law depends on Emerson's sort of submissive individualism.

2. Markets and Corporations

Race must be regarded as an essential part of the concentration and privatization of economic power. But how do these features of U.S. life go together? Is it simply a tragic accident that our ostensibly democratic, individualistic free-market system has been plagued with irratio-

nal racism? Is the answer to minimize racism in favor of the nondiscrim-
inating valuations of consumption, circulation, and trade?

This latter has long been a belief essential to liberalism, which argues
that market ideals and racism are completely separable, even if the market sometimes fails to oppose racism. Moreover, the market, if freed up,
can ease racism and diminish its scope. The market offers an equality of
opportunity for the self-reliant that will yield racially just outcomes once
some surface racism is wiped away. Civil rights will provide a truly color-
blind equality of opportunity and produce a "good enough" cross-racial
social equality down the road.[9] In such a case, rough equality will be
achieved without cumbersome and controversial government intervention and its divisive political conflicts. The market will provide the
mechanism that decides which individuals become equal, at what time,
and to what extent without penalizing anyone for their group identity.
The strategy continues to this day, as many reform liberals advocate
color-blind public investment programs on the theory that these will
avoid white backlash while doing a better job of lifting racialized communities than would race-targeted funds.

Northern reform liberals after the Civil War claimed that freedom,
freedom for everyone, black and white alike, "meant not economic autonomy or the right to call upon the aid of the activist state, but the
ability to compete in the marketplace and enjoy protection against an
overbearing government."[10] The market possessed a wisdom, offered a
freedom, expressed a tie to natural law that political activity almost always destroyed. Liberals, sometimes dragging radicals in their wake,
were uncertain about plans to remake Southern social relations without
waiting for manufacturing capital and trade to do the work for them.
They preferred to

> cultivate the moral attributes of honesty, hard work, and frugality . . . The
> inexorable operation of natural economic laws would insure the triumph
> of thrifty, industrious freedmen over adversity. . . . Political stability
> would be maintained sufficiently to facilitate the influx of Northern capi-
> tal freely and with slight risk. The South then would be integrated into
> the nation's economy to serve the manufacturing North both as a source
> of raw materials and as a market for finished goods. . . . Political stability,
> to the Republican helmsmen, meant that Southerners must defer to the
> national leadership of Northern politicians and their allies in the busi-
> ness community.[11]

Capital and trade were wiser than any feat of social legislation.

As I noted in the previous chapter, Emerson periodically makes his essays ring with a call to free-market commitment. Writing in "Wealth," the third essay in *The Conduct of Life,* he says,

> Wealth brings with it its own checks and balances. The basis of political economy is non-interference. The only safe rule is found in the self-adjusting meter of demand and supply. Do not legislate. Meddle, and you snap the sinews with your sumptuary laws. Give no bounties: make equal laws: secure life and property, and you need not give alms. Open the doors of opportunity to talent and virtue, and they will do themselves justice, and property will not be in bad hands. In a free and just commonwealth, property rushes from the idle and imbecile, to the industrious, brave, and persevering.
>
> The laws of nature play through trade, as a toy-battery exhibits the effects of electricity. The level of the sea is not more surely kept, than is the equilibrium of value in society, by the demand and supply: and artifice or legislation punishes itself, by reactions, gluts, and bankruptcies.[12]

Emerson twice identifies "legislation" as a violation of natural law, while these laws are expressed and preserved in untrammeled trade. Trade in turn quantifies justice in the form of property. Poverty and prosperity are accurate indices of corruption and virtue. Emerson's official views on this as an economic question changed little during his life, and at nearly every point they conformed to laissez-faire orthodoxy.[13] He opposed cruelty and suffering for others, but never modified his vision of the natural economy of market relations to justify democratically determined public-sector intervention. As he noted quite accurately in his journal after the war, "my faith in freedom of trade, as the rule, returns always."[14] Trade, or natural law, takes precedence over legislation, or public sovereignty.

When Emerson's thoughts turned to Reconstruction, his wishes for justice were genuine and strong but showed the same intent to trace racial change to free trade and free labor. In Reconstruction he sought an end to "false relations," which would occur

> only when, at last, so many parts of the country as can combine on an equal & moral contract, — not to protect each other in polygamy, or in kidnapping, or in eating men, — but in humane & just activities, — only so many can combine firmly & durably.
>
> I speak the speech of an idealist. I say let the rule be right. If the theory is right, it is not so much matter about the facts. . . . All our action now is new & unconstitutional, & necessarily so. To bargain or treat at all with the rebels, to make arrangements with them about exchange of prisoners or hospitals, or truces to bury the dead, all unconstitutional & enough to drive a strict constructionist out of his wits. Much more in our future

action touching peace, any & every arrangement short of forcible subjugation of the rebel country, will be flat disloyalty, on our part.

Then how to reconstruct. I say, this time, go to work right. Go down
to the pan, see that your works turn on a jewel. Do not make an impossible mixture. . . .

Leave slavery out. Since . . . God is God, & nothing satisfies all men
but justice, let us have that, & let us stifle our prejudices against commonsense & humanity, & agree that every man shall have what he honestly
earns, and, if he is a sane & innocent man, have an equal vote in the state,
and a fair chance in society.

And I, speaking in the interest of no man & no party, but simply as a
geometer of his forces, say that the smallest beginning, so that it is just,
is better & stronger than the largest that is not quite just.[15]

Though Emerson sounds like a radical Republican, he is not calling to
replace slavery with racial reconstruction but with open markets. Free
contract prevails, and a new order can be erected on equal opportunity
for "every man [to] have what he honestly earns." Emerson regarded
these as nonpartisan ideas.

In a wartime note to himself, Emerson summed this up by saying,
"History of Liberty / He is free who owns himself."[16] Freedom is self-
ownership, and the end of slavery means the end of the violation of the
most fundamental right to property — property in oneself. At Boston's
Jubilee celebration of the Emancipation Proclamation, Emerson wrote
a "Boston Hymn" which read, in part:

> Pay ransom to the owner
> And fill the bag to the brim.
> Who is the owner? The slave is owner,
> And ever was. Pay him.[17]

Emancipation meant emancipation into self-ownership. Slavery stole
the property that is the slave's labor and it stole the slave's property in
himself. The antidote to slavery, then, was its possessive opposite: self-
reliance defined as self-ownership and the possession of one's productive
work. Civil rights and equality before the law must enhance this kind
of self-reliance. Attempts to legislate social relations would need to be
designed not to interfere with one's right to property in oneself. Reconstruction would only work if it proceeded in accordance with the moral
law of property in person.

An 1868 editorial in the *Nation* spelled out these ideas by advising
freedpersons to seek success only through individual competition. "The
great burden which weights the negroes in the [foot] race is one which

neither Government nor philanthropists can remove, and that is the
want of all the ordinary claims to social respectability. . . . The negro
race must, in short, win a good social position in the way other races
have won it; and when it has its roll of poets, orators, scholars, soldiers,
and statesmen to show, people will greatly respect it; but not till then,
no matter how many novels are composed in its honor or how many
sermons are preached against 'the sin of caste.'"[18] Postbellum liberalism
returned again and again to this idea that freed individual achievement,
and it alone, would dissolve caste. Whatever Emerson's interest in intersubjectivity, race encouraged him to combine it with liberalism's classical
preoccupation not just with the right to but the redemptive power of
property incentives and private initiative.

The market, then, served as a neutral matrix that allowed all free individuals to demonstrate their attainments and express their real natures.
In Emerson's vision, this led to a spontaneous democracy of natural
equals. Even in 1870, he was writing as though Jefferson's rural America
underwrote an exceptional destiny. "Schelling, is called in, when Hegel
dies, to come to Berlin, & bend truth to the crotchets of the king &
rabble. Not so here. The paucity of population, the vast extent of terri-
tory, the solitude of each family & each man, allow some approximation
to the result that every citizen has a religion of his own, — is a church
by himself, — & worships & speculates in a new quite independent fashion."[19] Relations are voluntary and democratically self-regulated. No
governing power stands above. The market, in such a vision, is simply
a living and uniform principle of noninterference, which, when contact
does result, underlies the practice of gregarious liberty, a vision of contract's autonomous yet reciprocal self-determination.

But all this faith in self-ownership and free labor in a free market
collided with another economic attitude, one that, deliberately or not,
favored corporate consolidation.

Though as a resident of Concord, Emerson dwelt in the byways of
industrial civilization, he kept as abreast of business developments as
any private investor who, as in his case, depended for much of his financial support on investment success. His correspondence from the
mid-1850s on reflects a particularly steady interest in railroad companies, which pioneered many changes in corporate structure and management. Like other liberals, Emerson opposed monopoly. In 1868, he remarked in his journal that "a banker, Mr Manger, told me, that such is
the promise of the investments of the undertakers of the Pacific Railroad, that vaster fortunes will be made in this country, than were ever

amassed by private men; that men now alive will perhaps come to own a thousand millions of dollars. 'Tis well that the Constitution of the United States has forbidden entails, and the only defence of the people against this private power is from Death the Distributer."[20] Emerson was not clear about exactly how much redistribution he wanted. Among reformist, centrist opponents of monopoly abuse, this kind of ambivalent tolerance prevailed. To take one well-known example, Charles Francis Adams Jr. wrote a devastatingly critical narrative about the battle for control of the Erie Railroad, "Chapters of Erie," but also opposed restrictive legislation and, while a member of the Massachusetts railroad commission that he had helped to found, "speculated in railroad bonds and lands near proposed lines; his behavior did not appear to differ markedly from that he had condemned in 'Chapters of Erie.'"[21] Opponents of excessive corporate monopoly ended up supporting most corporate activities in part because of their belief in free-labor development. But their interest in the market and their opposition to monopoly was mixed with support for corporate governance, or, more accurately, with what I've called a corporate understanding of the link between subjectivity and law.

Liberalism's corporate thinking was compatible in a general way with a transcendentalist interest in predetermining law.[22] The "first systematic exposition of the new liberalism," in David Montgomery's view, was an 1868 legal treatise by Michigan Supreme Court Justice Thomas Cooley, which argued for a "higher moral law" "greater than the sovereignty of the people, an unwritten law which stands behind the Constitution and in the light of which the organic law must be interpreted."[23] Deploying terms that had been Emerson's lifelong touchstones, Cooley claimed that the unwritten moral law restricted both constitutional government and democracy itself. Laissez-faire social philosophy was not simply a recipe for competitive fitness but, with its deep and prior ties to an Emersonian liberal spiritualist cultural sensibility, was also a prescription for a fulfilling corporate governance of personal agency.

Emerson's liberal corporatism has a specific structure, reflected in the three-step articulation of self-reliance I first outlined in chapter 1: the rhetoric of autonomous individualism comes first and foremost as a remedy for the apparent futility of all social relations; democratic group relations complement and supplement self-reliance; but this collective agency is rapidly reinterpreted to mean individual submission to an unappealable natural or spiritual law. This latter stage translates self-reliance into what I've been calling submissive individualism: self-reliance remains a moral obligation, and group forms remain important, particularly democratic visions of marketplace contract turned into a model of general, reciprocal cooperation; but self-reliance is actually achieved through various forms of obedience and happy inferiority. The corporate individual consists of all three of these stages coexisting simultaneously, found, that is, in a coexistence that eliminates what would otherwise be a contradiction between the individual's independence and submission. Submission is folded into a hierarchical unity, in which agency and relation, steps 1 and 2, veil the rule of a providentially authoritarian law.

The practical payoff of this formation was the translation of despotism into rational management. Power would continue to flow from on high but through structures so collectivized, dispersed, and orchestral that it would seem much like the mode of the functioning of all organisms. At the same time, the structure of the business corporation was in sufficient conflict with liberalism's free-labor and free-market values to cause a large group of liberal Republicans to oppose the corporation's increasing legal latitude. A set of *Nation* editorials, almost certainly the work of its liberal editor Edwin Lawrence Godkin, nicely illustrates the means by which the cultural benefits of corporate individualism—in addition to other attractions like wealth and prosperity—helped lead reformist opponents of corporate power to consent to corporate governance of the public realm.

In the issue for June 8, 1871, Godkin strung together four commentaries: "'The New Departure'," "The Next Stage in the French Revolution," "The Labor Question in Massachusetts," and "The Borrowing Power of Corporations." Each of these pieces seeks the republican middle between the extremes of monarchy and communal self-rule, the latter recently represented by the Paris Commune. Like his fellow liberal Republican Horace Greeley, Godkin appears to distinguish between communism, which establishes an equality of property in common, and "Association," which renders cooperation and the division of labor compatible with private ownership.[24] Association is a fundamental principle of republicanism, for it unites the labor of countless hands without ceding their supervision to public government. Thus Godkin, though afraid of the "mob," could advocate profit sharing with workers as a cooperative form of "insurance against strikes."[25] By 1868, he had outlined a model of industrial partnerships between labor and management that would furnish cooperative production and social order. In 1878, Edward A. Atkinson would describe a similar middle-way association

that was neither oligarchic nor democratic: "[The] absence of communism—that is to say, inequality in respect to possession or property—
leads, as time goes on, to practical communism in consumption; that is,
to a more and more equal distribution of the products or means of
subsistence that are necessary to comfort."[26] For Godkin, corporations
could become the essence of the republic. They build "Railroads, tele-
graphs, banks, life and fire insurance," and so on, "in an age marked by
a growing indisposition to entrust to governments any powers," and
they build them through "that union and concentration of numberless
individual efforts which we describe as the principle of association."[27]
These two features of association—organizing a multitude and the priority of private to public agency—imply a third, inequality of power
and reward within the association. As in Atkinson, such inequality of
possession and wealth leads to a higher kind of distributive equality
sometime down the road. The second and third features—private governance and inequality—distinguish an association from a commune.[28]

In his editorial, "The Borrowing Power of Corporations," Godkin
sought to preserve the corporation as a healthy republican form of association by assaulting unrestricted borrowing as "corporate tyranny."
Rather than praising corporations for safeguarding economic management from meddling voters, he protested "the insufferable tyranny,
fraud, plunder, and corruption of the great corporations, who are today the masters, not the servants, of the people."[29] Tyranny arises from
the increasing separation of directors from the investors made possible
by borrowing funds. While the healthy association of the past provided
for "the control of the capital by the owners and contributors by means
of the selection of managers," the corporate board that can borrow from
large numbers of small investors breaks free from the will of those investors. The corporation, Godkin argued, is becoming "nothing but a
device by means of which a few individuals can borrow enormous sums
of money without personal responsibility."[30] In this way it was
breaching a republican social contract, and actual events, of course, bore
out Godkin's fear that the postbellum corporation possessed legal freedoms that encouraged fraud.[31] "Of all the railroad companies formed in
the United States within the last five years, not five per cent ever had
any capital of their own." The result was that self-elected directors of a
corporation could "commit a variety of acts which not one of them
would dare to do as an individual unprotected by his official character
. . . Money is borrowed in enormous sums on the security of a mort-
gage upon property which does not exist." Modern corporations are

associations which lack "control over the actions of their representatives."[32] Borrowed money, freed of the control of the lenders—the shareholders—"is used to corrupt legislators, to buy privileges, to influence judges and sustain armies of lawyers, to resist the just claims of the public." Godkin concluded by calling for the "restoration of the old original rule that the capital of an association must be furnished by the associates, and that borrowing must be restricted within very narrow limits, if not entirely prohibited."[33]

But in offering this solution, Godkin used the corporate form against a "democratic" association; he did not democratize the corporation. He was not seeking to block corporate tyranny with increased public supervision, for he assumed that capital is best left in private hands. He supported the economic power of private boards of directors, and wanted to improve this private authority by eliminating two contemporary defects. The first of these was the autonomy of directors from shareholders, for corruption ensues when directors "are responsible as directors only to themselves as stockholders, and as stockholders they are responsible to nobody," since they are stockholders who have often not even "invested capital in the enterprise."[34] But Godkin wished to restore the priority not of uncorrupted individual judgment but of the impartial laws of profit and loss. With one's own money on the line, decisions are effectively made by the logic of business itself. The best decisions are those which most perfectly conform to this logic as applied to specific economic conditions. Corrupt directors are those who possess a power to make their own decisions, whether to rob their own investors (as happened continuously) or to act for the "common good" without regard to profit. Godkin certainly had excellent reasons to desire better controls over corporate activities, but the control consisted of reimposing the iron laws of profit (unimpaired by fraud and malfeasance) on directors who were too self-reliant.

The second defect of private boards was an excessive populism. While Godkin certainly disliked boards which had achieved oligarchical detachment from their investors, his cure was not to enhance the directoral power of a multitude of small investors but to cast the multitudes out of the corporation. Borrowing was not so bad when it drew mostly on "great capitalists, wealthy firms, or other large associations" which had the knowledge and power to exert indirect control over the directors. This necessarily limited the circle of "associates" to other members of what Emerson called one's own order—in this case, wealthy or powerful businessmen. Godkin's cure was to narrow the circle again to those

capable of contributing capital in amounts large enough to give themselves direct governing power. The shareholders would be limited to
capitalists (although they would not be called that).[35] Though Godkin
was right to lament the loss of investor power in most shareholder structures, he had no interest in imagining the alternative to be a mass democracy of the shareholders. That would have required him to advocate
a structure of control that could express the collective agency of a multitude of noncapitalists, rather than the individual agency (ruled, as noted
above, by business logic) of capitalists. The problem (or promise) of
"scattered influence" is endemic to representative democracy and to the
"borrowing" corporation alike, but Godkin envisioned the restoration
of maximum power to the representatives and not their cooperation
with the multitude of shareholders.

These are the features of Godkin's improved and liberal corporation:
at the moment in which the rights of the small shareholders were being
defended, he called for increased sovereignty for a small group of directors limited to those who controlled large amounts of capital and who
submitted their judgment to impersonal economic law. Corporate tyranny meant the excessive self-legislation of leaders who draw on the
masses for support. Its elimination required the severing of the directors
from a benighted public, and the recovery of their identity as an exclusive group formed in obedience to established law.

Godkin reproduced what I've been describing through Emerson as
corporate individualism: First, the rights of responsible and private individuals are defended (shareholders and directors, the small and the
great alike). Second, the collective nature of the corporation is celebrated, and despotic indifference to the masses of investors is condemned. Finally, however, the cure is an inner circle's power to obey
preconstituted law without dislodging the appeals to individualism and
collectives. Just as Reconstruction is seen in the *Nation* to be disgracing
itself by legislating for a heterogeneous population rather than trusting
investment and developing uniform civil service codes, the corporation
was failing by setting its own priorities with the use of the financial
resources of the mob.

Postbellum Republicans imagined themselves to be advocates of free
labor and free trade, of protecting the individual producer, the sanctity
of property, and the rights of private selves. At the same time, they sponsored ("reformed") corporate forms that offered a different understanding of property ownership, personal agency, and the sources of prosperity. In their latter view, agency depended on collective cooperation, and

cooperation was regulated by an inaccessible law. This is not a law that liberates the cooperative individual will but one that predetermines it. Republicans, rooted in the market, and officially opposed to monopoly, were sliding toward a centralized, corporate alternative.

We are left with a couple of questions. How could the centralized corporate form seem as attractive as the free market and free labor? And once the former was in place, how could the contradiction between them be erased?

One answer is that the market and the corporation shared a common interest in natural, incorporeal, inhuman, unmodifiable laws that govern human affairs. In chapter 6, I argued that Emerson managed to extract a powerful determinism from a market idea of freedom, and this certainly brought the market closer to a corporate devotion to a transcendent order, thereby doing its part to support the bridge between market and corporate notions of social and economic order. But the market nonetheless retained strong overtones of individualist independence and equal dealings. And the corporation, as I discussed in chapter 3, could also imply public sovereignty and collective legislation. The postwar sense that the new national identity would depend on expanded equality also made the move to transcendent authority less likely. In the next sections, I will argue that crucial ingredients in the management of these forms of independence and equality were liberal attitudes toward race.

3. Mediations of Race: Englishness

The rise of corporate governance within liberal reform's free-labor, free-market vision pivots on the normalization of superior, external, determining law in a society officially devoted to expressions of individual will. Simple assertions that a corporate will expresses an individual will are not enough.[36] Additional translations and linkages must be embedded in popular consciousness. Liberal reformers were crucial to the process of making unilateral, even authoritarian rule compatible with democracy, and they supported several important strategies toward this end.

The first of these was to discredit the unsupervised, self-directed group relations that might ordinarily be thought to be the heart and soul of a free-labor democracy. Godkin prepared the way for his backhanded defense of (reformed) corporate centralization with his editorial "'The New Departure.'" As a liberal or centrist Republican, he suggested that the Democrats' new departure into ostensible support for a number of once-Republican policies was a plausible "bid for the support of that large body of Republicans who [like Godkin himself] are very sick of Republican doings, and who long for a decent excuse for trying both new measures and new men."[37] Writing only a few months before the formation of the breakaway Liberal Republicans, when he approvingly declared that the new party was done with "Reconstruction and slavery,"[38] Godkin attacked the Republicans not only for certain extreme policies but also for a general elevation of democracy over constitutional law. Godkin correctly estimated Reconstruction to be bound up with an effort on the part of many congressional Republicans to affirm the sovereignty of the legislative branch as superior to the executive and judicial in the making of national policy.[39] He disapproved of this and was receptive to the Democrats' offer to "oppose the dangerous tendency which the Republican party has for some time been manifesting to treat the [Thirteenth, Fourteenth, and Fifteenth] amendments as having practically abrogated the whole Constitution; or, in other words, as having practically constituted the majority of both Houses as supreme judges of what is or what is not constitutional."[40] Godkin did not regard the Constitution as the foundation of legislative supremacy but as the legislature's limit. Founding law, rather than sustaining and supporting the representative body, exists in structural opposition to its powers. Godkin did not see constitutional law as finding its primary living expression in Congress, but regarded this law as Congress's needful manager. Reconstruction became not simply excessively interventionist but excessively democratic. Its direction should, in unspecified particulars, remain safe from public control. Reconstruction should be not at all like a commune and much like a corporate enterprise, and Godkin felt strongly enough about the dangers of popular legislation to look outside his own party for correction.

Discussion of Reconstruction as a series of legislative deeds can hardly be separated from its effects on race relations. Not surprisingly, Godkin associated excessive legislative power with the presence of nonwhite peoples. In "The New Departure," the latter appear as the residents of the Dominican Republic, which many Republicans, following the Grant administration's lead, wished to annex to the United States in 1870. Godkin described the country as "a semi-barbarous island occupied by a turbulent population unused to civil government."[41] This description is part of a second means of restricting the democratic politics of free labor: to "primitivize" legislative agency by associating it with those allegedly uncivilized non-Anglo-Saxon societies that were said to be incapable of either democracy or order.[42]

A third mode of restriction is the most important, and it received some elaboration in Emerson's views on race. Godkin showed the possibility of setting constitutional authority — the Constitution as authority — above legislative power, and of racializing the legislature to associate it with the uncivilized, but these two strategies could only be pushed so far before an aroma of racist despotism began to creep in. As noted above, a liberal society was one possessed of a continuous potential for achieving equality, particularly by fulfilling the promise of "equality of opportunity." Inherent inequality, rooted in race or some natural economic law, and therefore prior to and independent of the inequalities of performance and ability thought to express individuality, violated the vision of a liberal society as a place in which actually existing hierarchies flow naturally from contingent differences of performance. Liberals sometimes extended this ideal to black Americans: "Even those who harbored doubts about blacks' innate capabilities insisted that to limit on racial grounds the egalitarian commitments central to American political culture made a mockery of republican institutions. There was no room for a legally and politically submerged class in the 'perfect republic' that must emerge from the Civil War."[43] Saturday Club member and Massachusetts radical Charles Sumner insisted that freedom depends on equality: "If you would maintain [the freedman] in his freedom, you must begin by maintaining him in the equal rights of citizenship."[44] Emerson, writing about West Indian emancipation in 1844, defined it as the end of all lordship and bondage relations: this "moral revolution" showed "the masters revolting from their mastery."[45] Most Republicans, liberal ("moderate") or radical, associated any kind of incipient caste system with the return of Southern rebellion, consolidated Black Codes, and the mockery of all the bloody war had stood for. Similarly, some branches of the labor movement argued that any sanction of inferiority for the negro would mean decline for white labor in the South and, eventually, in other parts of the country as well.[46] Particularly after the war, inequality required rather elaborate justification for antislavery liberals.

Under these circumstances, it would be more effective to normalize the unapproachable superiority of corporate forms of governance by redefining its constitutive superiority as equality. The presence of inequality would be read as equality itself. No further equality need be sought. This kind of pseudo-equality would negate the appearance of top-down, unrevisable, or coercive power. Corporate governance could look like the sort of voluntary exchange crucial to the free-labor ideal; unequal power would appear in the guise of equal relations. And it turned out that Emerson helped to redefine equality in this way by identifying it with white racial mixtures. This is the third strategy for reconciling authoritarian and democratic rule. Whiteness—or more accurately, English culture—establishes an essential and ineradicable equality among white people that remains unaffected by any actual inequality among them. Conversely, any obvious inequality can be linked to racial differences. I will take these points in order—first, Emerson's view of intraracial white relations, and then of differences between races.

Emerson's views about white races appears most fully in *English Traits*, where he was attempting to define and describe Englishness. I should say in advance, as background to the discussion below, that nothing in Emerson's views about race inhibited him from a long frolic among stereotypes. The English are an "anthology of temperaments" and a great jumbling of histories of a kind that might give the physiognomist pause, a combination "of well-marked English types, the ruddy complexion fair and plump, robust men . . . ; a Norman type . . . , a Saxon. . . ." Then the Roman has implanted his dark complexion in their "trinity or quaternity of bloods."[47]

And yet Emerson could trace nearly any distinctive feature of English society to something about the race creating itself in history. Racial essentialism and culturalism could produce either an analysis of political and economic factors or racist generalizations. Emerson makes little distinction, and thus both kinds of statements can be found sprinkled throughout his work. In thinking about Englishness, Emerson was moved to exclaim, "It is race, is it not? that puts the hundred millions of India under the dominion of a remote island in the north of Europe. Race avails much, if that be true, which is alleged, that all Celts are Catholics, and all Saxons are Protestants; that Celts love unity of power, and Saxons the representative principle. Race is a controlling influence in the Jew, who, for two millenniums, under every climate, has preserved the same character and employments. Race in the negro is of appalling importance."[48] This outburst, however, follows a very different statement two pages earlier, at the "Race" chapter's outset, when he notes that "the individuals at the extremes of divergence in one race of men are as unlike as the wolf to the lapdog. Yet each variety shades down imperceptibly into the next, and you cannot draw the line where a race begins or ends."[49] He notes the experts' obvious inability to agree on the number of races ("Blumenbach reckons five races; Humboldt three.").

The chapter "Race" in *English Traits* demonstrates that, although one can still use the concept, race lacks biological or genetic cogency for Emerson. He tends to use *race* and *nation* interchangeably; his history of the formation of England is a chronicle of national invasions (Vikings, Normans) and cultural intermixings that he sprinkles with countervailing assertions about racial essence. He also sees racial character as constituted in part by race's sociocultural opposites, by "the counteracting forces to race." "Civilization is a re-agent, and eats away at the old traits." Physiognomy is adduced not as a biological but as a religious trait, suggesting that environmental or cultural factors alter racial features: "Trades and professions carve their own lines on face and form."[50] Englishness is fundamentally affected by "certain circumstances of English life . . . as, personal liberty; plenty of food; good ale and mutton; open market, or good wages for every kind of labor; high bribes to talent and skill; the island life, or the million opportunities and outlets for expanding and misplaced talent; readiness of combination among themselves for politics or for business; strikes; and sense of superiority founded on habit of victory in labor and in war; and the appetite for superiority grows by feeding."[51] Rabelais might have come up with such a miscellaneous list of the ingredients of the English race. Why not also mention long noses, linen breeches, and rains of frogs? Emerson thinks as a Lamarckian, suggesting that race is determined by social life as well as determining it. Among the antiracial forces that comprise race, "Credence is a main element. 'Tis said, that the views of nature held by any people determine all their institutions. Whatever influences add to mental or moral faculty, take men out of nationality, as out of other conditions, and make the national life a culpable compromise."[52] It is not nature but a people's views of nature that create nature; it is always culpable for their national life because as a social group it is coeval with nature, and makes continual compromises between nature and culture.

Not only does race lack essence, but its features undergo continual modification. One might want to conclude from such passages that Emerson combines historicist and racialist thinking. But he sees so little tension between these two modes of viewing populations that the labels become meaningless. It would be more accurate to say that race is natural and cultural, inherent and continuously modified, physiological and historical. Race is where nature controls society, but also where society has access to the modification of nature. Race is fate, but also the conquest of fate as evidenced in the way that the Saxons transformed the barren English isles into the center of the world: "If the race is good, so is the place."[53] Race is simultaneously agency as well as destiny. A first feature of Emerson's thought on the white races is that he can combine a belief in racial determinism — race explains why England colonized India and not the other way around — with a sense of the flexibility and even the inessentiality of a racial category.

Second, Emerson favors a mixing of the white races rather than any kind of purification: "As the scale mounts, the organizations become complex. We are piqued with pure descent, but nature loves inoculation. A child blends in his face the faces of both parents . . . The best nations are those most widely related; and navigation, as effecting a world-wide mixture, is the most potent advancer of nations. . . . The English composite character betrays a mixed origin. Everything English is a fusion of distant and antagonistic elements."[54] All the races that make Englishness are white, and in this case, the more the blending the better the stock.

Third, in thinking about the highly hybridized English, Emerson links race to national equality: "An electric touch by any of their national ideas, melts them into one family, and brings the hoards of power which their individuality is always hiving, into use and play for all. It is the smallness of the country, or is it the pride and affection of race, — they have solidarity, or responsibleness, and trust in each other. . . . A great ability, not amassed on a few giants, but poured into the general mind, so that each of them could at a pinch stand in the shoes of the other; and they are more bound in character, than differenced in ability or in rank. The laborer is a possible lord."[55] Race furnishes a commonality that brings everyone together and brings them to more or less the same level. Any inequalities among the English are displaced to the outside. Their racial "pride and affection" brings their power into play, and every laborer becomes at least potentially a ruler in society. Racial union allows social equality to replace domination (domination of the economic kind Emerson witnessed in all-English London). English "racial" identity is an expression of a "great ability" or national agency, even of a kind of democratic art which, through the "general mind," takes control over the crude destinies of the English soil and its foreign enemies: England is a "nation whose existence is a work of art; — a cold, barren, almost arctic isle, being made the most fruitful, luxurious and imperial land in the whole earth."[56] This work arises from the solidarity of their national character.

For Emerson, the interest in Englishness is not that it allows him to specify race and race's social effects — Englishness refuses to help him to any single, fixed, definable, essential definition of race. Again, it is biological and not biological. It interacts with climate, but climate is also subordinate to its "civilization." English race determines cultural beliefs but is also the expression of cultural beliefs. Race is a national history but also the mixing of many nations into one polity. Race is nature, but also a spirit that precedes nature and lives within individuals. But Englishness does make sense as something besides a meaningful theory of race: it is an "electric touch" and a set of "national ideas" that provides solidarity, interchangeability, a general will, an activated individuality, and a "potential" lordship of self-rule, all without actualization in social relations. All these things are delivered by the sheer existence of Englishness itself. Increasing social equality and exercising democratic power need not consist of anything more than having the English mentality. Rather than grounding *white* American identity by establishing its Anglo-Saxon homeland, Emerson's Englishness symbolizes *social* equality without actual equality, collective agency without actual political agency. Englishness is a "race" that, while incoherent literally, is coherent figuratively as a symbol for a purely abstract social equality.

This equality as race coexists with the air of irreversible governance that the idea of race always invokes. English "race" expresses an egalitarian social life and the natural determinism to which all the English submit. The equality of English identity acts as concomitant to the subject's inequality before a higher law of (cultural) race. By calling it "race" rather than English culture, Emerson helps wed otherwise incompatible free-labor ideals to the preexisting authority of corporate union. Englishness furnishes a two-sided corporate equality, in which all of the citizenry is equal in spite of its actual inequality and subordinate to the national ideas that form its racial unity. This kind of equality among the white English of course depends on the exclusion of the African descended, as I will discuss below. My point here is that Emerson in effect adheres to notions of herrenvolk democracy among the best white strains. But he does not only invoke race as a foundation of English superiority, for he uses race to install corporate democracy.[57] This builds equality both on the exclusion of the racially inferior *and* on the subordination of individual whites to the rules of union.

4. Mediations of Race: Africans

I'm still in the midst of considering the third means by which corporate governance is reconciled with market-style equality. It involves the

double linking of white intraracial unity to equality, and interracial relations to inequality.

For Emerson, inequality defines relations between different races.
This is true between two white races as well as between white and black.
Emerson's love of white mixtures does not prevent him from making
sharp discriminations between the English and the Scotch.

> What we think of when we talk of English traits really narrows itself to a
> small district. It excludes Ireland, and Scotland, and Wales, and reduces
> itself at last to London, that is, to those who come and go thither. . . . As
> you go north into the manufacturing and agricultural districts, and to
> the population that never travels, as you go into Yorkshire, as you enter
> Scotland, the world's Englishman is no longer found. In Scotland, there
> is a rapid loss of all grandeur of mien and manners; a provincial eagerness
> and acuteness appear; the poverty of the country makes itself remarked,
> and a coarseness of manners; and, among the intellectual, is the insanity
> of dialectics. In Ireland, are the same climate and soil as in England, but
> less food, no right relation to the land, political dependence, small ten-
> antry, and an inferior or misplaced race.[58]

Political and economic problems, and the lack of the broad cultural experience found in the capital, handicap the outlying regions, but Emerson translates these as racial difficulties, whether the race is intrinsically
"inferior" or just "misplaced." Emerson's oblivion to the nature versus
culture distinction that founds our own thinking about race shows one
consistent feature here, which is that extraracial relations involve explicit
hierarchy. Hierarchy is fundamental to the representation of racial
difference. "Men hear gladly of the power of blood or race. Every body
likes to know that his advantages cannot be attributed to air, soil, sea,
or to local wealth, as mines and quarries, nor to laws and traditions, nor
to fortune, but to superior brain, as it makes the praise more personal
to him."[59] This is of course a major purpose of talking about racial identity in the first place — to establish quasi-innate superiority, to take ownership of a permanent advantage. When racial crossing exists between
white and black within one nation, inequality becomes an explicit principle of governance.

Emerson's views on U.S. race relations are usually assessed in the context of his antislavery convictions, which cannot be doubted. He had
always regarded slavery as a fundamental crime against natural and spiritual law, and he expected absolute opposition to it. As the 1850s drew
the country closer to war, Emerson had supported radical abolitionists
like John Brown, and had denounced those who favored union at the

cost of sustaining slavery. Excoriating the physical attack on Senator Charles Sumner on the floor of the Senate in 1856, an attack that followed directly from the vehemence of Sumner's abolitionist views, Emerson asked his audience incredulously whether "every sane human being were not an abolitionist, or a believer that all men should be free." He saw only one right answer on the slavery question: "I think we must get rid of slavery, or we must get rid of freedom."[60] He placed abolition above national union, saying, "There is no Union. Can any citizen of Massachusetts travel in honor through Kentucky and Alabama and speak his mind?" "I am glad to see that the terror at disunion and anarchy is disappearing," he continued. "Massachusetts, in its heroic day, had no government — was an anarchy. Every man stood on his own feet, was his own governor." The only cure for the slavish peace is open war, a fulfillment of the colonial tradition of armed citizenship in which, for "the Saxon man," "it was known that instant justice would be administered to each offense."[61] The opposition to slavery drew more passion from him in a single page of one of these occasional speeches on slavery than can be found in entire chapters of the middlebrow *English Traits*, his major publication of the mid-1850s. Emerson had been more single-minded about slavery than about any issue other than the existence of the moral law itself.[62]

But like many other opponents of slavery, his commitment to abolition did not lead to support for radical Reconstruction. It also coexisted with a liberal kind of racism. Antislavery opinion often rested on some kind of paternalistic benevolence, in which the opponent of slavery could reject the system for its cruelty, its brutalization of whites and blacks alike, its imperial designs (as "the slave-power"), its immorality, or its dehumanization, while still believing that African Americans were weaker, more childlike, less rational, or otherwise not yet ready for modernity. Antislavery sentiment did not eliminate racism but liberalized it: it meant one could believe in racial hierarchy while opposing hierarchy's crueler outcomes. George Fredrickson in particular has stressed the amazing variety of complicated racialist theory that coexisted with the antislavery and then the pro-Reconstruction Northern liberal and radical positions before and after the Civil War. There seem to have been more full-blown varieties of antislavery racism than there were states in the union, enough to hold a new and putatively benevolent explanation of African inferiority for each new week of the year.[63] Horace Bushnell, Theodore Parker, Charles Francis Adams, Jr., along with free-soil humanitarians like Salmon P. Chase and Gamaliel Bailey, liberal reform journalists such as Horace Greeley, and Emerson's admired associates and fellow members of the Saturday Club Louis Agassiz and Dr. Samuel Gridley Howe, generally agreed in picturing former slaves continuing as servants or disappearing once the end of slavery had allowed nature to take its course.[64] The glorious future foretold for the reunited, rapidly industrializing, racially just, fully continental nation coincided with visions of the former slaves using their freedom to drift southward into the alien tropics or nobly to bear their biologically fated racial death.[65]

Emerson's lifelong objection to slavery had strong cultural precedent for its coexistence with a commonplace racism. At the age of eighteen, Emerson proclaimed that "no ingenious sophistry can ever reconcile the unperverted mind to the pardon of *Slavery*."[66] And yet, only a few pages earlier he recorded that he "saw ten, twenty, a hundred large lipped, lowbrowed black men in the streets who, except in the mere matter of language, did not exceed the sagacity of the elephant. . . . In comparison with the highest orders of men, the Africans will stand so low as to make the difference which subsists between themselves & the sagacious beasts inconsiderable."[67] Emerson's belief in the inequality of the races was not merely the product of his youth. In the period 1856–58, long after he had publicly denounced the Fugitive Slave Act and had come to support radical abolitionist activity in Kansas and Nebraska, he remained a white supremacist. "When the apostle of freedom has gained his first point of repealing the negro laws, he will find the free negro is the type & exponent of that very animal law; standing as he does in nature below the series of thought, & in the plane of vegetable & animal existence, whose law is to prey on one another, and the strongest has it."[68] Abolition or emancipation free the Negro to go the way of natural law.

In his most canonical late essay, "Fate," Emerson argued that "the scale of tribes, and the steadiness with which victory adheres to one tribe, and defeat to another, is as uniform as the superposition of strata. We know in history what weight belongs to race. . . . See the shades of the picture. The German and Irish millions, like the Negro, have a great deal of guano in their destiny. They are ferried over the Atlantic, and carted over America, to ditch and to drudge, to make corn cheap, and then to lie down prematurely to make a spot of green grass on the prairie."[69] Where the active racial hostility of 1822 sought, like most such hostility, to establish or confirm a racial distinction, by 1856 Emerson had successfully attached racial hierarchy to the permanent order of things. He did not even single out the Negro for a unique degree of inferiority, but serenely consigned him or her to the mulching phase of a regenerative natural cycle. In this framework, slavery was unnatural not because it violated the African American's basic human right of liberty of person but because it violated the natural law by which all inferior races are plowed under. Similarly, Emerson espoused a flexible version of the climatic theory that correlated the Negro's low position on the scale of culture with his tropical origins: "The highest civility has never loved the hot zones. Wherever snow falls there is usually civil freedom."[70]

I have found no indication that Emerson ever conceived of the possibility of black-white social equality, though such views sometimes marked other liberals of moderate racial opinion. Saturday Club member Richard Henry Dana Jr. for example, though opposed to many aspects of the radical program, suggested that African Americans must be "built up into a self-governing, voting, intelligent population."[71] In his address on Edward Everett, Dana praised Everett for urging "that the negro must and could civilize Africa. He met the argument that the negro was not capable of self-government, — of constructing and maintaining a civilized empire, — that he is essentially inferior and must be governed by the white, by saying, 'I do not believe it.' He not only contended that, as a human being, the negro was substantially equal, but he drew proofs from all history."[72] Dana was still not advocating social equality and mixing between black and white, but Emerson did not go even this far. He remained silent on whether the Negro's capacity for democracy is equal to that of the whites. Linking the Negro to "animal law," Emerson's defense of abolition was humanitarian: the slaveholder "pleads Fate. Here is an inferior race requiring wardship. . . . The argument of the abolitionist is, It is inhuman to treat a man thus."[73] Emerson regarded the slave as a "man" deserving humane treatment without contesting the slaveholder's claim that the enslaved race is inferior.

Where Emerson *does* explicitly imagine the Negro surviving, it is not as a Negro: "How to pay the war-debt"; "the way to wash the negro white is to educate him in the white man's useful & fine Arts, & his ethics"; "honesty by temperament."[74] Eliminating the war-debt requires washing Negroes white because Negroes are a major part of that outstanding debt. Full emancipation means emancipation from blackness, which will disappear in the forward march of natural history. Social coexistence between black and white depends on the transfiguration of black into white. The preservation of racial difference, on the other hand, would perpetuate inequalities and block the reestablishing of a postwar national identity, one determined by the electric interchange-ability and equality of the English version.

For Emerson, multiracialism means inequality and the threat of so-cial disintegration. Brazil offered him an example of a struggling society whose poverty and trouble could be blamed on its racial mixtures.

Emerson considered the problem in a postbellum journal entry about Louis Agassiz's account of his journey there. We should recall that Emerson admired Agassiz as a leading natural scientist whose scientific racism, polygenicism, climatic theories of cultural difference, and in-tense phobias about cross-racial sexuality did not noticeably impair his reputation as a beacon of the biological enlightenment. Emerson ig-nored some of Agassiz's views — Emerson was a monogenicist, for ex-ample, believing that the races are not so different as to have sprung from multiple and unrelated biped races.[75] But Agassiz fused his opposi-tion to slavery with a combination of racism and a hatred of social equal-ity. In quarters as close as the Saturday Club's, it must have been a hard fact for Emerson to ignore.

Agassiz wrote that "we have already to struggle, in our progress, against the influence of universal equality, in consequence of the diffi-culty of preserving the acquisitions of individual eminence, the wealth of refinement and culture growing out of select associations. . . . Im-provements in our system of education . . . may sooner or later counter-balance the effects of the apathy of the uncultivated and of the rudeness of the lower classes and raise them to a higher standard. But how shall we eradicate the stigma of a lower race when its blood has once been allowed to flow freely into that of our children?"[76] This transition from education to procreation suggests how fully Agassiz sexualized racial contact. No transfer of knowledge can withstand a countervailing mix-ing of blood. Similarly, his description of his horror at first sighting Negroes in Philadelphia in 1846 is rather full:

> It is impossible for me to repress the feeling that they are not of the same blood as us. In seeing their black faces with their thick lips and grimacing teeth, the wool on their head, their bent knees, their elongated hands, their large curved nails, and especially the livid color of the palms of their hands, I could not take my eyes off their faces in order to tell them to stay far away. . . . What unhappiness for the white race — to have tied their existence so closely with that of negroes in certain countries! God pre-serve us from such a contact![77]

Agassiz's solution was to deal with "the colored races" through "a full consciousness of the real differences existing between us and them, and a desire to foster those dispositions that are eminently marked in them, rather than by treating them on terms of equality."[78]

Though Emerson could not, in adulthood, have shared Agassiz's racial shock, it was nonetheless this Agassiz whose 1866 visit left him with a strong impression.

> On 31 August visited Agassiz by invitation with Lidian & Ellen . . . He is a man to be thankful for, always cordial, full of facts, with unsleeping observation, & perfectly communicative. In Brazil he saw on a half mile square different kinds of excellent timber, — & not a saw mill in Brazil. A country thirsting for Yankees to open & use its wealth. In Brazil is no bread . . . No society, no culture; could only name three men . . . For the rest, immense vulgarity . . . A. explained, that the Emperor said, "Now you, when you leave your work, can always return into cultivated society, I have none." — Agassiz says, the whole population is wretchedly immoral, the color & feature of the people showing the entire intermixing of all the races. Mrs. Agassiz found the women ignorant, depressed, with no employment but needle-work, with no future, negligent of their persons, shabby & sluttish at home, with their hair about their ears, only gay in the ball room: The men well dressed.[79]

Agassiz traced economic and cultural deficiencies to Brazil's racial mixtures, and Emerson found this unexceptional enough to mention it in passing between remarks on the absence of culture and the depravity of the women. Brazil was still a slave society at the time of this writing, but Emerson seemed to accept Agassiz's belief that Brazil's social and economic problems arose not from the immorality of slavery but from the immorality of racial blends. Miscegenation violates the moral law, which is in turn expressed in economic prosperity or its lack. Economic virtue depends on a racial purity whose absence is manifested as Brazil and whose realization appears as Yankee. Cross-racial inequality must be maintained if society is to function as well as a successful business.

Such success does not require racial purification. It requires only that economic markets function to enforce a stratified unity. For example, Maurice Gonnaud reports that, "Invited to speak during an 1868 reception for the Chinese ambassador, Emerson heralded the influx of Asian immigrants on the West Coast with wholehearted acclaim, saying that 'their power to continuous labor, their versatility in adapting themselves to new conditions, their stoical economy, are unlooked-for virtues' sure to benefit the entire community."[80] Asian immigrants are not a threat in that their racial or cultural differences are subsumed by their "economy," which makes them entirely tractable surplus labor.[81] The Chinese can be included within a system that, translating them into laborers, makes them like everybody else. Emerson did not picture a free labor negotiation between distinct parties meeting as equals on the market but a corporate union in which racial or cultural differences had already been neutralized even as they were used to assign social station (here, the Chinese as flexible laborer).

One of the payoffs of Emerson's racial beliefs, which remained relatively stable throughout his life, was a white cultural supremacy that was attributed to the immanent workings of social order rather than to racism. I will discuss this issue in the next section. Another major payoff was the stabilization of corporate subjectivity. First, self-reliance remains central, and at no point does the stress on a determinism of the individual by group characteristics absolve the individual of full responsibility for his or her condition. Second, white racial identity provides a symbolic equality which comprises an official egalitarianism undiminishable by any actual inequality. And third, all cross-racial relations, and, in a class by themselves, all black-white relations, express and justify the subordination of individuals and groups to a higher, supervisory, unifying law.

Corporatism, I'm saying, would be far weaker in facing competing ideas of free labor or of public welfare without the racialist core of liberal thought. Corporatism in turn makes this racial thought more plausible. Liberal racism sustains corporatism by simultaneously providing a social equality that exists regardless of actual social conditions (white intra-racial relations), and an actual social inequality (interracial relations) that mandates the rule of preexisting and unappealable law. It assists corporatism's already existing tendency to be simultaneously democratic and authoritarian, to uphold equal rights while insisting on actual inequality. The values of equality and individualism are upheld, and so are racial inequality and the subordination of corrective, lawmaking power to higher law.

5. Civil Rights as Substitute for Civil Agency

Emerson's theories of white and black races translate a market ideal of negotiating differences into the three-part combination of corporate subjectivity. The latter, fusing self-reliance, abstract group equality, and submission to law, limits the meaning of civil rights after the war. If antiblack racism sustained corporate individualism, the converse is also true. Liberal racism, at least in Emerson's case, could not rest easily on a belief in the biological inferiority of African Americans which, as we've seen, Emerson did not uphold. This racism hinged on naturalizing black passivity and on the natural hierarchies of meritocracy. These two moves correspond to corporate individualism's steps 2 and 3 (as first outlined in chap. 1), and I consider them in turn in this section and the next.

Black civil rights arise from a political act which, for Emerson, does not inaugurate a black capacity for political action. The force of the Emancipation Proclamation, Emerson claims, "is that it commits the country to this justice, — that it compels the innumerable officers, civil, military, naval, of the Republic to range themselves on the line of this equity. . . . With a victory like this, we can stand many disasters. It does not promise the redemption of the black race; that lies not with us: but it relieves it of our opposition. The President by this act has paroled all the slaves in America; they will no more fight against us: and it relieves our race once for all of its crime and false position." [82] Once again, Emerson never suggests in this address that Emancipation will find in the former slaves an equal capacity for self-rule. Though the "crime" was white, the parolees are black, as though they were complicit in the theft of their own freedom. Since they are merely paroled, they will not be admitted into the full agency of free citizenship. Emerson's view had not changed much since the 1840s, when he described emancipation in the British West Indies as the "masters revolting from their mastery," as coming "mainly from the concessions of the whites." Any agency present here is white. When he continues to admit "that in part it is the earning of the blacks," he immediately qualifies this earning as reflecting the action of long-term natural laws. "Their powers and native endowments" manifest "the harmony of Nature," which always has its "[e]aters and food." The black man must "serve, and be exterminated," if he is "not on a parity with the best race," but will "play his part" if "the black man carries in his bosom an indispensable element of a new and coming civilization. . . . The anti-slavery of the whole world is dust in the balance before this." [83]

Whites are both the agents and the beneficiaries of Emancipation. Emancipation is self-emancipation for whites — emancipation from the burden of their "crime and false position." Redemption is expressly not promised to "the black race" even as relief is accorded to the white, and it is this relief that Emerson regards as the lead story. "With this blot removed from our national honor, this heavy load lifted off the national heart, we shall not fear henceforward to show our faces among mankind. We shall cease to be hypocrites and pretenders, but what we have styled our free institutions will be such."[84] Emerson's addresses on the end of slavery often described Emancipation as the restoration of white Americans to the bosom of the natural order, which accorded them a new freedom from shame, a new public mobility.

In another essay of 1862, published in the *Atlantic Monthly*, Emerson concentrated on Emancipation's power to deliver not freedom to African Americans but union to the nation. "The power of Emancipation is this, that it alters the atomic social constitution of the Southern people. Now, their interest is in keeping out white labor; then, when they must pay wages, their interest will be to let it in, to get the best labor, and, if they fear their blacks, to invite Irish, German and American laborers. Thus, whilst Slavery makes and keeps disunion, Emancipation removes the whole objection to union. Emancipation at one stroke elevates the poor-white of the South, and identifies his interest with the Northern laborer."[85] Emancipation frees the white citizens of the South, who can then reunite with those in the North. Emancipation establishes, first and foremost, a white republic whose relations to its black citizens will be settled later, in the power struggles of Reconstruction.[86]

National union — based on racial union — expresses the reunion of the nation with transcendental law. "But the laws by which the universe is organized reappear at every point, and will rule it. The end of all political struggle is to establish morality as the basis of all legislation. It is not free institutions, it is not a republic, it is not a democracy, that is the end, — no, but only the means. Morality is the object of government."[87] Similarly, his fullest journal entry on Emancipation linked it to restored law rather than to a rectification of race relations. Of the three "urgent motives point[ing] to the Emancipation," two concern "military necessity" and foreign relations with Europe; the lone reason of principle consists of five words: "The eternal right of it."[88]

Not only did Emerson link national union with union to eternal law, but he also argued that this law of union is the true agent of Emancipation. Even white agency, though always taking precedence over black, is itself subordinated to law. The real Great Emancipator is not Lincoln but this higher power for whom Lincoln was an agent in the field. Regarding the war on slavery, Emerson said that "this revolution is the work of no man, but the effervescence of nature. It never did not work. But nothing that has occurred but has been a surprise, & as much to the leaders as to the hindmost. And not an abolitionist, not an idealist, can say without effrontery, I did it. It is the fly in the coach, again. . . . It is elemental, it is the old eternal gravitations; beware of the swing, &

of the recoil!"[89] Writing in 1863, Emerson pushed what might have
been a comment about the way the best laid plans go astray into a
wholesale denial of antislavery agency. Slavery will end because nature
opposes it, and for no reason of human will or "legislation." This rule
applies equally to the giants of the historical stage. In his Concord eulogy for Abraham Lincoln, whose presidency Emerson celebrated as "a
triumph of the good-sense of mankind, and of the public conscience,"
he closed with a celebration of the

> serene Providence which rules the fate of nations, which makes little ac-
> count of time, little of one generation or race, makes no account of disas-
> ters, conquers alike by what is called defeat or by what is called victory,
> thrusts aside enemy and obstruction, crushes everything immoral as inhu-
> man, and obtains the ultimate triumph of the best race by the sacrifice of
> everything which resists the moral laws of the world. It makes its own
> instruments, creates the man for the time, trains him in poverty, inspires
> his genius, and arms him for his task. It has given every race its own
> talent, and ordains that only that race which combines perfectly with the
> virtues of all shall endure.[90]

Emerson did not trace the new racial order to the president or to other
collective action but to intervention from on high. His claim here is
quite extraordinary. He translated the nation's supreme totem of nation-
saving self-reliant initiative into an adjunct of invisible forces. If Lincoln
lacks agency in creating a new racial system, then so does everybody.
This is precisely Emerson's point.

For liberalism, race relations after slavery are to be governed by civil
rights. But contrary to our everyday understanding, civil rights are not
rights to power but a principle of governance. Emerson attributes civil
rights to African Americans but defines their origin such that civil rights
do not convey civil agency. A market context for civil rights would at
least theoretically enable the individual to create the rules of the immediate game and to eliminate irrational impediments to equal opportunities to enter contracts, own property, sell labor power, and so on. But
the act of Emancipation which creates civil rights for African Americans,
in Emerson's imagination of it, does not simply express natural law but
also prevents civil rights from implying a power to write social laws.
Although civil rights issued in black suffrage, and though nothing I am
saying here should be taken to imply doubts about their importance,
they nonetheless, as conceived by Emerson's liberalism, derive from a
change which separates a revolution in race relations from individual or
social agency. Though civil rights endowed freedmen with various civil

and political abilities, such as freedom to contract, to own property, and so forth, that had been unjustly stolen from them through slavery, it did not thereby endow them with the power to write and rewrite the basis of these rights. They could not revise the racial contract, which sets the ground rules for the deployment of black agency in a white free-labor society. Racial subjects remain inferior to the transcendental law that grants their freedom. Emancipation, in Emerson's description, structurally rejects attempts to move beyond equal rights to an equality of sociopolitical agency that would mean equality with the source of laws and hence an equal power to write them.

Thus, black civil rights assumed black submission to laws created through providential powers that mingle together with white actions. This racial submission was a principal source of the aforementioned combinations of equality and inequality that pervaded Reconstruction. The concept of equality was generally exhausted by equality before the law, equality as a subject of the law. The African American could achieve a potential equality with whites. "The white servant is deemed not on an equality with his employer — yet recognized the right to rise to that equality." Black Americans should have "an equal right with the white servant to gain" equality.[91] At the same time, actual equality was taboo. "Throughout Reconstruction, . . . the term 'social equality' conjured up fantastic images of blacks forcing their way into whites' private clubs, homes, and bedrooms. 'Negro equality, . . . ' [the Radical Thaddeus] Stevens assured the House, 'does not mean that a negro shall sit on the same seat or eat at the same table with a white man. That is a matter of taste which every man must decide for himself.'"[92] Emerson's understanding of Emancipation drew the line precisely between the two kinds of equality, one potential and sought, the other actual and forbidden. He defined proper equality as subordination before the law, and thus had no hesitation supporting equality of opportunity. This is the equality guaranteed by civil rights. But, in keeping with his corporatism, he avoided forms of equality in which higher law grants lawmaking agency to its subjects. Equal agency, equal social resources, and equal positions, might well lead to equality of outcome, social equality, and just as much power to sit at a table as that of white people. Ideas about this kind of equality were blocked by the convergence of Emerson's racist and corporatist thinking. To repeat, American "race relations" — as a replacement for master/slave relations — came into existence around a notion of civil rights that was constructed as an alternative to egalitarian powers of civil legislation.

An observation like George Fredrickson's can now be more fully appreciated. He says, "That northerners could oppose slavery without a commitment to racial equality helps explain why the Civil War resulted in the emancipation of the Negro from slavery but not from caste discrimination and the ravages of racism."[93] I would revise this point to suggest that northern liberals could not sustain racism or racial inequality without their commitment to civil rights as group submission.

6. Race and Merit Aristocracy

I'm denying something in particular here — the notion that Emerson as a liberal centrist believed in democratic equality and evenly distributed self-reliance but had a blind spot about race that prevented extending full equality to African Americans. I'm also denying that such liberals can easily repudiate a belief in racial inferiority and act affirmatively to encourage social equality among the races. One hundred thirty years after these issues were formulated by Reconstruction liberals, remedies that mandate equal social powers among races remain nearly unthinkable. In the last few years, equal rights liberals have joined the conservative attack on proposals that confront unequal outcomes — such as systems of "proportionate-interest representation" — proposals that would allow those groups primarily affected by a piece of legislation to have veto power over its passage even when they constitute a numerical minority.[94] Mandates for social equality are often met with claims that they interfere with personal freedom, disrupt market mechanisms, cover up actual inequalities of merit and performance, impair efficiency, and so on, but their real offense may be much simpler: mandated social equality might lead to actual social equality. It could provide not just equal rights but equal sovereignty over the rules that decide how these rights will be negotiated.

There is some evidence that Emerson consciously intended to reject an interpretation of Emancipation that implied equal sovereignty. In his essay, "Aristocracy," he hopes that the postwar United States will not shrink from maintaining class distinctions: "The existence of an upper class is not injurious, as long as it is dependent on merit. For so long it is provocation to the bold and generous."[95] This might sound like a straightforward advocacy of competition over prejudice, but Emerson also suggests that meritocracy retain a feature of slavery.

It will be agreed everywhere that society must have the benefit of the best leaders. How to obtain them? Birth has been tried and failed. Caste in India has no good result. Ennobling of one family is good for one generation; not sure beyond. Slavery had mischief enough to answer for, but it had this good in it, — the pricing of men. In the South a slave was bluntly but accurately valued at five hundred to a thousand dollars, if a good field-hand; if a mechanic, as carpenter or smith, twelve hundred or two thousand. In Rome or Greece what sums would not be paid for a superior slave, a confidential secretary and manager, an educated slave; a man of genius, a Moses educated in Egypt? I don't know how much Epictetus was sold for, or Aesop, or Toussaint l'Ouverture, and perhaps it was not a good market-day. Time was, in England, when the state stipulated beforehand what price should be paid for each citizen's life, if he was killed. Now, if it were possible, I should like to see that appraisal applied to every man, and every man made acquainted with the true number and weight of every adult citizen, and that he be placed where he belongs, with so much power confided to him as he could carry and use.

In the absence of such anthropometer I have a perfect confidence in the natural laws.[96]

Merit did not replace slavery but carried on its finest feature. Slavery was a system for the pricing of individuals, and Emerson here appreciates it for its certainty that individuals have a specific price and place that transcends all contingent social appraisals. The problem with contemporary America, he says a bit later, is that "we venture to put any man in any place."[97] Slavery, to the contrary, wedded market prices to absolute hierarchy. Emerson rejected American slavery's use of color or race as a discriminating feature, but he explicitly preserved slavery's system of placing a fixed price on a head. Slavery thus had a relevance to this postwar Northerner as an emblem of "anthropometric" courage. It remained valuable as a symbol of candor about sharply unequal abilities and about the need for society to reflect these inequalities. By also invoking Greek slavery, the English state, and the bondage of geniuses like Moses, Emerson made it clear that postwar, postracial hierarchy would not be reserved for the lowly, but would extend from top to bottom. Market circulation tends to distribute qualities anywhere; it can and even must be grounded in a general, absolute power of hierarchy. Value is not changingly created by community judgment but is to be sought by the community as innate.[98]

Emerson makes the leaders of democracy an aristocracy, and links this to the only native aristocracy in the history of U.S. culture, the slaveholding planters of the antebellum South. The principle of this aristocracy is merit, but merit maintains a hierarchy as comprehensive as that of slavery. The meritocracy that rises from this explicit precedent will also render judgments of innate and absolute value and establish a hierarchy on that basis. Meritocracy allows for independence, and yet it issues in a kind of caste: the chief duty of "the brave and the generous" is "loyalty to your own order."[99] Meritocracy may uproot and eliminate slavery's old planter class but preserves its belief in preventing a mixing of grades of people in which the low could have power equal to the high.

Emerson's liberal moderation, then, does not reluctantly place limits on liberty and equality, limits which most liberals claim to be forever beating back. Emerson replaces liberty and equality with a corporate individualist alternative: liberty thrives in the form of individual competition; equality appears in the constitutive relations between these individuals and their social group, relations that are almost always racialized and that replace agency; but both liberty and equality arise from a hierarchy of unappealable and transcendental laws.

The encroachment of private, corporate governance on the public realm accelerated during and after the 1870s, in the wake of liberalism's triumph over the older generation of radicals formed in the abolitionist movement. Liberalism grafted its racial attitudes onto this corporatist structure: racism is a problem of individual consciousness, rather than a system; the United States is held together by a common culture that transcends and subsumes racial difference; the rules that govern interracial relations must come from Euro-American values (democracy, equal justice, etc.).[100] These principles form an undemonstrative but pervasive resistance to efforts to produce cultural equality, racial equality, equality of outcome among communities historically differentiated by race. They oppose equality of social agency between racial groups, and as such, through their participation in a corporatist three-part equilibrium, form the last redoubt of respectable racism.

These principles comprise liberal racism. This means, again, three linked ideas: racism is not embedded in the major assumptions and practices of the social system but consists of local, irrational prejudice. A common, national culture, a moral union, supersedes racial and cultural differences; it replaces and substitutes for intergroup equality. And sociocultural interactions have as their highest court of appeal European principles in general (democracy, the rule of law) and the rule of merit in particular. This is the same merit that develops into a hierarchical system of appraisal from roots as a white philosophy of natural rank. Not all evaluation is tied to slavery, obviously. But meritocracy is a particular system with a specific history, one that arises in part from liberal attempts to turn freedpersons into corporate individuals of the kind I have described here. Meritocracy needs to be reevaluated in light of its ties to a symbiosis between corporate individualism and liberal racism.

Transcendental corporatism appears in the parable that closes Emerson's last "strong" work, *The Conduct of Life,* published the year before the beginning of the Civil War. Picturing the attempt to find the "central reality" of law beneath a life full of illusions, Emerson imagines a "young mortal enter[ing] the hall of the firmament" for a glimpse of the gods face-to-face, of the truth of being. Unfortunately, "on the instant, and incessantly, fall snow-storms of illusions." These illusions are particularly bad when they consist of life in a mob, a "mad crowd" that "drives hither and thither, now furiously commanding this thing to be done, now that." The worst of illusions, in other words, is the will of a mass democracy, no one in his or her proper place, all movement the overturning of "system and gradation."[101] Mercifully, the crowd evaporates: "when, by and by, for an instant, the air clears, and the cloud lifts a little, there are the gods still sitting around him on their thrones,— they alone with him alone."[102] The new democracy must use market mechanisms, but its necessary structure is as absolute as slavery's: society is led, finally, by a secret society of lords. At this meeting, there are no strangers present; everyone that had jostled him has vanished, leaving the young man and his gods free of such intrusive otherness. Here the rule of the lords does not make a still-Young America less democratic. It just enchants American democracy with an ascent into divine regions. The professional middle-class version of such divinity — fully adapted to corporate living — is success in a meritocracy with roots in slavery.[103]

CHAPTER

EIGHT

Continuations
Liberation from Management

In the 1990s, American democracy is everywhere being revitalized. But not in public. As the business corporation claims to become more egalitarian and to listen to all of its voices, the public sector becomes increasingly passive and elitist. One reason is simple: the corporate world can control democracy with a flexible yet overpowering authority that a diverse society lacks. The question I've attempted to address in this book is why the American mainstream favors this control. A major answer is the Emerson Effect, which makes the ceding of sovereignty to some higher or more automatic power seem like emancipation and progress. In the United States, this sensibility underwrites mainstream liberal positions which, while generally supporting valuable improvement and change, have not supported strong public sovereignty over economics, society and history.

Although my examples in this conclusion will be taken from the literature of social and business policy, I believe that the corporate individualism I've described extends beyond the boundaries of these areas of practice. The exact relevance of this tradition and its effects in any particular context are, of course, for the reader to decide. But in discussing this tradition's network of submissive individuality and corporate surrogates for democracy, I have imagined that these components are psychological as well as social forms. They appear as consciousness, feeling, practice, and as imaginations of a socially embodied self. These help create and yet pass beyond the particular histories and institutions of the middle-class European-American masculinity on which I have focused here. In concentrating on Emerson, I have specified influential work where these components were developed and amazingly combined. But their effects show up well beyond that frame. Here I will not be explicitly tracing these outside a broadly Emersonian cohort of liberal men in our own time, and yet I know that in American and perhaps European life, these apples do fall far from the tree.

The liberal consensus that ended the Reagan-Bush years is explicitly describing social rejuvenation as a business affair. Bill Clinton's Progressive Policy Institute issued a book after his election called *Mandate for Change,* which systematically avoids mention of any mandate for expanded personal freedom or popular democracy. It identifies five core themes for its vision: opportunity, reciprocal responsibility, community, democracy, and entrepreneurial government. Each of these is a staging ground for enhanced discipline and efficiency. *Opportunity* rejects redistribution in favor of pro-growth policies monitored and propelled by "fair rules of market competition." *Reciprocal responsibility* repudiates both neglect and entitlement, and requires instead that citizens show a "willingness to work, support their families, play by the rules, and give something back to their communities and country." *Community* means those voluntary associations that allow people to solve their own problems without making demands on public institutions. *Democracy* means "democracy and free markets" or "democracy and free enterprise" (*democracy* never appears unchaperoned by the market). It means a "realistic, tough-minded policy that keeps America strong," a "stabilizing force," and "free institutions [that] act as a check on government's conduct abroad." Democracy, in other words, implies *alternatives* to public government. Finally, public government has become entrepreneurial by "introducing choice, competition, and market incentives into the public sector."[1]

Fin-de-siècle liberalism has arrived. It has a mission which is far more traditional than its self-proclaimed transcendence of earlier (New Deal) liberalism would imply. Its traditionalism, in keeping with the preceding analysis of Emerson's version of liberalism, lies in the undermining of the major components it tries to balance. First, *Mandate for Change* is unable to name the forms of individual agency—other than paid labor—which it is attempting to enhance. Its rediscovery of "its traditional middle-class values" is not a reference to any strong kind of self-reliance or to collaborative sovereignty. It means the "real security concerns of middle-class voters."[2] And second, public participation does not involve mutual sovereignty among equals; each of the categories above, even democracy itself, is cleansed of egalitarian undertones. Public life consists of working for others, following rules, and relieving "public programs" of their financial obligations. Individuality and democratic rule are both submitted to the transformative yet unmodifiable processes of business.

Another example of this syndrome is Mickey Kaus's *The End of Equality*.[3] Kaus has done serious thinking and research, but his book is riven by contradictory desires that provide a useful snapshot of the crisis of liberalism today. He wants to replace "Money Liberalism" with "Civic Liberalism." While the former is an effort to redistribute wealth and reduce economic inequality, with civic liberalism one gives up on that while trying to achieve "social equality." The proponent of civic liberalism "worries about rebuilding, preserving, and strengthening community institutions in which income is irrelevant, . . . reduc[ing] the influence of money in politics, . . . reviv[ing] the public schools as a common experience" and rehabilitating a "public, community sphere" as a place where "money doesn't 'talk.'"[4] This sphere is a place where people "of all incomes actually meet under conditions of equal dignity." On an issue like health care, the civic liberal thinks that "what matters is that everybody wait in the same waiting rooms."[5] Civic liberalism allows us to see that economic inequality can be rendered irrelevant by common life, so that we can exclaim, with Kaus, "Will the success of new industry *X* create a new crop of moguls who will wear gold Rolexes and eat $200 meals? Well, so what! Let it all hang out! That's capitalism."[6]

Kaus's supposedly egalitarian attack on equality of power and resources fulfills rather than rejects traditional liberalism. Emerson's three-step again provides the generic prototype. Kaus celebrates entrepreneurial individualism, accepting its need for a market economy that he believes will produce increasing economic inequality. Second, he calls for "social equality," for a democratic life in common that grants everyone "equal dignity." This common life hinges on "a value, shared by rich and poor alike," and for this shared value "there is only one real candidate: work."[7] Social equality, it turns out, consists not of political negotiation or collective sovereignty but of a common value. In this perennial third step of Emersonian liberalism, public, reciprocal, rule-making agency is replaced by unity, by a common principle, a higher law which is out of reach of the public sphere. Work is precisely that activity whose strings are pulled by economics, whose law lies beyond the reach of public policy. Kaus's book does not simply insist on social equality but liberates economics from its egalitarian demands.

When he tries to describe the threat to social equality, Kaus looks down rather than up. He blames the obvious deterioration of the public sphere on an "underclass" that receives welfare payments rather than on the affluent who have encouraged the increasingly radical independence of economic decisions from public will.[8] Corporate culture, all its market institutions and vast mythology, once again has supplied the third step which suppresses group or democratic sovereignty. Kaus insists that economic life supersedes egalitarian relations even as he reveres the latter. Hence the double meaning of Kaus's title *The End of Equality:* in order to preserve equality as an end, it must be ended.[9]

This is also the double meaning of liberalism itself. There is nothing erroneous or hypocritical in Kaus's position, for it carries on the mainstream liberalism I have been analyzing here. Born in the hybrid "aristicrato-democractical" world of the early nineteenth century, it has helped to maintain that mixture ever since. While celebrating both liberty and equality, it has concealed the weakening and loss of both of these, and has even sought the loss itself. While attacking aristocracy and despotism, it has preserved some of their crucial elements in their democratic successors. Following the 1960s, liberalism has more than ever before aligned itself with mainstream business conservatism in branding strong equality as socialist excess — sometimes in the name of a weak equality of shared attitudes, values, or innate dignity — and reducing liberty to economic competition. The result has been that liberalism has all but buried itself as a public philosophy (evaporated to the "l-word" in the 1988 presidential campaign). Its weak forms of liberty and equality now live primarily as corporate versions of emancipation.

During the 1980s, the "social control" tone of management philosophy increasingly gave way to the languages of self-fulfillment, empowerment, and cross-cultural understanding that may have seemed the distinctive franchise of the populist left. Conservative and moderate business forces picked up some element of a countercultural interest in flexibility, flux, fragmentation, multiple identities, fused it with market-oriented management theory, and helped produce the neoliberal consensus of the 1990s. Ideas that had sought to liberalize public laws in the 1960s were now liberalizing private enterprise. Individualism and equality alike were fulfilled in corporate form.

A remarkable work of contemporary liberal thought is *Liberation Management,* Tom Peters's chaotic encyclopedia of the moment.[10] Peters there describes a garden of corporate delights. He begins by announcing the market death of the Fortune 500's tyrannical bureaucracies. He declares the future to be "horizontal" and all successful power to lack hierarchy. He combines a "just do it" individualism with a "relationship revolution" on behalf of flexible collaboration. He ratifies the "shift to soft" while reassuring us that "soft is hard."[11] He shows the new economic order offering unending personal liberation and total business fun through activities like "Building 'Wow Factories.'"[12] Peters proclaims a French Revolution for the businessperson — liberty ("just do it" in a "world gone bonkers"), equality ("going 'horizontal'"), and fraternity ("toward projects for all").[13]

Peters's corporate revolution is a utopian vision of liberating the performance principle as monitored by markets. Freedom requires maximum "businessing": "we are indeed trying 'to business' everyone: to turn all employees into mom-and-pop enterprises, into real, whole businesspersons, responsible for customers from order to delivery of a service or product."[14] The businessed self is a free agent in a nexus of production whose dispersed and delayered state makes the circulation of performance opportunities all the more efficient. Once fully businessed, the creative individualist should build and rebuild the product according to personal passion.

> I beg you to start a list like mine, to go berserk over floors labeled two that should be labeled one, shampoo containers that a pointy-toothed genius couldn't crack, and watch straps that snag sweaters. Don't be like that company secretary and assume it's your fault. . . . I urge you to become aware. Allow design and usability of everyday objects to worm their way into your consciousness. Allow yourself to become irritated, even furious, at the designer instead of feeling frustrated at yourself. It should convince you of how much can be done better, how big a little difference can be, and how important the whole idea is.
>
> The battle for competitive advantage is increasingly over nonobvious sources of value-added.[15]

In Peters, corporate individualism achieves its contemporary apotheosis, on the now-familiar three-step plan. Self-reliance is proclaimed as the negation of servility before conventional authority (don't be "that company secretary"; be irritated; trust thyself). Self-reliance, in the second step, turns out to be a function of systemic design, and its aim is structural enhancement undertaken with a reverence for the "whole idea." Finally, both the individuating fury of faultfinding and collaborative redevelopment are ruled by the laws of the competitive global market. As Peters notes toward the end, you should "get turned on" and "follow your bliss" because in "a knowledge-based economy, you must — to survive — add some special value, be distinctively good at something. And the truth is, we usually only get good at stuff we like."[16]

The corporation in this vision is increasingly individualist and democratic. At the same time, all individuality and democracy are corporate. Radically individual and collective agency have been relinquished in the same gesture that liberates the self to produce.

Peters, however, is not describing a new global reality which requires corporate pleasure for survival. He is expressing the perennial vision of American liberalism in the moment of its global aspiration. It has been one of the strengths of liberalism to have adapted individualism so well to the coming of the corporation, and Peters is one of the more infectious commentators working this corporate turf today. It would be absurd to suggest that liberalism could now or at sometime in the past have evaded dealing with corporate democracy and the subjectivity that it facilitates. I have no doubt that the immediate future is corporate as well. But recovering control over our various parts of the world system will require recovering the forms of individuality and equality whose abandonment by liberals had eroded that control in the first place. That control may be seriously redefined. I have no doubt that even weirder conjunctions of public and private, submission and agency await us down the road. But they will hardly be different enough, will not mix in much sovereignty of any kind, if they don't begin to confront the twin suppressions of liberalism that I've been discussing here.

Does a culture still dominated by liberalism have the resources for such a confrontation? Can it do that kind of reinvention? The undiminished Emerson Effect, after all, is to offer adaptation as a surrogate for lawmaking control. As in Peters's liberation of the business self in everyone, it labels as new freedom an enhanced service to inexorable rules. Emerson continually demanded a revolution, a permanent revolution, against ossified and archaic external authority. He did not demand a revolution against the liberal within. He ignored many of the forces that made him what he was. By this I don't mean that he stayed too detached from specific political, social, and economic questions; subjectivity was his jurisdiction, and he made his culturally powerful choices there. The revolution within would have required a more fundamental review of these features that constituted his own basic habits for living in the sociocultural world. Emerson's work raises questions on the same terrain today—not so much institutional arrangements in themselves, but our feelings about them. Several of his effects have been especially important to my preceding discussion, and those I list now remain in effect.

Emerson grew up in a deference culture, and he attacked some of its most important aspects, such as the clergy's franchise on scriptural interpretation.[17] But U.S. culture remained profoundly influenced by authoritarian elements that comprise a diffuse psychology, a habitual outlook, a political unconscious that go well beyond explicit institutional manifestations. Emerson was as likely as the next person to ignore these within structures that lacked an official reputation as oppressive. The market is one example, male friendship a second, and post-Emancipation's race relations a third. These, like the others I have analyzed, played a major role in Emerson's life, yet in his treatments he is often oblivious to their mechanisms of bondage and control. Most important, he ignored his own divided mind, a large part of which sought and relished the rewards of obedience. This is not such a horrible or surprising fact about oneself, this desire to be taken care of, to submit to a benevolent guardian when one's powers are so damnably weak. But it is a fact that, for a variety of reasons, remained off limits in Emerson's thought. He continually summoned supplemental, preemptive powers to take over for an incapacity he refused to acknowledge or attempt to overcome on his own.

Thus without necessarily intending to, he contributed to a perennial American "democracy and free-markets" nationalism that harbors a seemingly unlimited faith in freedom through hierarchy. The U.S. cultural mainstream can be profoundly anti-individualist, antiegalitarian, and antidemocratic. In a realm like economics, it makes no apologies for this, and, at least since Emerson, it has been rendering more and more of its cultural life in economic terms. It is a lot like other countries in this way. Its need for control is colossal. Its mistrust of sharing, equality, the untechnological, the nonproductive, the ordinary, is gigantic. Such feelings comprise the spontaneous psychology of its self-designated representative group, the European-descended middle class. About these feelings, Emerson is as self-censored as our Cold War reform liberals, including remarkable figures like Louis Hartz, author of *The Liberal Tradition in America,* whose unease and periodic contempt for American liberalism was buried in a cheerfully fatalistic sense that it is the best—if not the only—idea U.S. political culture ever had. But the Cold War is over. Maybe now we can talk, at least here in the academic midst of the professional middle class. Maybe we can talk about the other stuff matter-of-factly, the fascination with and fear of equality, the submissive liberty, and so on, perhaps with a sense of learning things others have already known about us.

Liberalism has never been so much about individual autonomy as

about inclusion.[18] It acculturates middle-class professionals into views
requisite to membership: truth as achieved through consensus-based
method, prejudice as irrationality, democracy as peer review, the cen-
trality of knowledge to happiness and of education to wealth, the importance of revision and intellectual change. Liberalism brings selves
into a well-administered structure. Liberty comes before equality, but
in a way that does not unleash individuality. Liberalism still has little
idea of what to do with things like racial or sexual identity, since it has
trouble imagining distinctive identity doing much more than injecting
bias or partiality into knowledge processes. The contemporary premium
on high-level functionalism (it's "skill-eat-skill," Tom Peters intones) has
a long history in a U.S. liberalism in which freedom is defined as self-
reliance in the sense of self-discipline. "Pray Without Ceasing," Emerson's first sermon, could be read as an early self-help tract, where the
idea is to achieve more effective praying by knowing more about your
real desires, which will place you in closer allegiance to God. Each of
these moves involves liberalism in norming and conforming. Exponents
of liberalism have had a very hard time regarding individualism as a
mode of political agency, by which I have meant a mode in which individuals or groups rewrite their basic rules of order.

I have been unable to detect much change in Emerson's general outlook toward individualism over the course of his life. The later doctrine
of self-reliance does not differ much, as I read it, from the 1826 composition of "Pray Without Ceasing." If we must locate a change and a decline in Emerson's work, I would place it not with a falling away from
his faith in self-reliance, which I think has been wrongly construed, but
with his seizing on self-reliance in the first place. The latter is a far more
misleading version of the pious deference and the trust in rescue that
rarely left him, even in moments of rebellion against the falsehoods of
his society. Self-reliance implies personal or collective agency where
there is usually none. On this score, I prefer the openness and consistency of Emerson's Unitarian sermons, where he says that "the minds
of men are not so much independent existences, as they are ideas present to the mind of God," so that "every desire of the human mind is a
prayer uttered to God and registered in heaven."[19] Here his individualism is honestly submissive and far more coherent for that. Its purpose
is to make him belong to somebody better or something higher, something not himself.

Emerson's utopian imagination continually embedded the solitary
soul in an association or system. His imagination tied this to equality

or reciprocity for only a few lines at a time. Equality meant that everyone had a ticket to get inside, and once there it would not interfere with the experience. The experience consisted of submitting to transformation and flux. Other people brought on the possibility of metamorphosis and the endlessly repeatable "moment of transition." "Rotation is [nature's] remedy. The soul is impatient of masters, and eager for change. . . . We touch and go, and sip the foam of many lives."[20] The problem of being mastered is solved by change. Equality in the network of interdependence would simply freeze and fix and obstruct the fluid movement of genuine freedom. Shifting to Tom Peters, we can see that business has finally caught up with this idea: the people inside the organization are to be as perpetually mobile as commodities outside; their relations are to be as incessantly liquified as those of price and consumer demand; their own identities are to molt and transfigure with each cycle of retooling. This kind of movement feels like freedom — freedom to end relationships, alter structure, start a new project. Freedom, equality, and democracy are all rolled into the power of individuals to respond to a world of flow, randomness, unbundling, and fractal effects. As Western thought frequently proclaims, always as though for the first time, and whether it be through the pre-Socratic philosophers, the conservative market theorist F. A. Hayek calling "competition . . . a discovery process," neopragmatism, or international commodity trading, freedom comes into existence through the acceptance of perpetual flux. None of this, however, addresses what shapes the flux itself. Emerson or Peters might have stressed feedback effects, such as the way the rustling butterfly wings of the individual actor create a hurricane three weeks later in the boardroom of the Bundesbank. Neither does: the flux and its rules are generally out of reach.

Such are the inclinations of this middle-class progressive culture: the forgetting of its authoritarian elements; individualistic, consensual submission to inexorable authority; the replacement of individual agency with inclusion; and seeing freedom as an uncontrollable system's flexibility. Emerson's submissive and corporate individualism sponsors each of these positions.

Still, my insistence on his corporate solution should not drown out the democratic middle step in Emerson's thinking. He was never content with isolated individualism, and intermittently socialized the possessive selfhood that seemed to people of average means to give them a share of concentrated capital and impregnable economic management. Some other kind of democratic subjectivity constantly haunted him, and has haunted idealistic, structurally middle-class readers like me. Writing a few years after Emerson's death, the liberal political economist Richard T. Ely remarked, "Pure communism in America is of the same age as American independence." Over a hundred years later, Robert Reich, in a passage I quoted in the introduction, insists that civic republicanism is as central to U.S. life as liberal individualism. American liberalism is permanently tormented by a remembrance of a lost relation, a lost sovereignty — an imagined past in which self-reliance and collaborative self-rule went naturally together. Emerson's writing bears witness to the confusions that ensue from forgetting to imagine this again.

Emerson, in fact, proscribes the kind of individualism that would be most useful in separating democratic groups from their pervasively corporate ancestry. This is an individualism realized through equality, equality of agency. This does not mean equality of opportunity or of outcome exactly, but an equality with the sources of the rules by which governing forces are structured. Such equality does not suggest particular modes of negotiation or specific results but envisions a redistribution of capacity away from the various versions of transcendental law. The capacity to make and unmake rules would inhere in self-reliance — other people's self-reliance. Equality would thus mean full agency for everyone, with the result to be worked out in the absence of superior, coercive authority. Collectively, this agency would reconstitute a public sector by bringing all the great powers into its field of influence, including those which, under corporate systems, create practices without being in turn revisable by their subjects. This democratic individualism, the individualism of Emerson's beleaguered step 2, would require the rejection of attempts to balance liberty and equality with unchangeable, unifying laws manifest as corporate markets. Its preliminary, reductive motto: if you aren't equal (to the laws), then you aren't free.

In this book, I have attempted to spell out the extent to which the obstacles to any sort of full reciprocity and collaboration belong not just to limited institutions or capitalism or business politics or conservative dominance but to the structure of liberal subjectivity. It is through this subjectivity that nondemocratic modes of democratic governance continue to actualize themselves. Liberalism is a transitional ideology, midway between authoritarian and democratic structures. Without our renewed effort, this transition could last another century. Emerson himself, a century and a half ago, frequently had other ideas. "Build, therefore, your own world," he said. Good idea, but it will require overcoming his submissive individualism to follow his advice.

NOTES

INTRODUCTION

1. Robert B. Reich, *The Resurgent Liberal (and Other Unfashionable Prophecies)* (New York: Random House, Vintage, 1991), 85.

2. Reich, *Resurgent Liberal,* 81. For other well-reviewed examples of this "communitarian" neoliberalism, see Robert Bellah et al., *The Good Society* (New York: Vintage, 1992); Amitai Etzioni, *The Spirit of Community: Rights, Responsibilities and the Communitarian Agenda* (New York: Crown Publishers, 1993); Will Marshall and Martin Schram, eds., *Mandate for Change* (New York: Berkeley Books, 1993). Often, liberal ideas did not conflict with conservatism, which deregulated the economic self while demanding more moral control of personal behavior.

3. Communitarians generally insist on their democratic credentials, often unconvincingly. The Bellah group exemplifies this problem. They note that we "live through institutions" and must develop modes of "public participation and accountability that alone will keep administrative structures from being despotic" (*Good Society,* 27). But this claim clashes with a deceptively similar theme, the priority of the "common good" over individuality: we must also "conjure a vision of an expanded and inclusive society in which the search for a common good would be central" (29). Participation is governed by this ideal, and not the other way around.

4. Robert Reich, *The Work of Nations* (New York: Vintage, 1991), 77.

5. Reich notes the "growing segregation of Americans by income"; predicts an increasingly passive dependency of "the lower four-fifths of the population" on the top fifth, which, since it moves in the global economy, has interests so different from those of its fellow citizens as to incline it to "secede"; and notes that the "renewed emphasis on 'community' in American life has justified and legitimized . . . economic enclaves" defined around similar incomes, educations, and vocations (ibid., 274, 294, 278).

6. For Reich's "positive economic nationalism," see ibid., 311–14.

7. Although Reich presumes democracy is an obvious good, in practice he replaces democracy with market corporatism. His only discussion of democracy ties it to eighteenth-century economic nationalism (ibid., chap. 1).

8. See Reich, "The Politics of Secession," in ibid., chap. 24, 282–300.

9. For a recent attempt to define authoritarianism broadly enough to include U.S. society, see Philip Slater, *A Dream Deferred: America's Discontent and the Search for a New Democratic Ideal* (Boston: Beacon Press, 1991). Slater identifies four features of authoritarianism that are not culturally or nationally specific: "the practice of deference or submissiveness"; "systematic oppression through brutality and terror"; "secrecy"; and "deflection" of discontent away from the actual sources of control or benefit (27–28). I concentrate on the first of these, which is usually sidelined in discussions of U.S. society although it is a prerequisite for the others.

10. George Catephores, "The Imperious Austrian: Schumpeter as Bourgeois Marxist," *New Left Review* 205 (May/June 1994): 29.

11. See James Weinstein, *The Corporate Ideal in the Liberal State: 1900–1918* (Boston: Beacon Press, 1968); R. Jeffrey Lustig, *Corporate Liberalism: The Origins of Modern American Political Theory, 1890–1920* (Berkeley and Los Angeles: University of California Press, 1980); Martin J. Sklar, *The Corporate Reconstruction of American Capitalism, 1890–1916: The Market, the Law, and Politics* (Cambridge: Cambridge University Press, 1988).

12. The sources of the republicanism revival who have had the greatest effect on my own thinking have been Joyce Appleby, Bernard Bailyn, J. G. A. Pocock, Sean Wilentz, and Gordon Wood. This revival has transformed a heterogeneous body of beliefs into liberalism's competitor as a candidate for the major American tradition. Republicanism is favored by those who believe that the earlier emphasis on liberalism overstated the importance of the "autonomous individual." I entirely agree with these revisionists that the prominence of autonomous individualism in American history has been seriously exaggerated. I disagree when they (less and less frequently) suggest a clear separation between liberalism and republicanism. These traditions seem entirely woven together to me, as the most subtle of the revisionist work suggests. See, e.g., Joyce Appleby, *Liberalism and Republicanism in the Historical Imagination* (Cambridge: Harvard University Press, 1992). The interweaving of liberalism and republicanism appears in her usage of both terms: for example, she describes John Adams as "liberal in the sense of cherishing public freedom and venerating the rule of law" (199). Liberalism here goes far beyond an exclusive (and very partial) emphasis on individual autonomy, and constitutes itself with "republican" traits. For an account of the dualism within modern liberalism, see Charles Taylor, *Multiculturalism and the Politics of Recognition* (Princeton, N.J.: Princeton University Press, 1992).

13. On the subject of Whig thinking I have particularly benefited from Daniel Walker Howe, *The Political Culture of the American Whigs* (Chicago: University of Chicago Press, 1979); for instances of their continual attempts at liberal "balance," see 129, 181, and 187. For an excellent account of Emerson's Federalist milieu, see Mary Kupiec Cayton, *Emerson's Emergence: Self and Society in the*

Transformation of New England, 1800–1845 (Chapel Hill, N.C.: University of North Carolina Press, 1989), chaps. 1–2. Cayton's reading differs from mine when she regards Emerson as breaking with or significantly rewriting the deference culture into which he was born.

14. Edward Everett, *An Oration delivered at Cambridge on the Fiftieth Anniversary of the Declaration of Independence* (Boston: Cummings, Hilliard, & Co., 1826).

15. Yehoshua Arieli, *Individualism and Nationalism in American Ideology* (Baltimore: Penguin Books, 1966), 113–14. Arieli is citing Adam Ferguson, *An Essay on the History of Civil Society* (Edinburgh: A. Millar & T. Caddel, 1767).

16. Stephen Whicher, *Freedom and Fate* (Philadelphia: University of Pennsylvania Press, 1953); Stanley Cavell, *Conditions Handsome and Unhandsome: The Constitution of Emersonian Perfectionism* (Chicago: University of Chicago Press, 1990).

17. Valuable synopses of the conflict between liberalism and democracy and of the issues involved in creating a liberal democracy can be found in Norberto Bobbio, *Liberalism and Democracy,* trans. Martin Ryle and Kate Soper (London: Verso Press, 1990); and Benjamin R. Barber, "Liberal Democracy and the Costs of Consent," in *Liberalism and the Moral Life,* ed. Nancy L. Rosenblum (Cambridge: Harvard University Press, 1989), 54–68. Barber's criticisms of liberalism do not extend to a critique of their retention of the authoritarian. He believes, as I do not, that though liberalism "did not necessarily entail democratic arrangements," it nonetheless "emancipate[ed] us from authority" of more traditional kinds (56, 66). As I will argue throughout, such authority has been more continuous, and continuously top-down, than liberalism is willing to recognize.

18. Thus David Leverenz displays a focus somewhat different from mine when he argues that "Emerson's various paradoxes reflect contradictions in the emerging ideology of individualism, which erected an ideal of free, forceful, and resourceful white men on the presumption of depersonalized servitude from several subordinated groups" (*Manhood and the American Renaissance* [Ithaca, N.Y.: Cornell University Press, 1989], 44).

CHAPTER ONE

1. Robert H. Wiebe, *The Opening of American Society: From the Adoption of the Constitution to the Eve of Disunion* (New York: Knopf, 1984), 146. Similarly, Karen Halttunen writes that "the early republican period between 1789 and 1840 marked the gradual transition from traditional deferential politics focusing on the political leader to modern egalitarian politics focusing on the electorate" (*Confidence Men and Painted Women: A Study of Middle-class Culture in America, 1830–1870* [New Haven, Conn.: Yale University Press, 1982], 15).

2. Daniel Walker Howe, *The Unitarian Conscience: Harvard Moral Philosophy, 1805–1861* (Middletown, Conn.: Wesleyan University Press, 1988), 209.

3. Ronald P. Formisano, *The Transformation of Political Culture: Massachusetts Parties, 1790s–1840s* (New York: Oxford University Press, 1983), 23.

4. Howe, *Unitarian,* 204.

5. Anne C. Rose, *Transcendentalism as a Social Movement, 1830–1850* (New Haven, Conn.: Yale University Press, 1981), 43, 42.

6. Benjamin R. Barber, "Liberal Democracy," 57. For a development of this balance through readings of Emerson and some contemporaries, see George Kateb, "Democratic Individuality and the Meaning of Rights" in Rosenblum, ed., *Liberalism* (see intro., n. 17).

7. George Ripley, "Discourses on the Philosophy of Religion" (1836), in *The Transcendentalists*, ed. Perry Miller (Cambridge: Harvard University Press, 1950), 136.

8. Ralph Waldo Emerson, "The Transcendentalist," *Essays and Lectures*, ed. Joel Porte (New York: Library of America, 1983), 195, hereafter *Es and Ls.*

9. The former phrase is explained in Michel Foucault, *The Order of Things: An Archaeology of the Human Sciences* (New York: Random House, 1970), chap. 9.

10. Bobbio, *Liberalism and Democracy*, 43.

11. Andrew Jackson, veto message July 10, 1830, cited in Arthur M. Schlesinger, Jr., *The Age of Jackson* (Boston: Little, Brown, 1950), 90.

12. Lawrence Frederick Kohl, *The Politics of Individualism: Parties and the American Character in the Jacksonian Era* (New York: Oxford University Press, 1989), intro. and chap. 1.

13. Orestes A. Brownson, "Emerson" (1839), in P. Miller, ed., *Transcendentalists*, 432.

14. Margaret Fuller, "The Great Lawsuit" (1843), in ibid., 461, 460, 459.

15. George Bancroft, "On the Progress of Civilization" (1838), in ibid., 425.

16. E. H. Chapin, "The Relation of the Individual to the Republic," election sermon, Massachusetts, January 3, 1844 (Boston: Dutton & Wentworth, 1844), 19.

17. Emma Goldman, "Anarchism: What It Really Stands For," *Anarchism and Other Essays* (New York: Dover Publications, 1969), 52.

18. Ibid., 56. Goldman can work with Emerson's thought not because he is an incipient socialist but because she remains an American liberal in remaining a transcendentalist. Rather than being a radical individualist, the anarchist is one who, as Karl Mannheim notes, "regards the existing order as one undifferentiated whole" (*Ideology and Utopia: An Introduction to the Sociology of Knowledge*, cited in Anne C. Rose, *Transcendentalism as a Social Movement, 1830–1850* [New Haven, Conn.: Yale University Press, 1981], 117). The refusal to oppose individual and community is a long tradition in American culture. Thomas Paine, e.g., writes that "public good is not a term opposed to the good of individuals; on the contrary, it is the good of every individual collected. It is the good of all, because it is the good of every one: for as the public body is every individual collected, so the public good is the collected good of those individuals" (cited in Stephen Lukes, *Individualism* [Oxford: Basil Blackwell, 1973], 49).

19. Cornel West, *The American Evasion of Philosophy: A Genealogy of Pragmatism* (Madison: University of Wisconsin Press, 1989), 213.

20. Cavell, *Conditions Handsome and Unhandsome,* 12, 125. As I note in my final chapter, this notion of self-reliance as self plus other dominated Emerson scholarship in the 1980s. For other insightful instances, see John Michael, *Emerson and Skepticism: The Cipher of the World* (Baltimore: Johns Hopkins University Press, 1988): "That which the seer says is the report of himself, and that report is simultaneously the abandonment and the recovery of the self proclaimed. Only in this *renunciation* of the self to the judgment of the other can the law of the self's authority be realized" (26). See also Phyllis Cole, "Emerson, England, and Fate," in *Emerson: Prophecy, Metamorphosis, and Influence,* Selected Papers from the English Institute, ed. David Levin (New York: Columbia University Press, 1975), 101–2; Ann Douglas, *The Feminization of American Culture* (New York: Doubleday, Anchor, 1988), 91, 129; Amy Schrager Lang, *Prophetic Woman: Anne Hutchinson and the Problem of Dissent in the Literature of New England* (Berkeley and Los Angeles: University of California Press, 1987), 117–21; David Robinson, *The Apostle of Culture: Emerson as Preacher and Lecturer* (Philadelphia: University of Pennsylvania Press, 1982), 89–91; Barbara Packer, "Origin and Authority: Emerson and the Higher Criticism," in *Reconstructing American Literary History,* ed. Sacvan Bercovitch, Harvard English Studies, no. 13 (Cambridge: Harvard University Press, 1986), 88; John Peacock, "Self-Reliance and Corporate Destiny: Emerson's Dialectic of Culture," *ESQ* 29, no. 2 (1983): 64; David Van Leer, *Emerson's Epistemology: The Argument of the Essays* (Cambridge: Cambridge University Press, 1986), chap. 6.

21. Offering a more one-sided reading of Emerson as a liberal, Bercovitch has recently noted that Emerson's interest in combining individuality with union did not mean he wanted social union. Emerson militated against all kinds of collective sovereignty then going under the name of socialism and rejected embodied collective governance. "The real point, Emerson seems about to say, is not my plan for society against yours. It is perfect union, a utopian hope we both share, based on a dream of individuality — something 'spiritual and not to be actualized' — which by definition sets the individual *at odds with* society as it is, anywhere, at any time" (Sacvan Bercovitch, "Emerson, Individualism, and the Ambiguities of Dissent," *South Atlantic Quarterly* 89, no. 3 [Summer 1990]: 635, emphasis added; revised as chap. 9 of *The Rites of Assent: Transformations in the Symbolic Construction of America* [New York: Routledge, 1993]).

22. Emerson, "Friendship," *Es and Ls,* 350–51.

23. For a different reading of what she calls Emerson's "tender hierarchy," see Julie Ellison, "The Gender of Transparency: Masculinity and the Conduct of Life," *American Literary History* 4, no. 4 (Winter 1992): 585. Our readings overlap where she says "The crucial point about Emersonian intimacy is that hierarchy is the medium of desire" (591).

24. Emerson, "Over-Soul," *Es and Ls,* 385. The "one blood" passage from the journal, when inserted into this essay, refers to the "union of man and God" (399).

25. Some recent commentators have taken the cultural importance of male, individualistic submission seriously. These include Bercovitch, *Rites of Assent,*

20; Richard H. Brodhead, "Sparing the Rod: Discipline and Fiction in Antebellum America," *Representations* 21 (Winter 1988): 67–96; Myra Jehlen, "The Novel and the American Middle Class," in *Ideology and Classic American Literature,* ed. Sacvan Bercovitch and Myra Jehlen (Cambridge: Cambridge University Press, 1986), 125–44; and on Emerson specifically, Lou Ann Lange, *The Riddle of Liberty* (Atlanta: Scholars Press, 1987). Jehlen, e.g., notes that "the case for social constraints, for law and order, for conformity to conventional roles, is powerfully argued throughout American fiction, and particularly in those very works of the first part of the nineteenth century which are usually cited as evidence of America's intractable commitment to individual freedom. For it is in these writings, of Hawthorne and Melville especially, that the representation of such freedom is most tense and guilt-ridden, and its exercise most often sinful and/or fatal" (137). I comment on these accurate and illuminating readings in due course. Social critics are being blunter than their counterparts in culture. Two recent examples are Slater, *Dream Deferred* and Lewis Lapham, *The Wish for Kings: Democracy at Bay* (New York: Grove Press, 1993).

26. Christopher Lasch is more accurate than Bloom in noting that Emerson, without expressing "weakness," holds that "submission, not defiance, is the way of true virtue . . . freedom lies in the acceptance of necessity" (*The True and Only Heaven: Progress and Its Critics* [New York: Norton, 1991], 264). Though Lasch shows an unusual grasp of the real purport of Emerson's position in major essays like "Fate," he does not explain how submission to necessity can be freedom in any sense of the word. He perpetuates the problem I'm describing by redefining freedom as submission.

27. Michael Kammen, *Spheres of Liberty: Changing Perceptions of Liberty in American Culture* (Ithaca, N.Y.: Cornell University Press, 1989), chap. 2.

28. Jay Fliegelman, *Prodigals and Pilgrims: The American Revolution against Patriarchal Authority, 1750–1800* (New York: Cambridge University Press, 1982), 126.

29. Lang, *Prophetic Woman,* 134.

30. Howard Horwitz, "The Standard Oil Trust as Emersonian Hero," *Raritan* 6, no. 4 (Spring 1987): 98.

31. Sacvan Bercovitch, *The Puritan Origins of the American Self* (New Haven, Conn.: Yale University Press, 1975), 19, 176, 184, 60, 173.

32. Louis Hartz, *The Liberal Tradition in America* (New York: Harcourt, Brace & World, Harvest, 1955), 111, and for the fusion of faith in individual and entrepreneurial property with democracy, see 106, 112, 116, 118, 122 passim.

33. On the differences between Hegel's highly influential scheme and the U.S. case, see Kendall Thomas, "A House Divided against Itself: A Comment on Mastery, Slavery, and Emancipation," Hegel and Legal Theory, pt. 2, *Cardozo Law Review* 10 (March/April 1989): 1481–1515. Among Emerson's contemporaries, one of the most powerful exposures of the master's synthesis of vulnerability and tyranny is Harriet Jacobs, *Incidents in the Life of a Slave Girl* (1861). For other critiques, see, e.g., Karl Marx, "On the Jewish Question" (1843),

in *Early Writings*, trans. Rodney Livingstone and Gregor Benton (New York: Random House, Vintage, 1975), 211–41; Herbert Marcuse, "The Affirmative Character of Culture," in *Negations: Essays in Critical Theory*, trans. Jeremy J. Shapiro (Boston: Beacon Press, 1968), 88–133 (among many other writings on this subject); and Carole Pateman, "Sublimation and Reification: Locke, Wolin and the Liberal-Democratic Conception of the Political," in *The Disorder of Women* (Stanford, Calif.: Stanford University Press, 1989): 90–117. A long and philosophically profound history of critiques of reciprocity between social unequals has had little visible impact on mainstream American Studies.

34. Michel Foucault, *The History of Sexuality*, trans. Robert Hurley (New York: Random House, Vintage, 1980), 92.

35. See, e.g., Richard H. Brodhead's deft revision of Foucault's *Discipline and Punish* for the American case in *Cultures of Letters: Scenes of Reading and Writing in Nineteenth-Century America* (Chicago: University of Chicago Press, 1993), chap. 1. His focus is on the shift from the obvious tyranny of corporal punishment to a loving, often maternal "disciplinary intimacy." Though he sees intimacy as disciplinary, and in that way like whipping, such discipline produces nothing more submissive than ordinary socialization. For discussion of domestic socialization, see chap. 5 below.

36. Bercovitch, *Rites*, 20. Avery Gordon has suggested to me that, were American studies scholars trained as sociologists, this would be considered a variant of Talcott Parson's functionalism.

37. Ibid., 21.

38. Emerson, "Montaigne," *Es and Ls*, 708.

39. Ibid., 705–6.

40. Ibid., 705.

41. Ibid., 687.

42. Stanley Cavell has a similar moment of pleasure in Emerson when he defines Emersonian liberation simply as "founding as finding, of grounding as lasting; the conversion of American success and Kantian succession into a passive practice, the power of mourning" (*This New Yet Unapproachable America: Lectures after Emerson and Wittgenstein*, The 1987 Frederick Ives Carpenter Lectures [Albuquerque, N.M.: Living Batch Press, 1989], 116).

43. Though models of mourning and abjection have been usefully applied to Emerson, and though they correctly suggest the power that ensues at the end of an intensively patterned loss, they tend to assume too easily that a wish to end hierarchy is really an attempt to recover a powerful place in one. In Julia Kristeva's words, the "inaugural *loss* that laid the foundations of its own being" coincides with an enabling identification with the father and with an (ambivalent) repudiation of the abject other (*Powers of Horror: An Essay on Abjection*, trans. Leon S. Roudiez [1980; New York: Columbia University Press, 1982], 5). See also Sharon Cameron, "Representing Grief: Emerson's 'Experience,'" *Representations* 15 (Summer 1986): 15–41; and Mark Edmundson, "Emerson and the Work of Melancholia," *Raritan* 6, no. 4 (Spring 1987): 120–36. Some nonpsychoanalytic analyses also conclude that in Emerson, weakness is strength

and loss leads to recovery. In "Scarcity, Subjectivity, and Emerson," Wai-chee Dimock argues that "the self's felt lack — its experiential scarcity — . . . sets it apart from the world of abundance and, paradoxically, underwrites its autonomy. To make the paradox even more apparent, we might say that, for Emerson, subjective deficiency is the ground for self-sufficiency" (*boundary 2* 17, no. 1 [Spring 1990]: 91). Richard Grusin similarly observes that "privation is eventually repaid by the 'incoming of God'" ("'Put God in Your Debt': Emerson's Economy of Expenditure," *PMLA* 103, no. 1 [January 1988]: 38).

44. Walter Benn Michaels makes a strong case for such defensiveness in "Romance and Real Estate," in *The Gold Standard and the Logic of Naturalism* (Berkeley and Los Angeles: University of California Press, 1987).

45. I am describing a kind of crowd psychology here which, as I argue in some detail in chap. 5, does not describe democratic mobs but group behavior in nondemocratic contexts.

46. This phrase is from the closing paragraphs of "Montaigne; or, the Skeptic," where Emerson's most famous doubts about the presence of higher powers — and closest approximations of an interconnected self-reliance — are woven together with his affirmation of these higher powers (*Es and Ls*, 707).

47. Emerson, "Fate," *Es and Ls*, 968. Marx offers the classic account of liberalism's vision of an (egalitarian) collective life that remains imaginary: the bourgeois individual "lives in the *political community*, where he regards himself as a *communal being*, and in *civil society*, where he is active as a *private individual*, regards other men as means, debases himself to a means and becomes a plaything of alien powers. The relationship of the political state to civil society is just as spiritual as the relationship of heaven to earth. . . . Man in his *immediate* reality, in civil society, is a profane being. . . . In the state, on the other hand, where he is considered to be a species-being, he is the imaginary member of a fictitious sovereignty, he is divested of his real individual life and filled with an unreal universality" ("Jewish Question," 220).

48. Etienne Balibar, *Masses, Classes, Ideas: Studies on Politics and Philosophy before and after Marx,* trans. James Swenson (New York: Routledge, 1994), xiii. Balibar is alluding to what he regards as the central, radical claim of the *Declaration of the Rights of Man* (1789), which he calls the "proposition of equaliberty." For a more sustained examination of these and related issues in the context of contemporary forms of racism, nationalism, citizenship, and democratic governance, see Balibar, *Les frontières de la démocratie* (Paris: Editions La Découverte, 1992). Balibar's concerns are close to my own here, but I encountered both of these texts too late to make use of them.

49. Eve Kosofsky Sedgwick, *Epistemology of the Closet* (Berkeley and Los Angeles: University of California Press, 1990), 23.

50. See chap. 4 for my argument that particular sexual liberties and social equality were stigmatized together, as though their connection were particularly potent.

51. On radical democracy, see esp. Ernesto Laclau and Chantal Mouffe, *Hegemony and Socialist Strategy* (London: Verso Press, 1985). For an appraisal of

the concept in light of contemporary U.S. society, see the special section, "Radical Democracy," in *Socialist Review* 93, no. 3 (1994).

52. Bloom, Bercovitch, and Cavell all exemplify this notion of freedom as the freedom to chose one's bonds, bonds already structured.

CHAPTER TWO

1. Jürgen Habermas, *Theory and Practice,* trans. John Viertel (Boston: Beacon Press, 1973), 145–46.

2. From fragment 116 of Friedrich Schlegel, *Athenaeum,* cited in Tzvetan Todorov, *Theories of the Symbol,* trans. Catherine Porter (Ithaca, N.Y.: Cornell University Press, 1982), 195.

3. John Keane paraphrases Fichte this way in *Public Life and Late Capitalism: Toward a Socialist Theory of Democracy* (Cambridge: Cambridge University Press, 1984), 125.

4. Sacvan Bercovitch, *The Office of the Scarlet Letter* (Baltimore: Johns Hopkins University Press, 1991), 126.

5. Harold Bloom, "Mr. America," *New York Review of Books* (22 November 1984): 19.

6. Cavell, *This New Yet Unapproachable America,* 101, 109; Bloom, "Mr. America," 22.

7. Emerson, "Language," *Es and Ls,* 20. Further references will be found in the text.

8. Plato, *Cratylus* 429b; see James H. Stam's explication in *Inquiries into the Origin of Language: The Fate of a Question* (New York: Harper & Row, 1976), 83. Socrates, unlike Cratylus, holds that "the knowledge of things is not to be derived from names" as the resemblance between word and thing is inexact (439b); he says to Cratylus, "I quite agree with you that words should as far as possible resemble things, but I fear that this dragging in of resemblance, as Hermogenes says, is a shabby thing, which has to be supplemented by the mechanical aid of convention with a view to correctness" (435c).

9. Emerson's realism is not a quirk of his Neoplatonic youth, for it is reiterated again in "The Poet," published in 1844. Though his views on language had changed by the time of later essays like "Quotation and Originality," they did not change in favor of nominalism so much as in favor of a kind of market realism, where timeless essences appear in endless circulation. See chap. 6 for discussion of this point.

10. Bloom, "Mr. America," 19.

11. See Cavell's invocation of Kant in *Conditions Handsome and Unhandsome,* 31, and elsewhere; for an important Kantian reading that stresses the influence on Emerson of the first over the second critique, see the early chapters of Van Leer, *Emerson's Epistemology.*

12. Within the *Biographia Literaria,* the term *degree* appears at several theoretical landmarks: only degree separates fancy from imagination and primary from secondary imagination (Samuel Taylor Coleridge, *Biographia Literaria*

[Princeton, N.J.: Bollingen–Princeton University Press, 1983], 1:82, 304). *Degree* distinguishes two modes or structures which do not differ in kind so much as in aspect.

13. Emerson modifies this statement shortly: "Every word which is used to express a *moral or intellectual* fact . . . is found to be borrowed from some material appearance" ("Language," *Es and Ls,* 20, emphasis added). I will shortly discuss this tacit shift from "words" to moral or intellectual words, but I take seriously Emerson's first formulation as intending to invoke the authoritative context of theories about language's material origins.

14. Elizabeth Palmer Peabody, review of J. G. Herder, *The Spirit of the Hebrew Scriptures, Christian Examiner* 16 (May 1834): 175.

15. Bercovitch, *Puritan Origins,* 159.

16. Jacques Derrida, "White Mythology," in *Margins of Philosophy,* trans. Alan Bass (Chicago: University of Chicago Press, 1982), 213. Derrida is describing a fable of language's fall that he finds in Anatole France, *The Garden of Epicurus.* This fable of the *"usure* (of metaphor), the ruining of the figure," is quite similar to Emerson's (and Plato's and others'): "'The vocabulary of mankind was framed from sensuous images'"; the sensuous image, Derrida notes, "is not exactly a metaphor. It is a kind of transparent figure, equivalent to a literal meaning *(sens propre)."* France's Polyphilos "undertakes an etymological or philological work which is to reawaken all the sleeping figures" (210–12). Polyphilos names the opposite of this awakened language a "white mythology": "Any expression of an abstract idea can only be an analogy. By an odd fate, the very metaphysicians who think to escape the world of appearances are constrained to live perpetually in allegory. A sorry lot of poets, they dim the colours of the ancient fables, and are themselves but gatherers of fables. They produce white mythology" (quoted in Derrida, 213). Much like Polyphilos, Emerson assumes that penetration to original meaning involves awareness of law rather than free legislative power.

17. Emerson's rewriting of cognate views tends to render them absolute and ahistorical. Peabody relishes the mind's "original principles" and nature's "original simplicity," but her version of man's fall into society differs from Emerson's claim that "duplicity and falsehood take place of simplicity and truth." Peabody says, "As society becomes ramified, and people act upon each other, and talk by imitation and custom, and not from within, a thousand arbitrary and accidental associations connect themselves with words, and even with things, which deaden and shut out the impressions they would naturally make. . . . Words that were once pictures become counters. This is prose" (Peabody, 175). What Peabody calls "prose" (or symbol-language) Emerson redescribes as "falsehood" even as he follows her account of the decline. Original language for her expresses not so much the absolute as "sensibility" (176); Herder, interested in the "spirit" of Hebrew poetry, offers concrete instances of Hebrew's historical influence on later languages that Emerson skips. Again, Emerson's account is not so much independent or unique as it is a borrowing well Platonized.

18. Paul de Man, "Intentional Structure of the Romantic Image," in *Romanticism and Consciousness: Essays in Criticism,* ed. Harold Bloom (New York: Norton, 1970), 68.

19. Charles Feidelson Jr., *Symbolism and American Literature* (Chicago: University of Chicago Press, 1953), 132, 297n, 132.

20. Bercovitch, *Puritan Origins,* 159, 164–65.

21. See also Philip Gura, *The Wisdom of Words: Language, Theology, and Literature in the New England Renaissance* (Middletown, Conn.: Wesleyan University Press, 1981), 94–95, and Larzer Ziff, *Literary Democracy* (New York: Viking, 1981). Ziff claims that "the American language was to differ [from Europe's] in its radical return to the natural physical base," but that Emerson also saw in the American "advance upon chaos . . . not an extension of the sacred cosmos [the "natural physical base"] but rather a reassertment of man upon the unspoiled in a series of restartings" (202, 38).

22. To take one more example: Emerson says that "because of this radical correspondence between visible things and human thoughts, savages, who have only what is necessary, converse in figures ("Language," 22). Here is a phenomenological balance between preestablished forms and individual agency: mind-nature correspondence does not lead to the engraving of literal signs on the passive mind but to active figuration which speaks the truth of the natural thing. These figures arise from individual "passion," "thought," being "earnest" (23), and they mean that "good writing and brilliant discourse are perpetual allegories" (23). The wise poet is not a scribe but an inventor, though of course he is an inventor of true images. But even this freedom, which remains within the careful restrictions of Aristotelian logocentrism, where figural meaning may be plural but must be determinate and finite (Derrida), is too much for Emerson. The allegories that arise "from the present action of the mind" are in reality "the working of the Original Cause through the instruments he has already made" ("Language," 23). Degree 2, mind, exists only to collapse into its immediate origin in degree 3, consuming Spirit. Truest consciousness is again the purest imitation.

23. A. Bronson Alcott, "Psyche" (1836), in *Emerson the Essayist,* ed. Kenneth Walter Cameron (Raleigh, N.C.: Thistle Press, 1945), 117.

24. Gura, *Wisdom of Words,* 94.

25. Blair, *Lectures on Rhetoric and Belles Lettres* (Dublin, 1783), 102. Similarly, Emerson quite likely distinguishes between "sign" and "symbol" through Blair: "Words, as we now employ them, taken in the general, may be considered as symbols, not as imitations; as arbitrary, or intuited, not natural signs of ideas" (106). This reverses the more familiar romantic or at least Coleridgean pairing of sign and symbol, in which "sign" describes an arbitrary and "symbol" an innate relationship between sign and thing (see, e.g., Derrida, "White Mythology," 212). Nonetheless, Emerson's usage is closer to Blair's than to Coleridge's.

26. Emerson's lack of originality here is nearly total, but so is his grasp of the capacity of Locke's views to sustain a realism of nature as much as a nominalism of words: "It may also lead us a little towards the Original of all our Notions and Knowledge, if we remark, how great a dependance our *Words* have

on common sensible *Ideas*; and how those, which are made use of to stand for Actions and Notions quite removed from sense, *have their rise from thence, and from obvious sensible* Ideas *are transferred to more abstruse significations,* and made to stand for *Ideas* that come not under the cognizance of our senses; *v.g.* to *Imagine, Apprehend, Comprehend, Adhere, Conceive, Instill, Disgust, Disturbance, Tranquility,* etc. are all Words taken from the Operations of sensible Things, and applied to certain Modes of Thinking. *Spirit,* in its primary signification, is Breath; *Angel,* a Messenger: And I doubt not, but if we could trace them to their sources, we should find, in all Languages, the names, which stand for Things that fall not under our Senses, to have had their first rise from sensible *Ideas.* . . . Nature, even in the naming of Things, unawares suggested to Men the Originals and Principles of all their Knowledge: whilst, to give Names, that might make known to others any Operations they felt in themselves, or any other *Ideas,* that came not under their Senses, they were fain to borrow Words from ordinary known *Ideas* of Sensation" (*An Essay Concerning Human Understanding,* ed. Peter H. Nidditch [Oxford: Oxford University Press, Clarendon, 1979]: Bk. III, 1.5, p. 403).

27. This excludes, e.g., David Hume and Adam Smith. The latter has no interest in the nature of the first relation between a proper name and its object, which he deems some "appellatio[n]" these "savages . . . might think proper, in that primitive jargon, to mark" the most familiar objects (Adam Smith, "Considerations Concerning the First Formation of Languages, and the Different Genius of Original and Compounded Languages," in *The Early Writings of Adam Smith,* ed. J. Ralph Lindonen [New York: Augustus M. Kelley, 1967], 225). He suggests that language as a genuine public system more importantly "originates" in the process by which a proper noun for an individual thing is generalized to cover similar objects until it becomes a common noun.

28. Locke, *Human Understanding,* 403; *Selected Works of Noah Webster* (Boston: Little, Brown, 1824), 183–84.

29. Horace Bushnell, "Language and Doctrine," *Christ in Theology* (Hartford, Conn.: Brown & Parsons, 1851), 15, "A Preliminary Dissertation on the Nature of Language, as Related to Thought and Spirit," *God in Christ* (Hartford, Conn.: Brown & Parsons, 1849), 43–44. On Bushnell's statements about language, see Michael Kramer, "Horace Bushnell's Philosophy of Language Considered as a Mode of Cultural Criticism," *American Quarterly* 38 (Fall 1986): 573–90; and the valuable study by Donald A. Crosby, *Horace Bushnell's Theory of Language in the Context of Other Nineteenth-Century Philosophies of Language* (The Hague: Mouton, 1975).

30. Bushnell, "Nature of Language," 55.

31. Samuel Taylor Coleridge, *Treatise on Logic II,* 403–4, quoted in Owen Barfield, *What Coleridge Thought* (Middletown, Conn.: Wesleyan University Press, 1971), 20.

32. James Marsh, "Review of Stuart on the Epistle to the Hebrews," in Gura, *Wisdom of Words,* 43.

33. Philip Gura, "Elizabeth Palmer Peabody and the Philosophy of Language," *ESQ* (1977), 160.

34. Cited by Derrida, in "White Mythology," 255, for a different purpose.

35. Hans Aarsleff, *From Locke to Saussure: Essays on the Study of Language and Intellectual History* (Minneapolis: University of Minnesota Press, 1982), 378.

36. Blair, "Lectures," 115, 289.

37. These include catachresis, abstraction, naming, mixing of languages, the expression of passion, and others.

38. Emerson seems interested in empirical questions of the origins of language not for their literal content but for their figuration of lawfulness. The period abounds in theories of language origin and if he were interested, Emerson might have referred to Socrates' (at least half-facetious) description of the physical origin of words in *Cratylus,* or have drawn on the Adamic tradition of the first words naming essences of things, or have invoked Horne Tooke's researches into universal linguistic radicals. Such is Noah Webster's move: "Now the Hebrew word *iheue* or *iove,* from the verb *heue,* or *eue, to exist,* that is, to *breathe,* is a mere onomatope; an imitation of a strong expiration, or forceable emission of breath, intended to express an idea of *breath* or *life,* and of course *spirit.*" In such an account, words are bound to things not by "their sounds — which *did* vary greatly for the same object in different tongues — but in the very *articulations* of sound" (Gura, "Peabody," 158). Emerson also avoids taking literally another available explanation of the concrete "imitation" that links thing and word (he alludes to it as a kind of figure in the second section of "Language"): the first words were pictures or "images" of things in "that picturesque language" (23) of "savages and children." The idea of the "picturesqueness" of natural language stemmed in part from contemporary discussions of Egyptian hieroglyphs: language develops, in this tradition, from "figurative" characters, "which literally represented the object meant to be expressed" (John Irwin, *American Hieroglyphics* [Baltimore: Johns Hopkins University Press, 1980], 6). Emerson avoids the speculations about the first sort of natural language that were already current in the mid-1830s in the work of Socrates, Dugald Stewart, Tooke, Samuel Henshall, Webster, Walter Whiter, Coleridge, Reed and Everett on Greppo, and Peabody's review of Herder. These arguments had enough currency to reappear in Thoreau's famous railroad-bank passage in *Walden,* where he suggests that the physical shape of vowels and consonants are literal imitations of the everyday processes of nature (Thoreau's Socratic precedent is *Cratylus* 426c-247d). Again, Emerson has little interest in the literal details but much interest in the general principle, which is of determination through nature.

39. Derrida, "White Mythology," 248.

40. Harold Bloom, on the contrary, has most forcefully argued that Emerson's "American Sublime" invokes a "self-rebegetting" when one becomes "one's own father" (*Poetry and Repression: Revisionism from Blake to Stevens* [New Haven, Conn.: Yale University Press, 1975], 244). Emerson's point usually seems to me to be to devise a fathering that can never be internalized as one's own autonomous power, but which can be called autonomy nonetheless. See chap. 7 for a discussion of the ongoing links between slavery and benevolent paternalism in the context of Emancipation and Reconstruction.

41. The first phrase is David Simpson's, by which he refers to transcendentalism's organicism (David Simpson, *The Politics of American English, 1776–1850* [New York: Oxford University Press, 1986], 240). His discussion includes a description of its "social and political correlative" with which I agree, and which I press further below: "In the nineteenth century this notion tended to function, as it still does, as a consoling mythology softening the implacable inequalities that were more and more noticeable with the increased pace of industrialization" (258).

42. Derrida observes the "metaphor of metaphor" to be "the metaphor of *domination,* heightened by its power of dissimulation which permits it to escape mastery: God or the Sun?" ("White Mythology," 266).

43. Again, one of the most luminous expressions of this position belongs to Bercovitch: "One could find no better gloss on that representative act of American dissent than the strategies by which, in his writing from *Nature* (1836) through *Essays: First Series* (1841), Emerson develops his utopian vision of the self. He transforms earlier concepts of autonomy (Descartes' *cogito,* Locke's self-possessive individualism) into a self-emptying mode of 'visionary possession,' one that requires us to discard in order to incorporate" (Bercovitch, "Emerson," 631–32 [see chap. 1, n. 21]). I remain perplexed by the contradictory nature of this reconciliation of "dissent" and "self-emptying" (which still allows the self to "incorporate"). Were this to lead toward some kind of socialist or collective identity, it would make more sense, but in this essay Bercovitch is explaining how Emerson rejects socialism. As it stands, this reconciliation is characteristic of a long line of liberal claims that subjecting the self yields the self's freedom.

44. Critics of liberalism who work in political philosophy have argued that liberalism is constituted by the loss of individual sovereignty. A name change might disrupt this insight. For an excellent condensation of the issues, see Pateman, "Sublimation," 90–117 (see chap. 1, n. 33).

CHAPTER THREE

1. Emerson, "Prospects," *Es and Ls,* 46.

2. Maurice Gonnaud, *An Uneasy Solitude: Individual and Society in the Work of Ralph Waldo Emerson,* trans. Lawrence Rosenwald (Princeton, N.J.: Princeton University Press, 1987), 254.

3. Alexis de Tocqueville, *Democracy in America,* trans, George Lawrence, ed. J. P. Mayer (Garden City, N.Y.: Doubleday, Anchor, 1969), 692.

4. Jean Baudrillard, *America,* trans. Chris Turner (New York: Verso Press, 1988), 96.

5. The most fully elaborated claim for the identity of personal autonomy and national destiny comes from Bercovitch. As I've noted elsewhere, he describes an individualism in which immersion in corporate providence invariably confirms autonomous power (*Puritan Origins,* 173, 176). Emerson's transcendentalism appears to be essentially identical to antebellum liberalism when Ber-

covitch describes the latter as a "pluralistic faith [which] compels resolution through the higher laws of both/and" that avoid choice and produce "bipolar complementarity . . . ; liberalism hold[s] the self intact by holding it in check" in accordance with an "expanding continuum of liberal reciprocity ("A-Politics in *The Scarlet Letter,*" *New Literary History* 19, no. 3 [Spring 1988]: 637, 643, 638, 641). I value these statements as myth description rather than as social analysis (and it is a myth that resonates most for a narrow range of antebellum society). Even the early, ebullient, and always patrician Emerson is more conflicted than this.

6. Bercovitch, *Puritan Origins,* 134.

7. See, e.g., George B. Forgie, *Patricide in the House Divided: A Psychological Interpretation of Lincoln and His Age* (New York: Norton, 1979); and Eric J. Sundquist, *Home as Found: Authority and Genealogy in Nineteenth-Century American Literature* (Baltimore: Johns Hopkins University Press, 1979).

8. Cavell, *Conditions Handsome and Unhandsome,* 31. Cavell's term is not "best self" but "further self," which he often associates with obeying an other who is your spouse. Remarriage is "the basis for them of moral encounter, of the constraint that announces the moral law, the standard attesting to the realm of ends, as developed in Emersonian Perfectionism. (The bond to the other as a function of the further self — Emerson also pictures it as the onward self — will at some stage have to be understood in contrast with bonds of narcissism — of the 'mirror stage' — and those of erotic fanaticism" [117].)

9. Emerson, "The American Scholar," *Es and Ls,* 54.

10. Quoted in Kohl, *Politics of Individualism,* 12.

11. David Henshaw, *Remarks upon the Rights and Powers of Corporations* (Boston, 1837), 5.

12. Robert Hessen, "The Evolution of Corporations: A Survey Article for the New Palgrave Dictionary of Political Economy," Working Papers in Economics E-86-57 (Stanford, Calif.: Hoover Institution, October 1986), 9.

13. R. Jeffrey Lustig, *Corporate Liberalism: The Origins of Modern American Political Theory, 1890–1920* (Berkeley and Los Angeles: University of California Press, 1980), 10.

14. Horwitz, "Standard Oil Trust," 98–99.

15. Walter Benn Michaels, *The Gold Standard and the Logic of Naturalism: American Literature at the Turn of the Century* (Berkeley and Los Angeles: University of California Press, 1987), 213.

16. Ibid., 206.

17. Ibid., 205.

18. Horwitz, "Standard Oil Trust," 99.

19. Ibid., 99, 119.

20. Kohl, *Politics of Individualism,* 16.

21. David Leverenz, "The Politics of Emerson's Man-Making Words," *PMLA* 101 (1986): 49, 52.

22. Gary G. Hamilton and John R. Sutton, "The Problem of Control in the Weak State: Domination in the United States, 1880–1920," *Theory and Society*

18, no. 1 (1989): 34. This article offers an excellent (and critically sympathetic) short history of the rise of administrative government in the United States.

23. Review of *Slavery*, by William Ellery Channing, *Boston Quarterly Review* 1, no. 2 (1838): 258.

24. Hannah Arendt's comments on the Greek polis suggest a more permanent haunting of democracy by slavery: "The mastery of necessity then has as its goal the controlling of the necessities of life, which coerce men and hold them in their power. But such domination can be accomplished only by controlling and doing violence to others, who as slaves relieve free men from themselves being coerced by necessity. The free man, the citizen of the *polis*, . . . not only must not be a slave, he must own and rule over slaves" ("What is Authority?" cited in Drucilla Cornell, *Transformations: Recollective Imagination and Sexual Difference* [New York: Routledge, 1993], 160).

25. Horwitz's account of "transcendent agency" is brilliantly correct as a description of an ideology.

26. Marx describes the "abstractness" of the communal as the principal mode by which this false reconciliation is put in place ("Jewish Question," 220).

27. In recent years, feminism has sponsored the historical work most apt to acknowledge that New England corporate life produced not only traditional individualism but concrete collective structures. Elizabeth Ammons, Nina Baym, Ann Douglas, Mary Ryan, Jane Tompkins, and others have described structures like the matriarchal home that imagine "escape for people as a group . . . into some larger and more perfect corporate system, one modeled not on individualism but on motherhood" (Elizabeth Ammons, "Stowe's Dream of the Mother-Savior: *Uncle Tom's Cabin* and American Women Writers before the 1920s," in *New Essays on "Uncle Tom's Cabin,"* ed. Eric J. Sundquist [Cambridge: Cambridge University Press, 1986], 157). Such readings suggest that a mixed range of antebellum corporate forms, though always entwined with an individualistic political culture, produced individualist fictions and other kinds of underanalyzed subjectivities.

28. Emerson, "The Over-Soul," *Es and Ls,* 385–86.

29. Horwitz, "Standard Oil Trust," 99; for a similar point, see works cited in chap. 1, n. 20.

30. Emerson, "Spirit," *Es and Ls,* 41.

31. "Man is all symmetry," Herbert writes, "Full of proportions, one limb to another, / And to all the world besides. / Each part may call the farthest, brother"; man, Herbert continues, "is in little all the sphere"; "Man is one world, and hath / Another to attend him" (quoted in Emerson, "Prospects," *Es and Ls,* 44–45). In each stanza of his poem, Herbert, who for Emerson is a kind of genteel naturalist, elaborates on a traditional identity between microcosm and macrocosm in which the individual mirrors the preexisting structure of being.

32. Quoted in Emerson, "Prospects," *Es and Ls,* 45.

33. Ibid., 46.

34. Quoted in Todorov, *Theories of the Symbol,* 176.

35. Emerson, "Prospects," *Es and Ls,* 43.

36. Thomas Taylor, "A Dissertation on the Life and Theology of Orpheus," in *Thomas Taylor the Platonist* (Princeton, N.J.: Bollingen-Princeton University Press, 1971), 166.

37. John Locke, *Two Treatises of Government,* ed. Peter Laslett, rev. ed. (Cambridge: Cambridge University Press, 1988), 271.

38. Taylor, "Orpheus," 166.

39. Michael, *Emerson and Skepticism,* 150.

40. Howe, *Political Culture,* 29 (see intro., n. 13).

41. William Ellery Channing, "Remarks on Associations," in *The Works of William E. Channing, D. D.* (Boston: American Unitarian Society, 1882), 143.

42. Ibid., 148.

43. Ibid., 149, 145.

44. Ibid., 145, 147.

45. Lawrence M. Friedman, *A History of American Law,* 2d ed. (New York: Simon & Schuster, Touchstone, 1985), 532.

46. Ibid., 275, 276.

47. Edwin Merrick Dodd, *American Business Corporations until 1860, with Special Reference to Massachusetts* (Cambridge: Harvard University Press, 1954), 37; Friedman, *American Law,* 534; Morton Horwitz, *The Transformation of American Law, 1780–1860* (Cambridge: Harvard University Press, 1977), 112.

48. L. Ray Gunn, *The Decline of Authority: Public Economic Policy and Political Development in New York, 1800–1860* (Ithaca, N.Y.: Cornell University Press, 1988), 133.

49. William Story, quoted in Morton Horwitz, *Transformation,* 203.

50. Horwitz, *Transformation,* 174.

51. Ibid., 39, 44.

52. Emerson, "Commodity," *Es and Ls,* 12.

53. Catherine Gallagher, "Marxism and the New Historicism," in *The New Historicism,* ed. H. Aram Veeser (New York: Routledge, 1989), 47.

54. Emerson, "Prospects," *Es and Ls,* 45–46.

55. Emerson, "The American Scholar," *Es and Ls,* 70–71.

56. Emerson, "Self-Reliance," *Es and Ls,* 268–69.

57. Gunn, *Decline of Authority,* 106.

58. Ibid., 100, 111.

59. Henshaw, *Remarks,* 5.

60. Ibid., 6.

61. *Bard v. The Bank of Washington,* cited in Joseph K. Angell and Samuel Ames, *A Treatise on the Law of Private Corporations Aggregate* (Boston: Hilliard, 1832), 81.

62. James W. Hurst, *The Legitimacy of the Business Corporation in the Law of the United States, 1780–1970* (Charlottesville: University of Virginia Press, 1974), 16.

63. Ronald E. Seavoy, *The Origins of the American Business Corporation, 1784–1855* (Westport, Conn.: Greenwood Press, 1982), 6.

64. Henshaw, *Remarks*, 11; cf. Charles J. Ingersoll, "Speech . . . in the convention of Pennsylvania, on Legislative and Judicial control over Charters of Incorporation," *United States Magazine and Democratic Review* 5 (January 1839): 99–144.

65. Cited in Dodd, *American Business Corporations*, 26. Although I reverse his stress on the corporate form's subordination to contract, I have benefited from Brook Thomas's reading of *Fletcher v. Peck* (1810) and *Dartmouth College v. Woodward* (1819), in his *Cross-examinations of Law and Literature: Cooper, Hawthorne, Stowe, and Melville* (Cambridge: Cambridge University Press, 1987), 49 and chap. 2 passim. My reading is similarly counter to M. Horwitz's authoritative interpretation, particularly chap. 4. Horwitz's research endorses the widely accepted view that legislative franchise was all but vanquished by the legal favor granted to economic development and its imperatives of "fair and equal competition," private contract, and "market" decision (134). But for a contemporary survey of the surprisingly irregular course of judicial opinion, see Angell and Ames, *Treatise*, esp. chaps. 5 and 7.

66. Dodd, *American Business Corporations*, 28.

67. In 1993, a resident of New York State named Robert Schultz sued to block a $6 billion bond issue authorized by the Metropolitan Transportation Authority and the Thruway Authority on the grounds that these public agencies had deprived New York citizens of "their state constitutional right to approve or disapprove an incurrence of debt" (James Ledbetter, "Of Human Bondage: A Maverick Activist Holds the State at Bay," *Village Voice*, 5 October 1993, 11). The constitutional article in question reflects attitudes that developed during Emerson's time: "No debt shall be hereafter contracted by or in behalf of the state, unless such debt shall be authorized by law for some single work or purpose to be distinctly specified therein. No such law shall take effect until it shall, at a general election, have been submitted to the people and have received a majority of all the votes cast for and against at such an election" (art. VII, sec. 11, cited 11). The lawsuit has sufficient legal merit for "an anonymous legislative aide" to have told the *New York Times*, "We view this as a big problem. We think that the state could very well lose on this one." Although fully private corporations have long been liberated from such legislative will, their increasingly transnational independence from not only the "public" but the "national" interest may in the future encourage parallel legal challenges to their sovereignty.

68. The latter phrase comes from Dewey, who also discusses "association" (John Dewey, "Corporate Personality" [1926], in *John Dewey: The Later Works, 1925–1953*, vol. 2, 1925–27, ed. JoAnn Bodyston [Carbondale and Edwardsville: Southern Illinois University Press, 1984], 22–43). Dewey also chronicles the tremendous historical variation of concepts of corporate personality and emphasizes the difficulty of keeping the private individual distinct from public entities even where the latter are conceptually modeled on the former.

69. L. R. Gunn, *Decline of Authority*, 105 passim; John Mayfield, *The New Nation, 1800–1845*, rev. ed. (New York: Hill & Wang, 1982), 74.

NOTES TO PAGES 92–96

CHAPTER FOUR

1. This chapter owes its existence to excellent feminist work on the subordination of women through Anglo-American notions of freedom and equality, but it focuses on redescribing the nature of heterosexual, patriarchal bonds between men. "Gays in the military" also revolved around male intimacies, as much commentary observed.

2. For a chronology of the term's American appearance, see Jonathan Ned Katz, *Gay / Lesbian Almanac: A New Documentary* (New York: Harper & Row, 1983), 147–48. On Wilde, see Ed Cohen, *Talk on the Wilde Side: Toward a Genealogy of a Discourse on Male Sexualities* (New York: Routledge, 1993), esp. chap. 5.

3. Sigmund Freud, *Group Psychology and the Analysis of the Ego,* trans. James Strachey (1921; New York: Norton, 1959), 73.

4. Sedgwick explains her term "homosexual panic" in *Epistemology of the Closet,* chap. 4, esp. 182–88.

5. [Rufus W. Griswold], *New York Criterion,* 10 November 1855, in *Walt Whitman: The Critical Heritage,* ed. Milton Hindus (New York: Barnes & Noble, 1971), 32–33.

6. Edward Coke, "Buggery, or Sodomy," *Laws of England* (London, 1644).

7. [Charles A. Dana], *New York Daily Tribune,* 23 July 1855, cited in Hindus, 22.

8. Katz, *Gay / Lesbian Almanac,* 45. Alan Bray notes a similar connection in Elizabethan England, which he says continues medieval traditions: "Homosexuality was defined . . . as part of a universal potential for disorder which lay alongside an equally universal order" (*Homosexuality in Renaissance England* [London: Gay Men's Press, 1982], 26). The nineteenth-century American middle class was a medieval culture precisely in this imagination of universal order, thus sodomy could retain the cosmic and political force of an earlier epoch in Europe. See also Jonathan Goldberg, "Bradford's 'Ancient Members' and 'A Case of Buggery . . . Amongst Them,'" in *Nationalisms and Sexualities,* ed. Andrew Parker et al. (New York: Routledge, 1992): "The truth of the history, as I am reading it, is the entanglement of the 'ancient members' with and the desire to separate from the figure of the sodomite who represents at once the negation of the ideal and its literalization" (68).

9. George Lippard, *The Monks of Monk Hall,* ed. Leslie Fiedler (New York: Odyssey Press, 1970), 390, 393. The novel was originally published as *The Quaker City; or, the Monks of Monk Hall. A Romance of Philadelphia Life, Mystery and Crime* (Philadelphia, 1845).

10. "Instead of legal references to sodomy, Americans, following the English common law, adopted the terms 'crime against nature' or the 'crime which could not be named,' and it is not at all clear that most Americans knew just exactly what these acts constituted" (Vern L. Bullough and Martha Voght, "Homosexuality and Its Confusion with the Secret Sin in Pre-Freudian America," *Journal of the History of Medicine and Allied Sciences* 28, no. 2 [April 1973]: 144).

Current usage still refers ambiguously to anal intercourse between men, between a man and a woman, and to bestiality. In antebellum America, sodomy denoted a "category of forbidden acts" and did not yet indicate a homosexual as a "personage, a past, a case history, and a childhood in addition to being a type of life, a life form" (Foucault, *History of Sexuality,* vol. 1, 43). These forbidden acts were variations of nonreproductive sexuality: sodomy invoked a biblical abomination, the "unnatural" act of spilling the procreative seed that offended the laws of God and nature. It sometimes stood for anal intercourse, but also masturbation, particularly in its confused connection with onanism. It often denoted intercourse between men, but also that between man and beast, and bestiality was more of a concern to the authorities of early America than was male homosexuality (Jonathan Katz, *Gay American History: Lesbians and Gay Men in the U.S.A.* [New York: Thomas Y. Crowell, 1976], 56; Katz outlines four definitions of sodomy on 56–57).

11. For the combination of taboo and polyvocality, see John D'Emilio and Estelle B. Freedman, *Intimate Matters: A History of Sexuality in America* (New York: Harper & Row, 1988), 122. These associations change as they cross national boundaries. For example, Theo van der Meer claims that the courts in Amsterdam had started, in the eighteenth century, to consider "sodomy exclusively as anal intercourse (or bestiality), and only then when the act had been committed to full: namely penetration and ejaculation in the body of a partner" ("The Persecutions of Sodomites in Eighteenth-Century Amsterdam: Changing Perceptions of Sodomy," in *The Pursuit of Sodomy: Male Homosexuality in Renaissance and Enlightenment Europe,* ed. Kent Gerard and Gert Hekma, *Journal of Homosexuality,* special issue, 16, nos. 1–2: 265). The history of sexuality is now accounting more systematically for national variations in the construction and ongoing redefinition of the homosexual by correlating these with discourses known to vary by nation, race, religion, and other factors.

12. Bullough and Voght, "Homosexuality and Its Confusion," 144.

13. Katz, *Gay / Lesbian Almanac,* 40–42. David F. Greenberg links prohibitions against nonproductive male deviance to the enforcement of the discipline demanded by "market economies": "Like it or not, an entrepreneur who permits ties of affection, solidarity with competitors, or sympathy for employees and customs to temper his competitiveness risks losing out to someone who pursues profits more singlemindedly" (*The Construction of Homosexuality* [Chicago: University of Chicago Press, 1988], 356; cf. 366).

14. Michael Moon, "Disseminating Whitman," in *Displacing Homophobia: Gay Male Perspectives in Literature and Culture,* ed. Ronald R. Butters, John M. Clum, and Michael Moon (Durham, N.C.: Duke University Press, 1989), 243.

15. Sodomy laws targeted eroticized male friendships far more than other types of threats to order: "The epithet 'sodomite' was certainly one to be feared throughout the nineteenth century," and my interest in the political deployment of sodomy should not be mistaken for indifference to the ungeneralizable experiences specific to the underexamined, largely unrecoverable, "embryonic urban, male-homosexual subculture of streets, taverns, and brothels" which were fitfully but increasingly the targets of a homophobia in the early stages of modern

crystallization (Jeffrey Weeks, *Sex, Politics & Society: The Regulation of Sexuality since 1800*, 2d ed. [London: Longman, 1989], 99; Moon, "Disseminating Whitman," 243).

16. Ralph Waldo Emerson, *Journals and Miscellaneous Notebooks* (Cambridge, Mass.: Harvard University Press, 1953–81), 1:39 (hereafter *JMN*); also cited in Katz, *Gay American History*, 457. Emerson's gazing at other men makes him quite compatible with Whitman, for whom, much later, he is the object of a similar attention. "Walt Whitman turned up in Concord to gaze, much in the attitude of a worshiper, upon his silent friend. At Sanborn's house, where the literati were gathered, Whitman cared little whether he was thought stupid in the conversation of the roomful of company, for he was spending what he called 'a long and blessed evening with Emerson,' though this meant almost nothing but staring at his cornered man. 'My seat and the relative arrangement were such that, without being rude, or anything of the kind,' he explained, 'I could just look squarely at E., which I did a good part of the two hours'" (Ralph L. Rusk, *The Life of Ralph Waldo Emerson* [New York: Charles Scribner's Sons, 1949], 505).

17. Emerson, *JMN* 1:94–95; "Although . . . me" is written in Latin and translated by the editors (cited in Katz, *Gay American History*, 460).

18. Alan Bray notes, e.g., that "Thomas Browne could write of his longing to be in the arms of his friend . . . [but he] would have been astonished at the suggestion that the rarified and platonic friendship of which he was writing could have been construed as having anything to do with homosexuality" (*Homosexuality*, 60).

19. For an overlapping reading of Emerson's interest in male friendship, see Julie Ellison, "Gender of Transparency," 584–606. Ellison describes Emerson's relation to Gay as a "fantasy world of masculine affection" which, in her view, does not conflict with the "homophobic logic" of Emerson's interest in male intimacy (592, 595). Ellison's essay is particularly significant for placing hierarchy at the center of Emerson's views about masculinity. Ses also Mary Kupiec Cayton, *Emerson's Emergence*, chap. 8.

20. Ralph Waldo Emerson, "Considerations By the Way," in *The Conduct of Life* (1860), *Es and Ls*, 1094.

21. Ibid., 1094, 1093.

22. Emerson, "Friendship," *Es and Ls*, 341.

23. Ibid., 350. Friendship may also have been chosen on the basis of youth. One reader of Emerson's sexuality concludes that Emerson "concentrated in his adult years on developing friendly relations with young men who, in the words of the *Symposium*, 'had just begun to show some intelligence'" (Erik Ingvar Thurin, *Emerson as Priest of Pan: A Study in the Metaphysics of Sex* [Lawrence: Regents Press of Kansas, 1981], 98). He often expressed his "elective affinities" for men with a romantic ardor, as when he notes, apparently alluding to his correspondence with John Sterling, "that he feels 'as warmly' when his friend is praised 'as the lover when he hears applause of his engaged maiden'" (Thurin, 171).

24. Emerson, "Friendship," *Es and Ls*, 351.

25. Ibid., 349.

26. Emerson, "Gifts," *Es and Ls,* 538.

27. Emerson, *JMN* 7:269.

28. Emerson, "Gifts," *Es and Ls,* 537.

29. I am citing the original version of this passage found in Emerson, *JMN* 13:112.

30. Emerson, "Considerations," 1081. These attitudes persisted through the Civil War period. Emerson blamed the draft riots in New York City in July 1863 on "the wild Irish element, imported in the last twenty-five years into this country, and led by Romish priests, who sympathize, of course, with despotism" (Gay Wilson Allen, *Waldo Emerson: A Biography* [New York: Viking, 1981], 622). For a kindred liberal perspective, see E. L. Godkin, "The Mob Spirit," editorial, *Nation,* 19 November 1868: 410–11.

31. This fear continued to organize liberal politics in the Northeast after the Civil War. John G. Sproat argued that "to liberal reformers . . . [Benjamin F. Butler, Democratic governor of Massachusetts] was the epitome of political villainy. '"Butlerism," whether in Massachusetts, New York, or South Carolina,' *The Nation* charged [in 1874], 'is simply a plan for the embodiment in political organization of the desire for the transfer of power to the ignorant and the poor, and the use of Government to carry out the poor and ignorant man's view of the nature of society.'" Not surprisingly, by 1868, "Emerson appealed to George William Curtis to speak in Massachusetts and 'save our district from the ignominy and mischief of Butler.'" Cited in John G. Sproat, *"The Best Men": Liberal Reformers in the Gilded Age* (New York: Oxford University Press, 1968), 49, 291–92n.

32. Cited in Paul Boyer, *Urban Masses and Moral Order in America, 1820–1920* (Cambridge: Harvard University Press, 1978), 89.

33. Edwin Chapin, *Humanity in the City,* (New York: DeWitt & Davenport, 1854), 18–19.

34. Richard Riker, cited in Paul O. Weinbaum, *Mobs and Demagogues: The New York Response to Collective Violence in the Early Nineteenth Century* (Ann Arbor, Mich.: UMI Research Press), 48–49.

35. Weinbaum, *Mobs and Demagogues,* 66, 35.

36. Ibid., 82–83.

37. From *The Boston Daily Bee,* reprinted in *The Workingman's Advocate,* 26 October 1844.

38. Boyer, *Urban Masses,* 97.

39. Ibid., 96.

40. Christine Stansell, *City of Women: Sex and Class in New York* (Urbana: University of Illinois Press, 1987), 41, 49.

41. As a fraction of the large and excellent literature on these varieties of working-class political economy, I have been particularly helped by Alan Dawley, *Class and Community: The Industrial Revolution in Lynn* (Cambridge: Harvard University Press, 1976); Paul G. Faler, *Mechanics and Manufacturers in the Early Industrial Revolution: Lynn, Massachusetts, 1780–1860* (Albany: State Uni-

versity of New York Press, 1981); Brian Greenberg, *Worker and Community: Response to Industrialization in a Nineteenth-Century American City, Albany, New York, 1850–1884* (Albany: State University of New York Press, 1985); Bruce Laurie, *Artisans into Workers: Labor in Nineteenth-Century America* (New York: Farrar, Straus & Giroux, Noonday Press, 1989); and Sean Wilentz, *Chants Democratic: New York City and the Rise of the Working Class, 1788–1850* (New York: Oxford University Press, 1984).

42. Valentine Nicholson, "The Fighting Family. No. 1," *The Workingman's Advocate* 7 (September 1844).

43. A particularly useful survey of the earlier writers can be found in Wilentz, esp. chaps. 4 and 5.

44. Walt Whitman, "Democratic Vistas," in *Prose Works 1892*, ed. Floyd Stovall (New York: New York University Press, 1964), 2: 379–80.

45. Ibid., 414–415n.

46. Jacques Derrida, "The Politics of Friendship," *Journal of Philosophy* 85 (November 1988): 640.

47. Elias Canetti, *Crowds and Power*, trans. Carol Stewart (New York: Farrar, Straus & Giroux, 1984), 29.

48. G. H. Barker-Benfield, *The Horrors of the Half-Known Life: Male Attitudes toward Women and Sexuality in Nineteenth-Century America* (New York: Harper & Row, 1976), 171, alluding to John Todd's masturbation phobia.

49. Kristin Ross, *The Emergence of Social Space: Rimbaud and the Paris Commune* (Minneapolis: University of Minnesota Press, 1988), 22.

50. Ibid., 24.

51. Ibid., 100.

52. Mikhail Bakunin, cited in ibid., 101.

53. This dependency of self on the (collective) other also cannot be understood as male feminization. Whitman generally refrains from compensating for his passive, receptive, stereotypically "feminized" moments with elaborate masculine protests.

54. Another middle-class proponent of a "link of sympathy" was the reformer Charles Loring Brace. With some loss of nuance, I associate notions of organic community with demagogue theories in that, for different reasons, neither imagines the group to be self-directed, but instead to be directed by a higher, prior, or stronger force. Paul Boyer suggests that the attempt to reproduce in the city "what had been an organic feature of village life" was part of a desire to "devise an urban analogue to the informal, but continuous and pervasive, scrutiny of behavior upon which the pre-urban moral order rested" (Boyer, 19). On Brace, see Thomas Bender, *Toward an Urban Vision: Ideas and Institutions in Nineteenth-Century America* (Lexington: University Press of Kentucky, 1975), chap. 6.

55. D'Emilio and Freedman, *Intimate Matters*, 69. John Todd's most famous treatment of masturbation is in the chapter "Reading" in *The Student's Manual, Index Rerum or Index of Subjects: Intended as a Manual, to Aid the Student and the Professional Man, in Preparing himself for Usefulness, With an Introduction,*

Illustrating its Utility and Method of Use" (Boston: W. Pierce, 1835), hereafter, *Student's Manual.*

56. Barker-Benfield, *Horrors of the Half-Known Life,* 179.

57. John Todd, *The Moral Influence, Dangers and Duties, Connected with Great Cities* (Northampton, Mass.: J. H. Butler, 1841), 152.

58. Barker-Benfield, *Horrors of the Half-Known Life,* 179, 167.

59. For a critique of the costs of "Whitman's chorus of merger and inclusion," which at times reiterate "the bloody, physical differentiations of plantation life" and "encompass and mediate all otherness," see Karen Sánchez-Eppler, *Touching Liberty: Abolition, Feminism, and the Politics of the Body* (Berkeley and Los Angeles: University of California Press, 1993), 57, 134, and chap. 2. Granting that authoritarianism, racism, and appropriation coexist with Whitman's politics of male love, I am questioning whether the latter should be seen as the former's cause.

60. For example, see Allan Stanley Horlick's analysis of middle- and upper-class business clubs and associations in *Country Boys and Merchant Princes: The Social Control of Young Men in New York* (Lewisburg, Pa.: Bucknell University Press, 1975); and Michael Moon, "'The Gentle Boy from the Dangerous Classes': Pederasty, Domesticity, and Capitalism in Horatio Alger," *Representations* 19 (Summer 1987): 87–107.

61. Oliver Wendell Holmes, *The Autocrat of the Breakfast-Table* (New York: Dutton-Everyman, 1906), 88–89.

62. Freud, *Group Psychology*; Gustave Le Bon, *Psychologies des foules,* published in English as *The Crowd: A Study of the Popular Mind* (New York: Ballantine Books, 1969). For a detailed and somewhat different reading of *Group Psychology* from the one I offer here, see Mikkel Borch-Jacobsen, *The Freudian Subject,* trans. Catherine Porter (Stanford, Calif.: Stanford University Press, 1988).

63. For this summary I am indebted to Susanna Barrows, *Distorting Mirrors: Visions of the Crowd in Late Nineteenth-Century France* (New Haven, Conn.: Yale University Press, 1981); and Robert A. Nye, *The Origins of Crowd Psychology: Gustave Le Bon and the Crisis of Mass Democracy in the Third Republic* (Beverly Hills, Calif.: Sage Publications, 1975); see also Laurence Rickles, *The Case of California* (Baltimore: Johns Hopkins University Press, 1991).

64. Freud also expands Le Bon's focus on spontaneous or "natural" groups to include "those stable groups or associations in which mankind pass their lives" (*Group Psychology,* 15; Serge Moscovici notes Freud's choice of groups in *The Age of the Crowd: A Historical Treatise on Mass Psychology,* trans. J. C. Whitehouse [Cambridge: Cambridge University Press, 1985], 239).

65. Freud, *Group Psychology,* 52–53.

66. Ibid., 26.

67. Ibid., 53.

68. Ibid., 59. It is beyond my scope to link these ideas to European fascism, though fascism propelled much group and social psychology on both sides of the Atlantic. Most work that I have seen—especially what was written before the 1960s—concurs with Freud's reading of group formation, and much offers

advice for the exploitation of the leader's authority. Even the masses' defenders accept Freud's fundamentals, in part because his views were already so deeply traditional. Wilhelm Reich, for example, yokes his call for the emancipation of the masses through their own efforts to his charge that the masses have indeed rejected freedom throughout history (*The Mass Psychology of Fascism*, ed. Mary Boyd Higgins and Chester M. Raphael, trans. Mary Boyd Higgins [New York: Farrar, Straus & Giroux, 1970], esp. chap. 12).

69. Freud, *Group Psychology*, 34–35.

70. Groups, for Freud, manifest a "desexualized, sublimated homosexual love for other men, which springs from work in common"; it is also compatible with the "sexual love of women." Ibid., 35.

71. Ibid., 56n. The editor references Freud, *Totem and Taboo*, standard ed., 13: 144.

72. Gilles Deleuze and Félix Guattari, *Anti-Oedipus: Capitalism and Schizophrenia*, trans. Robert Hurley, Mark Seem, and Helen R. Lane (Minneapolis: University of Minnesota Press, 1983), 62.

73. Freud himself is unwilling to claim that mutual identification drives out desire altogether. "Is it quite certain that identification presupposes that object-cathexis has been given up?" (*Group Psychology*, 46). For an argument that identification in fact generates desire as part of its own structure, see Michael Warner, "Homo-Narcissism; or, Heterosexuality," in *Engendering Men: The Question of Male Feminist Criticism*, ed. Joseph A. Boone and Michael Cadden (New York: Routledge, 1990), 190–206: "In the very action of taking an ideal, the subject apprehends a difference between the ideal and the actual ego. And that difference is just what produces our sense of longing and our search for the recognition of others" (193).

74. Freud, *Group Psychology*, 40.

75. Ibid., 48; emphasis in original.

76. Freud's logic is associative here: he does not continue to analyze identification within groups but switches to "identification . . . in some other cases which are not immediately comprehensible" (ibid., 40). He links two separate kinds of cases: "male homosexuality" and "melancholia" (40–41). The domination of the ego ideal is in place by the end of this chapter, and receives confirmation in the following chapter on being in love as hypnosis. Once love is shown to be slavery to the ego ideal, the importance of being in love to group life, in all its available homoeroticism, poses no threat to the father's power to demand homosexuality's sublimation in service to himself.

77. Ibid., 40–41.

78. Sigmund Freud, *The Ego and the Id* (New York: Norton, 1962), 22. In this work, Freud undermines one of the major determinations by which he differentiates homosexual from heterosexual outcomes: "the more complete Oedipus complex, which is twofold, positive and negative," is more common than the simple Oedipus complex. In the former case, "a boy has not merely an ambivalent attitude towards his father and an affectionate object-choice towards his mother, but at the same time he also behaves like a girl and displays an

affectionate feminine attitude to his father and a corresponding jealousy and hostility towards his mother" (23). "At the dissolution of the Oedipus complex the four trends of which it consists will group themselves in such a way as to produce a father-identification and a mother-identification" (24). The superego is a "precipitate in the ego, consisting of these two identifications in some way united with each other" (24, emphasis omitted).

79. Even orthodox attempts to identify the heterosexual son's ego with the superego (and the superego with the father-image) run afoul of the divided nature of the castration complex. Freud remarks, "I am accustoming myself to regarding every sexual act as an event between four individuals" (Freud, *Ego and Id,* 23n).

80. Freud, *Group Psychology,* 40–41.

81. Kenneth Lewes, *The Psychoanalytic Theory of Male Homosexuality* (New York: New American Library, Meridian, 1988), 38.

82. Lest we doubt that Freud's point here is less to describe the nature of male homosexual desire than to equate it with subjection, he continues his discussion by turning in the following paragraph to the melancholic ego. The melancholic ego is "fallen apart into two pieces," one, the ego "which contains the lost object" (the boy entirely identified with his mother), and the other, the cruel superego.

83. Freud, *Group Psychology,* 37.

84. Ibid., 56n.

85. Emerson, "Discipline," *Es and Ls,* 31.

86. "Jesus as a glorified friend retains the terrible power of judgment, the awful power to approve or reject. In his attention to what Jesus, as glorified friend, will or will not approve more, Emerson cannot help representing in the figure of Christ the authority of the community whose approbation he has yet to win. Thus, even when he most forcefully advances the claims of his inner sense, Emerson demands the confirmation of another's regard. The 'free way of friendship' links the sentiment of the self to the judgment of others, and this point in turn links the self to the law" (Michael, *Emerson and Skepticism,* 18 [see chap. 1, n. 20]).

87. *Es and Ls,* 10.

88. Todd, *Student's Manual,* 168. Freud notes that the individual in the horde has "only a passive-masochistic attitude" toward the father "to whom one's will has to be surrendered, — while to be alone with him, 'to look him in the face,' appears a hazardous enterprise" (*Group Psychology,* 59).

89. "Gifts," *Es and Ls,* 537.

90. "Friendship," *Es and Ls,* 342.

91. *JMN* 7:268. Emerson revised this passage for "The Over-Soul," *Es and Ls,* 399, where its meaning is altered by its context.

92. "Friendship," *Es and Ls,* 342.

93. "The American Scholar," *Es and Ls,* 54.

94. "Uses of Great Men," *Es and Ls,* 629–30. Pestalozzi appears to opposite effect in "The American Scholar": "'I learned,'" said the melancholy Pestalozzi, 'that no man in God's wide earth is either willing or able to help any other man.'

Help must come from the bosom alone. . . . The world is nothing, the man is all" (70). I discuss this more familiar individualism below.

95. Ralph Waldo Emerson, "The Young American" (1844), *Es and Ls,* 222.

96. Ibid., 223.

97. Ibid., 223.

98. Emerson, "New England Reformers" (1844), *Es and Ls,* 598.

99. Cited in Perry Miller, ed., *The Transcendentalists,* headnote, 465.

100. Sacvan Bercovitch, "Emerson," 632. Bercovitch is elaborating a nineteenth-century distinction between "individuality" and "individualism" as a theory of society.

101. P. Miller, *Transcendentalists,* 464.

102. Emerson, "New England Reformers," 599.

103. Bercovitch, "Emerson," 643.

104. Ibid., 642.

105. Emerson, "New England Reformers," 598–99.

106. Ibid., 599.

107. I am not proposing that the preferable alternative is strict equality between individuals, an equality that would deny the vulnerabilities and vicissitudes of all transferential relations. I am saying that the hardening of transference into submission to a paternalized object goes beyond the requirements of transference itself.

108. The third section of Maurice Gonnaud's *Uneasy Solitude,* "From Ideal Democracy to Natural Aristocracy," bears witness to Emerson's frequent preference for elites over the masses but says little about the tension between these ideas. For Emerson, he says, democracy is "an equalization, if one likes, but an equalization at the top" (372). "Every man prefers the company of his superiors to that of his equals, he had asserted in 'New England Reformers,' because the natural movement of the soul leads it to look upward" (372). Exhibiting the Emerson Effect, in which a certain basic conceptual precision feels petty, Gonnaud generally ignores his own insights into Emerson's intermittent but repeated rejection of democratic aims, broadly conceived.

109. Emerson, *JMN* 16:45.

110. Heidi Hartmann, "The Unhappy Marriage of Marxism and Feminism: Towards a More Progressive Union," cited in Sedgwick, *Epistemology of the Closet,* 184.

111. Sedgwick, *Epistemology of the Closet,* 94.

112. D. A. Miller, *Bringing Out Roland Barthes* (Berkeley and Los Angeles: University of California Press, 1992), 4. The phrase is part of Miller's remarkable opening paragraph that tells how, years earlier, he learned of the possibility of glimpsing Roland Barthes at the Saint Germain Drugstore in Paris: "Although in frequenting the Drugstore by night (as soon after this intelligence I began to do), I may initially have hoped to see Barthes, I eventually contented myself with *doing* Barthes, experiencing this promiscuous emporium as I imagined he might. Now the various displays of luxury would provoke my hot imitation anger with their repulsive evidence of bourgeois *myth* in the process of

naturalizing an oppressive class bias; now they would lend themselves to my cool imitation appreciation as so many relaxed *signifiers* stiffening in no hierarchy but the continually flexible one instituted by desire" (3–4). Residually heterosexual at the time, Miller imagines Barthes's feelings to be polarized into a revulsion for the veiled inequalities of mass life and an attraction to the mobile inequalities of desire. This oscillation between resisting inequality and seeking it in the "relaxed" order of desire is precisely what is not resolved by the homosexual panic that concludes the paragraph, and when this younger Miller flees his identification with Barthes after a male cruiser asks him the time, his confirmed straightness preserves the dependence of Miller's desire on his inferiority to Barthes.

113. There are different approaches to this issue: Ed Cohen investigates the construction of the *we* in "Who Are 'We'? Gay 'Identity' as Political (E)motion (A Theoretical Rumination)," *Inside / Out: Lesbian Theories, Gay Theories*, ed. Diana Fuss (New York: Routledge, 1991), 71–92. Lauren Berlant and Elizabeth Freeman supplement their discussion of lesbian and gay activism's use of multiple approaches to diverse spaces with an account of the exposure of the privileged: "In their drive to embody *you*, the citizen / spectator / reader / lover, by negating your disembodiment, the zines represent the horizon of postpatriarchal and postnational fantasy" ("Queer Nationality," *boundary 2* 19, no. 1 [Spring 1992]: 180).

114. "Straightness" does not exclude men who identify as gay. I am not arguing that a move from straight to gay identity or practice moves the subject from hierarchical to egalitarian thinking; both of these positions are compounded of variable formations of straight paternalism.

CHAPTER FIVE

1. Rose (*Transcendentalism* [see chap. 1, n. 5 above]) notes that although women were active in theorizing the need for and founding communes such as Brook Farm, and though they sustained these communes with grossly disproportionate amounts of domestic labor, and though their visions of "social freedom" and consociational emancipation were as developed as the men's, the outcome was the perpetuation of their conventional role. In spite of all their efforts, "women made little progress in a movement that promised to revolutionize society" (195).

2. Ibid., 192.

3. Brodhead, *Cultures of Letters*, chap. 1 (see chap. 1, n. 35); Mary P. Ryan, *The Empire of the Mother: American Writing about Domesticity, 1830–1860* (New York: Harrington Park Press, 1985), 49–58.

4. Anne C. Rose, *Victorian America and the Civil War* (New York: Cambridge University Press, 1992), 158. Tocqueville was already insisting that democracy had produced a new father, one who had replaced autocracy with affection (see n. 9 below). My discussion in this chapter has benefited from the following treatments of the feminization and liberalization of the patriarchal family through the first half of the nineteenth century: Gillian Brown, *Domestic*

Individualism: Imagining Self in Nineteenth-Century America (Berkeley and Los Angeles: University of California Press, 1990); Carl Degler, *At Odds: Women and the Family in America from the Revolution to the Present* (New York: Oxford University Press, 1980), esp. chaps. 5–7; Douglas, *Feminization of American Culture*, esp. intro. and chap. 3 (see chap. 1, n. 20); Jay Fliegelman, *Prodigals and Pilgrims,* esp. chaps. 5 and 8 (see chap. 1, n. 28); Mary P. Ryan, *The Empire of the Mother,* esp. chaps. 1 and 2; Carroll Smith-Rosenberg, *Disorderly Conduct: Visions of Gender in Victorian America* (New York: Oxford University Press, 1985), esp. pt. 1; and Jane Tompkins, *Sensational Designs: The Cultural Work of American Fiction, 1790–1860* (New York: Oxford University Press, 1985), esp. chaps. 5–6. Valuable treatments of women's extradomestic agency include Mary P. Ryan, *Women in Public: Between Banners and Ballots, 1825–1880* (Baltimore: Johns Hopkins University Press, 1990); and Stansell, *City of Women.*

5. T. Walter Herbert, *Dearest Beloved: the Hawthornes and the Making of the Middle Class Family* (Berkeley and Los Angeles: University of California Press, 1993), 77.

6. Leverenz (*Manhood*, 44 [intro., n. 18]) usefully redefines Emersonian manhood through an "inward experience of spontaneous metamorphosis" rather than the more traditional "public rivalry for dominance."

7. Tocqueville, *Democracy in America,* 601.

8. Some excellent work has been done on male feminization, however. Eric Cheyfitz and Erik Ingvar Thurin, among others, have detailed Emerson's life-long belief that the "complete" man must also be part woman. See esp. the chap. "Androgynous Completeness" in Thurin, *Emerson as Priest of Pan* (chap. 4, n. 23). Thurin is useful throughout on Emerson's perennial ambivalence about masculinity and agency. See also Eric Cheyfitz's chapter, "The Decline of the Father" in *The Trans-parent: Sexual Politics in the Language of Emerson* (Baltimore: Johns Hopkins University Press, 1981).

9. Tocqueville, *Democracy in America,* 585, 590, 595.

10. Jeffrey Steele, ed. *The Essential Margaret Fuller* (New Brunswick, N.J.: Rutgers University Press, 1992), 392.

11. Emerson, *JMN,* 15: 181 (sentence incomplete in original). This passage appeared with little change near the end of "Civilization," in *The Complete Works of Ralph Waldo Emerson,* Centenary Edition (Boston: Houghton Mifflin, 1903–4), 32 (hereafter *ECW*).

12. Emerson, "Uses of Great Men," *Es and Ls,* 629–30. As is usual for Emerson's most headlong moments, this one is juxtaposed with counsels to "serve the great. Stick at no humiliation. Grudge no office thou canst render. Be the limb of their body, the breath of their mouth. . . . Never mind the taunt of Boswellism" (629). As I've argued, such conjunctions express a basic contradiction in Emerson's understanding of democracy: everyone is great; everyone must submit to the great. Emerson tries to solve the problem with the *mobility of relations,* a point I will return to in chap. 6, below.

13. Ibid., 625.

14. Emerson, *JMN* 7: 108–9.

15. Albert Brisbane, *The Social Destiny of Man; or, Association and Reorganization of Industry*, in Rose, *Transcendentalism*, 191.

16. For treatment of Emerson's actual Concord, Massachusetts, see David Hackett Fischer, *Concord: The Social History of a New England Town, 1750–1850* (Waltham, Mass.: Brandeis University, 1984).

17. Rose notes that Emerson's distress at the marriage of his friends Anna Barker and Samuel Ward suggests that "everyone assumed the conjugal bond would prevent the free interaction of either husband or wife with the group. 'Farewell, my brother, my sister,' Emerson wrote in a strange celebration of marriage" (*Transcendentalism*, 182). Emerson may also be expressing dismay at the impossibility of an ideal state in which their marriage, and all the conventional forms of domestic life, would not disrupt intermingling.

18. Harriet Beecher Stowe, "The Cathedral"; cited by Lynn Wardley, "Relic, Fetish, Femmage: The Aesthetics of Sentiment in the Work of Stowe," in *The Culture of Sentiment: Race, Gender and Sentimentality in 19th Century America*, ed. Shirley Samuels (New York: Oxford University Press, 1992), 207. Wardley's essay, tracing aspects of sentimental culture to African practices, offers a valuable exploration of precisely the "unseen opposition" in "little things" that Emerson often misses, while refraining from generalizations about the political effects of Stowe's use of sentimentalism.

19. Emerson, *JMN* 7:228.

20. These remarks are wholly compatible with Emerson's reputation as an affectionate father. Writing about William Ellery Channing's esteem for Emerson's routine in the late 1860s, his biographer Ralph Rusk notes that "what most impressed the impressionable Channing was the charm of the family life and the pride Emerson took in his children. . . . He was teaching his children entire independence of his own personal faith" (Rusk, *Life of Emerson*, 444).

21. Emerson, *JMN* 7:229.

22. Ibid.

23. Ibid., 184. A further example of domestic harassment is found in the text a few pages on: "The whole world seems to be in conspiracy to invade you, to vanquish you with emphatic details, to break you into crumbs, to fritter your time. Friend, wife, child, mother, fear, want, charity all knock at the student's door at the critical moment, ring larums in his ear, scare away the muse, & spoil the poem. Do not spill thy soul, do not all descend, but keep thy state; stay at home in thine own heaven & let fingers do the fingers' work. Unite & break not" (ibid., 189).

24. Ibid., 171.

25. For a discussion of Whitman's applications of amative and adhesive love, see Michael Lynch, "'Here is Adhesiveness': From Friendship to Homosexuality," *Victorian Studies* 29, no. 1 (Autumn 1985): 67–96.

26. Emerson sometimes declares that "Friendship requires that rare mean betwixt likeness and unlikeness, that piques each with the presence of power and of consent in the other party. . . . The only joy I have in his being mine, is

that the *not mine* is *mine*" ("Friendship," *Es and Ls,* 350). See also such journal parables as that of the "rude village boy" who sees "one fair child" who "distances him instantly"; "These two little neighbors" are learning "to respect each other's personality" (*JMN* 7:171).

27. Emerson, "Love," *Es and Ls,* 334.

28. Ibid., 337.

29. Ibid.

30. Ibid. This romanticized Neoplatonic ascent remains an influential expression of male ambition in our century. One of the purest expressions of the genre is Nick Carraway's description of the younger Jay Gatsby's love for Daisy, in which her beauty is his solitary stairway to heaven (F. Scott Fitzgerald, *The Great Gatsby* [New York: Charles Scribner's Sons, 1925], 112).

31. Emerson, "Love," *Es and Ls,* 337.

32. Emerson, "Swedenborg," *Es and Ls,* 679–80. An earlier version of this passage was composed in November 1840, during the period when, Maurice Gonnaud observes, Emerson was most preoccupied with ideas about women's direct line to God (*Uneasy Solitude,* 268 [see chap. 3, n. 2]).

33. Emerson, *JMN* 7:455.

34. Ralph L. Rusk, ed. *The Letters of Ralph Waldo Emerson,* cited in Gonnaud, *Uneasy Solitude,* 269.

35. Ibid., 270.

36. Ibid.

37. Ralph Waldo Emerson, "Woman. A Lecture Read Before the Woman's Rights Convention, Boston, September 20, 1855," *ECW* 11:419.

38. Catharine Beecher, *Treatise on Domestic Economy for the Use of Young Ladies at Home and at School* (Boston: Marsh, Capen, Lyon and Webb, 1841), 131.

39. By contrast, Beecher describes women's agency as the freedom to choose a bond: "In most other cases, in a truly democratic state, each individual is allowed to choose for himself, who shall take the position of his superior. No woman is forced to obey any husband but the one she chooses for herself; nor is she obliged to take a husband, if she prefers to remain single. . . . Each subject, also, has equal power with every other, to decide who shall be his superior as a ruler" (*Treatise on Domestic Economy,* 131).

40. Emerson, *JMN* 4:72.

41. Ibid., 299.

42. Ibid., 7:77.

43. Lidian Emerson to Waldo Emerson, April 1836, quoted in Rose, *Transcendentalism,* 170.

44. Emerson, *JMN* 4:53. Emerson remarked on Webster's "great cinderous eyes," eyes which Thurin thinks inspired a rhapsodic journal passage about being beheld by a man with "great serious eyes," which "were a great river like the Ohio or the Danube which was always pouring a torrent of strong, sad light on some men, and tinging [*sic*] them with the quality of his soul" (Thurin, *Emerson as Priest of Pan,* 179).

45. Emerson, *JMN* 4:263, 264.

46. Ibid., 7:544.

47. Emerson, "Woman," *ECW* 11:405–6.

48. Ibid., 406–7.

49. Ibid., 418–19.

50. Ibid., 426.

51. Emerson, "Montaigne; or, the Skeptic," *Es and Ls,* 708.

52. Emerson, "Domestic Life," *Society and Solitude, ECW* 7:107.

53. Ibid., 132–33.

54. Ibid., 122.

55. Emerson, "Clubs," *Society and Solitude, ECW* 7:235, 234.

56. Emerson, *JMN* 15:215.

57. Ibid., 231. Here, in Journal War, Emerson labels this passage "West Point Notes"; a very similar passage appears in the concurrent Journal DL, this time labeled "Friendship" (ibid., 25).

58. Ibid., 216.

59. The countervailing complexities of outside life do not mix in: "The discipline is yet so strict, that these military monks, in years, never pass the limits of the post, & know nothing of the country immediately around them. It is pleasant to see the excellence & beauty of their fences" (ibid.).

60. For a trenchant critique of the idea that middle-class culture was feminized in this period, see Lora Romero, "Vanishing Americans: Gender, Empire, and New Historicism," in *Culture of Sentiment,* ed. Samuels, 115–27. On the importance of family as a figure for national union, and its role in forming antebellum middle-class masculinity, see George B. Forgie, *Patricide in the House Divided: A Psychological Interpretation of Lincoln and His Age* (New York: Norton, 1979). My own reading has attempted to avoid the castration thesis so often applied to antebellum liberal ministers and intellectuals: such men were made to feel effeminate and their work shows the strain of compensatory thinking. Leverenz offers a subtle version of this fundamentally unsubtle thesis in *Manhood*; see also Douglas, *Feminization.*

61. Julian Hawthorne, *Nathaniel Hawthorne and His Wife,* quoted in Herbert, *Dearest Beloved,* 12–13.

CHAPTER SIX

1. F. O. Matthiessen, *American Renaissance: Art and Expression in the Age of Emerson and Whitman* (New York: Oxford University Press, 1941), viii.

2. Emerson, *JMN* 5:466, cited in Porte, *Representative Men: Ralph Waldo Emerson in His Time* (New York: Columbia University Press, 1988), 107.

3. West, *American Evasion,* 212.

4. Cavell, *New Yet Unapproachable America* (see chap. 1, n. 42), and *Conditions Handsome and Unhandsome* (see intro., n. 16).

5. Julie Ellison, *Emerson's Romantic Style* (Princeton, N.J.: Princeton University Press, 1984), 200, 113.

6. Richard Rorty, *Philosophy and the Mirror of Nature* (Princeton, N.J.: Princeton University Press, 1979), 169, 132, 157. Most of Rorty's writing since

this influential book has argued against the foundationalist enterprise, and he usefully anatomizes this argument in "Solidarity or Objectivity?" in *Post-Analytic Philosophy,* ed. John Rajchman and Cornel West (New York: Columbia University Press, 1984), 3–19. For a comment on the relation of "foundational" claims to the overall "representational" theory of knowledge, see Charles Taylor, "Overcoming Epistemology," in *After Philosophy: End or Transformation?* ed. Kenneth Baynes, James Bohman, and Thomas McCarthy (Cambridge: MIT Press, 1987), 464–88. Among literary theorists, sustained critiques of foundationalist positions can be found in Jonathan Culler, *On Deconstruction* (Ithaca, N.Y.: Cornell University Press, 1982); Howard Horwitz, "'I Can't Remember': Skepticism, Synthetic Histories, Critical Action," *South Atlantic Quarterly* 87, no. 4: 787–820; Walter Benn Michaels, *The Gold Standard and the Logic of Naturalism* (Berkeley and Los Angeles: University of California Press, 1987); and Barbara Herrnstein Smith, *Contingencies of Value: Alternative Perspectives for Critical Theory* (Cambridge: Harvard University Press, 1988).

7. Stanley Fish, *Doing What Comes Naturally* (Durham, N.C.: Duke University Press, 1989), 344.

8. Fish has most fully insisted that antifoundationalism is not "an argument for unbridled subjectivity . . . [but] for the situated subject, for the individual who is always constrained by the local or community standards and criteria of which his judgment is an extension" (ibid., 323).

9. For versions of this pragmatic antifoundationalism, see Giles Gunn, *Thinking across the American Grain: Ideology, Intellect, and the New Pragmatism* (Chicago: University of Chicago Press, 1992); and for the radicalization that Rorty receives from Ernesto Laclau, see Laclau, "Community and Its Paradoxes: Richard Rorty's 'Liberal Utopia,'" in *Community at Loose Ends,* ed. Miami Theory Collective (Minneapolis: University of Minnesota Press, 1991), 83–98. Laclau says that "antifoundationalism, together with a plurality of other narratives and cultural interventions, has created the intellectual climate in which [radical democracy is] thinkable" (83). Antifoundationalism and freedom are linked in his piece insofar as the former leads to an understanding that "antagonism exists because the social is not a plurality of effects radiating from a pregiven center, but is pragmatically constructed from many starting points. But it is precisely because of this, because there is an ontological possibility of clashes and unevenness, that we can speak of freedom" (92).

10. Barbara Herrnstein Smith, *Contingencies of Value,* 131.

11. Emerson, "Swedenborg; or, The Mystic," *Es and Ls,* 676.

12. Emerson, *Es and Ls,* 463.

13. Emerson, "Swedenborg," *Es and Ls,* 679.

14. Barbara Packer, "Origin and Authority," 87–88 (see chap. 1, n. 20).

15. Emerson, "Quotation and Originality," *ECW* 8:177. Emerson did not fully supervise the editing of his collections following *Society and Solitude* (1870), and yet, as I mention in "Note on Emerson's Texts," I am not convinced that the work of his editors was as disruptive as it appears at first. The static nature of Emerson's thought is consistent with what I regard as its fondness for

pure authority. Fluidity is often only apparent. "Whilst the eternal generation of circles proceeds, the eternal generator abides. That central life is somewhat superior to creation, superior to knowledge and thought, and contains all its circles" ("Circles," *Es and Ls*, 412). Consistency can mark either the little or the transported mind, mind lost or mind centered. Some of my readings of the later essays may require revision as better texts become available. But though I am sure his editors did damage to Emerson's texts, I think the juxtaposition of writing separated in time would create less intellectual disjuncture than do many other readers of Emerson.

16. Ibid., 178.

17. Ibid., 181, 182.

18. Ibid., 193.

19. Ibid., 198–99. See also the end of "Illusions" (in *ECW*), which uses very similar language.

20. "Quotation and Originality," *ECW* 8:181–82, 193.

21. Emerson, "Shakespeare; or, the Poet" (1850), *Es and Ls*, 711.

22. Emerson, "Quotation and Originality," *ECW* 8:182.

23. Ibid.

24. Ibid., 189.

25. Emerson, "The Poet," *Es and Ls*, 448.

26. Emerson, "Shakespeare," 711, 712.

27. Ibid., 713.

28. Ibid., 712.

29. Remaining consistent with the traditional reception of Emerson as a straightforward individualist, Mark R. Patterson suggests that Emerson used a "derogatory tone" to describe the poet as "the organ of social expression without original thought" (*Authority, Autonomy and Representation in American Literature, 1776–1865* [Princeton, N.J.: Princeton University Press, 1988], 179). Packer's rejection of this kind of reading marks an admirable break with the tradition.

30. Emerson, "Quotation and Originality," *ECW* 8:189.

31. Emerson, "Nature," *Es and Ls*, 13.

32. Emerson, "Shakespeare," *Es and Ls*, 711.

33. Emerson, "Quotation and Originality," *ECW* 8:191.

34. Ibid., 191.

35. Emerson, "Shakespeare," *Es and Ls*, 715.

36. Emerson, "Quotation and Originality," *ECW* 8:200. An entire chapter on Goethe concludes *Representative Men*, perhaps as though he synthesized the traits embodied by Plato and Swedenborg on the one hand, and Montaigne, Shakespeare, and Napoleon on the other. As "the Writer," Goethe represents a universal function by comparison to the roles of "Philosopher," "Mystic," "Skeptic," "Poet," or "Man of the World". The writer, in this role, fuses the individual will to the common sense.

37. Emerson, "Quotation and Originality," *ECW* 8:179.

38. Emerson, "Wealth," *Es and Ls*, 991.

39. For a brief outline of the marketing of U.S. writing into an "American" literary canon, see Richard Brodhead, *The School of Hawthorne* (New York: Oxford University Press, 1986), esp. chap. 3, and *Cultures of Letters* (see chap. 1, n. 35).

40. Michael Gilmore, *American Romanticism and the Marketplace* (Chicago: University of Chicago Press, 1985), 30.

41. Emerson, "Quotation and Originality," *ECW* 8:204.

42. Chamber of Commerce of the U.S.A., *Socialism in America* (Washington, D.C.: Chamber of Commerce of the U.S.A., 1950), 69–70.

43. Richard Rorty, *Contingency, Irony, and Solidarity* (Cambridge: Harvard University Press, 1989), 51–52, emphasis in original.

44. Emerson, *JMN* 16:85.

45. Emerson, "Quotation and Originality," *ECW* 8:192.

46. Stanley Fish is one market antifoundationalist who has been explicit about this. New methodologies, e.g., must conform to existing ones even when they seem to be taken from unrelated disciplines. "The imported product will always have the form of its appropriation rather than the form it exhibits 'at home'": if it doesn't it cannot be appropriated at all. The imported machinery is "brought in in terms the practice recognizes; the practice cannot 'say' the Other but can only say itself, even when it is in the act of modifying itself by incorporating material hitherto alien to it" ("Being Interdisciplinary Is So Very Hard to Do," *Profession* 89 [1989]: 19). But, as with Emerson, this does not make Fish a crude determinist: "neither interpretive communities nor the minds of community members are stable and fixed, but are, rather, moving projects—engines of change—whose work is at the same time assimilative and self-transforming" ("Change," *Doing What Comes Naturally*, 152). It makes Fish a liberal necessitarian, giving and withdrawing "change" in the way that keeps American culture permanently off balance about the kind of greater changes it could plausibly demand.

47. Emerson, "Quotation and Originality," *ECW* 8:200–201; "Poetry and Imagination," *ECW* 8:8.

48. Emerson, "Quotation and Originality," *ECW* 8:201.

49. Ibid., 201–2, 204.

50. Emerson, "Language," *Es and Ls,* 20.

51. Ibid., 25.

52. Emerson, "Poetry and Imagination," *ECW* 8:3.

53. Ibid., 5.

54. Ibid., 6.

55. Ibid., 6, 8.

56. Ibid., 3.

57. Ibid., 25.

58. Emerson, "Culture" (1860), *Es and Ls,* 1030–31.

59. Emerson, "Fate," *Es and Ls,* 958.

60. Emerson, "Nominalist and Realist," *Es and Ls,* 584.

61. Emerson, "Uses of Great Men," *Es and Ls,* 625.

62. Ibid.

63. Daniel Webster, "The Currency, September 28 and October 3, 1837," in *The Papers of Daniel Webster: Speeches and Formal Writings*, vol. 2, 1834–1852, ed. Charles M. Wiltse (Hanover, N.H.: University Press of New England, 1988), 165, 162, 193.

64. Edward Atkinson, "An Easy Lesson in Money and Banking," *Atlantic Monthly* 37 (August 1874): 195, 196, 205.

65. Again, I am not claiming that we can avoid submission through an escape to an imagined "outside" of the market. But among American critics, a post-Foucauldian insistence that there is no outside to power or to the market from which to level a detached critique has often obscured the coercive effects of these systems by naturalizing them as inevitable.

66. Foucault, *History of Sexuality*, 92. Packer comes close to locating liberation in meaning's "slow but massive accumulation" in the public realm ("Origin and Authority," 89), but as far as I can tell remains within the liberal notion of freedom as "a perpetual play of tropes" (87) and the "'instant eternity' which is the present moment" (91).

67. Emerson, "Quotation and Originality," *ECW* 8:189.

CHAPTER SEVEN

1. Gonnaud, *Uneasy Solitude*, 461.

2. Emerson, "Prospects," *Es and Ls*, 48.

3. W. R. Brock, *An American Crisis: Congress and Reconstruction, 1865–1867* (New York: Harper & Row, 1963), 286.

4. Eric Foner, *Reconstruction: America's Unfinished Revolution, 1863–1877* (New York: Harper & Row, 1988), 237.

5. Brock, *American Crisis*, 288. Brock offers an astute and compact survey of the fate of equality under Reconstruction in chap. 8.

6. Quoted in Du Bois, *Black Reconstruction in America, 1860–1880* (New York: Atheneum, 1992), 244.

7. Robert Higgs, *Competition and Coercion: Blacks in the American Economy, 1865–1914* (Cambridge: Cambridge University Press, 1977), 13. For important accounts of the role American race relations played in supporting coercive forms of American freedom, see David Brion Davis, *The Problem of Slavery in the Age of Revolution, 1770–1823* (Ithaca, N.Y.: Cornell University Press, 1975); and Edmund S. Morgan, *American Slavery, American Freedom: The Ordeal of Colonial Virginia* (New York: Norton, 1975).

8. Emerson, "Civilization," *ECW* 7:30.

9. Cavell discusses his concept of "good enough justice" in *Conditions Handsome and Unhandsome*, xxii (see intro., n. 16).

10. Foner, *Reconstruction*, 498.

11. Sproat, *"Best Men"* (see chap. 4, n. 31), 28–29. I will discuss below the Liberals' increasing interest in "association" and "partnership" as models of industry that complement the market.

12. Emerson, "Wealth," *Es and Ls*, 999–1000.

13. Even Emerson's reformist moments almost always equate the lawfulness

of things with a particular kind of right to property. In his essay "Politics," written and rewritten in the early 1840s, he affirms that "the whole constitution of property, on its present tenures, is injurious, and its influence on persons deteriorating and degrading; that truly, the only interest for the consideration of the State, [should be] persons: that property will always follow persons" (Emerson, "Politics," *Es and Ls,* 561). One page later, he affirms property's eternity. "Things have their laws, as well as men; and things refuse to be trifled with. Property will be protected. Corn will not grow, unless it is planted and manured; but the farmer will not plant or hoe it, unless the chances are a hundred to one, that he will cut and harvest it. Under any forms, persons and property must and will have their just sway. They exert their power, as steadily as matter its attraction" (ibid., 562). Though rules about property in things may change, one rule of property must be permanent: the right to property in oneself and in one's labor. Valuable corrective readings that explore Emerson's transcendentalism as a pro-market, pro-property viewpoint can be found in Lang, *Prophetic Woman,* chap. 7 (see chap. 1, n. 20); and Howard Horwitz, *By the Law of Nature: Form and Value in Nineteenth-Century America* (New York: Oxford University Press, 1991), chap. 2.

14. Emerson, *JMN* 16:85.

15. Ibid., 15:301–2.

16. Ibid., 203.

17. Emerson, "Boston Hymn: Read in Music Hall, January 1, 1863," *ECW* 9:204.

18. *Nation,* 12 November 1868, 387. There is reason to think that the moderate liberalism of E. L. Godkin, the *Nation's* founding and longstanding editor, was not remote from Emerson's views. Writing to Godkin on January 31, 1868, Charles Eliot Norton somewhat flatteringly observed that "Emerson who had been cold toward [the *Nation*], who thought a mistake had been made in putting you at the head of it, spoke to me last week in warmest terms of its excellence, its superiority to any other journal we have or have had" (Charles Eliot Norton, *Letters of Charles Eliot Norton,* vol. 1 [Boston: Houghton Mifflin, 1913], 297).

19. Emerson, *JMN* 16:211.

20. Ibid., 87.

21. Foner, *Reconstruction,* 475.

22. On the connection between transcendentalism and the rise of the business trust, see Horwitz, *By the Law of Nature,* chap. 6. Horwitz shrewdly establishes a codependence between individual independence and corporatism. At the same time, I suggested in chap. 3 that he underplays the contradiction between the two terms, and overstates the possibility (and desirability) of a "corporate" independence.

23. Thomas McIntyre Cooley, *A Treatise on the Constitutional Limitations which Rest upon the Legislative Power of the States of the American Union* (Boston, 1868), paraphrased in David Montgomery, *Beyond Equality: Labor and the Radical Republicans, 1862–1872* (New York: Alfred A. Knopf, 1967), 381.

24. Greeley's thoughts on this distinction in 1845 are quoted in Charles

Sotheran, *Horace Greeley and Other Pioneers of American Socialism* (New York: Humboldt Publishing Co., 1892), 149–51.

25. E. L. Godkin, "Insurance Against Strikes," *Nation*, 19 June 1866, 777.

26. E. L. Godkin, "Co-operation"; and Edward A. Atkinson, *Labor and Capital Allies Not Enemies*, both quoted in Montgomery, *Beyond Equality*, 384.

27. Godkin, "The Borrowing Power of Corporations," *Nation*, 8 June 1871, 398.

28. "The idea of equal rewards for all Greeley rejected (as did most other American Associationists); he felt it unjust that the 'ingenious, efficient' person should receive no more than others" (Howe, *Political Culture* [intro., n. 13], 193).

29. Godkin, "Borrowing Power," 400.

30. Ibid., 399.

31. See, e.g., Friedman, *History of American Law*, chap. 8 (see chap. 3, n. 45).

32. Godkin, "Borrowing Power," 399.

33. Ibid., 400.

34. Ibid., 399.

35. Postbellum elites usually "referred to themselves as part of the 'producing class,' or as 'labor,' or even as 'workingmen,' as distinct from the 'capitalists' (i.e., the old elite). . . . The nation's economic system was not called 'capitalism' but the 'free-labor system'" (Montgomery, *Beyond Equality*, 14).

36. For criticisms of this position, see chap. 3.

37. Godkin, "'The New Departure'," *Nation*, 396.

38. Godkin, quoted in Foner, *Reconstruction*, 500.

39. On the relation between Reconstruction and asserting "the right of the legislative branch within the national government," see Brock, *American Crisis*, 254–62.

40. Godkin, "'New Departure'," 396.

41. Ibid.

42. Godkin shared this feeling with many of the annexation effort's critics. Carl Schurz argued that "tropical peoples could not rule themselves democratically," and thus "annexation would introduce a 'poison' into the nation's public life, leading inexorably down the road to despotic government." Elsewhere, Godkin claimed that the Dominican Republic's population of "ignorant Catholic spanish negroes" could never become American citizens (quoted in Foner, *Reconstruction*, 496).

43. Ibid., 231.

44. Charles Sumner, speech to the Senate of the United States, 5 February 1866, quoted in Du Bois, *Black Reconstruction*, 194. Du Bois calls this speech "a Magna Charta of democracy in America" (193).

45. Emerson, "Address delivered in Concord on the Anniversary of the emancipation of the Negroes in the British West Indies, August 1, 1844," *ECW* 11:135.

46. Arguing that "it is impossible to separate the question of color from the question of labor" in the South, "for the reason that the majority of the laborers

... throughout the Southern States are colored people," the *Washington Weekly Chronicle* claimed that, "if now, through the success of the scheme for the disfranchisement of the negro, color is made a badge of subjection, no power can prevent the same idea from being associated with labor" ("Practical Effects of Negro Disfranchisement," *Washington Weekly Chronicle,* 15 August 1868, 5).

47. Emerson, *English Traits, Es and Ls,* 794–95.

48. Ibid., 792.

49. Ibid., 790.

50. Ibid., 792. On Lamarck and Emerson, see Philip Nicoloff, *Emerson on Race and History: An Examination of "English Traits"* (New York: Columbia University Press, 1961), 110–15. Emerson derives Lamarckian ideas from a number of sources, and one of these is Swedenborg: "Swedenborg says, that, 'What parents have so thoroughly acquired by use & education that it become a part of their nature, is implanted in their posterity in the form of an inclination,'" (*The Topical Notebooks of Ralph Waldo Emerson,* vol. 2, ed Ronald A. Bosco [Columbia, Mo.: University of Missouri Press, 1993], 314).

51. Emerson, *English Traits,* 792.

52. Ibid.

53. Ibid., 807.

54. Ibid., 793.

55. Ibid., 819–20.

56. Ibid., 819.

57. David R. Roediger identifies the concept of *herrenvolk democracy* with the sociologist Pierre L. van der Berghe, for whom it denotes "the ideology of 'regimes like those of the United States or South Africa that are democratic for the master race but tyrannical for the subordinate groups'" (*The Wages of Whiteness: Race and the Making of the American Working Class* [London: Verso Press, 1991], 59). Roediger provides much astute commentary on the interplay of rebellion and bondage in white working-class efforts to distinguish free labor from slavery in part by distinguishing white from black workers. George F. Fredrickson invokes the same passage in *Black Image in The White Mind: The Debate on Afro-American Character and Destiny, 1817–1914* (Middletown, Conn.: Wesleyan University Press, 1987), 61.

58. Emerson, *English Traits,* 794–95.

59. Ibid., 791.

60. Emerson, "The Assault Upon Mr. Sumner: Speech at a Meeting of the Citizens in the Town Hall, in Concord, May 26, 1856," *The Works of Ralph Waldo Emerson,* Standard Library Edition (Boston: Riverside-Houghton Mifflin, 1883), 11:250, 248, hereafter *Works.*

61. Emerson, "Speech at the Kansas Relief Meeting in Cambridge, Wednesday Evening, September 10, 1856," *Works* 11:260–62.

62. A standard survey of Emerson's views on slavery is Marjory M. Moody, "The Evolution of Emerson as an Abolitionist," *American Literature* 17, no. 1 (March 1945): 1–21; Moody's examination of Emerson's opposition to slavery

does not extend to his views on race. Len Gougeon has offered a more comprehensive and complex survey of similar issues in *Virtue's Hero: Emerson, Antislavery, and Reform* (Athens, Ga.: University of Georgia Press, 1990) but exagger-
ates Emerson's reform instincts. Nicoloff's more critical *Emerson on Race and
History* has influenced my thinking about Emerson's racial determinism. Cornel
West notes that "as a trope in his discourse, race signifies the circumstantial, the
conditioned, the fateful — that which limits the will of individuals, even exceptional ones" (*American Evasion of Philosophy*, 31 [see chap. 1, n. 19]). In spite of
his valuable summary of Emerson's racial thought, West follows the vast majority of Emerson readers in trivializing the destructive effect of his so-called
"mild racism" on his beliefs about freedom, equality, democracy, and corporate
capitalism: Emerson's understanding of the American self "cannot but be shot
through with certain xenophobic sensibilities and racist perceptions of the
time" (28).

63. See, in particular, Fredrickson, *Black Image*, chaps. 4–6.

64. Howe was one of three members of the War Department's American
Freedmen's Inquiry Commission, which recommended the formation of the
Freedman's Bureau. During this period he occasionally corresponded with
Agassiz about his views on racial biology.

65. Fredrickson notes that for some "antislavery racists," emancipation was
tacitly regarded as "a step toward genocide by natural causes" (*Black Image*, 159;
most of the figures named above are discussed on 152–59 passim).

66. Emerson, *JMN* 2:57.

67. Ibid., 2:48.

68. Ibid., 13:35.

69. Emerson, "Fate," *Es and Ls*, 950.

70. Emerson, "Civilization," *ECW* 7:25–26. Emerson continues, "Where
the banana grows the animal system is indolent and pampered at the cost of
higher qualities: the man is sensual and cruel. But this scale is not invariable.
High degrees of moral sentiment control the unfavorable influences of climate;
and some of our grandest examples of men and of races come from the equato-
rial regions, — as the genius of Egypt, of India and of Arabia" (26).

71. Richard Henry Dana Jr., "The 'Grasp of War Speech'" (1865), *Speeches
in Stirring Times and Letters to a Son*, ed. Richard Henry Dana III (Boston:
Houghton Mifflin, 1910), 256.

72. Richard Henry Dana Jr., "An Address Upon the Life and Services of
Edward Everett; Delivered Before the Municipal Authorities and Citizens of
Cambridge, February 22, 1865" (Cambridge, Mass., 1865), 49–50.

73. Emerson, *JMN* 13:114.

74. Ibid., 16:19.

75. Nicoloff argues that Emerson's move to monogenicism was gradual and
encouraged by his abolitionism, *Emerson on Race and History*, 123.

76. Agassiz, correspondence to Samuel Gridley Howe (August, 1863),
cited in Stephen Jay Gould, *The Panda's Thumb: More Reflections in Natural History* (New York: Norton, 1980), 174–75. Gould finds most of these passages in

Harvard's collection of Agassiz's unpublished manuscripts, which had been altered without comment by Agassiz's widow Elizabeth Cary Agassiz when first published in the *Life and Correspondence of Louis Agassiz.*

77. Agassiz, quoted in Gould, *Panda's Thumb,* 173.

78. Ibid., 172.

79. Emerson, *JMN* 16:34–35.

80. Emerson, "Speech in Honor of the Chinese Embassy," Boston, 1868, *Works* 11:474.

81. See Ronald Takaki, *Iron Cages: Race and Culture in 19th-Century America* (New York: Oxford University Press, 1979), chap. 10. Takaki notes that the Chinese were "Negroized" but finds the *Vicksburg Times* welcoming them as improved Negroes: "Emancipation has spoiled the negro and carried him away from the fields of agriculture. Our prosperity depends entirely upon the recovery of lost ground, and we therefore say let the Coolies come" (219).

82. Emerson, "The Emancipation Proclamation. An Address Delivered in Boston in September, 1862," *ECW* 11:319–20.

83. Emerson, "British West Indies," *ECW* 11:143–44.

84. Emerson, "Emancipation Proclamation," *ECW* 11:321.

85. Emerson, "American Civilization. Lecture at the Smithsonian Institution, January 31, 1862," *ECW* 11:307. An editor's note suggests that Emerson was deliberately limiting his discussion of emancipation to its effectiveness as a "war measure" (607).

86. For a comprehensive analysis of this kind of white egalitarianism, see Alexander Saxton, *The Rise and the Fall of the White Republic: Class Politics and Mass Culture in Nineteenth-Century America* (London: Verso Press, 1990), and Roediger, *Wages of Whiteness.*

87. Emerson, "American Civilization," *ECW* 11:309.

88. The entry is dated August 30, 1862; *JMN* 15:206–7.

89. Ibid., 15:405.

90. Emerson, "Abraham Lincoln: Remarks at the Funeral Services Held in Concord, April 19, 1865," *ECW* 11:337–38. Emerson is consistent on this linkage between the great middle-class president and providential guidance. "[G]reat as the popularity of the President has been, we are beginning to think that we have underestimated the capacity and virtue which the Divine Providence has made an instrument of benefit so vast. He has been permitted to do more for America than any other American man" ("The Emancipation Proclamation: An Address Delivered in Boston in September, 1862," *Miscellanies, ECW* 11:317).

91. William C. Jewell, correspondence with Charles Sumner, 19 February 1866, quoted in Foner, *Reconstruction,* 235.

92. Foner, *Reconstruction,* 231.

93. George Fredrickson, *The Arrogance of Race: Historical Perspectives on Slavery, Racism, and Social Inequality* (Middletown, Conn.: Wesleyan University Press, 1988), 204.

94. The tremendous stigma attached to such ideas was demonstrated by

President Bill Clinton's dumping of Lani C. Guinier, his own nominee to head the Civil Rights Division of the Justice Department, when she became publicly associated with them. She describes "proportionate-interest representation" in the aptly titled "Minority Goal Must Be Equality in Fact," *Los Angeles Times* 27 May 1993, sec. B, 7. Although the attack on Guinier was led by the right, it was fortified by Clinton's own think tank, the Progressive Policy Institute, whose Will Marshall charged that "[m]any of Guinier's views 'fall way outside the American tradition of equal opportunity, individual versus group rights, and majority rule'" (Ronald Brownstein, "Nomination May Add Race Issue to Democrats' Schism," *Los Angeles Times* 26 May 1993, sec. A, 21).

95. Emerson, "Aristocracy," *ECW* 10:38. This text is unreliable, and in this way resembles the other late texts edited by J. E. Cabot without Emerson's supervision. Most of these compilations were based on lectures that Emerson repeatedly rewrote and redelivered, sometimes over a period of decades. Reconstruction may clarify the turns in Emerson's thinking, but those discussed here are close enough to longstanding difficulties to suggest that this text represents his feelings; see chap. 6, n. 15.

96. Emerson, "Aristocracy," *ECW* 10:48–49.

97. Ibid., 50. Only a certain "class" should be leaders, and Emerson goes on to say that the test should be whether he is "a man of talent" (51) and whether he has a "will," both of which are "gift[s] of nature."

98. The passage cited above continues on to suggest that, "in the absence of such anthropometer" the "natural laws" will "in the long run give the fairest verdict and reward" to each citizen if they are interpreted by "the community—every community, if obstructing laws and usages are removed" (ibid., 49).

99. Ibid., 57. This order is often unapparent: "The Golden Table never lacks members; all its seats are kept full; but with this strange provision, that the members are carefully withdrawn into deep niches, so that no one of them can see any other of them, and each believes himself alone" (60–61).

100. For a fuller discussion of these features as the components of post-civil rights "liberal racism," see Avery Gordon and Christopher Newfield, "White Philosophy," *Critical Inquiry* 20 (Summer 1994): 737–57.

101. Emerson, "Illusions," *Es and Ls,* 1123.

102. Ibid., 1124.

103. In "Aristocracy," Emerson repeatedly insists that the great man, "like all magnanimous men, . . . is a democrat," and that "no great man has existed who did not rely on the sense and heart of mankind as represented by the good sense of the people." He simply rejects the idea of contradiction between democracy and aristocracy. Sometimes the mediation occurs through pseudocompromise: the "man of honor" should "accept the position of armed neutrality, abhorring the crimes of the Chartist, abhorring the selfishness of the rich, and say, 'The time will come when these poor *enfans perdus* of revolution will have instructed their party, if only by their fate, and wiser counsels will prevail'" (63–64). Sometimes it involves the power of the artist to "establish a wider dominion" over the masses on whom he draws (54).

CHAPTER EIGHT

1. Marshall and Schram, eds., *Mandate for Change*, xvi-xviii (see intro., n. 2).

2. Seymour Martin Lipset and Martin Schram, "Interpreting the 1992 Election," foreword to *Mandate for Change*, xxi, xx.

3. Mickey Kaus, *The End of Equality* (New York: Basic Books, 1992).

4. Ibid., 21, 20.

5. Ibid., 93.

6. Ibid., 21.

7. Ibid., 104.

8. Ibid., 104, 121, 129.

9. Kaus offers a different account of his two meanings on 5–6.

10. Tom Peters, *Liberation Management: Necessary Disorganization for the Nanosecond Nineties* (New York: Knopf, 1992).

11. Ibid., 5; Thomas J. Peters and Robert H. Waterman, Jr., *In Search of Excellence: Lessons from America's Best-Run Companies* (New York: Warner Books, 1984), 319.

12. Peters, *Liberation Management*, 701.

13. Ibid., 66, 33, 448, 222. Peter's two subsequent pocket manuals are even more anarchistic in form and content: see *The Tom Peters Seminar: Crazy Times Call for Crazy Organizations* (New York: Random House, Vintage, 1994), and *The Pursuit of Wow!: Every Person's Guide to Topsy-Turvy Times* (New York: Random House, Vintage, 1994). Loose-tight, anarchy-control, the motto of *Crazy Organizations*, comes from Andy Grove, Intel's discipline king: "only the paranoid survive."

14. Peters, *Liberation Management*, 235.

15. Ibid., 737.

16. Ibid., 757.

17. A particularly useful reading of Emerson's early political culture can be found in Cayton, *Emerson's Emergence*, chaps. 1–2 (see intro., n. 13).

18. A contemporary corroboration of this claim: concluding a discussion of the Cold War liberal Arthur Schlesinger Jr.'s ideas about race relations, Stanley Fish describes the picture of a younger Schlesinger on his book jacket. Schlesinger's "face is a young one—the year is 1958—and unformed; the features are ethnic, Semitic, even a bit negroid; the look is quizzical, as if he were asking, 'what will I become?' The answer he hopes for is represented in the picture by a figure in its middle ground—elegantly dressed, erect, self-contained, finished, looking not at us but at the far horizon. It is Arthur Schlesinger Sr. . . . obviously at home in the landscape which just happens to be Harvard Yard. . . . The picture suggests that Protestant America has not yet enclosed the younger Schlesinger in its bosom and that it is not yet certain that he will be able to complete the passage from the heritage of his Jewish grandfather to total assimilation" (Stanley Fish, *There's No Such Thing as Free Speech and it's a Good Thing, Too* [New York: Oxford University Press, 1994], 88).

19. Emerson, "Pray Without Ceasing," first preached 15 October 1826, in

Young Emerson Speaks, ed. Arthur Cushman McGiffert Jr. (Port Washington, N.Y.: Kennikat Press, 1968), 4, emphasis omitted. Other sermons collected here, such as "Self-Culture" and "Trust Yourself" (both 1830), demonstrate the conjunction of god-reliance and autonomy too often pulled apart and placed in different periods of the career.

20. Emerson, "Uses of Great Men," *Es and Ls,* 623.

INDEX

abolition-democracy, 175
abolitionism, 195
Adams, Charles Francis, Jr., 182, 195
African Americans: black emancipation,
175; civil rights for, 200–205; on
emancipating them from blackness,
197; Emerson on inequality of, 196;
Emerson on race relations in America,
194–200; equality for, 175, 189; political freedom for as freedom to work,
176; position ascribed to tropical origins, 197; predictions for after slavery,
196; self-reliance for, 175. *See also* racism; slavery
Agassiz, Louis, 196, 198–99
Alcott, Bronson, 51, 57
America: alleged feminization of American culture, 149–50, 250n.60; alleged
loss of common culture in, 171; as
anti-individualist, antiegalitarian, and
antidemocratic, 215; antipathy between liberty and equality in, 34, 35–
37, 38, 175–77, 212; Asian immigration, 199–200, 259n.81; associations
in antebellum, 67–72; as authoritarian
as it is nonconformist, 63; authoritarianism profoundly influencing, 215;
competitive economic system and coercive racial system of, 177; democracy
made despotic in, 63; democracy revitalized in 1990s, 209–18; dissent privileged in American liberalism, 30;
economic segregation in, 219n.5; economic system as "free-labor" not "capi-

talist," 256n.35; economy losing its national identity, 3–4; exaltation of the
individual and search for perfect community, 27; faith in freedom through
hierarchy, 215; familial democracy in,
131; freedom narrative of, 17; gays in
the military controversy, 92; herrenvolk democracy in, 193, 257n.57; homophobia in, 92, 94; husband as head
of the household in, 130; laissez-faire
hierarchies as compatible with ideals
of, 176; liberalism as pervasive common sense in, 26; liberalism's victory
over socialism in, 36; loss of autonomy in modern, 4; maximum freedom
in, 2; moderation as cause of success
of, 1; race relations in, 194–200; Reconstruction, 179–81, 186, 187–88,
195; refusal to oppose individual to
community as tradition of, 222n.18;
social restraints and conformity in
American fiction, 224n.25; success of
due to moderation, 1; synthesis of liberty and order in, 27. *See also* African
Americans; middle class; working class
"American Scholar, The" (Emerson), 83
Ammons, Elizabeth, 234n.27
anarchism, 21, 122, 222n.18
antifoundationalism: as basis for democratizing culture, 155; in Emerson, 24,
26, 154–57, 167; Fish on, 251n.8;
freedom and, 251n.9; as ground for
autonomy, 155; liberalism and, 156,
165; markets as antifoundationalist,

263

antifoundationalism (*continued*)
    156–57, 165, 170, 253n.46; in po-
    etry, 172; truth for, 154, 165; as up-
    dating power relations installed by
    foundationalism, 171
Appleby, Joyce, 220n.12
Arendt, Hannah, 234n.24
"Aristocracy" (Emerson), 205, 260nn.95,
    103
aristocracy, merit, 205–8
Aristotle, 58–59
Asian immigration, 199–200, 259n.81
associations: in antebellum America,
    67–72; artificial, 78; autonomy and
    unity linked in, 67; clubs, 147; Emer-
    son on, 119, 122–24; freedom ex-
    tended by, 77–78; as fundamental prin-
    ciple of republicanism, 183; Godkin
    on, 183–84; inequality of power in,
    184; middle-class obsession with, 67;
    natural, 78; partnerships, 86; society
    as an association writ large, 77; wom-
    en's role in, 234n.27. *See also* business
    corporations; corporatism
Atkinson, Edward, 170, 183
authoritarianism: America as authoritarian
    as it is nonconformist, 63; American
    culture profoundly influenced by, 215;
    authoritarian command replaced by lib-
    eral exchange, 165; authority in the
    market, 170; corporate individualism
    naturalizing hierarchy, 39; Emerson as
    liberal authoritarian, 26; Emerson de-
    manding a revolution against author-
    ity, 214; Emerson feminizing unap-
    pealable authority, 137; in Emersonian
    individualism, 6, 22–26; Emerson's
    theory of language as authoritarian,
    60–61; features of, 220n.9; founda-
    tionalism associated with, 171; the
    market as liberal authoritarian, 171;
    normalizing of, 29; retention in liberal-
    ism, 221n.17; social restraints and con-
    formity in American fiction, 224n.25;
    sovereignty without grounds in post-
    authoritarian society, 171; as structure,
    28. *See also* submission to authority
autonomy: antifoundationalism as ground
    for, 155; autonomous individualism
    replaced by corporatism, 38; autono-
mous individualism stressed by liberal-
    ism, 220n.12; confused with subjec-
    tion, 25; Emerson's insistence on total,
    44; in Emerson's rejection of social-
    ism, 122; equality and, 31; as function
    of corporate existence, 69; liberalism
    as about inclusion not, 215–16; linked
    to unity in associations, 67; loss of in
    modern America, 4; markets homoge-
    nizing multiplicity not underwriting,
    169; in tenements, 103

Balibar, Etienne, 226n.48
Bancroft, George, 20–21
Barber, Benjamin R., 221n.17
Barker, Anna, 140–41, 143, 248n.17
Barthes, Roland, 245n.112
Baudrillard, Jean, 63
Beecher, Catherine, 141, 249n.39
Bellah, Robert, 219nn. 2, 3
Bercovitch, Sacvan: on antebellum liberal-
    ism, 232n.5; on associations synthesiz-
    ing self and law, 67; on co-optation
    and dissent, 30; on Emerson's rejec-
    tion of collective sovereignty, 223n.21,
    232n.43; on Emerson's rejection of so-
    cialism, 122; on Emerson's theory of
    language, 49
Berghe, Pierre L. van der, 257n.57
Berlant, Lauren, 246n.113
Bible, the, 159
black Americans. *See* African Americans
Blair, Hugh, 53–54, 58, 229n.25
Bloom, Harold, 25, 231n.40
Bobbio, Norberto, 19, 39
bondage: always-constructed freedom as,
    28; in Hegel's master-slave relation,
    28–29; in Holmes's view of friend-
    ship, 110; of homosexuals to a substi-
    tute father, 116; loving bondage, 129–
    50. *See also* slavery
"Boston Hymn" (Emerson), 180
Bourdieu, Pierre, 13
Boyer, Paul, 241n.54
Brace, Charles Loring, 102–3, 241n.54
Bray, Alan, 237n.8, 239n.18
Brazil, 198–99
Brisbane, Albert, 135
Brock, W. R., 175
Brodhead, Richard H., 225n.35

Brook Farm, 91, 121, 246n.1
Brown, John, 153, 194
Browne, Thomas, 239n.18
Brownson, Orestes, 20, 70
Bushnell, Horace, 55, 56–57, 195
business corporations: assuming distinc-
    tive characteristics after 1850, 68; be-
    coming private, 84; business liberal-
    ism, 170; as compatible with public
    life, 85; as a contract, 80; as the es-
    sence of the republic, 184; Godkin on,
    183–86; interest in natural law, 187;
    mobility inside as well as outside, 217;
    monopoly, 181–82; new management
    philosophies in, 212; partnerships, 86;
    postbellum development, 181–87;
    state-corporation alliance, 84; un-
    restricted borrowing by, 184–85
Butler, Benjamin F., 240n.31

Cabot, James Elliot, 260n.95
capitalism. See market capitalism
castration thesis, 250n.60
catachresis, 49, 56, 57
Cavell, Stanley: on Emerson as philoso-
    pher, 154; on Emersonian liberation,
    225n.42; on Emersonian self-reliance,
    21; on Emersonian Perfectionism, 66,
    233n.8; on Emerson's individualism, 9
Cayton, Mary Kupiec, 220n.12
centrism: Emerson removing collective in-
    dividualism from, 7; liberal centrism,
    205; moderation, 1, 2; in professional
    middle classes, 13; reconciling the
    differences of modern societies, 1
Channing, William Ellery, 77–78,
    248n.20
Chapin, Edwin, 100–101
Chapman, John Jay, 93
charity, 81, 99
Cheyfitz, Eric, 247n.8
"Circles" (Emerson), 252n.15
civic friendship, 91, 93
civic liberalism, 211
civic republicanism, 3, 8, 218
civil rights, 200–205
Clinton, Bill, 171, 210, 260n.94
clubs, 147
Coke, Edward, 95
Coleridge, Samuel Taylor, 56, 229n.25

collective entrepreneurship, 3, 7
collective labor, 120
collective sovereignty: culture as, 157–61:
    Emerson's rejection of, 223n.21,
    232n.43
communitarianism, 219n.3
communities, utopian. See utopian com-
    munities
community: American refusal to oppose
    individual to, 222n.18; America's
    search for perfect, 27; democracy as
    community self-rule, 105; Emersonian
    self-reliance dependent on egalitarian
    community, 137; liberalism's balance
    of individual and, 33; Mandate for
    Change on, 210; the One allowing a
    community controlled by private inter-
    est, 88; submission as part of dialectic
    of individuality and, 31
Condillac, Etienne Bonnot de, 57
Conduct of Life, The (Emerson), 208
consent: in corporations, 85; Emerson's
    denial of, 59–61; freedom and order
    balanced through, 66; obedience re-
    quiring in liberalism, 60–61, 65; sub-
    mission as another name for, 28
conservatism: attacks on proposals con-
    fronting unequal outcomes, 205; eco-
    nomic individualism stressed by, 3;
    Emerson's conservative-liberal views,
    153; on equality impairing liberty, 35;
    liberalism aligning itself with, 212
"Considerations By the Way" (Emerson),
    98
contract: the business corporation as, 80;
    corporate charter as, 86; identity as
    personal in, 79; intimacy trans-
    gressing, 98, 238n.13; personal free-
    dom resting on, 26; and possession,
    79–82
conventionalism, 47–48
Cooley, Thomas, 182
corporate individualism: the corporate in-
    dividual, 69, 70–72, 76, 87–88, 183;
    corporate liberalism and, 7–8; defined,
    5; democratic prophecy and, 62–88;
    democracy and, 5, 76; equality and,
    35–39; extending beyond social and
    business policy, 209; as following
    from Emerson, 5, 26, 38; in Godkin,

corporate individualism (*continued*)
186; hierarchy naturalized in, 39; oedipal and orphic readings of, 76–77; in
Peters's three-step plan, 213; public
sovereignty undermined by, 5; on submission, 41–88; sustained by racism,
200–201; tension of liberty and equality overcome in, 38
corporate liberalism: in Cooley, 182; corporate individualism and, 7–8; as democratic, 69; Emerson's domestic theory
as fulfilling, 149; individual and transcendent agency combined in, 75;
move from republican liberalism to, 8;
on self-possession and exchange as
symbiotic, 82; synthesizing private
and transcendent powers, 68–69
corporate republicanism, 91
corporatism: autonomous individualism
replaced by, 38; consent in corporations, 85; corporate charters, 84–87;
the corporate fiction, 86; the corporate
personality, 86, 236n.68; corporate republicanism, 91; the corporation as a
body politic, 86; the corporation as
neither private nor public, 87; corporatist solution to submission, 41–88;
as democracy, 77–78; democracy in
the public aspects of, 87–88; democracy rendered superfluous by, 38–39;
of Emerson, 126; Emerson's refusal to
separate from spiritualism, 83–84;
equality and, 35–39; genesis of liberal
racism and, 174–218; market corporatism, 171; oedipal and orphic, 72–77,
79, 85; private property and corporate
form consolidated, 84; public basis of
the corporation, 82–87; racism
strengthening, 200; shift from public
to private corporation, 84; submission
without a discrete superior in, 38–39.
See also associations; business corporations; corporate individualism; corporate liberalism
Cratylus, 44–45, 227n.8
crowd, the (the group; the mob): collective attachments as homosexual for
Freud, 113; crowd psychology and
submissive male friendship, 117–21;
crowds with a leader, 100–105; Emer-

son's hatred of, 97; Freud on group
psychology and male homosexuality,
109–17; Freud on the individual in,
244n.88; groups of built of love, 112–
13, 243nn. 70, 76; group ties making
men into sheep, 113; the primal father
as the group ideal, 112; riots, 101–2,
104; same-sex crowd subjectivity resisting submission, 108; science of,
93; sodomy and, 96, 97; Todd on,
108, 109; women as diverting investments from the group leader, 113. *See
also* associations; masses, the
culture: alleged loss of common culture,
171; antifoundationalism as basis for
democratizing, 155; as collective sovereignty, 157–61; the cultural market,
168; as private property, 164; Tocqueville on authoritarianism in American,
63
"Culture" (Emerson), 168

Dana, Richard Henry, Jr., 197
Dartmouth College, Trustees of, 86
Dartmouth College v. Woodward, 236n.65
degrees, 46, 49, 55, 227n.12
demagogue theory of rioting, 102, 104
democratic individualism: in Emerson,
24; as individualism realized through
equality, 218; public sovereignty in, 5;
the state in, 19
democracy: abolition-democracy, 175; absorbed in sociability by Emerson
effect, 39; American culture as antidemocratic, 215; American democracy
revitalized in 1990s, 209–18; antifoundationalism as basis for democratizing
culture, 155; Bobbio on autocratic
power of, 39; as community self-rule,
105; contradictions in Emerson's view
of, 247n.12; corporate individualism
and, 5, 76; corporate individualism
and democratic prophecy, 62–88; corporate liberalism as democratic, 69;
corporatism as, 77–78; corporatism
rendering superfluous, 38–39; democratic patriarchy, 112; as despotic in
America, 63; Emerson on creative democracy, 153; Emerson on mass democracy, 208; Emerson's as halfway

democracy, 13; Emerson's repudiation of, 22; Emerson's spontaneous democracy of natural equals, 181; Emerson's weakening of, 6; familial democracy, 131–37; free-labor democracy, 187; Freud on, 111, 116, 117; in friendship, 91–92; Godkin on non-Anglo-Saxons as incapable of, 188, 256n.42; herrenvolk democracy, 193, 257n.57; homoeroticism and radical, 92; husband's role not undermined by, 130; and individualism balanced in liberalism, 22, 26; Jacksonian, 19; leaders of as aristocrats, 206; liberal democracy built on submissiveness, 126; male friendship and 91–92, 105–6; *Mandate for Change* on, 210; mass democracy and sodomy, 97, 100; mass democracy in Paris Commune, 106–7; maximum freedom in American, 2; middle-class fear of mass democracy, 100; natural associations as democratic, 78; non-Anglo-Saxons as incapable of, 188, 256n.42; in public dimension of corporations, 87–88; and radical individualism repudiated by Emerson, 22; scattered influence in representative, 186; Transcendentalism on, 17–18, 20–21; Whitman on mass democracy, 105, 106; Whitman's definition of, 105. *See also* democratic individualism

Derrida, Jacques, 58–59, 106, 228n.16, 232n.42

Dewey, John, 86, 236n.68

Dimock, Wai-chee, 226n.43

domestic life. *See* family, the

"Domestic Life" (Emerson), 147, 148, 149

Dreiser, Theodore, 81

Du Bois, W. E. B., 175, 256n.44

Ellison, Julie, 154, 223n.23, 239n.19

Ely, Richard T., 218

Emancipation Proclamation, 201

Emerson, Lidian, 142

Emerson, Mary Moody, 142

Emerson, Ralph Waldo: as abolitionist, 195; on the active soul, 21; on African Americans, 196, 197; "The American Scholar," 83; antifoundationalism in, 24, 26, 154–57, 167; apparent self-contradictions in, 45; "Aristocracy," 205, 260nn. 95, 103; on Asian immigration, 199–200; on associations, 119, 122–24; authoritarianism in, 6, 22–26; Barker and, 140–41, 143, 248n.17; on black emancipation, 175; Blair's influence on, 53–54, 58, 229n.25; "Boston Hymn," 180; Brook Farm invitation declined, 91, 121; Christianity liberalized by, 25; "Circles," 252n.15; on civil rights, 200–205; on Civil War as triumph for liberty, 174; on class distinctions, 205–6; on collective labor, 120; collective sovereignty rejected by, 223n.21, 232n.43; on the complete man being part woman, 247n.8; *The Conduct of Life,* 208; conservative-liberal views of, 153; conservative policies opposed by, 153; "Considerations By the Way," 98; contradictory view of democracy, 247n.12; on controlling the voice, 56; on conventionalism, 47; on the corporate individual, 87–88; corporate individualism following from, 5, 26, 38; corporatism of, 126; Cratylus compared to, 44–45; on creative democracy, 153; on crowds, 97; "Culture," 168; democratic individualism in, 24; democracy and radical individualism repudiated by, 22; democracy weakened by, 6; on domestic life, 146–47, 148–49; "Domestic Life," 147, 148, 149; double legacy of, 26; editing of essays of, 251n.15; elective affinities with younger men, 239n.23; on emancipating African Americans from blackness, 197; on Emancipation Proclamation, 201; empiricist aspects of theory of language of, 51–56, 58, 231n.38; on Englishness, 190–93, 194; *English Traits,* 190, 195; epistemology of, 154–57; on equality, 99, 123–24, 177; equality redefined by, 190; eulogy for Lincoln, 203, 259n.90; eye-fascination and, 97–98, 118, 239n.16; on the family, 132–37, 248n.23; fatalism of, 33; "Fate," 149,

Emerson, Ralph Waldo (*continued*)
224n.26; feminizing unappealable authority, 137; on figuration having its source in the Father, 59; Fourierist socialism and, 135, 146; on freedom, 2, 26, 72; freedom and otherness reconciled in, 22; on freedom as rapturous servitude, 22–23, 224n.26; on friendship, 98–99, 118–19; "Friendship," 125, 137; Gay and, 97–98; on genius, 23, 162, 167; German idealism and, 43; growing up in a deference culture, 214–15; halfway democracy of, 13; on the harlot, 141–43; on Herbert, 73, 80, 234n.31; on his children, 136, 248n.20; homoeroticism and, 91–128; homoeroticism of, 98; as illuminating difference between structured and submissive individuality, 28; on the individual, 26; individualism repudiated by, 22; on instinct, 83; intersubjectivity in, 24, 26, 154, 181; on intimacy, 98–99; as Lamarckian, 191, 257n.50; on language, 46–61, 167–68, 172; on legislation, 179; as liberal authoritarian, 26; on liberalism of moral relations, 9–10; "Love," 138; on love of women, 137–43; on male friendship, 23–24, 98–100, 117–21, 125, 248n.26; on marriage, 139, 144, 248n.17; on mass democracy, 208; on the masses, 99–100, 102, 120, 240n.30; mild racism of, 258n.62; monogenicism of, 198; monopoly opposed by, 181–82; "Montaigne; or, the Skeptic," 146, 149, 226n.46; moving between Whig and Democratic parties, 8; on multiracialism, 198; as the national Orpheus, 43–44; Neoplatonism of, 43, 50–51, 83, 165; on nonidentity, 82; on originality, 158–60, 163, 167; "The Over-Soul," 24–25; Perfectionism of, 66; on perpetual transition, 154; as philosopher, 153–57; as Plotinus-Montaigne, 31; "The Poet," 51, 157; "Poetry and Imagination," 26, 167; "Politics," 255n.13; positive notion of power, 33; postwar writing of, 174; "Pray Without Ceasing," 216, 261n.19; preference for

elites, 125, 245n.108; on property, 255n.13; on quotation, 161–64, 165, 166; "Quotation and Originality," 158, 162, 164, 167; on race mixing in Brazil, 198–99; on race relations in America, 194–200; racism of, 196, 258n.62; radical individualism of, 22, 44; as realist, 44–45, 227n.9; on Reconstruction, 179–81, 195; as reformist, 254n.13; refusal to separate corporatism from spiritualism, 83–84; *Representative Men,* 252n.36; revolution against authority demanded by, 214; as sage of professional middle classes, 13; self-censorship of, 215; "Self-Reliance," 22–23, 83, 130; on the self's infinitude, 19; the servants invited to dinner by, 122; the skeptical Emerson, 31–34; slavery opposed by, 194–97; on socialism, 91, 121–22, 135, 146, 223n.21, 232n.43; *Society and Solitude,* 251n.15; society's authority rejected by, 6; as spokesman for the market, 82; on spontaneous democracy of natural equals, 181; submission in individualism of, 6, 7, 182; submission to tradition in, 1–2; substantial forms of equality and liberty rejected by, 177; as theorist of laissez-faire individualism, 6–7; three-step argument of, 22–23, 26, 33, 38, 46, 170–71, 182–83; on too little government, 123; on total autonomy, 44; in tradition of social individualism, 9; Transcendentalism of, 17–22; Unitarian heritage of, 17, 18; on utopian communities, 120–21, 121–24; utopian imagination of, 217–17; "Wealth," 179; on West Indian emancipation, 189, 201; on West Point, 148; as white supremacist, 196; on women, 130, 136–37; on women's rights, 141, 145–46; workingman's republicanism in, 21; Yankee pragmatism in, 51; "The Young Americans," 124. *See also* Emerson effect; Emersonian self-reliance; *Nature*
Emerson effect: defined, 4; democracy absorbed into sociability in, 39; making ceding sovereignty seem like emancipa-

tion, 209; offering adaptation as surrogate for control, 214

Emersonian self-reliance: Bloom on, 25; Cavell on, 21; as complex relation to society, 23; contradictions in, 22; as corporate agency, 69; as dependent on egalitarian community, 137; Emerson's pious deference compared to, 216; as god-reliance, 25; the self listening to its own instincts first, 6; as self plus other, 223n.20; the self-reliant individual as seeking submission, 28; the self's relation to intersubjectivity, 24

End of Equality, The (Kaus), 211–12

Englishness, 190–93, 194

English Traits (Emerson), 190, 195

entrepreneurial individualism, 211

entrepreneurship, collective, 3, 7

equality, 37; for African Americans, 175, 176, 189, 204; American culture as antiegalitarian, 215; antipathy between liberty and, 34, 35–37, 38, 175–77, 212; autonomy and, 31; black emancipation and, 175, 189; conservatives on equality impairing liberty, 35; corporatism and, 35–39; democratic individualism realized through, 218; Emersonian self-reliance dependent on egalitarian community, 137; Emerson on, 99, 123–24, 177; Emerson on women's rights, 141, 145–46; Emerson's redefinition of, 190; Emerson's spontaneous democracy of natural equals, 181; *The End of Equality*, 211–12; equal agency, 33–34, 218; in the family, 131–32; Freud on, 111; gender equality, 20; of homoeroticism, 109, 126; homophobia as about, 93; inequality of power in associations, 184; inequality read as a kind of, 189; Jackson on, 19–20; as key to avoiding submission, 31, 33; nineteenth-century understanding of, 176; as obsolete and inefficient, 176; of opportunity offered by the market, 178; possibility of achieving equality in liberal society, 189; of power, 5–6; in queer sexuality, 127; race and, 192, 193, 194, 204; racial equality rejected

in America, 176, 204; social equality, 204, 205, 211; submission to right law making irrelevant, 34; working-class egalitarianism, 104–5

equivalence, logic of, 168, 172

Everett, Edward, 8–9, 197

faculty psychology, 77

family, the: Emerson on, 132–37, 248n.23; Emerson on domestic life, 146–47, 148–49; equality in, 131–32; familial democracy, 131–37; men's place in antebellum, 130, 131; women's role in antebellum, 129–31

fascism, 242n.68

"Fate" (Emerson), 149, 224n.26

Feidelson, Charles, 48

feminism, 234n.27

filiopiety, 66

Fish, Stanley, 251n.8, 253n.46, 261n.18

Fletcher v. Peck, 80, 236n.65

Foner, Eric, 175

Fontanier, Pierre, 57

Forbes, John Murray, 153

Foucault, Michel, 29, 172

Fourier, Charles, 135, 146

Frederickson, George F., 195, 205, 257n.57, 258n.65

freedom: American faith in freedom through hierarchy, 215; antifoundationalism and, 251n.9; black emancipation, 175, 176; bondage as, 28; to choose laws already given, 39, 227n.52; corporate capital as preserving, 70; to differ, 36–37; as endless flexibility in Emerson, 26; extended by associations, 77–78; fluid movement feeling like, 217; freedom narrative of nineteenth-century America, 17; intellectual freedom, 161; as liberal principle, 2; maximum freedom in American democracy, 2; as obedience, 72; and order balanced through consent, 66; orphic freedom, 77; and otherness reconciled in Emerson, 22; personal freedom only through mass freedom, 107; personal freedom resting on contract, 26; professional middle class denying to itself, 13; public sovereignty providing form of, 5; as rapturous ser-

freedom (*continued*)
    vitude for Emerson, 22–23, 224n.26;
    regulated freedom in the middle class,
    64; as relinquished freely, 65; subordi-
    nated to law, 60. *See also* liberty
Freeman, Elizabeth, 246n.113
Freud: on active homosexuality, 114–16,
    126, 243n.78, 244n.82; on civiliza-
    tion as managing homosexuality, 93;
    on democracy, 111, 116, 117; on
    equality, 111; fascism and group psy-
    chology of, 242n.68; *Group Psychology
    and the Analysis of the Ego,* 93, 109–17;
    on group psychology and male homo-
    sexuality, 109–17; on groups as built
    of love, 112–13, 243nn. 70, 76; on
    the individual in groups, 244n.88; so-
    cialism and democracy rejected by,
    111; submission in incorporation and
    interjection, 29
friendship: civic friendship, 91, 93; Emer-
    son on, 98–99, 118–19; intimacy in,
    98–99, 118–19; as little society, 91,
    117; platonic, 98. *See also* male
    friendship
"Friendship" (Emerson), 125, 137
Fujimori, Alberto, 62
Fuller, Margaret, 20, 131–32, 149

Gay, Martin, 97–98, 118
genius, 23, 162, 167
Godkin, Edwin Lawrence: on Associa-
    tion, 183–84; on business corpora-
    tions, 183–86; corporate individual-
    ism in, 186; Emerson compared to,
    255n.18; on non-Anglo-Saxons as in-
    capable of democracy, 188, 256n.42;
    on Reconstruction, 186, 187–88; on
    unrestricted corporate borrowing,
    184–85
Goethe, Johann Wolfgang von, 162–63,
    252n.36
Goldman, Emma, 21, 122, 222n.18
Gonnaud, Maurice, 63, 174, 199,
    245n.108, 249n.32
Gougeon, Len, 258n.62
government: Emerson on legislation as vi-
    olation of natural law, 179; Emerson
    on too little government, 123; losing
    their real authority, 3–4; the market as

a uniform government, 170; as provid-
    ing lords, 124; morality as object of,
    202; Transcendentalism on, 18. *See
    also* laissez-faire government; state, the
Greeley, Horace, 183, 196, 256n.28
Greenberg, David F., 238n.13
Griswold, Rufus, 94–95, 105
group, the. *See* crowd, the
Group Psychology and the Analysis of the Ego
    (Freud), 93, 109–17
Grusin, Richard, 226n.43
Guinier, Lani C., 260n.94

Hartmann, Heidi, 126–27
Hartz, Louis, 1, 27, 62, 215
Hawthorne, Nathaniel, 43, 91, 224n.25
Hawthorne, Sophia, 149–50
Hayek, F. A., 217
Hazard, Rowland, 54
Hazlitt, William, 57
Hegel, George Wilhelm Friedrich, 28–29
Henshaw, David, 85
Herbert, George, 73, 74, 75, 76, 80,
    234n.31
Herder, Johann Gottfried von, 228n.17
herrenvolk democracy, 193, 257n.57
heterosexual homoeroticism, 93–94
Holmes, Oliver Wendell, 110, 118
homoeroticism, 91–128; egalitarianism
    of, 109, 126; of Emerson, 98; figuring
    faith in radical democracy, 92; Freud
    on archaic threat of, 117; genealogy
    of, 94; heterosexual homoeroticism,
    93–94; as spoiled by groups for Emer-
    son, 100; as tacit threat to hierarchy,
    127. *See also* homosexuality; male
    friendship
homophilia, 128
homophobia, 92, 93, 94
homosexuality: as in bondage to a substi-
    tute father, 116; collective attachments
    as homosexual for Freud, 113; Elizabe-
    than English view of, 237n.8; as essen-
    tialist identity for Freud, 110; first
    development of the term, 93; Freud
    on active, 114–16, 126, 243n.78,
    244n.82; Freud on group psychology
    and, 109–17; gay rights repealed by
    referenda, 97; gays in the military con-
    troversy, 92; homophilia, 128; homo-

phobia, 92, 93, 94; homosexual panic, 94; ignorance of details of same-sex intercourse, 96; link between male bonds and, 109–10; and melancholia in Freud, 116, 117, 243n.76, 244n.82; queer sexuality as egalitarian, 127; same-sex crowd subjectivity resisting submission, 108; science of, 93; straightness as including men who identify as gay, 246n.114; submissiveness associated with 126; Wilde, 93. *See also* homoeroticism; sodomy

Horwitz, Howard, 69, 236n.65, 255n.22

Howe, Daniel Walker, 17

Howe, Samuel Gridley, 196, 258n.64

identity: homosexuality as essentialist identity for Freud, 110; influenced by political subjectivity, 5, 10; as mutual and relational, 64; nonidentity, 82; as personal in contract, 79; as a problem for liberalism, 216; straight male identity, 93

imitation (mimesis): dialectical relation to invention, 49; distinction from invention denied by Emerson, 55; as dominating market poetics, 165; invention governed by, 56, 60; in the origin of language, 49, 231n.38; in realist view of language, 45; truest consciousness as purest, 229n.22; words arising by, 53

incorporation, 29

individual, the: American exaltation of, 27; centrists reconciling society with, 1; the corporate individual, 69, 70–72, 76, 87–88, 183; Emerson on, 26; Freud on the individual in groups, 244n.88; liberalism's balance of community and, 33; refusing to oppose to the community as American tradition, 222n.18; the self-divided individual, 123; submission as part of dialectic of individuality and community, 31. *See also* individualism

individualism: American culture as anti-individualist, 215; anarchism as socialized, 21; authoritarianism in Emersonian, 6, 22–26; autonomous individualism replaced by corporatism, 38;

autonomous individualism stressed by liberalism, 220n.12; collective, 7; contradictions of, 63–67; corporation stockholders as representative of, 67; cultural effects of, 45; and democracy balanced in liberalism, 22, 26; and democracy repudiated by Emerson, 22; democracy weakened in Emersonian, 6; economic individualism stressed by conservatives, 3; Emerson as illuminating difference between structured and submissive individuality, 28; Emerson as theorist of, 6–7; Emerson in tradition of social, 9; entrepreneurial, 211; and freedom balanced in liberalism, 22; as interdependence for Reich, 3; Lockean, 3; market individualism, 82; possessive, 32, 78, 82, 88, 126; postindividualism, 91; real individualism as social, 7; radical individualism of the Transcendentalists, 18; republicanism interwoven with, 220n.12; slavery as source of Southern, 70; submission in Emersonian, 6, 7, 182; and submission in private life, 89–150; true individualism as yielding union, 27. *See also* corporate individualism; democratic individualism; individual, the

instinct, 83

intersubjectivity: in Emerson, 24, 26, 154, 181; in Freud, 29; in Whitman, 107

intimacy: domestic life uniting higher law and, 147; erotic energy of, 140; in friendship, 98–99, 118–19; middle-class norms of male, 110; need to elevate women's, 141; as transgressing contract, 98, 238n.13. *See also* love

introjection, 29

invention: dialectical relation to imitation, 49; distinction from imitation denied by Emerson, 55; governed by imitation, 56, 60; as having an external source, 158; in nominalist theory of language, 45; only an inventor knowing how to borrow, 163; by the poet, 48, 229n.22

Jackson, Andrew, 19–20

Jacksonian Democracy, 19

Jehlen, Myra, 224n.25
Johnson, Andrew, 176

Kant, Immanuel, 45, 65, 69, 227n.11
Kaus, Mickey, 211–12
Kohl, Lawrence, 69
Kristeva, Julie, 225n.43

labor, collective, 120
Laclau, Ernesto, 251n.9
laissez-faire government: conventionalism,
    47–48; Cooley on, 182; Emerson as
    theorist of, 6–7; faculty psychology rul-
    ing out, 77; hierarchies of as compa-
    tible with American ideals, 176; Jackso-
    nian Democracy and, 19; liberalism as
    ideology of, 6; liberalism departing
    from, 68; liberty linked to, 177; in
    nineteenth-century New England, 7;
    replaced by big government, 8. *See also*
    market capitalism
Lamarck, Jean-Baptiste de Monet, 191,
    257n.50
language: Bushnell on spiritual significa-
    tion, 56–57; catachresis, 49, 56, 57;
    degrees of, 46, 49, 55, 227n.12; Emer-
    son's theory of, 46–61, 167–68, 172;
    Emerson's theory of as authoritarian,
    60–61; as grounded in a nature linked
    to spirit, 157; imitation in the origin
    of, 49, 231n.38; language of nature,
    52–53, 157, 231n.38; Locke's conven-
    tionalist theory of, 47–48, 58; making
    language one's own as form of liberty,
    165; metonymy, 168; Peabody's defi-
    nition of prose, 228.17; as in perpet-
    ual metamorphosis, 157; private lan-
    guage, 161; realist and nominalist
    theories of, 44–45, 227n.9. *See also*
    poetry
Lasch, Christopher, 224n.26
law: associations synthesizing self and, 67;
    corporate and market interest in natu-
    ral, 187; disjuncture between individu-
    ality and, 146–47; Emerson on legisla-
    tion as violation of natural, 179;
    freedom as choosing laws already
    given, 39, 227n.52; freedom subordi-
    nated to, 60; Kant on free submission
    to, 65, 69; Oversoul shifting from a

Law to a Father, 50; the poet as law-
    giver, 49; the poet obeying and creat-
    ing, 48; the poet transcribing, 51; sub-
    mission to right law making equality
    irrelevant, 34
Lawrence, D. H., 120
Leaves of Grass (Whitman), 94–95
Le Bon, Gustave, 93, 110–11, 112
Leverenz, David, 69, 130, 221n.18,
    247n.6
liberalism: as about inclusion not auton-
    omy, 215–16; as acculturating middle-
    class professionals, 216; aligning itself
    with conservatism, 212; alleged femini-
    zation of American culture as liberaliza-
    tion, 149–50; antebellum liberalism,
    232n.5; antifoundationalism and, 156,
    165; antipathy between liberty and
    equality in, 34, 35–37, 38, 175–77,
    212; authoritarian retentions in,
    221n.17; autonomous individualism
    stressed by, 220n.12; business liberal-
    ism, 170; change from republican to
    corporate form, 8; civic liberalism,
    211; corporate individualism follow-
    ing from, 5; corporatism and genesis
    of liberal racism, 174–218; democracy
    and individualism balanced in, 22, 26;
    dissent privileged in American, 30;
    Emerson as liberal authoritarian, 26;
    Emerson's conservative-liberal views,
    153; Emerson's liberalism of moral re-
    lations, 9–10; fin de siècle liberalism,
    210; freedom as principle of, 2; ideals
    corrupted by circumstances of history,
    11–12; identity as problem for, 216;
    individual and community balanced
    in, 33; laissez-faire individualism ex-
    changed for corporate model, 68;
    latter-day, 174–77; as of the left, 2; lib-
    eral centrism, 205; liberal democracy
    built on submissiveness, 126; liberal
    exchange replacing authoritarian com-
    mand, 165; loss of autonomy and sov-
    ereignty made to feel good by, 4; the
    market as liberal authoritarianism,
    171; moderate reformism as element
    of, 2; negative liberty, 9; nineteenth-
    century liberalism, 7; obedience requir-
    ing consent in, 60–61, 65; originating

as ideology of laissez-faire, 6; as pervasive common sense in America, 26; political-cultural constituents of liberal self, 5; positive principles of, 2; possibility of achieving equality in liberal society, 189; private property as principle of, 2, 6; on racism, 207; reformism as element of, 2; reform liberals after Civil War, 178; republicanism interwoven with, 220n.12; as statist, 165; as structure, 26–31; tensions in, 7; as transitional ideology, 218; victory over socialism in America, 36. *See also* corporate liberalism

Liberation Management (Peters), 11, 212–14

liberty: antipathy between equality and, 34, 35–37, 38, 175–77, 212; Civil War as triumph for, 174; conservatives on equality impairing, 35; as created and protected by moral sentiment, 34; Emerson rejecting substantial forms of, 177; laissez-faire economics linked to, 177; in liberalism of moral relations, 10; making language one's own as form of, 165; negative liberty, 9; ordered liberty, 27; slavery as demonstration of relation of equality and, 175. *See also* freedom

Lincoln, Abraham, 203, 259n.90

Lippard, George, 95–96

Locke, John: conventionalism of, 47–48, 58; Lockean individualism, 3; on origin of words, 53, 54, 229n.26

logic of equivalence, 168, 172

love: Emerson on love of women, 137–43; Freud on groups as built of, 112–13, 243nn. 70, 76. *See also* intimacy

"Love" (Emerson), 138

Lowell, James Russell, 31

Lustig, Jeffrey, 35

male friendship: bondage in Holmes's view of, 110; crowd psychology and submissive male friendship, 117–21; democracy and, 91–92, 105–6; Emerson on, 23–24, 98–100, 117–21, 125, 248n.26; European tradition of, 106; love of women compared to, 137–39;

middle-class norms of male intimacy, 110; oedipal structures and, 92; as a principle of public life, 94; submission veiled in, 138

Mandate for Change (Progressive Policy Institute), 210

Mannheim, Karl, 222n.18

market capitalism: accumulation required for, 164; American economic system as "free-labor" not "capitalist," 256n.35; authority in the market, 170; chamber of commerce-type economy, 165; compatibility of revolution and uniformity in, 171; contradictions in, 79; the cultural market, 168; Emerson as spokesman for the market, 82; equality of opportunity offered by, 178; exchange of quotations, 165, 168–69, 170; exchange only of what can find its equivalent, 172; as homogenizing multiplicity not underwriting autonomy, 169; interest in natural law, 187; intimacy transgressing, 98–99, 238n.13; the market as liberal authoritarian, 171; the market as a uniform government, 170; market corporatism, 171; market individualism, 82; markets as antifoundationalist, 156–57, 165, 170, 253n.46; markets as webs of relations, 168; racism and the market, 177–81; as a uniform government, 170. *See also* business corporations; laissez-faire government; private property

marriage, 139, 144, 248n.17

Marsh, James, 57

Marx, Karl, 83, 107–8, 226n.47

masses, the: Emerson on, 99–100, 102, 120, 240n.30; Emerson on mass democracy, 208; mass democracy and sodomy, 97, 100; mass democracy in Paris Commune, 106–7; middle-class fear of mass democracy, 100; neighborhoods of, 105; personal freedom only through mass freedom, 107; Whitman on mass democracy, 105, 106; Whitman's love of, 105–9. *See also* crowd, the

masturbation, 96, 106, 108, 118, 238n.10

Mattheissen, F. O., 153
Meer, Theo van der, 238n.11
melancholia, 116, 117, 243n.76, 244n.82
Melville, Herman, 224n.25
men: alleged feminization of American culture, 149–50, 250n.60; in the antebellum family, 130, 131; feminization of, 131, 247n.8; group ties making men into sheep, 113; intercourse with women robbing of their powers, 108; link between male bonds and homosexuality, 109–10; self-differentiation as point of male existence, 101; the straight homophiliac, 128; straight male identity, 93; straight men who identify as gay, 246n.114; women as source of male authority, 146. *See also* homosexuality; male friendship; patriarchy
merit aristocracy, 205–8
metonymy, 168
Michael, John, 223n.20
Michaels, Walter Benn, 69, 226n.44
middle class, 12–13; alleged feminization of, 149–50, 250n.60; battling against sensibility of from within, 14; centrism in politics of, 13; denying freedom to itself, 13; Emerson as sage of, 13; fear of mass democracy and sodomy, 100, 237n.8; fear of the purposeful mob, 102; gender roles in Transcendentalism, 129; liberalism acculturating, 216; liberalism as pervasive common sense among, 26; norms of male intimacy in, 110; obsession with association, 67; reformers, 103, 105; regulated freedom in, 64; submission in political psyche of, 28; traditional values of, 210; utopianism of, 176; women's role in the family, 130–31
Miller, D. A., 245n.112
Miller, Perry, 122
mimesis. *See* imitation
mob, the. *See* crowd, the
moderation, 1, 2. *See also* centrism
monogenicism, 198
monopoly, 181–82
"Montaigne; or, the Skeptic" (Emerson), 146, 149, 226n.46

Montgomery, David, 182
Moody, Marjory M., 257n.62
moral sense, 66
mourning, 32, 225n.43
multiracialism, 198

Nature (Emerson), 41–88; on corporate individualism, 62–88; Emerson's eye-fascination in, 118; Emerson's theory of language in, 46–61; "Language," 46–61; on language as grounded in a nature linked to spirit, 157; "Prospects," 62–88
Neoplatonism, 43, 50–51, 83, 165
Nietzsche, Friedrich, 65, 69
nominalism, 44–45, 227n.9
Norris, Frank, 69
Norton, Andrews, 58
Norton, Charles Eliot, 255n.18

oedipal structures: authoritarianism normalized in, 29; in Freud's account of active homosexuality, 114–15, 243n.78; Herbert as oedipal son, 73; male friendship and, 92; oedipal and orphic corporatism, 72–77, 79, 85
One, the: a community system controlled by private interest and, 88; individuality and, 43; as mediating self-positing and consent, 66; Transcendentalism on the Oneness of being, 46
originality, 158–60, 163, 167
Orpheus, 74–75, 76, 84
Oversoul, 49, 50
"Over-Soul, The" (Emerson), 24–25

Packer, Barbara, 252n.29, 254n.66
Paine, Thomas, 222n.18
Paris Commune, 106–7
partnerships, 86
passion, 5
patriarchy: in the antebellum family, 131; democratic, 112; male bonding and, 126–27; Transcendentalists' failure to critique, 129
Patterson, Mark R., 252n.29
Peabody, Elizabeth Palmer, 47, 228n.17
Pestalozzi, Johann Heinrich, 244n.94
Peters, Tom, 11, 212–14, 217
platonic friendship, 98

Poe, Edgar Allan, 57
"Poet, The" (Emerson), 51, 157
poetry: as alone infinite and free, 43; the
    antifoundationalist poet, 172; conven-
    tion stripped away in, 48; imitation in
    market poetics, 165; originality in,
    158–60; the orphic poet, 72–74, 83,
    88; as perpetual play of tropes, 157;
    the poet as an inventor, 48, 229n.22;
    the poet as lawgiver, 49; the poet as
    transcribing the law, 51; the poetic
    sign, 160–61; the poet obeying and
    creating the law, 48; realist theory of
    language and, 45. See also imitation; in-
    vention
"Poetry and Imagination" (Emerson), 26,
    167
"Politics" (Emerson), 255n.13
positive economic nationalism, 4
possession, contract and, 79–82
power: antifoundationalism updating
    power relations installed by founda-
    tionalism, 171; ceding to an ulterior
    source, 33–34; corporate power flow-
    ing as through an organism, 183; cure
    for centralized, 170; democracy's auto-
    cratic, 39; equality of, 5–6; erotic
    power of women, 109; Emerson's posi-
    tive notion of, 33; inequality of power
    in associations, 184; multiplicity of
    power relations, 29, 172; successful
    power denied to everyone, 32
"Pray Without Ceasing" (Emerson), 216,
    261n.19
private language, 161
private life: individualism and submission
    in, 89–150. See also family, the;
    friendship
private property: contract and possession,
    79–82; and corporate form consoli-
    dated, 84; the corporation as, 86; cul-
    ture as, 164; Emerson on, 255n.13; as
    just another commodity, 81; as liberal
    principle, 2, 6; as manifesting reciproc-
    ity of public and private, 165; the po-
    etic sign as, 161; quotation appro-
    priated as, 163; socialization as danger
    to, 67
professional and managerial middle class.
    See middle class

Progressive Policy Institute, 210, 260n.94
proportionate-interest representation,
    205, 260n.94
prose, 228n.17
Psychologie des foules (Le Bon), 93, 110
public sovereignty: corporate individual-
    ism undermining, 5; corporate sover-
    eignty and, 71; in democratic individu-
    alism, 5; trade taking precedence over,
    179

Quaker City, The (Lippard), 95–96
queer sexuality, 127
quotation, 161–64, 165, 166, 168–69,
    170, 172
"Quotation and Originality" (Emerson),
    158, 162, 164, 167

racism: antislavery racism, 195–96,
    258n.65; corporate individualism sus-
    tained by, 200–201; corporatism and
    genesis of liberal, 174–218; corporat-
    ism strengthened by, 200; Emerson as
    white supremacist, 196; Emerson on
    American race relations, 194–200; Em-
    erson on Englishness, 190–93; Emer-
    son on race mixing in Brazil, 198–99;
    Emerson's mild racism, 258n.62; liber-
    alism on, 207; the market and, 177–
    81; racial equality rejected in America,
    176, 204. See also slavery
realism, 44–45, 227n.9
reason, 20–21, 50
Reconstruction, 179–81, 186, 187–88,
    195
reformism: Emerson as reformist,
    254n.13; middle-class reformers, 103,
    105; moderate reformism as element
    of American liberalism, 2; reform liber-
    als after Civil War, 178
Reich, Robert, 2–4, 7–8, 218, 219n.5,
    220n.7
Reich, Wilhelm, 243n.68
Representative Men (Emerson), 252n.36
republicanism: association as fundamental
    principle of, 183; business corpora-
    tions as essence of American republic,
    184; civic republicanism, 3, 8, 218;
    corporate republicanism, 91; liberal-
    ism interwoven with, 220n.12; move

republicanism (*continued*)
  from republican to corporate liberal-
  ism, 8; revival of, 220n.12; working-
  man's republicanism, 21
Republicans, 186, 188
Riker, Richard, 101
riots, 101–2, 104
Ripley, George, 18, 91, 121
Roediger, David R., 257n.57
Rorty, Richard, 165, 250n.6
Rose, Anne C., 18, 129, 246n.1, 248n.17
Ross, Kristin, 106
Rotch, Mary, 142
Rousseau, Jean-Jacques, 56, 57
Royce, Josiah, 69, 86
Rusk, Ralph L., 248n.20

Schlegel, Friedrich, 49, 57, 73
Schlesinger, Arthur, Jr., 261n.18
Schultz, Robert, 236n.65
Schurz, Carl, 256n.42;
Sedgwick, Eve Kosofsky, 126
self-reliance: black emancipation and,
  175; the genuinely self-reliant person
  as a perfect member, 27; in Peters's
  three-step plan, 213; as self-ownership, 180; the self-reliant individual
  incorporating the other, 64; Transcendentalism and, 18; unregulated self-
  reliance as old-fashioned, 3. *See also*
  Emersonian self-reliance
"Self-Reliance" (Emerson): on the aboriginal self, 83; freedom as rapturous servitude in, 22–23; on women's role, 130.
  See also Emersonian self-reliance
Shakespeare, William, 159–60
Shelley, Percy Bysshe, 56, 57
signs: Bushnell on spiritual signification,
  56–57; Coleridge on sign and symbol,
  229n.25; exchanges of, 168; the poetic sign, 160–61; quoted signs, 166.
  See also language
Simpson, David, 232n.41
Slater, Philip, 220n.9
slavery: abolitionism, 195; as demonstration of relation of liberty and equality,
  175; Emerson's opposition to, 194–
  97; in the Greek polis, 234n.24; in
  Hegel's master-slave relation, 28–29;
  as source of Southern individualism,

70; as system for pricing individuals,
  205–6; as violation of property in oneself, 180
Smith, Adam, 56, 58, 230n.27
Smith, Barbara Herrnstein, 156
social equality, 204, 205, 211
socialism: American liberalism's victory
  over, 36; the corporation as privatized
  socialism, 68; Emerson on, 91, 121–
  22, 223n.21, 232n.43; Fourierist socialism and Emerson, 135, 146; Freud
  on, 111; Transcendentalists and, 91;
  Whitman's psychic socialism, 107
society: affection turning to charity in, 99;
  as an association writ large, 77; centrists reconciling the individual with,
  1; Emersonian self-reliance's complex
  relation to, 23; Emerson rejecting authority of, 6; friendship as "little society," 91, 117; possibility of achieving
  equality in liberal, 189; postauthoritarian, 171; social stratification increasing, 4, 219n.5
Society and Solitude (Emerson), 251n.15
Socrates, 227n.8, 231n.38
sodomy: acts considered as, 238nn. 10,
  11; colonial definition of, 95; the
  crowd and, 96, 97; as form of insurrection, 95; mass democracy and, 97,
  100; middle-class fear of, 237n.8; political deployment of, 238n.15; as social as well as sexual crime, 96; two
  sodomies, 93–100
"Song of Myself" (Whitman), 107
sovereignty: collective, 157–61, 223n.21,
  232n.43; Emerson effect making ceding sovereignty seem like emancipation, 209; loss of made to feel good by
  liberalism, 4; public, 5, 71, 179; without grounds in postauthoritarian society, 171
Sproat, John G., 240n.31
state, the: in democratic individualism,
  19; liberalism as statist, 165; Marx on,
  107; state-corporation alliance, 84. *See
  also* government
Sterling, John, 239n.23
Stevens, Thaddeus, 204
Story, William, 80, 86
strikes, 102

submission to authority: American moderation resting on, 1; as consent, 28; corporatist solution to, 41–88; crowd
psychology and submissive male
friendship, 117–21; in dialectic of individuality and community, 31; in Emersonian individualism, 6, 7, 182; equality as key to avoiding, 31, 33; freedom
as for Emerson, 23, 224n.26; in Hegel's master-slave relation, 28–29; homosexuality associated with, 126; in incorporation and interjection, 29; and
individualism in private life, 89–150;
as individuation through relation, 30;
Kant on free submission to law, 65,
69; liberal democracy built on, 126; in
middle-class political psyche, 28; political subjectivity determining how submission feels, 10; racial submission,
204; same-sex crowd subjectivity resisting, 108; self-possession linked to
by Emerson, 24; the self-reliant individual as seeking, 28; submission to
right law making equality irrelevant,
34; submission to tradition in Emerson, 1–2; the transcendent destiny to
which one must submit, 23; veiled in
male friendship, 138; without a discrete superior in corporatism, 38–39
Sumner, Charles, 189, 195, 256n.44
Swedenborg, Emanuel, 139, 158–59,
257n.50
symbolic analysts, 4

Takaki, Ronald, 259n.81
Taylor, Thomas, 74
tenement life, 103
Thomas, Benjamin Franklin, 153
Thomas, Brook, 236n.65
Thoreau, Henry David, 231n.38
Thurin, Erik Ingvar, 247n.8, 249n.44
Tocqueville, Alexis de: on authoritarianism in American culture, 63; on corporation stockholders as representative of
individualism, 67; on democracy in
the American family, 131; on friendship as a little society, 91, 117; on husband as head of household, 130,
246n.4
Todd, John, 108–9, 118, 241n.55

Tooke, Horne, 231n.38
Transcendentalism, 17–22; on democracy,
17–18, 20–21; on government, 18;
middle-class ideas on women in, 129;
on the Oneness of being, 46; radical
individualism of, 18; reluctance to
choose between naturalism and supernaturalism, 55; self-reliance and, 18;
socialism and, 91; the transcendent
destiny to which one must submit, 23;
two opposing poles in, 122

Trustees of Dartmouth College, 86
truth, 154, 165, 216

Unitarianism, 17, 18
United States. *See* America
utopian communities: Brook Farm, 91,
121, 246n.1; Emerson on, 120–21,
121–24; women in, 129, 246n.1

van der Berghe, Pierre L., 257n.57
van der Meer, Theo, 238n.11
Vico, Giambattista, 57

Walsh, Mike, 102
Ward, Samuel, 248n.17
Wardley, Lynn, 248n.18
"Wealth" (Emerson), 179
Webster, Daniel, 142, 169, 170, 249n.44
Webster, Noah, 54, 231n.38
Weinbaum, Paul, 101–2
West, Cornell, 21, 153, 258n.62
West Indian emancipation, 189, 201
West Point, 148
Whicher, Stephen, 9, 60
Whigs, 8, 77, 169
Whitman, Walt: on feelings for women
and men, 137, 248n.25; gazing at
other men, 239n.16; Griswold's re-
view of *Leaves of Grass,* 94–95; on ho-
moeroticism and democracy, 92; as
man of the herd, 94; on mass democ-
racy, 105, 106; on the masses, 105–9;
psychic socialism of, 107; "Song of
Myself," 107; Todd contrasted with,
108–9
Wiebe, Robert, 17
Wilde, Oscar, 93
women: alleged feminization of American

women (*continued*)
culture, 149–50, 250n.60; in the antebellum family, 129–31; in associations, 234n.27; in democratic patriarchy, 112; as diverting investments
from the group leader, 113; Emerson
on, 130, 136–37; Emerson on love of,
137–43; Emerson on the harlot, 141–
43; Emerson on women's rights, 141,
145–46; erotic power of, 109; feminism, 234n.27; genius for relations in,
20; intercourse with robbing men of
their powers, 108; as source of male
authority, 146; in tenement life, 103;
Transcendentalism on, 129; in utopian
communities, 129, 246n.1

Women's Rights Convention, 145
Wordsworth, William, 57
working class: egalitarianism of, 104–5;
elite considering itself as part of,
256n.35; labor-management partnerships, 183; strikes, 102; white and
black workers distinguished by,
257n.57; workingman's republicanism, 21. *See also* masses, the

"Young Americans, The" (Emerson), 124

Ziff, Larzer, 229n.22